WAR, JUSTICE, AND PUBLIC ORDER

WAR, JUSTICE, AND PUBLIC ORDER

England and France in the Later Middle Ages

RICHARD W. KAEUPER

Clarendon Press · Oxford

This book has been printed digitally and produced in a standard specification in order to ensure its continuing availability

OXFORD
UNIVERSITY PRESS

Great Clarendon Street, Oxford OX2 6DP

Oxford University Press is a department of the University of Oxford.
It furthers the University's objective of excellence in research, scholarship, and education by publishing worldwide in

Oxford New York

Auckland Bangkok Buenos Aires Cape Town Chennai
Dar es Salaam Delhi Hong Kong Istanbul Karachi Kolkata
Kuala Lumpur Madrid Melbourne Mexico City Mumbai Nairobi
São Paulo Shanghai Singapore Taipei Tokyo Toronto

with an associated company in Berlin

Oxford is a registered trade mark of Oxford University Press in the UK and in certain other countries

Published in the United States
by Oxford University Press Inc., New York

Reprinted 2002

ISBN 0-19-822873-2

Jacket illustration: The Great Seal of Edward III. Photos by Royal Chamberlain.

For my Mother and Father

Preface

On 21 April 1908, Theodore Roosevelt's guest of the day at a White House luncheon was James J. Walsh, whose recent book, *The Thirteenth—Greatest of Centuries*, had intrigued the president and left him 'somewhat converted' to the thesis so unambiguously proclaimed in its title.[1] Though initially rejected by six publishers, when printed by the Catholic Summer School Press in 1907, the book sold more than 70,000 copies. The idea of the thirteenth century as a glorious peak in the mountain range of medieval centuries was by no means an idiosyncrasy of Walsh, though his contention that this century towered over all others would have won less than general acceptance. But medieval historians before and after Walsh's time, and especially the great Victorians, ill-disguised their warm admiration for the thirteenth century; they admired its cathedrals; they approved of its universities; they marvelled at its philosophical structures (though often with Protestant reservations); and they discovered in its politics the foundations of modern government, complete with the essential checks of representative institutions and the rule of law. As a preface to the Silver Jubilee edition of his book, issued in 1929, Walsh collected some of the paeans of praise sung by the Victorians, ending with the veritable benediction of Henry Adams, 'The twelfth and thirteenth centuries were a period when men were at their strongest.'

The relevance of this historiographical tradition for any study with a focus primarily on the fourteenth century is obvious. From so great a height as the thirteenth century the way can only be down in the following age. Historians have, in fact, often viewed the fourteenth century as an age of decline, of waning, or breakdown, and have judged such slippage from the heights with an intensity ranging from nostalgic regret to outright condemnation. Reactions against such negative judgements have

[1] Kirwin, 'James J. Walsh—Medical Historian and Pathfinder'.

more recently produced a revisionist attitude, emphasizing the innovative qualities of the fourteenth century and often casting scorn on any emphasis on its problems. At its most vigorous such a view comes close to boosterism; scholars have found a forward movement in the fourteenth century and have argued that economic growth characterized an age more often discussed in terms of a great depression.

Moreover, if critical evaluation of the character of medieval civilization on a scale of centuries poses one problem for a fourteenth-century study, there is a second and no less troublesome issue. War and the control of violence were central issues to fourteenth-century people. Yet they are difficult subjects for historians, and they sometimes carry an emotional freight which complicates analysis. Historians have perhaps generally written about war with an aim not far different from that of Froissart, the recounting of great deeds as a celebration of the human spirit and an encouragement of heroism, even if in modern writing the beneficiary has become the impersonal state rather than the individual warrior demonstrating prowess and seeking profit. Far fewer historians seem to be inclined to take such a view in the late twentieth century, probably sharing what may be a widespread disinclination to glorify war. Calm appraisal of the effects of war fought in an age which revelled in its very sights and sounds thus becomes a challenge. Can we disengage our analysis from our own values? Should our analysis rest with an understanding of the medieval values?

Confronting the issues of value judgements is thus as important as it is obvious. The present book investigates and emphasizes a set of closely related problems concerning the role of the state and the effects of war organized by the state in north-western European society in the fourteenth century. These problems were numerous and they seem to have been serious. But such a focus does not imply a value judgement on the people involved or on the institutions they inherited or created. The study does, however, assume that there is some merit in considering the several centuries between the millenium and the late thirteenth or early fourteenth century, often termed the High Middle Ages, as having their own unity and that important new problems relating to the capacity of the state and an expansion of warfare, acting in conjunction with economic, demographic, and intellectual changes, mark off the fourteenth century as the beginning of a new era.

This study would not have been possible without the support and advice of a number of institutions and individuals. Major financial support came from the Harry Frank Guggenheim Foundation during the academic years 1978-81; I am indeed grateful to the Foundation for this essential help. The University of Rochester named me R. T. French Exchange Professor at Worcester College, Oxford, for the academic year 1979-80 and then generously added a year of leave in 1980-1. Throughout the former year the Provost and Fellows of Worcester College provided a warm welcome to the stimulating environment of Oxford. In 1982-3 the Center for Naval Analysis in conjunction with the University of Rochester provided a grant for basic research. At the invitation of the University of Wales I spent the summer term of 1982 as Visiting Professorial Fellow in the University College of Wales at Aberystwyth.

Among the individuals whose help I acknowledge with gratitude the oldest debt of thanks must go to Joseph R. Strayer whose interest in broad and comparative historical questions has long been an inspiration. James V. Capua, Bernard W. McLane, and Thomas G. Hahn listened patiently to my earliest formulations of themes and commented usefully on them. During my summer term in Aberystwyth Edmund Fryde not only gave me a room in his house and use of his personal library, he also gave me the benefit of his considerable knowledge. Elizabeth A. R. Brown, Janet Coleman, Fredric Cheyette, Charles Coulson, Edmund Fryde, Bernard McLane, and Brian Merilees provided copies of documents or of their own work in advance of publication. David Kaeuper helped me obtain microfilm copies of manuscripts in the Archives Nationales, Paris. Charles T. Wood read an early draft of chapters 2 and 3 and gave sound advice; Thomas Hahn and Gerald Bond performed the same service for chapter 4, part 2; Stanley Engerman gave helpful advice on the economic consequences of war. John Henneman, John Maddicott, and Bernard McLane read and commented on a first draft of the complete manuscript; Dr McLane and Dr Maddicott heroically read some chapters twice, commenting in considerable detail. The index was skilfully prepared by David Sterling. Jean DeGroat deserves a medal for typing the entire manuscript—repeatedly. My wife Margaret has been a source of constant help and wise advice.

R.W.K.

University of Rochester
Rochester, New York

Contents

Abbreviations

Actes	*Actes du Parlement de Paris*
An	Archives nationales, Paris
CCR	*Calendar of the Close Rolls*
CFR	*Calendar of the Fine Rolls*
CPR	*Calendar of the Patent Rolls*
JUST	Justices Itinerant, Public Record Office, London
l.p.	*livres parisis*
l.t.	*livres tournois*
Ordonnances	*Ordonnances des roys de France*
PRO	Public Record Office, London

Introduction

On opposite sides of the great seal by which they authenticated their solemn orders and grants, the kings of Medieval England presented two formal images of their kingship: on the obverse side the king appeared seated on the royal throne, bearing sceptre in one hand and orb in the other; on the reverse side the king appeared as a knight in armour, mounted on a war horse (a 'covered destrier'), charging with drawn sword. The great seal might be taken symbolically as a kind of political or constitutional *sic et non*, each face representing a set of potentially contradictory statements about the role of kingship in the emerging state: the king as fount of justice and giver of law; the king as chief chivalric war-lord. These contrasting images point to the central concern of this book, the relationship between law and war in the Medieval state. For as it emerged in the High Middle Ages the European state was both a war-state and a law-state. The growing demands of a more developed society across the High Medieval centuries promoted royal efforts in the fundamental areas of law, order, and justice and brought significant advances in the development of the Western state. The crown in both England and France was becoming the institution which dispensed justice and provided whatever regulation of violence was possible on the scale of the entire realm. These states could speak of their superior powers exercised for the public good and for the common utility, drawing upon their actual experience and upon the categories and concepts of Roman law. Kings in each country claimed, if not an outright monopoly of legitimate violence, at least some divinely sanctioned authority for the regulation of violence and the protection of the powerless. In two ways, then, the king's government worked toward the goals of justice and order. For the regulation of daily life and the resolution of the disputes which so easily disrupt it, the crown provided criminal courts and officials to prosecute offenders and civil courts and processes which might serve as alternatives to violent self-help. Claiming to be the final arbiter of legitimate violence, the royal government also acted against feud and private war, at least containing what it was never able to suppress. The advance of kingship, and of relative peace and order seemed to move in harmony across the High Middle Ages.

Yet by the late thirteenth century the medieval state was working under severe and obvious strains in both England and France. In part the rapid advance of the law state itself produced these strains. The powerful and privileged of society—lords, knights, and townsmen alike—were bound to view the expansion of royal justice with mixed feelings. All had some interest in order and found royal courts on occasion to be of great assistance in maintaining property or in chastizing opponents. Thus the high claims of the crown in public order might be heard with seriousness by people who would expect to receive all of the benefits so ambitiously promised by the crown. Yet basic ambiguities tempered and complicated their support. All of the powerful in society possessed rights of jurisdiction which were often valuable and which might be prized for symbolic worth even when no great source of income. The chivalric layers of society in particular, and especially in France, cherished a code which glorified the knightly right to settle through violence any affront to honour and which portrayed knights as the internal policemen of Christian society, the proper righters of wrong. How would chivalric claims intersect with the revival of effective kingship which had been so prominent a feature of the High Middle Ages? Of course for many generations knightly kings and king-like knights had co-operated with only the quarrels and adjustments (often settled at swordpoint) that one might expect in a group of proud and powerful men. There was so much work to be done and so much profit to be gained in doing it that any ultimate contradiction in roles was often masked. But as the capacity of the state and the idea of sovereignty waxed, the tensions became increasingly apparent, sometimes within the kings themselves, often between monarchy and chivalry.

The rapid growth of the law state created another problem that was especially apparent in England. Given its resources, a medieval government simply could not fulfil its grand claims to provide justice and an end to administrative and judicial corruption and violent self-help. A kind of collective 'Peter Principle' was at work: royal administrations claimed ever more judicial authority and competence until they found themselves seriously over-extended. The distance between the claims of the crown and its actual achievements in law and justice afforded room for considerable disenchantment. The results are recorded clearly in the often bitter and satirical literature of fourteenth-century England, so much of which takes as its focus the corruption and denial of justice measured by an obviously rising standard.

Perhaps even more important than the expansion of the royal effort in law was the great extension in the scale of warfare and the concentration of royal administrative energy on war. Considering once again the limited resources of medieval governments, a great increase in the resources and attention devoted to war could only mean a reduction of the royal interest in law; at the very least any increase in governmental activity would be directed to war and so would significantly alter the relative balance which had long operated in the state. Of course for many centuries kings had ridden forth at the head of a column of warriors to smite their enemies. But from the last decade of the thirteenth century a new stage is apparent. Following the long and significant period of peace which sheltered much of Europe across most of the thirteenth century, kings now harnessed the full powers of the state for the purposes of war on a grander scale and over longer periods than previously was thought possible.

The first signs of the new scale of warfare to come in the fourteenth century appeared in the English conquest of Wales carried out in the campaigns of 1276-7 and 1282-3. In order to conquer the remaining independent part of this small land Edward I marshalled massive force, financed his efforts via merchant bankers who could tap the supply of cash available in north-western Europe generally, and secured the conquest with an ambitious building programme which erected castles and walled towns at the most strategic sites. Already in the last quarter of the thirteenth century royal government in England was acting as the agency which transferred an increasing share of the wealth available in northern Europe to the enterprise of war. This enterprise achieved more dramatic momentum in the 1290s. The English not only faced a major Welsh rising, they also began their long and bitter effort to conquer the Kingdom of Scotland; the French tried to conquer the County of Flanders and found as bitter a war and as obdurate an enemy in the continental lowlands as the English confronted in the Scottish highlands. Even more significant, in 1294 the two great kingdoms went to war against each other, in effect beginning the series of Anglo-French wars which would last to the middle of the fifteenth century, one portion of which we are accustomed to isolate as the Hundred Years War (1337–1453).

Contemporaries emphasized the disruptive and destructive effects of this warfare in late Medieval society, though historians still debate the issues in detail. But they have focused less attention on the entire range of changes this warfare brought to the states themselves. Major works of scholarship have detailed the relationship between war and the growth of representative assemblies (so useful for war taxation); but scholars have less often discussed the way in which late Medieval warfare severely retarded the equally important royal activity in law.

The combination of royal over-extension in law and justice and the major effort devoted to war produced quite different results in England and France. Many Frenchmen whose views counted thought that royal activism in law and order had passed acceptable bounds in the early fourteenth century, as the movement of the provincial leagues in 1314–15 reveals. Yet the reaction was shorter and less severe in France than in England, and the English invasions of France soon necessarily worked a transformation in the view French monarchs took of the problem of order in their realm. It gradually became apparent to all that the peril was more likely to be royal incapacity than over-extended royal claims to secure public order. By mid-fourteenth century, as bands of soldiers under one banner or another (or under no banner at all) roamed the countryside, France resembled the near-anarchy of her early Capetian past more than the relative order of the thirteenth century. The 'crisis of order' in France was of the most obvious sort during the Hundred Years War.

In England the situation was quite different, though England, too, had her problems with former soldiers. A genuine sense of crisis became quite apparent as the gap widened between royal claims and the actual state of the peace; heightened expectations (in part generated by the crown) were not matched by effective royal measures. In fact, the crown found itself compelled to place extensive judicial powers in the hands of local gentlemen. These men cheerfully used delegated royal powers as a powerful weapon in their local feuding. Yet kings found it difficult to discipline the men whose martial energies they called upon for victories in the French wars. At the same time this costly war in France—requiring men, money, and supplies—strained the home populace sufficiently to raise great outcries about the wisdom of royal policies or at least about the justice of royal administrative methods; the strains finally created doubts about the usefulness of royal power as it had developed across the High Middle Ages. Perhaps the origins of English 'constitutionalism' and of French 'absolutism' were deeply rooted in the linked fourteenth-century problems of war, justice, and public order.

Each of the chapters which follow takes up one of these issues. Chapter 1 considers the kingdoms of England and France as war states. Though both kingdoms devoted major resources to war, significant differences mark the ways in which they had come to procure military force by the fourteenth century. England had at a much earlier time acquired the capacity to translate authority into military power through the agency of money, as the English use of mercenaries, the development of effective systems of direct and indirect taxation, and the utilization of credit on the grand scale (supplied largely by Italian merchant-banking companies) make clear. This heightened English capacity enabled her kings to carry on war with the kingdom of France, several times the size of England. The long Anglo-French warfare would hardly have been possible without English governmental precocity, relentlessly pressed forward by English kings' territorial ambitions on the continent. In order to gain a sense of the costs of such warfare, the focus must, in fact, be broad enough to give a view of the economy of north-western Europe, rather than of individual countries. It seems unnecessarily limited to debate which kingdom emerged from generations of war with a larger hoard of precious metal. The physical devastation, the disruption of trade and credit, the transfer of vast amounts of wealth via war taxation suggest rather that we must investigate and evaluate war as a factor of great significance in the economic problems of later medieval Europe. Equally important is the effect of continuous warfare on the states which organized it, especially since the fourteenth century marks a critical stage in the process by which the European state emerged.

Yet the warfare of great kingdoms was only the massive and elaborate end-point on a scale of violent action reaching down through the private wars and feuds of great lords, knights, and townsmen to the tavern murders and midnight robberies of village society. Chapter 2 moves down the scale of violence to consider the role of royal justice in internal order. The changes that so marked High Medieval European society insured that this royal role would increase with time; the growth of towns and trade, the production of more wealth, the demographic increase—all helped to intensify a desire for order and to generate an increased willingness to support some agency that could secure an acceptable level of peace and provide means for resolving disputes. Kings would be the ultimate heirs of such views, but the legacy was sometimes slow in coming to them and the process seemed uncertain at more than one point; it was, moreover, a process that proceeded at different rates on either side of the Channel. In the region that would become France, churchmen first stepped into the void left by absent or ineffective kingship and launched the peace movement in the decade before the millennium. Across the eleventh century this movement achieved greatest effectiveness as a legitimation of the power of lords of several great French fiefs. Only across the next century, or perhaps over the next two centuries could the kings of France transform the Peace of God into something like a royal peace. The kings of England, by contrast, maintained their association with public order without a serious break; Anglo-Saxon and Norman kingship possessed enough power to make a peace movement unnecessary in England; after the innovative work of Henry II English kings exercised the broadest secular jurisdiction in Europe. They continued to develop this jurisdictional competence into the fourteenth century and (despite certain parallels in the elaboration of cases begun by informal complaint in both countries), continued to exercise a much more direct and comprehensive public order jurisdiction than that of the kings of France. But from the late thirteenth century the gap opening between the high claims of the English royal administration on the one hand and the actual process of justice and the state of public order on the other provoked a crisis of order.

When thinking of the state of the peace on either side of the Channel we must not, however, confuse public order with crime, for one of the greatest threats to order came from the various strata of knights who not only practised violence openly, but claimed the right as a legitimate exercise of power. The code of chivalry, in short, encouraged as much violence as it curbed. The complex relationship between chivalry, the state, and public order is the theme of Chapter 3. As the Church had done earlier, fourteenth-century kings tried to co-opt the force of knighthood; they founded royal chivalric orders, they attempted to control tournaments and private fortification. Yet the central issue between kings and knights in the matter of public order was the knightly right to settle affairs by violence, codified in France as a right to private war. The kings of France, especially Philip IV and Philip V, worked creatively with a wide range of particular legal devices and prohibitions; but their success was limited. The kings of England did not recognize the right of private war at all, but they had to struggle with the somewhat lower level of feuding and violence carried out by lords and gentlemen. The effects of royal efforts seem as important to the political and constitutional history of England and France as to the legal history of each country: royal intervention in the area of public order powerfully affected the particular form of state emerging in England and France.

Large numbers of people gave allegiance to these states, which could scarcely have developed their powers in the absence of widespread popular support. Yet subjects might show complex or even contradictory responses as they witnessed kings in pursuit of the twin policies of vigorous and expensive war with external enemies and an internal exercise of power to preserve order and secure justice as defined by the crown. Some subjects only slowly and reluctantly yielded their private rights to legitimate violence and the dispensing of justice; most subjects at one time or another resented the intrusion of royal power into their lives; all subjects objected that the action of government (which they basically supported) came at so costly a price. Moreover, the standards by which the process of governance would be judged were constantly rising; generations of social and economic change had nourished more complex governmental apparatus and more sophisticated political and constitutional arrangements; but in performing their work and in securing support, particularly in times of crisis so often associated with war, royal administrations fed the desire for government purged of the local tyranny, extortion, and favouritism that so often were its hallmarks. Chapter 4 explores the ways in which subjects responded to the actions of the state and helped to shape the royal role in each kingdom. Cross-Channel similarities and differences are again instructive. In both realms a dialogue between king and subject brought constant adjustment of the legitimate role and administrative apparatus of government. Yet the timing of governmental reform differed in England and France and the two processes led to results highly important to each country. This sense of contrast is reinforced by the second subject of Chapter 4, an investigation of the image of the stage in works of literature. The Old French epic in the twelfth and thirteenth centuries and a broad range of English complaint literature in the fourteenth century are especially informative. The outbreak of popular revolts provides a third line of investigation. By the second half of the fourteenth century cumulative and bitter frustration with the state of justice and the costs of war in England and the rather more specific crisis of invasion and military disaster in France (combined on either side of the Channel with social and economic transformations common to all of north-western Europe), produced major revolts. A comparison of the 1358 Jacquerie in France and the 1381 Rising in England shows some similarities; but the contrasts are even more significant and again reflect the difference in the rates by which royal power grew in England and France.

The thematic and comparative nature of this study is apparent from even a brief prospectus of its major concerns. These concerns are admittedly broad: changes in the fourteenth century viewed against earlier developments in the High Middle Ages; the action of the state in England compared to that of the state in France; the role of royal law in both countries related to royal warfare; the problem of disorder linked to issues of war, justice, and chivalry. Such a broad study is possible only by accepting other limitations. This book lays no claim to coverage of the Hundred Years War nor to a comparative examination of all aspects of law and government in late Medieval England and France. The intent is simply to investigate an interlocking set of problems that resulted in England and France from the tension between the role of the developed medieval state in war and in law. This thematic focus requires a chronological sweep of some breadth. Most attention will be devoted to roughly the first phase of the Hundred Years War if we begin that phase with the 1290s (rather than with the somewhat more traditional 1330s) and if we are willing to look occasionally beyond the traditional closing date of the Peace of Bretigny in 1360. Even more often we will want to turn back into the twelfth and thirteenth centuries to watch the formative stages of some development important in the fourteenth century.

Of necessity such a study is in effect an extended interpretive essay involving a good deal of generalization. The approach would have been termed at least moderate realism in the medieval schools. Such an approach is regarded as suspect by more than a few historians; but I will follow Luther's advice to sin boldly, believing with Charles Davis that 'in the last analysis, all historians are realists and not nominalists, for otherwise how could they write history'.[1] To sin boldly is not to abandon reason nor to block the voice of conscience utterly; it is particularly hazardous, I know, to make broad, general statements in fields only partially illuminated by difficult evidence the meaning of which is still debated by specialists. Indulgence can only be sought in the hope that this inquiry redeems its shortcomings by stimulating further discussion and study, even if the answers suggested to the questions raised do not convince all. F. W. Maitland's advice is difficult, but apt: 'If only we can ask the right questions we shall have done something for a good end.'[2]

[1] Davis, 'Ockham and the Zeitgeist', 64.

[2] Maitland, *Doomsday Book and Beyond*, 2-3.

1

The Enterprise of War

1. THE EMPHASIS ON WAR

War was an essential and characteristic function of medieval states, commanding a vast share of the treasure of governments, a major part of the time and energies of kings and their advisers. That war has been an absorbing preoccupation of kingdoms and empires before and since the Middle Ages is equally obvious. But in recognizing this fact we are not reduced to homilies about the darker content of the human soul in any age or its likely expression through wars directed by some state-like mechanism. If the concentration of the medieval state on war is manifest, there were specifically medieval forces at work, and even factors specific to the emergence of the medieval states themselves.

At the broadest level we must take into account the deep and persistent influence of the warrior mentalité, the ethos which glorified war as the greatest test and expression of manhood. This ethos, of course, was already very old by the Middle Ages. But the characteristic medieval form seems to have emerged only from the late eleventh century as new cavalry tactics triumphed, as the social group to fill the ranks of knighthood rose in prestige and political status, as a sense of social exclusiveness was built and buttressed by new cultural (and especially literary) forms.[1] Some scholars have stressed even more the influence of the Peace Movement and Gregorian Reform. They note that Churchmen proclaimed that the mailed warriors were not merely fulfilling a

[1] Maurice Keen offers fascinating comments on the secular origins of knighthood in *Chivalry*, ch. 2. I am indebted to Dr Keen for the opportunity to read this book in manuscript. Georges Duby argues the case for the importance of clerical views and the peace movement in 'Les Origines de la chevalerie' and 'Les Laics et la Paix de Dieu'. An English trans. of these studies by Cynthia Postan appears in Duby, *The Chivalrous Society*, chs. 8 and 11. See also Morris, "Equestris Ordo": Chivalry as a Vocation in the Twelfth Century', 87-98.

role regrettably necessary in an age of iron; they were an *ordo*, one of the set orders of society prescribed by the divine intelligence for the proper functioning of the world.

The medieval state which had begun to form in these centuries was a creation of warriors and churchmen with definite notions about warfare and the role of knighthood. But once launched, these states quickly developed a momentum all their own. In other words, the internal logic of the growth of state power, no less than the chivalric *mentalité*, dictated the concentration of the emerging state on war. Nearly all of the forces linking the state and war proved to be positive catalysts, encouraging the involvement of the state in wars which over time could become progressively larger affairs.

As it developed, the royal drive for jurisdiction over public order and for some first, often faint, approximation of a monopoly of legitimate violence vested in the hands of royal agents had no limiting effect on violence beyond the frontiers. In fact, external violence may well have formed a counterpart for a policy of internal peace and a safety valve for releasing the tensions generated by such a policy. Borrowing a page, however unconsciously, from the ecclesiastics of the tenth and eleventh centuries, kings of the thirteenth and fourteenth centuries defined a zone within which they wanted to reduce violence, and tried to focus the violence of their knightly followers against some acceptable enemy beyond the increasingly well-defined sphere of the realm. At their most ambitious (and with severely limited success) ecclesiastics had attempted in the Peace Movement to consider Christendom to be the sphere of peace and pagans the foe. Kings, however, in an age in which such notions were visibly failing, achieved somewhat greater success by limiting their definition of the sphere of peace to their own realms; they then easily found the legitimate external enemy in another Christian realm.

This development met with no major impediment in the scholastic or canonistic thought on the topic of warfare. By the fourteenth century 'the just war theories had evolved into a right to war theory within the elastic restrictions of Christian morality. Warfare of monarchs was assumed by an indulgent clergy to be just unless directed against its own interests.'[2] Significantly, the

[2] Russell, *The Just War in the Middle Ages*, 301. Cf. Haines, 'Attitudes and Impediments to Pacifism in Medieval Europe', 369-88.

church may have moved closest to a blanket condemnation of violence in the Peace Movement, during a time when any form of reliable state authority had all but disappeared over much of Europe. But churchmen both by long habit and by theoretical prediliction deeply wanted a legitimate state authority on which they could rely, a 'secular arm' which could provide that degree of peace and protection within which the church could live and carry out its divine mission. A comment by Thomas Aquinas in the *Summa Theologica* (II. ii, q. 40, 1) illustrates the link between the ecclesiastical need for internal peace and the ecclesiastical blessing bestowed on just external warfare.[3] Aquinas wrote of kings, 'And just as when they punish criminals they are rightfully defending the State against its internal enemies by the exercise of their civil power . . . so must they also protect the state against its exterior foes by using the sword of war.' Royal policies of internal peace, vigorous external war, and the contemporary theories of just war and necessity thus were most conveniently congruent. As Frederick Russell observes,

> armed with a potent instrument of rule, secular rulers were able to oppose the violence of justice to the violence of private warfare, for to control justice was to limit internal warfare. The development of the just war can be seen as an aspect of the transition from 'segmentary' states in which private warfare was necessarily tolerated to 'unitary' or sovereign states enjoying a monopoly of licit violence. That this development also made possible ever larger wars between sovereigns is no surprise. . . .[4]

Nor it is a surprise that states which were increasingly exercising sovereign powers showed a distinct touchiness over boundaries which were increasingly acquiring greater definition.[5] By the late thirteenth and fourteenth centuries the feudal overlordship and the blurred concept of the realm which accompanied it were significantly becoming unacceptable; men sought definition of superior authority and clear delineation of political boundaries even as they sought clarity and precision in so many other areas of thought and action. Neutral words like clarity and precision, however, when applied to questions of jurisdiction and boundaries led easily to war.

3 Quot. Allmand (ed), *Society at War*, 17.
4 Russell, *The Just War in the Middle Ages*, 302.
5 Strayer, *On the Medieval Origins of the Modern State*, 58-9.

Finally, war was all the more likely in the medieval state because war advanced, or at least was thought to advance, the very specific material interests of those on whose political and financial support the crown relied. The development of taxation is so closely linked with war policies that we will not go far wrong if we roughly equate the growth of taxation with the pursuit of ever more grand and costly warfare. The doctrine of necessity which provided the theoretical support for taking subjects' money practically ensured this equation between taxation and war taxation. Only war represented that overriding necessity which allowed kings clear licence to command some portion of their subjects' goods.[6] Governments grew on this financial nourishment in the thirteenth and fourteenth centuries, as they have in more modern periods of warfare; directly or indirectly the flow of wealth from the countryside to the armies, passing through the fledgling bureaucracies, enriched and expanded the ranks of royal servants.

This flow of wealth likewise reached the purses of lords, knights, and their followers on whom the war depended, especially with the strong and persistent tendency towards paid armies on either side of the Channel. For the warriors, campaigning meant a happy combination of *la gloire* and a chance for riches, whether through a share in war taxation collected in their lands (as in France) or the prospect of rich booty (for English lords setting out on a *chevauchée* through some wealthy French province) or the assurance of pay and the prospects of ransoms (for both the English and the French). Let it be said at once that making a profit, and looking forward to it eagerly, was entirely compatible with the chivalric ethos;[7] only post-Medieval adaptations of the ideas of chivalry have considered profit-making a stain and a debasement of pure ideals.

Generalization about the attitudes of merchants and townsmen toward war is more difficult, but the warfare of the period could hardly have been financed without at least a grudging acceptance

[6] Harriss, *King, Parliament, and Public Finance;* Henneman, *Royal Taxation in Fourteenth-century France* (1971); Post, *Studies in Medieval Legal Thought*, 14-22, 196, 320, 346.

[7] Barnie, *War in Medieval English Society*, ch. 3, esp. p. 71; McFarlane, *The Nobility of Later Medieval England*, ch. 2. May McKisack, *The Fourteenth Century*, 133, comments on 'the profit motive which always operated so powerfully in the wars of chivalry . . .'.

by those whose hands were on so much of the liquid wealth of the realms. Clearly some merchants saw marvellous opportunities and seized the moment. That protracted war became an economic liability for many merchants is a position taken by some historians; the question must be examined later. But whether the medieval merchant clearly saw dangers outweighing his opportunities is open to doubt. For long years—especially the years decorated with showy victories—the English parliamentary commons supported the French war and select groups of merchants eagerly sought what profits were to be made from such wartime measures as royal manipulation of the wool trade. Likewise the merchants and townsmen of France, albeit with all the canny negotiating we would expect them to exercise in dealing with royal tax agents, funded the royal armies time and again. But, at least before the great crisis brought by the capture of King John in 1356, they balked at suggestions of peacetime tax proposals for purposes like the reform of the coinage, weights and measures.[8]

2. RESOURCES FOR WAR: MEN

Historians have long been troubled by the exact link between monarchy, money and military force across the Middle Ages. Each new scholarly analysis has seemingly pushed into a more remote past the era when adequate military force was procured simply by calling out the unpaid feudal host to ride down the enemy in cumbersome splendour. Correspondingly, the military revolution brought about by pay—larger armies, longer campaigns, better control of men and manœuvre—has been a much heralded phenomenon, claimed for every century from the eleventh to the fourteenth, so that notions of the rise of paid armies and particularly of mercenaries might be placed alongside their elder, the rise of the middle class.

Of course these related concepts say something true in a very general way about the transformation of early feudal society, the transition from the first to the second feudal ages, to use the terms of Marc Bloch. In the late Carolingian world imperial or royal

[8] Brown, 'Subsidy and Reform in 1321', 399-431.

authority was progressively divorced from real power; landed wealth was the only significant source of wealth and a host of mailed warriors serving by virtue of land tenure was as sensible a response to military needs as was virtual local control by these local strong men to the elementary requirements of politics and jurisdiction in a chaotic age. If something like this pattern held sway over most of north-western Europe around the millennium, the gradual reconstruction of political authority on a sound basis of power began in the course of the eleventh century. As new strength came to central authorities, and principally monarchies, across north-western Europe, it would everywhere be fuelled by the interlocking forces of economic, demographic, and urban change which generated new sources of wealth. Kings who could tap these sources of wealth could convert money into significantly heightened military capacity.

This pattern is well known and has often been elaborated. Yet by emphasizing the general transition from feudal to stipendiary forces as a common European phenomenon, we may lose sight of an important fact. The movement which is so apparent and widespread on the continent by the twelfth century was in progress much earlier in England. The Old English monarchy was the first, and by a considerable margin, to achieve the revenues which made possible a significant intrusion of money into military recruitment and reward.

England under the House of Wessex was, as James Campbell has suggested, 'the continuator and the heir of the Carolingian state' as it had been in its vigour.[9] Perhaps no consequence of Anglo-Saxon royal power was more remarkable than the revenues it commanded by means of a sophisticated financial system. 'The revenues flowing into the Anglo-Saxon treasury', C. W. Hollister writes, 'were very large indeed by comparison with the rest of Europe (there was apparently nowhere else anything quite like the danegeld), and by far the greater proportion of these revenues was devoted to military expenses—chiefly to the hiring of mercenaries.'[10] As Hollister suggests, most significant among these revenues was the danegeld, first collected in 991 to provide protection money paid

[9] Campbell, 'Observations on English Government', 54.

[10] Hollister, *Anglo-Saxon Military Institutions*, 19. For what follows see ch. 2 of this work.

over to invading Danes. From 1012 it was used instead for wages of mercenaries. Pre-conquest England in fact knew a great profusion of types of mercenaries: the English or Danish housecarles of great Anglo-Saxon lords; the bands of foreign warriors serving under their own leaders; the more shadowy lithsmen and butsecarls who served with equal facility on sea or land.

Mercenary is, of course, an amorphous term and must designate something more precise than a warrior who receives money.[11] He is sometimes said to be stateless, though this qualification is slippery in an era when states were yet to be formed over much of Europe. The best distinction seems to be that he served primarily for pay rather than as a consequence of customary obligation such as land tenure. Such a distinction can become blurred,[12] but in a general way it sets apart the mercenaries employed by the Old English kings; it also works for their successors in a long line of fighting men stretching across later centuries.

The importance of such mercenaries and the royal capacity to pay them in the early eleventh century is highly significant. But it should not lead to the conclusion that Old English military force was composed solely or mainly of mercenaries. The rank and file of the army was, in fact, filled by men who were there because of customary obligation. What Hollister terms the select fyrd was composed of warriors supplied from each area assessed at five hides (or in some cases six carucates) of land. The Germanic obligation of all free men to fight in an emergency produced a general levy which Hollister refers to as the great fyrd. On the ridge at Hastings, Harold's army included all of these elements: mercenaries; at least a part of the select fyrd; and the great fyrd of Sussex. The better troops, including the housecarles, were used

[11] Ibid. 9; cf. Contamine, *La Guerre au moyen âge*, 204-5.

[12] Philip II's favourite mercenary, Cadoc, became constable and later lord of Gaillon, was given the neighbouring fief of Tosny, and became bailli of Pont-Audemer. Richard's famous mercenary, Mercadier, accompanied the king to the Holy Land and was constantly at his side; he termed himself Richard's *famulus* and commander of his army; after Richard's death he served Queen Eleanor (see Powicke, *The Loss of Normandy*, 231-2. The position of household knights might also involve more than a relationship based solely on money. In general see Hollister, *The Military Organization of Norman England*, 189-90; Powicke, *Military Obligation in Medieval England*, 30 ff.

to stiffen the crucial shield wall along the front of the Anglo-Saxon position, with the more indifferent fighting material of the great fyrd massed behind.[13]

Once the Norman duke had become the English king after the Conquest of 1066, a powerful fusion of old Germanic and emerging feudal patterns of rule and armed might was possible. Of course contention over the nature of the military and political changes effected by the Norman victory has been almost as fierce and exhausting as the fight at Hastings. But for our purposes the significant facts are first, the likelihood that the Normans did not replace the Germanic military arrangements with the feudal, but rather tried to maintain fyrd and danegeld alongside knights fees and the feudal host;[14] and, second, that in the Anglo-Norman period money and mercenaries continued to play highly significant roles, possibly taking on even more importance in military arrangements.[15] J. O. Prestwich has emphasized that these hired troops probably even in the Conqueror's reign were fitted into the framework of a royal military household, and that this household was at least beginning to assume a role in military administration and in actual fighting that scholars once thought it took on only under the guidance of Edward I two centuries later. Especially under William Rufus and Henry I this household emerged as 'a natural, though not an inevitable, product of energetic monarchical government largely preoccupied with internal security, defense and conquest.'[16]

Mercenaries would be especially important to the Norman kings, and later to the Angevin kings, as they tried to keep their iron grip not only on England but on the congeries of continental feudal principalities which came under their domination. Use of the feudal host across the Channel always raised prickly questions from the English baronage; the limited duration of feudal service could only be further discouraging. Though Norman kings put the select fryd to good continental use more than once, it was an

13 Hollister, *Anglo-Saxon Military Institutions*, 134; id., *The Military Organization of Norman England*, 16.

14 A theme of Hollister's work in the two books cited in the preceding note.

15 Prestwich, 'War and Finance in the Anglo-Norman State', 19-43. Cf. Hollister, *Anglo-Saxon Military Institutions*, ch. 1; id., *The Military Organization of Norman England*, ch. 6.

16 Prestwich, 'The Military Household of the Norman Kings', 34.

institution rooted in social levels undergoing radical transformation after the Conquest and could not retain vigour indefinitely. Given their continental ambitions and the efficiency of their financial mechanisms in England there can be little surprise that 'it was evidently the Anglo-Normans who first used mercenaries on the Continent on a large scale.'[17]

The need was especially apparent to Henry II, trying to control a vast trans-Channel collection of territories. W. L. Warren attributes his military success to the employment of the mercenary footmen Henry made 'the mainstay of his military power'. He carefully sustained them, faithfully paid their wages, and above all trained and equipped them for siege operations. Because of his skilful use of specialist mercenaries Henry II was known for surprisingly swift moves to smash resisting castles. Such 'internal police duties' formed a large part of his military enterprises. But for occasional offensive expeditions Henry combined large numbers of feudal cavalry with his mercenary infantry. Warren thinks he never effected a really successful fusion of the two types of troops and concentrated more successfully on the holding and taking of castles with paid professional footsoldiers.[18] Such mercenaries seem usually to have been of low birth and thus were a scandal to some contemporaries. Ecclesiastical sources in particular described them with a set of names emphasizing their position as marginal men in society.[19] The antithesis of individual knightly prowess, such mercenaries' utility lay in their fighting in company with their fellows, most likely in some sort of phalanx bristling with spears and liable to lethal discharges of crossbow bolts. They had to be put in full harness and in good order before entering battle, which made their unusual speed and surprise tactics all the more important. Assured of these conditions they were often considered an irresistible force in attack, an immovable obstacle

[17] Hollister, *The Military Organization of Norman England*, ch. 8. For the quotation, see p. 169.

[18] Warren, *Henry II*, 232-3. He suggests (ibid. 144) that the significant use of footsoldiers made the road system as important to Henry as it had been to the Romans. In his view this explains why Berry, the crossroads of important trade routes, took on the importance formerly held by the Vexin in Angevin-Capetian rivalry. Cf. Powicke, *Military Obligation in Medieval England*, ch. 3.

[19] Powicke, *The Loss of Normandy*, 227-37; Duby, 'Guerre et société dans l'Europe féodale; 461-71; Verbruggen, *The Art of Warfare*, 117-25.

in defence. But Henry evidently knew that mercenary footmen had limitations, especially when they were confronted by opponents who understood their mode of fighting. If caught on the march, especially by cavalry, they were at a great disadvantage. The destruction of a major part of his mercenary force in the trap laid by Philip II and Richard in June of 1189 caused the effective end of Henry's power and brought the bitter close of his reign.[20]

Yet Henry did not simply rely on corps of mercenaries and feudal cavalry. His basically defensive military stance, his concern for internal order within his wide lands, even his 'insistence on calling upon the resources of the community as a whole in the work of government'[21] stand behind the Assize of Arms issued for England in 1181.[22] All free subjects of the realm were to be divided into four categories (holders of knights fees, possessors of rents and chattels worth 16 marks and 10 marks, all other freemen) ready to serve the king and to defend the realm with arms and armour appropriate to their status. There is a Janus quality to this reform, for if in its emphasis on status rather than tenure it looks forward to the transformation of knight service based on private tenures (in the arms ordinances of Henry III and Edward I, and in their practice of distraint of knighthood) it also looks backward to the Old English military recruitment of the select fyrd, based on hide and carrucate assessments of status. We can understand Bishop Stubbs's claim that Henry II in this assize achieved the reconstitution of the fyrd. That a similar assize was issued for Henry II's continental lands and that it seems to have been copied by Philip Augustus and Philip of Flanders not long after 'illustrates the importance of the sub-feudal military tradition on the continent as well as in England.'[23]

Although by this time the kings of England had been experimenting with military pay and with the tactical and strategic employment of mercenaries for the better part of two

[20] See esp. the two studies by Boussard: 'Les Mercenaires au XIIe siècle, 189-224; 'Services féodaux', 131-68. There is also much useful information and analysis in Verbruggen, *The Art of Warfare*, ch. 3.

[21] Warren, *Henry II*, 379.

[22] For what follows see Powicke, *Military Obligation in Medieval England*, ch. 2; Hollister, *The Military Organization of Norman England*, 258-60.

[23] Hollister, *The Military Organization of Norman England*, 258. Cf. Warren, *Henry II*, 379.

centuries, the French kings were just coming around to such methods. Under Louis VI and Louis VII the French crown had not acquired the financial capacity to use mercenaries on a significant scale although by the latter's reign Henry II's vigorous actions, so often dramatically crowned with success, were demonstrating how few were the military alternatives. While the Norman kings of England were developing a military household and employing corps of mercenaries who might ensure victory on far-flung battlefields and who repeatedly went over—or through—castle walls, the Capetian kings were forced by limitations of resources patiently to call out their vassals and communal levies and move time and again to reduce the independence and the castle keeps of petty lords in a field of action characteristically restricted to the Île de France. Louis VI of course saw the utility of Henry's methods, but could not find the necessary cash to duplicate such a policy. Once the French kings had the money in hand the men were easily enough obtained; no secret formula guarded the manner of making full use of them. By the last decades of the century Philip Augustus could collect the war chests needed. The king lived simply, said the *Grandes Chroniques de France*, in order to amass the treasure with which he could pay his knights and sergeants, for he thought that lack of money had crippled the efforts of his predecessors.[24] It was with largely paid forces that Philip II wrested Normandy, Maine, Anjou, and Touraine from King John in 1204 and then smashed his ambitious plans for an anti-French coalition in 1214. Whatever the contrasts between English and French leadership, the French crown could now work the formula by which revenues converted authority into realized power. In 1194 Philip's government had compiled the *prises des sergeants* which listed the sergeants and the carts (for military transport) owed to royal service by the prévôtés, communes, towns, villages, and abbeys of the royal domain. Even at this date the most important communes actually discharged the obligation by a cash payment calculated on the wages of sergeants and the value of carts owed;

[24] Quot. Contamine, *La Guerre au moyen âge*, 192-3. See the comments of Verbruggen, *The Art of Warfare*, 123, 139; he notes that the full use of mercenaries came late in Philip's reign and that his communal infantry was more useful on town walls than in the field.

by the time the 1202-3 royal account was drawn up, all of the service had been commuted.[25]

After the conquest of the rich and ordered provinces formerly in English control, the French crown of course had an enormous boost in resources to back any further conflict. Use of pay and employment of mercenaries could hardly have the impact that the Anglo-Norman and Angevin kings had achieved in the eleventh and twelfth centuries. When the kings of England and France could both employ them at will, mercenaries became one element among several in a common formula of military success closely linked to royal revenues.

Across the thirteenth century the place of feudal service in that formula of military success continued its steady decline. By the end of the century it was obvious that the obligation to feudal service had undergone a major transformation long in the making. Faced with rising costs of knighthood great lords had gradually secured reductions in the amount of knight services they owed to the crown. Both in England and in France a summons to the feudal host in the late thirteenth century would produce only a fraction of the number of knights expected from such a summons a century earlier. As Michael Prestwich writes of England, 'it does not seem that the forces yielded by the strict quotas were of any great importance. . . . Nor was the use of the feudal summons of any considerable financial benefit to the crown. At this time the Exchequer was fighting a losing battle to collect scutage on the old assessment of fees, rather than on the new reduced quotas.'[26] Philippe Contamine suggests a similar picture for France: 'Vers 1300, dans la royaume de France, le *servitium debitum* traditionnel est en pleine débâcle.'[27]

But for most of the thirteenth century, after the important French victories which so marked its opening,[28] Anglo-French conflicts all but disappeared, and in general north-western Europe enjoyed an era of relative peace. The great increase in French power achieved by Philip Augustus undoubtedly had something

[25] Fawtier, *The Capetian Kings of France*, 195; Fawtier and Lot, *Le Premier budget de la monarchie française*, 19; Powicke, *The Loss of Normandy*, 220-1.

[26] Prestwich, *War, Politics, and Finance*, 81-2.

[27] *La Guerre au moyen âge*, 181.

[28] Yves Renouard analyses the broad changes of the early thirteenth century in '1212-1216', 5-21.

to do with this; in England the civil wars which embroiled both John and Henry III and the long minority of Henry were additional factors; later the character of Henry III and even more of St Louis would become important, perhaps in particular Louis's sincere devotion to the idea of crusade.[29]

Yet when major warfare resumed late in the thirteenth century it was taken in hand by states whose capacity for fighting had mounted significantly in the general administrative development of those decades of peace.[30] The ambitions, claims, and sensitivities associated with these developing states likewise easily rekindled the flames of war. From roughly the last decade of the thirteenth century, and leading into the Hundred Years War, military action increased in scale and, some historians argue, produced new effects on the states, society, and economy of northern Europe.

On both sides of the Channel the opening of the era of more intensive warfare was marked by royal efforts to create massive military force by using the entire 'nation' in arms: the mailed horsepower of the several ranks of lords, knights, and lesser gentlemen; masses of footsoldiers provided by various rural territories or urban communities. Hired companies of specialists appear (such as the Genoese crossbowmen in the service of France or the mounted Gascon crossbowmen Edward I found so handy a force in his conquest of Wales) but from the warfare of Philip IV and Edward I through the first phase of the Hundred Years War, the reliance on specialist companies of mercenaries more or less available to the highest bidder, so prevalent in twelfth-century warfare, is overshadowed by a reliance on mustering—and paying—sufficient force among the king's subjects. As is well known, the Hundred Years War produced, in the second half of the fourteenth century, the free companies which seem so much like a new version of the twelfth-century mercenary phenomenon, perhaps raised to a higher power.

[29] A theme of Jordan, *Louis IX and the Challenge of the Crusade*.

[30] The comment of Philippe Contamine is appropriate: 'La guerre a profité du perfectionnement des rouages dans le gouvernement et l'administration des hommes. Il en fut pour les armées comme pour la justice, les finances ou la religion: l'encadrement devint plus complexe, plus rigoureux plus serré . . . les bureaucrates d'Edouard Ier et de Philippe le Bel montrent un remarquable savoir-faire dans le domaine de l'administration militaire', *Le Guerre au moyen âge*, 227.

Creating the free companies was certainly not the least important effect of fourteenth-century warfare on the social and economic life of the era, but this should not mask the earlier royal effort (of *c.*1290-1350) to produce large armies with a character we might, with perhaps pardonable anachronism, call national.

Perhaps this military policy reflects the medieval state at its most self-conscious phase, at the acme of its claims to a form of sovereign power over the military service as well as the litigation and the purses of its subjects. Compulsion was claimed as a royal right; Edward I and Philip IV would command the formation of armies they hoped would be irresistible. But if they commanded, they were also willing to pay; those who served in the king's armies would be given (or in the case of English lords at least offered) the king's wages.

Across most of the thirteenth century English military efforts earned low marks from contemporaries and have appeared in no better light to modern historians; but Edward I by the century's end has often been given credit for a new policy. The traditional view has been that he called large paid armies into being and in the process created the tactics which would win the famous set piece English victories of the Hundred Years War. That he produced large armies and used pay, extensively developing what Henry III had begun,[31] is clear; that his tactics foreshadowed Crécy and Poitiers is much more doubtful. The tactics so successful on these battlefields, basically a combination of longbowmen and dismounted men-at-arms, seem more likely to have emerged from Edward III's early campaigns in Scotland. The victories at Dupplin Moor in 1332 and at Halidon Hill in 1333 may represent the turning points.[32] Far more important than any anticipation of tactical combinations of archers and dismounted knights was Edward's combination of compulsion and pay, along with the willingness and capacity of his government to provide the wages and the flow of military supplies which this combination required.

Compulsion plus pay as the formula for achieving massive force is most evident in the procuring of footmen. Sizeable levies of infantry from the counties and boroughs generally brought

[31] Powicke, *Military Obligation in Medieval England*, 82, 95-6.

[32] Verbruggen, *The Art of Warfare*, 393; Prestwich, *The Three Edwards*, 62, 67, 197-200.

little outcry (except in times of acute political crisis, as in 1297) because in the Welsh wars the crown provided wages as soon as the troops left their county of origin, and in the Scottish wars from the time of the county muster.[33] Here Edward gave up a strong claim to free service in the interests of perceived efficiency and political expediency; precedent actually gave the king a claim to free service for forty days or two months.[34] The crown did not specify the arms of these footmen and early in the reign they were largely armed with spears, but by the time of the Scottish wars bowmen predominated. A change effected even more quickly was the replacement of sheriffs as recruiters by men holding special commissions of array. From 1282 men were specifically commissioned for this arraying of infantry; at first household and other officials were given the task, but it came increasingly into the hands of professional soldiers by the end of the reign. The size of the infantry forces could be impressive, though numbers fluctuated wildly during a campaign. Although in 1296 the king imperiously demanded a supply of cash from the Exchequer to support 60,000 footmen, he seems to have got less than half that number for this campaign and at one time or another in most campaigns had at maximum only a quarter of this number: perhaps 15,000 at one point in the Welsh war of 1277; 11,000 in 1287; 31,000 in several forces in Wales, and 16,000 at Chester in late 1294. Large forces of infantry were summoned for Scottish campaigns, but desertion usually reduced the masses of footmen quickly. Problems of inexperience, a marked inclination to desertion, and an inability to catch the elusive Scots must have raised questions about the wisdom of employing large bodies of men arrayed in the shires.[35]

Edward's cavalry forces were obtained in more complex ways and fit less easily into the formula of compulsion and pay. Both these elements appear, but they do not exhaust the possibilities. In the Welsh campaigns of 1277 and 1282 Edward issued traditional feudal summons to obtain his heavy cavalry (going

33 Powicke, *Military Obligation in Medieval England*, 82, 121-2; Prestwich, *War, Politics, and Finance*, 102; Maddicott, 'The English Peasantry and the Demands of the Crown', 34-5.

34 Powicke, *Military Obligation in Medieval England*, 118, 231.

35 Prestwich, *War, Politics, and Finance*, ch. 4; *The Three Edwards*, 68-70; Powicke, *Military Obligation in Medieval England*, ch. 7.

over to pay after the customary service was rendered), and again summoned the host for three Scottish campaigns. But the crown could scarcely rely on the feudal host alone. Over the course of the first half of the thirteenth century the new, reduced quotas for feudal service had reduced this contingent of the royal army to only about 500 fighting knights, a fraction of the force needed. Moreover Edward wanted the closest possible control over the heavy cavalry considered a key to military success.[36] A sizeable paid contingent from the royal household operated in most of Edward's armies and in the 1282 Welsh war Edward had, in fact, tried to summon an entirely paid cavalry force. But he had met significant opposition from lords—especially the earls—who were aware of the tangible economic benefits from scutage paid by their own tenants, and sensitive about any lessening of potential benefits from rights to booty and captured territories if they became a paid force, but above all wary of the loss of independence involved in accepting the discipline and subordination which came with royal pay.[37]

How many mounted warriors served in Edward's various campaigns is very difficult to know, but for the Falkirk campaign of 1298 more than 1,300 mounted men took the king's wages. Michael Prestwich has estimated the total number of cavalry in this army, however, at more than twice this number, perhaps as many as 3,000. The evidence in this instance seems in no way exceptional.[38] Thus not the king's willingness to offer pay nor the presence of a significant paid household contingent, nor the calling out of the feudal host, can explain the origins of Edward's cavalry *in toto*. Only a part of the horsemen came in response to feudal summons and only a portion of the total force seems to have accepted pay. Edward was characteristically willing to try compulsion to obtain his cavalry. Especially in the years of particular pressure late in the reign, Edward tried to distrain landowners with a certain level of income (£20 or £40 annually) not simply to take up knighthood and its administrative responsibilities, but to serve as paid cavalrymen in his Scottish

[36] Denholm-Young, 'Feudal Society in the Thirteenth Century,' 107-19; Powicke, *Military Obligation in Medieval England*, 104; Prestwich, *The Three Edwards*, 63-4.

[37] Id., *War, Politics, and Finance*, ch. 3.

[38] Ibid. 91.

wars.[39] This extension of service to all those whose landed wealth put them within the knightly class formed an important element in the crises of 1297 and 1300; in fact the opposition was serious enough for Edward to drop this attempt to link cavalry service with specific levels of landed wealth for the remainder of his reign. Edward's son would renew the effort in 1316, demanding service from fifty librate landowners; in 1324 he even tried to recruit county cavalry by means analogous to the levy of infantry forces from the shires.[40] But all these efforts were, in the final analysis, unsuccessful. There was to be no general obligation to cavalry service.

If significant numbers of cavalry were serving neither because of feudal obligation nor an agreement about wages, and were not twenty or forty or fifty liberate men compelled to serve by their level of landed wealth, they may simply have been serving at their own expense. Contingents of magnates who declined pay may, in fact, have outnumbered the paid men who were especially to be found in the royal household units. Royal writs, such as those summoning cavalry for the campaign which culminated in the capture of Caerlaverock in 1300, sometimes requested that the magnates appear not with the traditional feudal service owned (*cum servicio debito*) now so attenuated, but with all the military force they could provide (*quanto potencius poteritis*). Michael Prestwich emphasizes varied recruiting techniques that stand behind cavalry forces which, as they took the field in one campaign after another, would not have appeared to any observer to differ in their composition:

> There is no simple way of distinguishing the cavalry forces in the armies of Edward I's reign: they cannot with justice be termed either mercenary, feudal or contractual. . . . Many men served at their own expense. . . . The royal household provided a very substantial and important paid element in the armies, but in the major campaigns this was outnumbered by the contingents of magnates who refused to accept pay for themselves or for their men. Whether novel techniques of summons, based on wealth rather than on traditional obligations, or obsolete feudal methods forced on the crown by the opposition, were used, the armies as they assembled in the field were similar.[41]

[39] As early as 1282 he had tried to get twenty librate men to pay the crown for the service not performed in Wales; *ibid.* 83.

[40] Id., *The Three Edwards*, 65.

[41] Id., *War, Politics and Finance*, 168.

The flexibility and balance Edward showed in recruitment of both infantry and cavalry is stressed by Michael Powicke: 'The army of Edward I achieved a balance between contractual, feudal, and communal troops, which exceeded anything achieved before or after.'[42] Moreover, the very scale of his total effort deserves emphasis. As Michael Prestwich points out the army for the Falkirk campaign (perhaps 3,000 horse and 25,700 foot) may have been the largest single force raised by an English government to that time. In the Middle Ages it was exceeded only by Edward III's army for the siege of Calais. In the post-medieval era, English armies would exceed those of Edward I only in the middle of the seventeenth century.[43]

The armies of Philip the Fair have received less attention from historians. They seem to have been on roughly the same order of magnitude as the English; J. R. Strayer doubts that Philip 'ever had more than 30,000 men concentrated in one theater of war,' and estimated that the battlefield peak, achieved at Mons-en-Pévèle, might have been nearer 17,000 than 26,000 men.[44] The role of pay in producing these forces seems close to that scholars have in the past attributed to the armies of Edward I: the royal wages were transforming feudal service (combined with some volunteers) into a paid cavalry; and, drawing on the theoretical obligation of all free men to serve the crown in battle, large numbers of footsoldiers, perhaps as many as ten to fifteen for each horseman, were levied and paid. Philippe Contamine underscores the importance of pay to the continued recruiting of knightly cavalry across the fourteenth century:

> Les gages du roi: tel est le grand fait qui explique, conjointment à l'établissement ou à la consolidation de ses privilèges fiscaux, la facilité avec laquelle l'ensemble de la noblesse admit cette extension considérable du pouvoir monarchique et répondit largement aux mandements des souverains à travers tout le 14e siècle.[45]

The letters of retinue by which French nobles agreed to furnish troops had less the character of a contract than English indentures of the same period; the French agreements specified

42 Powicke, *Military Obligation in Medieval England*, 97.

43 Prestwich, *War, Politics, and Finance*, 113.

44 Strayer, *The Reign of Philip the Fair*, 379.

45 Contamine, *Guerre, état, et société*, 50.

the number of troops, but not the length of service and may have been in force for a month at a time, then being renewable.[46]

Confronting heavy military demands from the 1290s, Philip tried to collect direct taxes which would provide wages to hire troops, eliminating the lordly middleman. The great protest which countered this effort was calmed only by royal grants of tax exemptions or at least a sharing of tax proceeds with nobles. In 1303 Philip revived the *arrière-ban*, hoping to find in this crown claim on the military service of all free men the leverage to obtain men and money in the quantities needed. The similarity to the English tradition of general military service going back to the pre-Conquest great fyrd is obvious; both the *arrière-ban* and fyrd recall the obligation of all free men in Germanic society to give military service, especially at a time of emergency.[47] A combination of feudal summons and *arrière-ban* (providing either men or fines from those not serving) became the basis for French forces through the opening phase of the Hundred Years War in the first half of the fourteenth century. Seven times in the first two decades of the war, the French monarchy called out the *arrière-ban*: in 1338, 1340, 1342, 1346, 1347, 1355, 1356. But the king even more commonly called out the nobles specifically, paying them, even if they owed free service, freeing them from any debt prosecution while they were in royal military service, and sometimes exempting them from current taxation. When a summons was issued, some of the mounted men who appeared would be volunteers who owed no service, but were eager to fight at the king's wages. Towns, whether directly under the king's lordship or not, were expected to furnish companies of footmen, often crossbowmen; in the course of the fourteenth century some received tax exemptions and were, in effect, treated like fiefholders.[48]

Thus Philip, his sons, and the early Valois kings obtained the needed heavy cavalry and footmen, though often to the accompaniment of all the tedious negotiating so much a part of crown relationships with its mighty subjects individually and with its humbler subjects in their local communities. As in the

[46] Ibid. 64.

[47] Hollister, *The Military Organization of Norman England*, 16, 76-83, 112, 192, 217-19, 230.

[48] Contamine, *Guerre, état, et société*, 27-62.

case of England, though these composite forces may seem small by modern standards, they represent a medieval apogee; the size of French armies in the first half of the fourteenth century would scarcely be exceeded until the end of the reign of Louis XI in the closing decades of the fifteenth century.[49] But, again, as in the English case, the achievement of sizeable armies did not mean a satisfying level of military efficiency and capacity.

The armies of Edward I and Philip IV, in fact, proved often to be ill-coordinated and ill-suited for the needs of campaign and battlefield. Moreover, a significant financial and political cost had to be paid for producing them on either side of the Channel.[50] Resistance within each realm was recurrent; the end of Philip's reign and the last decade of Edward's reign were indelibly marked by the crisis caused by warfare on a new scale. In England beset by the political turmoil of Edward II's reign or in France making the uneasy transition from Capetian to Valois rule, an observer would have required the gift of foreknowledge to predict that the costly and intense warfare of Edward I in Wales and Scotland and that of Philip IV in Flanders and Aquitaine would be soon carried on by English armies in the heartland of the kingdom of France.

The changes enabling this outcome must be sought in French and English politics and in English military tactics as they developed in the 1330s. Uncertainty over the succession to the French throne after the exhaustion of the Capetian line seriously weakened Valois France. Edward III could hope that disaffected subjects of the French king might join his cause, or at least offer little assistance to Philip VI. The tactics, as briefly suggested above, were apparently learned slowly in Edward III's campaigns fought in Scotland, while English arms were still under the shadow of the terrible defeat at Bannockburn.[51] The new battlefield formation which triumphed at Dupplin Moor in 1332 and at Halidon Hill in 1333 combined archers and dismounted men-at-arms, and retained the possibility of a cavalry action as a decisive blow or for the pursuit of a fleeing enemy. The problem of mobility which had hampered the usefulness of the infantry

[49] Contamine, *Guerre, état, et sociéte*, 72.

[50] Powicke, *Military Obligation in Medieval England*, ch. 10; Strayer, *The Reign of Philip the Fair*, 147-91.

[51] For what follows see Verbruggen, *The Art of Warfare*, 393; Prestwich, *The Three Edwards*, 62, 67, 197-200.

raised by Edward I and Edward II was solved by the use of mounted infantry which appeared in 1333; not only could the archers now ride with the men-at-arms, they could be integrated into magnate retinues. Archers serving in such a retinue might very likely turn out to be fighting men of higher quality than those conscripted for service a generation earlier by commisioners of array.

The use of retinues to form a contract army makes a logical final link in this chain. But the contract army must not be hurried along any more swiftly than the paid army. During the first phase of the Hundred Years War armies led by the king in person were usually paid by the traditional agency of the wardrobe and formal contracts were apparently not drawn up with leaders of retinues. In 1337 Edward III raised the first army entirely on contract, but in the 1340s he 'revised and elaborated the system by which men were assessed according to their wealth to provide specific numbers of troops, who were then recruited by means of commissions of array.' The resulting outcry might have produced a serious crisis but for the great victories at Crécy and Calais which smothered widespread protest. Later in the Hundred Years War the importance of contracts grew at the expense of wardrobe payment of wages because so many expeditions were led by magnates rather than the king.[52] A final tactical development, as Michael Prestwich suggests, may have come from the early years of the reign of Edward III. Scottish raiding across the border and deep into northern England may have given the English a dramatic demonstration of the effectiveness of the medieval version of total warfare—widespread destruction wrought by troops who travelled lightly, living off the countryside. If so, the signposts pointed to the *chevauchées* which English armies would use to devastating effect in the provinces of France.[53]

During these same years the young Edward III was laying the foundations for the co-operation and trust of the magnates of England which ultimately would play as great a role in English victories in France as any changes in tactics, or rather which enabled the tactics to work so effectively. Edward III had clearly learned from the problems and errors of the first two Edwards and

[52] Id., 'English Armies in the Hundred Years War', 102-13; Sherborne, 'Indentured Retinues', 718-46.

[53] Prestwich, *The Three Edwards*, 67-8.

was determined to eliminate the internal political problems which had plagued his grandfather's later years and had brought his father's deposition.[54] As masterful patron of chivalric ceremonial he fulfilled the beau ideal of a king held by his magnates;[55] in the lavish nature of his generosity he significantly outdid the rather pinched quality of reward offered by his grandfather; by his widespread generosity reaching all who counted he avoided the critical problems of patronage created by the detested favourites of his father. Above all, Edward III was able to enlist the magnate class in the profitable business of war in France with its satisfying prospects of renown and loot. Moreover Edward III showed his willingness to yield gracefully on most matters other than the all-important matter of the war. Ten years after his father's deposition, then, on the eve of the Hundred Years War, Edward III had established the political environment and worked out the military techniques requisite for warfare on a major scale. Across the Channel the Valois claim on the French throne and on the loyalties of Frenchmen raised questions and presented opportunities for Edward III. What he needed—what any medieval king waging such war needed—was money.

3. RESOURCES FOR WAR: MONEY

Charles Victor Langlois described the Anglo-French war of 1297 as a struggle between the pound sterling and the livre tournois.[56] Whatever qualifications we might want to make, the statement serves to remind us how closely the war capacity of the thirteenth- or fourteenth-century state was linked to its economic well-being and to the efficiency of the mechanism of royal finance. How the English and French states filled their war chests is thus as important a question as how they filled their companies of cavalry and infantry. Three major differences between the English and French royal finances had appeared by the late thirteenth century. In the first place English kings had, considering the relative size of the two realms, more efficiently than their French counterparts found means of tapping the wealth

54 McKisack, 'Edward III and the Historians', 1-15.

55 Vale, *Edward III and Chivalry*.

56 Langlois, *Histoire de France*, II. 297.

of their subjects; above all they had moved beyond feudal-domainal revenues towards a system of direct and indirect taxation. Secondly, this English revenue and especially the tax revenue was closely linked to credit arrangements of a sort largely undeveloped by the French monarchs; the use of credit added greatly to the power and flexibility of action available to English kings. Thirdly, English credit finance in particular, as the English capacity for war in general, was closely linked to the great economic resource represented by English wool. The sizeable export trade in raw wool not only fed the looms in the low countries and even in northern Italy, it fed the machinery of war by providing revenues of sufficient size and sufficient constancy to serve as collateral for regular and systematic borrowing by the crown.

By the reign of Edward I the English crown had for nearly a century been slowly expanding the base of its revenues beyond those available after the Norman Conquest: the shire farm, profits of justice, feudal incidents, royal perquisites (such as tolls, fines, etc.) and such extraordinary grants as tallage on the royal demesne and danegeld.[57] Considerable though these revenues were, perceived needs were already outpacing the funds they produced, especially after the rapid inflation of 1180-1220.[58] Expansion of the revenues available from the feudal relationship of king and his tenants-in-chief, particularly the charges for taking up a fief (reliefs), was one avenue tried by Henry II and his sons; but they encountered customary and practical limitations and then Magna Carta proved a roadblock against further movement along that line.[59] The occasional aid for knighting a son or marrying a daughter would long be collected and provided revenue which kings surely welcomed. But the feudal aids and incidents were no foundation on which to build an active and costly royal policy; certainly the limited profits from feudal incidents and the sporadic profits from aids would not support a vigorous war policy. Such a policy would only be funded by a

[57] Mitchell, *Taxation in Medieval England*; Ramsay, *A History of the Revenues of the Kings of England*.

[58] Harvey, 'The English Inflation of 1180-1220', 3-31.

[59] Harriss, *King, Parliament, and Public Finance*, 8; Holt, *Magna Carta*, 107-8, 112, 208-9.

system of taxation which would effectively, even if only periodically, tap the wealth of the entire realm.[60]

Taxation in England

A tradition of taxation in England stretched back to the danegeld of the late tenth century, but this tax itself had been reduced by twelfth-century exemptions and could not be imagined the key to funding a vigorous military policy.[61] For a time the Anglo-Norman kings used a ramshackle collection of feudal and juridical revenues along with almost any other sources of coin that their position afforded; even Henry II's efforts have been termed 'less a system of taxation than a system of plunder.'[62] Of course system was less important than success to Henry and his sons, whose war finance astonished their contemporaries. F. M. Powicke suggest[63]

> The true answer to the problem is, as Gerald of Wales points out, that the extraordinary revenue (*accidentia*) was vastly increased during the second half of the twelfth century. The growth of a settled and industrious population, protected by the law in town and country, had multiplied these indirect proceeds of the land which were accessible to the government; if rents were inelastic, loans, tallages, and fines were capable of vast extension.

By the end of the twelfth century, however, new sources of money were needed. As noted above, inflation multiplied the cost of war several times over in the late twelfth and early thirteenth century.[64] Scutage was clearly unsatisfactory, being based on a list of knights' fees that was becoming progressively outdated. The financial opportunities of a forest eyre were clear by 1175, but these eyres were held only sporadically and the revenue they produced may have been hard to collect and was limited by the sale of exemptions from forest law.[65] The various aids and gifts kings could extract from their lands and towns were transformed into a uniform tallage in Henry II's reign and became for a few

60 Mitchell, *Taxation in Medieval England*.

61 What follows is based on Harriss, *King, Parliament, and Public Finance*, ch. 1.

62 Ibid. 7.

63 Powicke, *The Loss of Normandy*, 232-3, quoting Gerald of Wales, *Opera*, xiii. 316.

64 See n. 58.

65 Young, *The Royal Forests of Medieval England*, 37-58.

years in John's reign (1202-6) an annual imposition. But the yield was low and showed a tendency to decline. The same disabilities reduced the usefulness of the tax known as carucage, assessed on hides in 1194, on carucates in 1198 and 1217, and on plough teams in 1200 and 1220.

The breakthrough pointing toward the standard medieval English form of tax, the lay subsidy collected throughout the realm on assessed wealth, seems in retrospect to have come in 1207 when King John took a thirteenth on revenues and movable goods. Several opportunities in the second half of the twelfth century had helped to make the lay subsidy possible. Officials could argue that the tenth for the crusade collected in 1166 and that collected in 1188, known as the Saladin tithe, were needed for a cause of unassailable worthiness. In England the argument worked; significantly in France the outcry against a feudal aid on this basis was sufficient to end the effort, and sufficient as well to give feudal aid a bad taste in the mouths of royal officials into the reign of Louis IX.[66] Then the ransom of Richard I provided a justification for taxation in 1193 and 1194 almost as good as the Saladin tithe; the obligation of all vassals to contribute was easily generalized to all subjects. The French would not ransom a king until the disastrous first crusade of Louis IX in the middle of the next century, and would move towards a system of taxation only after the capture of King John in the middle of the fourteenth century. Though kings did not thoughtfully arrange capture to aid the finances of their successors, royal captivities did seem to have this effect. Moreover, both the Saladin tithe and a part of Richard's ransom were assessed as certain percentages of personal property, which proved to be simpler to collect and more lucrative than other taxes based on the assessed value of land. King John used this method in collecting his thirteenth in 1207. John's son, Henry III, collected four of these great taxes on personal property in his long reign, a fifteenth in 1225, a fortieth in 1232, a thirtieth in 1237, and a twentieth in 1269. Edward I increased the tempo only slightly in the first half of his reign, taking a fifteenth in 1275, a thirtieth in 1283, and a fifteenth again in 1290. But once across the mid-1290s' dividing line, the change was marked: six

[66] Favier, 'Les Finances de Saint Louis', 136.

taxes fell in the last fourteen years of the reign, a tenth and sixth in 1294, an eleventh and seventh in 1295, a twelfth and eighth in 1296, a ninth in 1297, a fifteenth in 1301, and a thirtieth and twentieth in 1306.[67] Moreover this general pattern continued into the opening years of the Hundred Years War. In the forty-one years 1294-1334 the crown levied sixteen taxes; equally important, it dramatically increased the rate.[68] By the opening of the great war with France the English crown had established a pattern of direct taxation on personal property which was of obvious importance for war on a major scale.

The resource of English wool

But direct parliamentary taxation tells only part of the story and met only part of the high cost of warfare. The finance of armies and sailing of fleets depended not only on direct taxation discussions by officials, lords, and commons in parliament, it also required the wealth represented by flocks of sheep in green countryside pasture. Indirect taxation of the trade in English wool and direct manipulation of the wool export *per se* provided a cornerstone for royal war finance. It is most difficult to imagine the conquest of Wales or the repeated campaigns in Scotland, let alone the English expeditions to France, in the absence of this major resource. In 1297 when the dissident earls and their supporters drew up the Monstraunces to document lay grievances they uncharacteristically waxed statistical and declared that wool approached half and the tax on wool a fifth of the total value of the land.[69] Accurate quantification was not one of the outstanding chivalric virtues and the estimates in the Monstraunces were certainly off the mark; but the contemporary sense of the great value of the wool trade and of the importance of the taxation of wool to the king's revenues is dramatically emphasized.

As Edmund Fryde has suggested,[70] kings could rely on the wool trade for support of their wars in two ways. First, they could increase the export duties on raw wool shipped to the continent

[67] In the double rates the towns and ancient demesne paid on the higher schedule. Prestwich, *War, Politics, and Finance*, 179.

[68] Willard, *Parliamentary Taxes on Personal Property, 1290-1334*, 3-5, 9-11.

[69] Miller, 'War, Taxation, and the English Economy', 12.

[70] Fryde, 'Financial Resources of Edward I in the Netherlands, 1294-1298' (1962), 1168-87.

by additions to the low custom of half a mark (6*s*. 8*d*.) established in 1275. Second, they might themselves enter the trade with stocks of wool acquired through taxation or compulsory crown purchase. Given the volume of the wool exported, between 30,000 and 40,000 sacks a year (with the sack weighing 364 English pounds), either choice offered tremendous financial possibilities. Unfortunately the choices were mutually exclusive. Customs revenues depended on a high volume of private export, yet royal woolmongering required close restriction or even prohibition of private wool export in order to obtain monopoly prices for royal wool sold abroad. The contradiction was no mere abstraction. Warfare on the scale intended by Edward I and Edward III put such massive and urgent pressure on resources that the crown was forced not only to try the two policies in quick succession but even side by side.

The problem is illustrated in Edward I's years of crisis. In 1294-7 the king first considered a forced loan in wool, but encountered such determined resistance from merchants that king and council substituted the heavier customs duties soon called the maltolt. The king was apparently influenced by an elaborate financial scheme submitted by an anonymous foreigner who might have been an agent of the Riccardi of Lucca, the royal bankers. The plan called for a sales tax of 2*d*, on the pound and sumptuary laws to free revenues for purposes of war by limiting certain domestic expenses; but its main feature was a heavy export duty of 5 marks per sack on wool which was expected to yield 110,000 marks within six months. The crown, in fact, began the infamous maltolt at this rate charging 5 or 3 marks per sack of exported wool, depending on quality, though opposition soon forced a lowering of the rate to 3 marks per sack.[71] The

[71] The document recording this plan is printed in Blaauw, *The Barons' War*, app. C and in Langlois, 'Project for Taxation Presented to Edward I', 517-21. Prestwich discusses the document in *War, Politics, and Finance*, 195. Langlois thought the author 'some agent of the Plantagenets' who was working in France but whose 'extremely incorrect' French style shows he was not French. His plan remains in the French archives because it was 'taken from its author before he had time to send it to England'. Though there can be no certainty, this description would perfectly fit an agent of the Riccardi of Lucca. The Riccardi maintained branches of their *societas* in France, they were extremely anxious to try to maintain their relationship with Edward I in the troubled period of the outbreak

maltolt brought overall customs revenue in 1294-7 to roughly £116,000, more than the proceeds of direct lay taxation in these years. This revenue was obviously of great assistance to Edward. Yet a sixfold increase in export duty had failed to produce anything like a proportionate increase in royal customs revenue; the cause was apparently a drop in the volume of wool exported in the first two years of the war to a level less than half that of the five years preceding the war. This decline was closely related to the war, but seems to have been a result of disruptions in trade and credit patterns as well as determined and successful resistance to the maltolt.[72]

Pressures to turn to the alternate policy of royal wool-mongering, even in the years of the maltolt, are evident in the occasional export bans with special licences for royal creditors and privileged Italian companies. But the decisive switch to direct royal trade in wool appeared in 1297, first in crown seizure of the wool of foreign merchants and soon by a rather hasty general wool seizure. Opposition to Edward's wool policies proved to be so weighty that abolition both of the wool seizure and the maltolt were among the concessions extracted from the government in England in 1297, during Edward I's absence on the continent. Higher indirect taxation of wool and the crown seizures had not only provoked outrage and resistance at home, they had failed to produce sufficient revenues to form the basis for the war chest Edward needed on the continent; as noted, the higher wool export duty was sizeable but not completely satisfactory; the seizures and wool sales of 1296-8 proved much more disappointing and may have given Edward I only £25,000, less than half the amount he

of Anglo-French warfare, and they suffered a seizure of their business records by the agents of Philip IV. See Kaeuper, *Bankers to the Crown*, 225-7. That the document remained in France does not mean the plan never reached Edward I. The regular company correspondence (fragments of which survive from 1296 and later) could easily have conveyed the scheme to the Riccardi in London for presentation to the king; it is equally likely that the plan was drawn up in London and that the document seized in France was a copy.

72 Fryde, 'Financial Resources of Edward I in the Netherlands, 1294-1298' (1962), 1179-82; and his 'Financial Policies of the Royal Governments', 833-4; Prestwich, *War, Politics, and Finance*, 196-7; Harris, *King, Parliament, and Public Finance*, ch. 3; Lloyd, *The English Wool Trade in the Middle Ages*, 75-98.

paid in subsidies to his continental allies in 1297-8. The political costs of both policies had been high.[73]

Edward III, like his grandfather, found it necessary to try both royal options connecting the resource of wool and war finance. After experiments with several wool subsidies for Scottish campaigns early in his reign,[74] Edward III, on the eve of his war with France, turned to an active role in the wool trade in hopes of finding the enormous resources his plans required. He could draw the elements of his plan from isolated policies carried out in the reigns of his father and grandfather: an embargo on wool exports; crown wool seizures; a staple port through which all legal export must pass. But he had to combine these elements skilfully, working with a body of merchants 'small enough to enforce the monopoly rigidly, and wealthy enough to sustain the delay between purchase and sale, while concurrently making large advances to the Crown on the expected profit.'[75] Edward III and his advisers planned on a grand scale.[76] To a group of perhaps 250 native merchants (the 'Contract Merchants') the king gave the monopoly of wool export; freed of competition, especially from foreign merchants, they contracted to ship 30,000 sacks of wool to the continent in three instalments. The king could also offer them the prospect of excellent prices for their exported wool, perhaps as much as 200 per cent profit; a strict embargo in effect since August 1336, would ensure continental customers willing to pay handsomely for English wool. In return Edward got an interest-free loan of £200,000 (100,000*m*. in advance of each of the three shipments of 10,000 sacks of wool), plus half the profit on the sale of the wool. A schedule of minimal prices for the purchase of the wool in England was to prevent a level of

[73] In addition to the sources cited in the previous note see Prestwich (ed.), *Documents Illustrating the Crisis of 1297-1298 in England*.

[74] Harriss, *King, Parliament, and Public Finance*, 426 ff.

[75] Ibid. 436. Working with the great wool merchant Lawrence Ludlow, Edward I may have considered some such scheme on a more modest scale in 1294, but if so the plan sank with Lawrence when he was drowned crossing the Channel with the wool fleet in late 1294 (see Fryde, 'Financial Resources of Edward I in the Netherlands, 1294-1298' (1962), 1180).

[76] What follows is based on several studies by Fryde: 'Edward III's Wool Monopoly of 1336'; 'Financial Resources of Edward I in the Netherlands, 1294-1298' (1967); 'Materials for the Study of Edward III's Credit Operations, 1327-1348'.

exploitation of wool producers which might generate enough resistance to ruin the entire scheme. Such a guarantee for wool producers was all the more needed since the Contract Merchants were empowered to use the royal prerogative of purveyance and could purchase wool forcibly and without immediate payment.

The first 10,000 sacks of wool were, in fact, collected and sent across the Channel to Dordrecht; but because of a delay in sending over this shipment the crown altered the original agreement with the merchants and gave the royal envoys rather than the merchants themselves full control over the wool. Faced with the king's war needs, the royal envoys, at a conference with the merchants at Gertruidenberg in Holland on 19 December 1337, demanded £276,000 by mid-Lent. When the Contract Merchants refused this demand as outrageous, the crown agents seized the entire supply of exported wool at Dordrecht. But if the king was to play woolmonger for his war finance he now had to arrange the sale of the first shipment (actually some 10,300 sacks) on his own, and also had to see to the shipment and sale of the second and third consignments of 10,000 sacks each. Though he had expected to increase his profit significantly by the Dordrecht seizure, Edward in fact made only a very little more from selling this wool than the Contract Merchants had promised him in their original agreement. Moreover, his efforts to bring over the second and third consignments of wool were even more troublesome and disappointing. The levy, often called the Moiety because royal agents were empowered to seize half of any wool found in England, seems to have been mismanaged and certainly proceeded slowly; it produced only 2,806 of the 10,000 sacks needed for the second shipment by August 1338.

By this time the king and his advisers realized that a new and more carefully planned wool levy was needed. They secured assent for a workable scheme for a tax in wool, based on precise assessment, at a Great Council assembled at Northampton. But three problems plagued this plan. First, the scheme was obviously coming too late to supply the king's needs for the current year; he could expect little relief until 1339. Second, and equally serious, when the wool arrived in the Netherlands it would be sold in a depressed market. Edward's need for war cash forced him to allow free export to increase customs revenue; the price to be paid by exporters was a schedule of higher rates (£2 and £3 per sack for natives and aliens respectively). Yet he allowed his magnate followers and his business creditors to export wool free of duty as a means of repaying the royal debts owed these men. Not only did the vast quantities of wool exported from England thus fail to generate proportionate customs revenues, they also drove down wool prices in the Netherlands. Finally, the wool levy yielded less than Edward expected, a little more than 14,000 sacks in place of the nearly 19,000 calculated; and even of the wool collected, much had to be paid over to royal creditors (9,303 sacks to the Bardi and Peruzzi, William de la Pole, William van Duivenvoorde, Paul Monte Florum)[77] or shipped to aid the defence of Gascony (397 sacks).

Plans for the two most ambitious military enterprises of our period, that of Edward I launched in 1294 and that of Edward III in the years following 1337, had thus been based in large part on the resources of the wool trade; considerable though these resources were, in each case the costs of warfare (or at least the cost of alliances designed for war) drained the war chests more swiftly than any wool schemes could fill them. In each the immediacy of wartime need pushed the crown into the alternate and even contradictory policies of indirect royal taxation of wool and direct royal appropriation of wool. In each effort the results were disappointing: the king was outraged that his finance slumped far below his goals; the merchants and wool producers could scarcely be pleased when their wool was seized under conditions promising uncertain or delayed repayment; moreover, the lesser merchants and the graziers bitterly resented the disruptive embargoes and the monopolies restricting opportunities to the relatively few intimately involved in high government finance, perhaps above all, the lower prices paid to home wool producers. Important consequences followed in a 'constitutional' vein and important questions were raised in parliament concerning the authorizing power and legitimacy for crown use of wool in war finance; the Commons resented the king's negotiations with assemblies of merchants; they also came to resent the narrow monopolies and the wool seizures which so often accompanied them. This entire pattern—the double royal policy of direct and

[77] Duivenvoorde was an influential Low Countries magnate and financier with links to the Count of Holland and the Duke of Brabant; Monte Florum was one of the chief royal paymasters in the Netherlands.

indirect taxation of wool, negotiations with merchant assemblies as well as parliament, narrow monopolies associated with wool seizures, and constant argument among king, great and small merchants, and producers—ended in the decade following the crisis of 1341. But the change is best understood in the context of the royal credit measures so closely connected with the wool trade and so essential to the prosecution of war.

English credit finance

In July 1338 the Great Crown of Edward III was shipped across the Channel, along with other royal jewels, to serve as security for the war loans needed to keep the king's continental campaign alive.[78] The incident provides a symbolic demonstration of the royal dependence on credit which was already old by the opening of the great war with France.

In fact, something like a first stage in the linkage of costly war and credit finance had appeared in the ambitious efforts of Richard and John to preserve their continental possessions against Capetian pressure in the late twelfth and early thirteenth centuries. Richard employed the prominent Rouen money-changer Geoffrey of Val Richer both in the payment of his sizeable ransom and in building the impressive fortress he named Château Gaillard. John relied on a network of money-changers which stretched from Piacenza and Genoa to Cologne and Rouen. He likewise instituted a rudimentary customs system 'the fifteenth of the merchants in the seaports', by the Winchester Assize of 1203. This may have been a wartime revenue measure 'to tide him over the struggle with France. . . .'[79] The appetite for power quickly developed a royal taste for credit. As F. M. Powicke observed, 'Richard and John were unable to resist the temptation to borrow and to go on borrowing. John borrowed from everybody, so that the records of the last months of his rule in Normandy give the impression that the revenue must have been far exceeded by his anticipations.'[80]

But if the effort to prevent the loss of Normandy brought a first stage in credit finance, drawing broadly on money-changers and Jewish financiers, the ambitious scale of Edward I's kingship

[78] Fryde, 'Financial Resources of Edward I in the Netherlands, 1294-1298' (1967), 1154.

[79] Gras, *The Early English Customs System*, 48-53.

[80] Powicke, *The Loss of Normandy*, 236-40.

would open a second stage of longer duration and greater scale. For roughly three-quarters of a century, *c.*1270-*c.*1340, the English crown relied heavily on a succession of major financiers: the Riccardi of Lucca to 1294; the Frescobaldi of Florence, 1299-1311; Antonio Pessagno of Genoa, *c.*1312-20; the Bardi, later in combination with the Peruzzi of Florence, *c.*1312-41. These merchant bankers provided the advances required if the considerable royal resources were to be translated into a capacity for decisive action. By the late thirteenth and fourteenth centuries English kings needed credit facilities to anticipate revenue even for peacetime expenditure. In the first four years of his reign, before the Welsh war of 1276-7, Edward I borrowed on average about £13,600 from the Riccardi.[81] In the calm before the French war the government of Isabella and Mortimer and then of Edward III (after his coup) borrowed in 1328-31, between £12,000 and £19,000 annually from the Bardi.[82] Major and sustained campaigning created demands which would have been inconceivable and unbearable without the crown bankers. The existence of sophisticated arrangements between the English crown and the Italian financiers was thus a critically important precondition for the type of warfare which emerged at the end of the thirteenth century. Throughout the High Medieval Ages demographic and economic growth across Europe had developed a remarkable and widespread, if uneven, prosperity. Several great Italian companies, in their role as English royal bankers, enabled kings to channel some portion of this wealth into grander and more continuous warfare than men had previously managed or imagined possible. Thus Edmund Fryde suggests that

> The system of regular borrowing made it easier for England to sustain the role of a great power which the ambitions of English kings and their possession of continental dominions imposed upon this country: it must be taken into account among the factors that encouraged Edward III to embark upon his Scottish adventure and that later made him ready to face war with France.[83]

The massive scale of Italian lending and the close integration of the companies into the financial structures and processes of the

[81] Derived from accounts in *CPR 1272-1281*, 131-2, and E101/126/1.

[82] Fryde, 'Edward III's Wool Monopoly of 1336', 10.

[83] Id., 'Loans to the English Crown, 1328-1331', 211.

English government deserve emphasis. When the system was working at its best, as launched by the Riccardi and Edward I, continued by Edward I and Edward II with the Frescobaldi and reconstituted by Edward III with the Bardi and Peruzzi, the companies were not formally approached for each loan needed to finance a diplomat in Rome or to pay a shire contingent marching into Wales. The crown entered into long range understandings with the merchants; it committed major sources of revenue to them and in return expected cash advances whenever and wherever the need arose, on a scale from a few pounds to many thousands; running accounts were kept and were settled periodically with interest on the loans (in addition to a flow of royal favours) easily concealed. Though the bankers had considerable resources of their own[84] they also served as links between the crown and the entire community of Italian merchant bankers active in England. As all of these companies were international in scope, operating by means of letters carried by their own couriers throughout a network of branches stretching from Rome to Dublin,[85] their potential for channelling into royal coffers the liquid wealth available in Western Europe is obvious.

The initial attraction bringing the Italians to England was the wool trade, along with the opportunities of involvement in papal high finance, and it was likewise this trade which enabled the king to employ them as his financiers.[86] Although Henry III had relied on various merchants of Cahors as lenders, wine agents, and purveyors of the household,[87] the origins of a royal credit structure which operated continuously and on a major scale appear only with Edward I; the development appears especially after 1275 when he instituted the custom of half a mark (6*s*. 8*d*.) per sack of exported wool, later called the Ancient Custom. This duty provided a certain and sizeable source of revenue admirably suited to serve as collateral for a continuous series of loans. Edward I would use this custom as the base on which to build a firm relationship

[84] Bardi assets in 1318 stood at 875,000*fl*., or roughly £130,000 sterling, at a time when Edward II's ordinary revenue did not much exceed £30,000 annually; (see Fryde and Fryde, 'Public Credit', 455.)

[85] See the Riccardi examples in Kaeuper, *Bankers to the Crown*, ch. 1, and the app. to the ch.

[86] Lloyd, *The English Wool Trade in the Middle Ages*, ch. 3.

[87] Ibid. 45-7.

with the Riccardi of Lucca,[88] the Italian *societas* he had found so helpful on his crusade in 1270 and on the return to take over the reins of government in England after his father's death in late 1272. The Riccardi helped establish the 1275 custom and for the next nineteen years were receivers of the customs in England (and for most of this time in Ireland as well), collecting the duties as repayment for their steady stream of loans, payments, and purchases on the king's behalf. They did not farm the customs, paying a set fee in the hopes of profit; they collected the customs for nearly two decades as the most certain sign and most significant support of their role as king's merchants, constantly receiving and paying on his business. Customs revenue repaid perhaps £211,000 out of the king's total obligation of £409,000 to the firm in 1272-94; proceeds of direct taxation in the same period repaid a little more than half as much, roughly £125,000. When the Riccardi lost the control of the wool custom in July of 1294, it was a clear sign that their long, positive association with Edward I was at an end. Averaged over the twenty-two years of their service as crown bankers, Riccardi loans stood at £18,500 per annum, nearly half as much as the annual receipts accounted for by the household, the principal agency of Edward I's government finance. This arrangement between king and banker seems to have come close to the ideal for both parties: while served by the Riccardi Edward I suffered no insurmountable problems of liquidity and carried out the most significant accomplishments of his reign; the Riccardi happily advanced money on the security of royal revenues in their charge, collected repayment with interest and enjoyed a flow of royal privileges nearly as constant as their stream of loans to the crown.

The effects of such financial capacity on military campaigning are apparent. Edward I's relationship with the Riccardi clearly stood behind his conquest of Wales.[89] During the first Welsh campaign in 1276-7 the Italians advanced £22,500 towards a total war cost estimated by John Morris at £23,149. Moreover, in comparison with the four years before the war, Riccardi loans

[88] On Edward I and the Riccardi see Fryde and Fryde, 'Public Credit', ch. 7; Kaeuper, *Bankers to the Crown*; Prestwich, 'Italian Merchants'; (1979); id., *War, Politics, and France*, ch. 9.

[89] Kaeuper, *Bankers to the Crown*, ch. 4; Morris, *The Welsh Wars of Edward I*, 74-80, 140-2, 196-8, 267-70.

in the three years covering the campaign and its financial aftermath showed a threefold increase. During the second campaign (1282-3) which ended the independent Welsh principality, Riccardi loans came to £72,600. Though not all of this money went specifically for war expenditure, the sum should be compared with a special war account (listing £101,621 received for the war) and with the usual account of wardrobe (the financial agency of the royal household), which brings the total royal expenditure in the war years to £204,573. Riccardi advances made up £39,196 or roughly two-fifths of the special war fund and £33,405 of the regular wardrobe account. By chance the relatively minor campaign to crush the rebellion of Rhys Maredudd in 1287 shows the role of Riccardi credit in warfare with greatest precision. In the absence of the wardrobe, travelling with the king on the continent, the Italians had, literally, to finance the war and their lending had to be recorded in a separate account. This account survives, as does the urgent letter from Edmund, Earl of Cornwall, the regent. This letter does not negotiate loans; it simply orders the Riccardi to pay the paymasters of horse and foot 'all funds, either our money in your possession or money as loans for our business, or money procured in any other way'; but it also notes that the king 'will cause allowance to be made' to the Riccardi in their account 'for the money thus to be paid' by them.[90] The advantage of credit arrangements in wartime could scarcely be made more obvious: in an emergency the dimensions of which were dangerously unknown in Westminster, a sizeable paid force could be assembled despite the absence of the wardrobe, and in disregard of the cash available in the treasury. The bankers did just what was expected of them. Several Riccardi agents accompanied the army into the field to supervise payments and their colleagues in London supplemented company resources in the usual way, by negotiating two general series of loans with twelve other Italian *societates* operating in England. Riccardi advances provided £8,288, about 98 per cent of the cost of actual campaigning (and about 80 per cent of the overall costs, including garrison expenses, of the suppression of the rising). For his part the regent could lay hands on only £823 at once: £430 extorted from the Jews; £300 from the Canterbury

[90] Discussed, with full citations to sources, in Kaeuper, *Bankers to the Crown*, 195-9.

mint; plus small sums from other sources. Equally interesting, the accounts of the constable of Bristol castle show the Riccardi had an additional £4,000 in waiting at Bristol, in case the Welsh rebellion proved more formidable than it in fact turned out to be. The bulk of Riccardi lending for this campaign was charged on the wool custom; in their account for wool export revenues 1286-9 the merchants were given allowances for £7,222 paid out in wages of horse and foot. It is noteworthy that during these same years the Riccardi were financing Edward's continental visit, paying out £103,733 for his household and diplomatic expenses in 1286-9.

When the collapse of the relationship came in 1294 and the years following, the cause was no failure of will in either partner, but rather a complex series of political and financial miscalculations by both.[91] The Riccardi slid into bankruptcy protesting in their private, internal correspondence that their greatest goal was recovery in order once again to serve the English king and the English lords; Edward, so soon as he could, established the Riccardi system anew, with the Frescobaldi as replacement bankers. It is no surprise that Edward II maintained this system with the Frescobaldi as long as he could, until the political revolution of 1310-11 wrecked it.[92]

The Frescobaldi moved warily and perhaps reluctantly into the Riccardi position. From 1299 their lending, although still on a small scale, became more regular and by 1301 Edward I promised them the wool custom, as soon as his Gascon creditors were satisfied from this revenue for advances provided in the war against Philip the Fair. But the promise, repeated in 1302, was no basis for a full agreement with the Frescobaldi. The queue of creditors waiting for repayment from the 1275 custom was distressingly long. Clearly the crown needed a new base for the renewal of the Italian credit arrangement which had proved so useful before 1294. Edward partially secured this base in the New Custom of 1303. In return for a charter (the *Carta Mercatoria*) which in effect gave them equal standing with Englishmen in business transactions, alien merchants would henceforth pay 50

[91] Ibid. 209-51.

[92] On the Frescobaldi see, in addition to the sources listed in n. 88, two studies by Kaeuper: 'The Frescobaldi of Florence'; 'Royal Finance and the Crisis of 1297'.

per cent higher export duties on wool in addition to a schedule of new duties on other imports and exports. But the general outcome may have fallen considerably short of Edward's highest hopes, for the native merchants were unwilling to pay the new duties and the increase on imports and exports of foreign merchants added only about £5,000 a year to his income. In itself the addition was inadequate as a base for a renewed credit structure with a major Italian company. The revenue was immediately put in Frescobaldi hands, but a year later, largely ignoring the claims of his Gascon creditors, Edward gave the Frescobaldi control over nearly all old customs revenue as well. The result was just what he intended: Frescobaldi loans 1302-10 jumped to £15,300 per year, three times the level of 1299-1302. Over the entire period 1299-1310 the crown debt to the merchants came to more than £155,531.

The credit system based on Italians only suffered a setback when in 1310-11 Edward II's political enemies, the Ordainers, exiled the Frescobaldi, required native control of the custom, and abolished the additional duties negotiated with foreign merchants in 1303. The advantages to the crown so obvious to the Ordainers were still present and the chance for high profits in royal service could still attract bold merchants, despite the risks. Edward II quickly found a new banker in Antonio Pessagno[93] who was willing and able, even in perilous times, to lend on the Riccardi scale for a number of years; in *c*.1310-*c*.1319 he lent Edward II at least £145,000 or more than £16,100 a year, on average.[94] In 1311 he was assigned the proceeds of the London customs and half those of Southampton in repayment of crown debts owed him; a letter written by a partner of the failing Frescobaldi in 1313 enviously mentions further customs assignments made to Pessagno.[95] But evidence of Pessagno's dealings with the crown does not permit the close analysis of crown repayment possible for the Riccardi and Frescobaldi.[96] In fact there is something of a maverick quality about Pessagno; he was the head of a shifting group of merchants rather than a great Tuscan company; his

[93] Fryde, 'Antonio Pessagno of Genoa'.

[94] Fryde and Fryde, 'Public Credit', 459, suggests Pessagno 'may have been actuated by a desire to establish his position at all costs.'

[95] Kaeuper, 'The Frescobaldi of Florence', 82-3.

[96] See Fryde, 'Antonio Pessagno of Genoa', app.

relationship with the crown, reflected perhaps in the less systematic arrangements for his repayment and accounting, seems more *ad hoc* than that of the Riccardi and Frescobaldi before him or the Bardi and Peruzzi who followed him. Given the very troubled state of England, the backlog of royal obligation borne by the Ancient Custom and the total abolition of the new custom in 1303, which Edward II was able to revive only after his *revanche* of 1322, the relationship was bound to show some peculiarities. Through it all Pessagno managed to lend sums Edward desperately needed and to leave England before any disaster befell him. His assistance in war finance had, at times, been highly significant. Edward II had relied heavily on the money and supplies provided by Antonio Pessagno for the campaign which ended so disastrously at Bannockburn. Pessagno supplied at least £21,000 between March and June of 1314, and in the following years kept the English border garrisons supplied; the latter service was impressive, for during the terrible famine affecting England and north-western Europe he shipped grain from the Mediterranean to the border fortresses in Genoese galleys.[97]

Edward II also began the close crown relationship with the Bardi who, later joined by the Peruzzi, would finance the crown through the opening years of the Hundred Years War. Edward II's connection with the Bardi was very close and at times they came to his aid when royal credit with other lenders was cripplingly low.[98] But the Bardi relationship with Edward II does not seem to have operated on the scale of the Riccardi or Frescobaldi in the reigns of Edward I and Edward II, nor of the Bardi themselves in the reign of Edward III; this seems a fair conclusion from what we presently know of the scale of their lending and the royal resources placed in their charge for repayment. Moreover, after 1322 Edward II began collecting a great store of treasure drawn from the properties of his defeated enemies, and after the 1323 truce with the Scots was able to 'pursue wholeheartedly one of his main passions, the accumulation of wealth.'[99] He used the Bardi in the last five years of his reign not so much for lending money as for foreign transfers, convenient support of diplomatic

97 Ibid. 170-3.

98 Fryde, *The Tyranny and Fall of Edward II*, 91-2.

99 Ibid. 94.

missions, special purchases, and the like. With a hoard which finally reached almost £62,000, Edward did not need many loans. He had accumulated enough wealth to pay for the War of Saint Sardos fought in Gascony in 1324-5 out of cash reserves, even though this minor war may have consumed £65,000. The Bardi role and the royal finances of this late period of Edward's reign are unusual for the era of the three Edwards and reflect both Edward's avoidance of major campaigns and his large scale series of confiscations of property from his domestic enemies. These were circumstances which would not be repeated in our period.

The new regime of Isabella and Mortimer was forced to buy support by returning vast tracts of confiscated land and to battle the Scots who quickly renewed the war in the north; the supplanters of Edward II spent his treasure hoard with remarkable speed and the pattern of warfare managed largely on credit returned. John of Hainault, whose support had been so important to Isabella and Mortimer in mustering the invasion force to overthrow Edward II, left England in March of 1327 with nearly £13,500 owed him; he returned in May when the Scottish war suddenly came to life and within two months had added £41,304 to the regime's debt to him. The regency government turned more than once to the Bardi for partial repayment of the debt owed John of Hainault (who also employed the Bardi as his agents).[100]

In fact, Isabella and Mortimer had been anxious to secure the services of the Bardi from the time they overthrew Edward II. In the troubles surrounding the king's fall the Londoners had pillaged the Bardi house, destroyed their valuable business records, and caused them to flee in terror. But Isabella, who had benefited from their loans while in France, quickly showed them favour by buying their looted property for the hefty sum of £700. In the fourteen months after August 1326, Mortimer borrowed £19,453, the bulk of it from the Bardi.[101] The brothers Richard and William de la Pole had promised to provide £20 a day for the household in May 1328, but by August, 1329, their payments were in arrears and had to be taken on by the Bardi. But even the Bardi may have been unwilling or unable to provide all the loans the regime wanted. They may have felt a certain caution about the finances

[100] Nicholson, *Edward III and the Scots*, 39-40.
[101] Fryde, 'Loans to the English Crown 1328-1331', 206.

of the English government under Isabella and Mortimer; they certainly complained about the inadequacy of customs and other revenues assigned to them in repayment.[102]

Once the young Edward III overthrew Mortimer and placed his mother in comfortable retirement he, too, wanted Bardi services and he seems gradually to have established a more satisfactory relationship with them. As Edmund Fryde has written of the Bardi, 'They had become part of the normal arrangements of government and, like the personnel of the administration, were little affected by political upheavals.'[103] Edward III's creation of a satisfactory relationship with the Bardi is of a piece with his general arrangements for harmony within English political society. For the first time since the expulsion of the Frescobaldi in 1311 something like the Riccardi system of public credit was operative again on the eve of the Hundred Years War. Edward III followed his grandfather's formula: he relied on a major firm, and he turned to customs revenue and the proceeds of taxation to repay their lending. One of the periodic accounts between king and banker for this period shows that of a cumulative debt of £53,040 owed them for 1328-31, at least £18,000 was repaid from the wool custom and £17,000 from Edward's share of four ecclesiastical tenths conceded to him by the pope.[104] Although records for the credit transactions of the early years of Edward III, before the launching of the Hundred Years War, are incomplete, those surviving indicate that the Bardi lent more to the king than all other crown creditors combined.[105]

In his seven years of personal rule before the opening of the great war with France, Edward III had thus clearly developed a good working relationship with the Bardi and by 1336 with the Peruzzi acting in concert with them.[106] He could lead his armies to the continent bolstered by the comfortable knowledge that the

[102] Fryde; *The Tyranny and Fall of Edward II*, 174, 193-4, 214, 271 n. 48.

[103] Fryde and Fryde, 'Public Credit', 459.

[104] Fryde, 'Loans to the English Crown 1328-1331', 204-8. Baker, 'The English Customs Service, 1307-1343', 19 n. 91, argues that the Bardi never placed their own attorneys in the ports to hold one part of the seal authorizing export, and thus to check local collectors. This would mean a difference from the Riccardi scheme; see Kaeuper, *Bankers to the Crown*, 148-9.

[105] Fryde, 'Loans to the English Crown 1328-1331', 200-1.

[106] Id., 'Materials for the Study of Edward III's Credit Operations 1327-1348', 106; Russell, 'The Societies of the Bardi', 99, 111 ff.

credit system which had collapsed in his grandfather's years of extreme need, 1294-7, was functioning at peak efficiency in 1337.

Crises in English war finance, 1294-1298, 1337-1340

In these two continental campaigns the medieval English state made its maximum military and diplomatic efforts; Edward I in 1294-8, and Edward III in 1337-40 pressed the resources of the state to the limit and in the process created major governmental crises. These two crises reveal much about the strengths and limitations of English war finance, especially about royal policies based on English wool and Italian credit. In several important regards the broad outlines of the campaigns were similar. Both involved grand and lavishly expensive continental alliances against the French king: Edward III concentrated his subsidies within the Low Countries; Edward I broadcast pounds sterling even more widely, and was especially anxious to secure the German king Adolf of Nassau as his ally. Edward I promised £250,000 to his allies and actually delivered at least £165,784 to them.[107] Edward III may have promised less, but he paid out subsidies on nearly as lavish a scale, £130,112 and possibly more.[108] The total cost of the campaigns show a similar pattern: staggering sums were spent by each king, with Edward I again outpacing his grandson. The French war (including the heavy charges in Gascony, perhaps as much as $400,000) may have cost Edward I £615,000; if the Welsh and Scottish wars of the same period are included his war expenses may have soared to £750,000 in 1294-8.[109] Half a century later Edward III raised and spent £400,000 in the Netherlands in three years, 1337-40[110] If the idea of an anti-French coalition and the scale of war finance are similar, the campaigns were also alike in their use of wool as a great resource for war finance. As we have seen, Edward I imposed a maltolte and later ordered general wool seizures; Edward III used wool even more elaborately with the company of

[107] Prestwich, *War, Politics, and Finance*, 173.

[108] Fryde, 'Financial Resources of Edward I in the Netherlands, 1294-1298' (1962), 1170.

[109] Prestwich, *War, Politics, and Finance*, 175.

[110] Fryde, 'Financial Resources of Edward I in the Netherlands, 1294-1298' (1967), 1142.

1337 and subsequently with wool seizures, taxation in wool and increased customs duties. Finally the campaigns were alike in their results. Each was a complete military failure and produced temporary royal bankruptcy.

But these important and broad similarities must not mask two significant differences in the financing of the campaigns; both suggest that in essentials Edward III's war finance might have been less troublesome than that of Edward I. He planned in the first place to make much better use of the wool trade than had Edward I. Exactly what Edward I expected from the wool trade for his war is unknown; he may have simply wanted as much as he could get in an emergency and his plans bear the mark of *ad hoc* response to crisis. The wool duty was increased to 40*s*. and the wool seizures of 1297 seem rather hasty. The situation created by the Flemish alliance against France produced an 'unavoidable, compulsory wool staple in the Netherlands' which 'did not however confer any striking financial benefits on the king.'[111] Edward I may have collected roughly £141,000 from wool: £116,000 from customs,[112] £25,000 after deduction of expenses, from the sale of wool seized in 1297.[113] Comparisons between the two kings' use of the resource of wool are difficult for we have some idea of what Edward I realized from wool but not what he may have hoped to get, and for Edward III we know his financial plans based on wool in detail, but can scarcely follow the thread of his profit through the maze of wool seizures, payments, sales, and loans which followed the Dordrecht seizures. As it was actually carried out the wool scheme conceived in 1336 and launched in 1337 involved serious miscalculations, but it failed more because of the king's haste and his excessive demands for funds to pay his allies than from any inherent implausibility in the plan as originally formulated. Edward III's arrangement with the Contract Merchants was designed to provide him with a £200,000 loan, interest free, plus perhaps another £30,000 representing half the profit on the sale of 30,000 sacks of wool abroad.[114] Could he

[111] Id., 'Financial Resources of Edward I in the Netherlands, 1294-1298' (1962), 1180.

[112] Prestwich, *War, Politics, and Finance*, 197.

[113] Fryde, 'Financial Resources of Edward I in the Netherlands, 1294-1298' (1962), 1183-5.

[114] Id., 'Edward III's Wool Monopoly of 1336', 12-13.

have realized these funds, deficiencies of war finance need not have been crippling.

But the contrast between the two campaigns is even greater when we turn to the critical question of credit finance, for which much more evidence is available. Especially after his elaborate wool scheme faltered, Edward III had to rely on loans. By October 1339 Archbishop Stratford could tell parliament without exaggeration that the king's indebtedness had mounted to £300,000 or more.[115] 'No medieval ruler', Edmund Fryde comments, 'ever borrowed so much in a comparably short time as did Edward between 1337 and 1340.'[116] His agents combed Brabant and Flanders and even went to the Rhineland in their search for willing lenders. Edward borrowed £150,000, half of his total loans, in the first four months after his arrival abroad in 1338. The Bardi and Peruzzi provided £71,522 in this period and royal agents raised another sum of £25,497 on the security of the Great Crown and other royal jewels, a gold cross, and two golden chalices from the abbeys at Reading and Bury St Edmunds.[117] Overall Bardi and Peruzzi loans came to £125,880 in less than two years, 1338-40. In time Edward came to accept loans available only on onerous and even humiliating terms; when other collateral was exhausted, he pledged not only his crown, but a war horse, and finally even obligated his companions to reside in a fixed place as virtual war captives. The problems for his major bankers were even more severe. The combination of English war finance in the Netherlands and the political and financial problems in Florence pushed the Bardi and Peruzzi beyond their capacity. Though they remained faithful to the English cause and active in Edward's service, the Italians could be of limited help to Edward after 1338. By the summer of 1339 they were defaulting on engagements undertaken for the king;[118] by 1342 the papal nuncio in England refused to transfer funds to them (preferring the Alberti and Acciaiuoli). The Peruzzi failed in the following year and the Bardi held out only until 1346.

115 Ibid. 24.

116 Fryde and Fryde, 'Public Credit', 460.

117 Fryde, 'Financial Resources of Edward I in the Netherlands, 1294-1298' (1967), 1152-4.

118 Ibid. 1169-70.

As the 1337 wool scheme failed and the Bardi and Peruzzi slipped, William de la Pole moved swiftly into their place;[119] he provided about half of the £28,974 Edward borrowed between July and September 1339, that is during the four months before the attack on French territory actually began; overall he advanced £111,000 between June 1338 and October 1339. Pole lacked the capital of the great Italian companies, but he was apparently able to borrow for the crown from other Englishmen abroad. Whatever he lacked in capital he seemed able to make up in calculation and ruthlessness throughout a roller-coaster career. Although he had been, along with the London merchant Reginald de Conduit, head of the 1337 wool company, its collapse did not prevent Pole from becoming chief crown creditor, 1339-40. When all efforts to raise funds were finally overcome by costs and virtual royal bankruptcy ended the campaign, Pole was one of the objects of Edward's wrath. He had to stand trial in 1341 and remained in disgrace until 1343. Pole's later career is closely entangled in Edward's efforts to revive a credit structure on which he could rest his ambitious war finance.

The decline of the Bardi and Peruzzi and the prominence of Pole mark an important stage not only in Edward's finance of his initial French campaign but in the general story of English war finance. By the end of this campaign the era in which war chests were filled at critical periods by the great Italian *societates* in crown employ had also come to an end. But the relentless royal drive for war financing on this scale, and with this level of flexibility and convenience, had not abated. If the Italians were not available, substitutes would have to be found; if native merchants inconveniently lacked the financial resources then they would have to be provided with whatever royal resources, favours, monoplies were required. This was the policy followed during the decade after 1340, as soon as Edward had got past the crisis which erupted in England in 1341. In 1343 he committed the customs revenue to a syndicate of English merchants who agreed to advance money to the king on the security of these export duties.[120] Thirty-three men were originally involved, drawn from

119 What follows is based on several studies by Fryde: 'Financial Resources of Edward I in the Netherlands, 1294-1298', (1967); 'The English Farmers'; *The Wool Accounts of William de la Pole*; and 'The Last Trials of Sir William de la Pole'.

120 Id., 'The English Farmers'.

most levels of merchants in England. Many joined out of a concern to recover payment on bonds given them at the time of the Dordrecht seizures in early 1338; in 1343 the crown had yet to pay for most of the wool seized, valued at £110,000. Though it operated under the nominal leadership of Thomas Melchebourn, this syndicate was in fact organized by William de la Pole, whose services were rewarded by a return to the royal favour lost in 1340. Pole soon reduced the company to himself and six other partners, two of whom were likely his agents. This narrower company began to farm the customs at a considerable profit; for prolonged periods they enjoyed a monopoly of wool export; and, finally, they were licensed to buy up old royal debts at a considerable discount, and to return them to the crown for credit at face value. The king got £50,000 annually for the farm of the customs and considerable loans. The arrangement lasted without major changes through 1345-9. Pole left the company to others in 1345, in retrospect a wise move, though it left his former associates most unhappy about his share of the liabilities. For the moment all seemed to go well; successive groups of English merchants took up the farm of the customs and provided Edward III with the war loans he needed:

Melchebourn Company	£60,000	1343-1345
Wesenham Company	£112,000	1345-1349
Cheriton and Company	£126,000	1346-1349
Sureties of Cheriton	£131,000	1349-1351

Once again credit translated into military capacity and in this period even into military success. Cheriton and Company financed the campaign leading to the victory at Crécy and the successful year of siege which took Calais.

But the English syndicates proved to be only a temporary expedient, lasting barely a decade; they were not to be a sound replacement of the Italian companies, providing another three-quarters of a century of crown credit. Essentially 'middlemen artificially boosted up by the king',[121] they could provide the advances expected of them only by borrowing themselves, often at high cost, from more substantial merchants (Londoners, Germans, York exporters) who were too wary to place their own fortunes in the king's hard grasp. Most of the syndicates ended in

121 Fryde, 'The English Farmers', 6.

exhaustion: Melchebourn failed to raise 20,000 marks promised to the crown; after outbidding Wesenham for the privilege of the customs farm, Cheriton and Company could not manage the demands of crown finance (especially the Crécy campaign and Calais siege), in combination with the Black Death and poor wool speculation; they landed in prison. Though their successors (the sureties) survived and even made a profit, by 1352 they had had enough. With new evidence of fraud ironically brought to light by the wool arrangements made in 1345-9, the crown put Pole on trial again in 1353-4, and secured his renunciation of all claims on the crown (including £21,844 in debts, a bond for 1,000 sacks of wool, and all rights to the great manor of Burstwick). What the majority of merchants and wool producers thought of monopolistic crown financiers emerged clearly at the same time. In order to end this phenomenon the Great Council in 1353 prohibited English merchants from participating in the wool trade. Though this exclusion remained in effect only four years, no English merchant would assume responsibility for the customs for twenty years; in 1376 Richard Lyons, who had tried to revive the customs farm, was impeached;[122] even in 1382 men prudently remembered the fate of Pole, Wesenham, Cheriton, and others 'who for . . . transactions made with the King in his great need and for a little gain' had been ruined.[123]

Edward III's opening campaigns in the French war thus caused the system of royal credit finance operative since the 1270s to buckle and collapse. But he had brought this result by excessive demands, by attempting an unreasonable use of this system and of the royal revenues on which it was based.

The situation of Edward I in 1294-7 could scarcely present a greater contrast. After twenty-two years of what seems the most sophisticated and satisfactory relationship between an Italian company and the English crown across the entire era of credit finance,[124] Edward I entered the great crisis of his reign without a regular financier. The outbreak of a major Anglo-French war had been a terrible shock both to Edward and the Riccardi of Lucca.

122 Fryde and Fryde, 'Public Credit', 463.

123 Fryde, 'The Last Trials of Sir William de la Pole', 30.

124 For detailed treatment of what follows see Kaeuper, *Bankers to the Crown*; id., 'The Frescobaldi of Florence and the English Crown'; id., 'Royal Finance and the Crisis of 1297'.

The merchants' assets (including a vast portion of the papal crusade tax collected on the continent and assigned to Edward) were apparently tied up in trade or immobilized in France, where the French king's seizures caused them considerable loss. In his great need Edward expected the Riccardi to provide an initial war chest with the speedy and significant loans they had always delivered. As their helplessness became apparent he broke off the special relationship in hot temper, depriving them of control over the customs in July 1294, a month after renouncing his homage to Philip IV for Gascony (the act equivalent to declaring war). As news of the Riccardi fall from the king's favour spread, creditors (including the pope) rushed to withdraw deposits and the company was swept into a whirlpool of decline that ended in bankruptcy. Edward could not find a replacement for at least five years; Frescobaldi lending became fairly continuous and voluntary only in 1299; it reached roughly the Riccardi scale only in the years following 1302. During his crisis years Edward could of course extract money from the Italian companies; he forced them to lend him nearly £29,000 in 1294-8. But forced loans were no substitute for a working relationship with a single major firm acting as crown banker. Such a firm would willingly lend large sums from its own resources and, equally important, act as a financial funnel for most other potential lenders who might otherwise be unwilling or uneasy about involvement in crown finance. Between the late autumn of 1294 and October 1295, for example, Edward could obtain only £16,133 from eleven Italian companies at a time when he was desperate for cash. So great was his need, in fact, that during the first seventeen months of the war (June 1294-November 1295) he seized the crusade tax money available in England (£32,480) and even private treasure on deposit in churches.[125] He likewise browbeat the clergy into an unprecedented tax grant of half of clerical income (which may have produced more than £100,000, using the new and higher assessment of 1291), and secured a parliamentary tax grant of a tenth and sixth (yielding between £75,000 and £82,000). The great increase in customs duties imposed during the period brought in £25,000 in England and customs payments and loans received in the Netherlands added

[125] The following is based on Fryde, *Book of Prests*, pp. 1-lii; Prestwich, *War, Politics, and Finance*, 179, 186, 208-9.

£6,098. Clearly an imperious king in command of an active administration could amass a vast war treasure without the willing co-operation of a major banker. Edward I would collect something like thirty per cent of the total lay taxation in his reign and more than forty per cent of the total clerical taxation in his reign during the short space of three years 1294-7.[126] As we have seen, when hard pressed Edward did not scruple to seize and spend money deposited for the crusade or as private savings. The resourceful and even ruthless quest for cash was remarkable in its effectiveness. In the first seventeen months of the war Edward probably raised and spent more than £250,000.

How important, then, was credit to war finance if Edward I's campaign, undertaken largely in the absence of major credit arrangements and Edward III's campaign, fought with the most complete medieval credit finance, both raised massive war funds and both failed? Two aspects of the question must be considered. In the first place, failure was a consequence in each case of so radical an imbalance between resources and expenditure as to be beyond correction by the temporary addition of funds a credit structure could provide. 'The plain fact is', as Edward Fryde writes, 'that the prolonged subsidizing of a continental coalition was beyond the means of an English king in this period.'[127] Overspending on over-ambitious alliances was the root problem, not the availability of credit resources however much they might smooth the process of collecting and dispersing vast sums on war.

In addition, the existence of credit resources might be of great import to the consequences the campaign had on the home front, even if the sheer scale of war expenditure obliterated any chance that credit might make a difference in the campaign abroad. The crises which followed the two campaigns show fascinating differences when viewed from this perspective. Although historians traditionally speak of the crisis of 1297, there are good arguments for seeing the problems which began in 1294 and which came to a peak of intensity in 1297 as actually grinding on to the end of the reign and beyond. When Edward I died there were fundamental problems between monarchy and the political community which were still very much alive; the recurrent

[126] Calculated from figures provided ibid. 191.

[127] Fryde, 'Financial Resources of Edward I in the Netherlands, 1294-1298 (1967), 1142.

debates over such issues as perambulation of the forest, purveyance, the military service owed the crown, show how much the strain of Edward's great effort of 1294-7 continued to trouble the minds and the purses of his subjects. In fact the reign ended in financial chaos and 'disguised bankruptcy'. Tout, who thought that the deficit in 1307 was £60,000, lamented 'thus tamely and ingloriously the great king's reign came to an end with broken-down finances.' Michael Prestwich quantifies the inglorious financial end of the reign differently. He thinks the deficit was closer to £200,000 and that the smaller figure represents the residue of Edward's debts left unpaid toward the end of his son's reign in the late 1320s.[128] A figure of about £200,000 would represent a backlog of debt equivalent to nearly seven years' ordinary crown income. The lay taxation which could retire such a debt seems to have carried an unacceptable political price tag. After parliament granted Edward a fifteenth in 1301 at the cost of royal concessions concerning the forest, purveyance, and military service, 'the crown virtually abandoned the attempt to pay its way' and found 'it was politically safer to incur heavy debts than to levy oppressive taxes and to seize private property.'[129] Tenths imposed on the clergy by the pope brought Edward some £70,000 in his last five years;[130] but this welcome revenue obtained at so little political cost, even when augmented by the lay thirtieth and twentieth of 1306 (worth £34,778), did not dam the mounting deficit. In fact, the heritage of debt and discontent Edward I left to his son probably set the stage for Edward II's troubles. The crisis of 1297 in this sense continued into the crisis of 1310-11 when the Ordainers temporarily took over management of the government of Edward II. The argument can even be made that the opposition to Edward I, as fearful of the bitter old king's wrath as they were mindful of his advanced age, simply waited to deal with his less daunting son.[131] Edward II, 'chicken-hearted and luckless in war', as a chronicler summed up his qualities,[132] could easily have appeared

128 Tout, *Chapters in the Administrative History of Medieval England*, ii. 125; Prestwich, *War, Politics, and Finance*, 221.

129 Ibid. 270.

130 Ibid. 191.

131 Ibid. 272.

132 The Lanercost Chronicle, quot. Prestwich, *The Three Edwards*, 53.

a better bet for lords, gentry, merchants, and townsmen wishing to settle the issues still pending from his father's excessive demands.

This long period of political and financial fallout from Edward I's crisis was not reproduced in the aftermath of Edward III's campaign. Edward III secretly left the Netherlands late in 1340 and returned in wrath to deal with the home government he considered responsible for his temporary but humiliating bankruptcy; his actions precipitated a sharp but relatively brief crisis.[133] If the virtual collapse of Edward I's ambitious finances in the last decade of his reign gives a measure of the severity of the reaction to his wartime demands, the rather speedy recovery of Edward III is noteworthy. By 1343 the king was again dealing with companies of the English merchants whose help he had given up prematurely in 1338. These English syndicates, as we have already seen, were artificial creations which would prove to be no long-term solution to the problem of war finance on the grand scale. But the significant point is that Edward III could climb down from the high finance of 1337 in two stages; he was largely supported by the Bardi and Peruzzi and Pole after the failure of the wool scheme in 1338, and then was able to continue with the English syndicates in 1343–9. Edward I had lacked such cushions after the Riccardi failure and found financial props for his high level of war expenditure only at the cost of problems in politics and governance which would seriously affect the political atmosphere for at least two decades. Credit arrangements allowed Edward III to steer a course further away from despotism and thus to provoke less lasting resentment on the part of his subjects. The Italian *societates*, Pole and the syndicates sustained his campaigning until roughly mid-century when basic changes appeared in the general pattern of his kingship.[134] The failure of the syndicates was one factor in this complex of changes which basically ran in the direction of concession and compromise. Edward III had learned that he must deal with English political society in parliament and that he must pay particular heed to the specific demands of those levels of society represented by the Commons. He could no longer rest his military plans on a grand continental alliance or spend on warfare the sums that had passed

133 Fryde, 'Edward III's Removal of his Ministers and Judges'.

134 Keen, *England in the Later Middle Ages*, ch. 7.

so quickly through his hands in 1337-40; but he could lead his magnates in campaigning on a reduced scale and maintain political peace at home if he adopted a less aggressive stance and gave the Commons more of what they wanted. If the absence of any major credit arrangements narrowed his choices, Edward at least had the wit to embrace a near necessity with skill and enthusiasm. It would indeed be foolhardy to try to eliminate differences in personalities or in the political and military situations in comparing the aftermath of 1340 with that of 1297. Yet the underlying connection between the nature of royal war finance and the depth and extent of governmental crises is real enough. A functioning credit system significantly reduced the political and financial strain imposed at home by even the most massive wartime demands. The more general results of warfare on this scale are another matter.

Taxation in France

The certainty and precision which are elusive goals in the study of English financial records become nearly hopeless goals for the study of French royal war finance. Archival losses, monetary fluctuations, local acquisition and expenditure of some funds—all work against any neat tabulation of income and expenditure on warfare. But the broad characteristics are recoverable, even if records providing details went up in flame and smoke in an eighteenth-century archival fire.

French royal revenues could be, in the first place, quite substantial. In the reign of St Louis the king's average annual income may have stood at about 250,000*l.t.*[135] By the late thirteenth century certain annual income had likely climbed to the range of 400,000 to 600,000*l.t.*, (66,000 to 100,000*m*: £44,000 to 66,000 sterling). By the opening of the Hundred Years War the figure had risen to a range of about 130,000 to 145,000*m*. From the late thirteenth century the clerical tenth was collected so regularly it can be counted in with the certain revenue, adding about 45,000*m* to the totals.[136] English certain

[135] Jordan, *Louis IX*, 78-9.

[136] Based on figures given in Strayer and Taylor, *Studies in Early French Taxation*; Strayer, *The Reign of Philip the Fair*, 142-91; Favier, *Philippe le Bel*. ch. 7; Henneman, *Royal Taxation in Fourteenth-century France* (1971), esp. ch. 1 and the apps.

royal income across this era is usually estimated at about 30,000*l.* or 40,000*m.* Whatever the uncertainties and approximations in such French figures, it is clear that the king of France could draw on a regular peacetime income in the range of three to five times that of the king of England. The question was whether even this royal income could cover ordinary expenses and meet the extraordinary demands of war. At least until the late thirteenth century French royal revenues matched royal ambitions nicely. In contrast to their English royal cousins, French kings exploited a rich and sizeable demesne and were content to live with a more limited ambition. 'The French kings grew rich without strain', Southern comments; 'the English kings strained every nerve but could never be rich enough.'[137]

Yet French kings, despite the size and wealth of France, were apparently unable to accumulate and spend more money on war than their English opponents. In the Anglo-French war of 1293–1303, the French governmental estimate of what it could theoretically spend and the surviving English governmental records of what was spent came very close (about 1,735,000*l.t.* in the former case and a minimum of 1,440,000*l.t.* in the latter) and no doubt actual expenditure was even closer.[138] Moreover, the French was effort seems to have suffered as much if not more than the English from a chronic shortage of funds. How did the French capacity to generate special wartime revenues compare with the English methods? As we have seen the English capacity to wage war was shaped by a precocious development of royal taxation, sophisticated credit mechanisms, and the great resource of the wool trade. Since none of these advantages undergirded the French crown, its war finance shows a distinctly more ramshackle, *ad hoc* character.

By the time medieval warfare took on new scope and intensity in the 1290s, the English government had for nearly a century been creating a working system of occasional taxation; these percentage taxes on personal property were in fact sufficiently established for the crown to make them regular impositions during the almost constant periods of warfare across the northern border and the Channel. In France, by contrast, Philip the Fair appeared to try to match the English taxation policy with almost

[137] Southern, *Medieval Humanism and Other Studies*, 152.
[138] Strayer, 'The Costs and Profits of War', 272.

none of the preparation which had occupied the centre stage of thirteenth-century English politics.[139] St Louis, it is true, had been able to raise perhaps 1,500,000*l.t.* for his crusade; but almost two-thirds of this sum came from special taxes on the clergy (partly raised in the emergency following the king's capture), and the effort did not launch general royal taxation in France.[140] For roughly a decade, 1292-1302, Philip sought new financial measures and above all from 1295 insisted that all Frenchmen owed the crown their financial support in war; he pressed the view that taxation was a common obligation, not the specific result of payments replacing service owed by military tenants. This argument stood behind the taxes of Philip's years of great stress—the hundredth of 1295, the fiftieth of 1296, the fiftieth of 1297. But opposition to the idea of direct taxation of all subjects mounted and in 1302-4, after the crushing defeat of Courtrai and the crisis of Anagni, the king returned to the more acceptable formula of taxation as a commutation of service owed. Compromise brought its reward, for the tax of 1304 brought in 735,000*l.t.* and paid for the army which defeated the Flemish at Mons-en-Pévèle. It was probably the largest tax collected by the French crown in the first half of the fourteenth century. In all, war subsidies of one kind or another were collected in seven of ten years, 1295-1304. But no general taxation of this sort could be collected in the ensuing years of peace, 1305-13, and for additional revenue Philip had to turn to feudal aids for the marriage of his daughter (1309) and the knighting of his eldest son (1313). Indeed in 1313 the king showed that he accepted the principle that no general subsidy could be collected in peacetime by returning a tax which was being collected in anticipation of a Flemish campaign which proved unnecessary and the principle was forced on him in 1314 by the provincial leagues when he tried to continue collection after a Flemish truce. This principle was written into the charters his son gave to the leagues in 1315.[141] After the effort of so strenuous an administration, the relative failure to find a solution to financial problems is significant. In the words of J. R. Strayer:

139 See esp. id., *The Reign of Philip the Fair*, 142-91, for what follows.

140 Jordan, *Louis IX*, 79-104.

141 Brown, '*Cessante Causa* and the Taxes of the Last Capetians'.

> . . . Philip's early prosperity turned to adversity with the coming of wars and . . . there was no real recovery even after the wars ended. Heavy taxation barely paid for military expenses from 1294 to 1305, and there was no large general tax after the subventicn of 1304. Philip improved French financial administration, but not to the point where it could meet ordinary expenses and still leave a surplus for an active foreign policy.[142]

This generalization is broadly true for French royal finance across the first half of the fourteenth century.[143] The French administration repeatedly found it impossible to find the funds required to raise the military force it wanted. In their short reigns Philip's sons were unable to advance royal finances significantly, though Philip V characteristically seems to have come closest to success. The new Valois line in the person of Philip VI, uncertain of its legitimate hold on the sacred crown of St Louis, was more cautious and compromising still. At the beginning of the Hundred Years War crown finances were at their lowest point in Philip's reign, perhaps the lowest point in several reigns.

Even the beginning of the war with England and the initial English invasions failed to generate the level of support Philip needed for really effective war finance. The French government had to try one expedient after another in the opening years of the war: coinage revaluation, seizures of Lombard property, fines for illegal fief acquisitions, sales taxes, hearth taxes, property taxes—an 'almost infinite variety of forms'[144] in 1340, but there was no real substitute for substantial war subsidies. To complicate matters the nobles expected high wages, but insisted that the crown not tax their subjects. The initial period of 'phoney war' and the stop and start pattern of short truces played havoc with efforts to convince the politically and financially important classes of the seriousness of the war effort. Bad harvests further complicated crown efforts to fill war chests. Royal coinage manipulations fed inflation; the price of silver had gone up fivefold in a decade. Philip made some progress by dealing with discontent over the coinage. In 1343, after careful negotiations with nobles and a meeting of the 'Estates-General', he obtained a

142 Strayer, *The Reign of Philip the Fair*, 191. Jean Favier came to a similar conclusion, *Philippe le Bel*, 204.

143 Henneman, *Royal Taxation in Fourteenth-century France* (1971), 152; Brown, 'Customary Aids and Royal Fiscal Policy'.

144 Henneman, *Royal Taxation in Fourteenth-century France* (1971), 152.

tax in return for coinage reform (a 76 per cent reduction in the price of silver). But coinage manipulation was now lost as a substantial contributor to war finance and by 1345 finances were again inadequate as actual fighting resumed. John Henneman summarizes the state of affairs concisely:

> The government had been forced to vacillate between coercive fiscal expedients and concessions to the privileged or influential. For the better part of five years it had been very difficult to raise money, especially among those of the king's subjects who did not feel a sense of danger. Coinage manipulation had been abused, challenged and temporarily repudiated. The one new tax of this period, the *gabelle du sel*, was increasingly unpopular.[145]

The Estates-General called in 1346 in separate meetings at Toulouse and Paris was more a sign of governmental weakness in the face of crisis than of any initiative. In response to the wave of criticism which swept over the administration, the king promised reforms and an end to unpopular taxes. The king's subjects had only to devise tolerable means of supplying him with an army. The Paris assembly agreed in principle on the need for a tax and left the specifics in providing the army for local negotiations. The grant of men-at-arms was not forthcoming in the south of France where the estates agreed, instead, to two hearth taxes. In fact, the English invasion of Normandy and the Crécy campaign disrupted government plans and forced the crown to fall back on calling out the *arrière-ban* to get quick results.[146] But this formula—a trade of taxation computed in the form of a certain number of troops in return for reforms obtained through use of assemblies, with room left for local variations in the form of the tax—would again be the basis for agreements in 1347-8 and 1355-6. In the mean time, Clement VI, the most pro-French of the Avignon popes, tided over Philip VI with generous loans: 622,000fl. (approximately 92,100*l.t.*).[147] Then the harsh realities of defeat at Crécy and the English siege of Calais revived the important plan to supply a tax computed in men-at-arms. Thus continuing papal support would come on top of the prospect

[145] Hennemann, *Royal Taxation in Fourteenth-century France* (1971), 190.

[146] Ibid. 215. He notes that most of the money collected in the south seems to have gone for local defence.

[147] Ibid. 233-4. By about 1360 the total had come to 3,517,000*fl.* for the crown, plus 100,000*fl.* to great lords.

of really substantial war taxation. Though comprehensive figures are lacking, the king's government may have counted on receiving as much as 3,000,000*l.t.* from the realm of France in 1348. In Henneman's opinion, 'there was thus considerable promise early in 1348 that a reformed royal government would be able to place the crown's finances on a sound footing at last'.[148] If this plan represented a chance for financial stabilization, co-operation between the crown and representative assemblies, and a chance for a vigorous military initiative, all such prospects were dashed by the ravages of the Black Death which spread across France in the spring and summer of 1348. At the same time as the Plague completed the ruin of the English syndicate struggling to finance Edward III it eliminated any hope of success for the ambitious French tax plan not only by causing drastic population reduction, especially in the south, but by causing chaos in the administrative ranks; at the royal court one-third of the notaries died, as did the Queen, and the Chancellor. It is hardly surprising that only a fragment of the tax was ever collected.[149]

From the viewpoint of royal war finance the realm was not back on its feet until 1351. The shaky equilibrium then established was destroyed in 1354 by the defection of the powerful Evreux family of Normandy from allegiance to the Valois cause. The subsequent loss of Norman revenues was a great blow to the French crown which had long leaned heavily on the duchy as a source of wealth and as a model for workable means to obtain it.[150] It is true that the French population was gradually becoming accustomed to regular taxation in one form or another and that local assemblies had met frequently enough to have developed a certain routine and a degree of self-confidence in matters relating to taxation. But major financing was not forthcoming and opposition had not lessened; it may even have increased. Consequently the level of tax revenue produced was far from adequate even when the fighting involved only local skirmishes.[151]

[148] Ibid. 234.

[149] Ibid. 234-8; Fryde suggests that no part of England was so devastated as Languedoc and Provence: 'Financial Policies of the Royal Governments', 845.

[150] Henneman, *Royal Taxation in Fourteenth-century France* (1971), 264-72, 307.

[151] Ibid. 289.

The summons for a meeting of the Estates of Languedoil late in 1356 once again was a sign of the utter financial frustration of the French crown. The process of 1347-8 seems to have been repeated on a grander scale. The cry for reform was even louder than before and the army promised in response would have cost the realm much more than before, no less than 5,000,000*l.t.* for one year. In fact, the troubles in Normandy increased, general resistance to paying taxes forced the administration into time-consuming local negotiations, and the proceeds were utterly inadequate. In the midst of negotiations and collections the English invaded lower Normandy, the French king took the field and in September 1356 brought the Black Prince and his allies to battle near Poitiers. The result was unmitigated disaster, the capture of John II, and the death or capture of many French nobles. 'The Battle of Poitiers', as John Henneman writes, 'was an event equaled only by the Black Death in its ultimate impact on royal taxation in France.'[152] For the moment the great war had to stop; the first phase of the Hundred Years War was over. A truce held through 1357-9 and then a treaty arranged at Bretigny lasted nearly a decade, 1360-9.

When we shift focus from the immediate chain of events to the long-range consequences, the turning-point represented by the capture and ransom of John II is apparent; it was then that 'the French began paying annual taxes without regard for the state of war or peace'.[153] The basic royal taxes of early modern France—*aides, gabelle,* and *fouage* (which later became the *taille*)—began to emerge in the decade after Poitiers as Frenchmen learned at the hands of the free companies (the brigands or *routiers*) that 'peace' could be more disruptive of their lives and fortunes than war.[154] But it is equally important to remember that few Frenchmen in the mid-fourteenth century could have seen important factors leading to the development of a French state in the defeat at Poitiers, the costly ransom of the king, and the unleashing of thousands of unemployed soldiers on the countryside. Governmental collapse and civil war, bloodshed and destruction were the realities to contemporary observers. When the regency government would not allow the great feudal

[152] Hennemann, *Royal Taxation in Fourteenth-century France* (1971), 302.
[153] Id., *Royal Taxation in Fourteenth-century France* (1976), 2.
[154] Ibid.

lords their traditional share of tax proceeds, some defied the collectors and even brought armed force against them.[155] Noble support for the regular taxation after 1360 was secured by handing over to important lords large shares of the taxes collected from their subjects. The indirect taxation of *aides* imposed on all mercantile transactions and the direct taxation of the *fouages* can only have raised the cost of living and deepened the poverty of a shrinking population.[156]

French credit finance

The striking point in comparison with England is that only at mid-century did taxation roughly in line with the needs of royal finance appear. Across the first half of the fourteenth century France remained a wealthy country, whatever her difficulties and French royal revenues were substantial; they may even have been sufficiently large to reduce somewhat the need for credit facilities. Yet like all medieval governments the French found that wartime financial needs outran income, sometimes disastrously. In particular the pattern of French taxation, as it emerged across the first half of the fourteenth century was ill-suited to producing quickly the large sums of money required for vigorous and successful military operations. Each tax required rounds of negotiations with local nobles, regions, and towns. Bargains had to be struck by sharing revenues or providing exemptions and special favours to important individuals or groups. As Edmund Fryde argues, 'Perhaps the greatest drawback of this French pattern of taxing was the excessive slowness in the mobilizing of resources and the uncertainty about the yield of any particular tax.'[157]

Thus the absence of a close and continuous connection with Italian *societates* was significant. Coupled with the absence of a single major and easily controlled export trade, it meant that credit would play a very different role in French war finance. A supply of continuous credit requires suitable collateral. Judging from the English case, the Italian companies, representing the major suppliers of credit, seem to have been most satisfied with

155 Fryde, 'Financial Policies of the Royal Governments', 848, citing Perroy, 'La Fiscalité en Beaujolais', 9-10.

156 Fryde, 'Financial Policies of the Royal Governments', 850-1.

157 Ibid. 837.

the relatively stable cash revenue from customs duties.[158] But England had a primary export and, lying at the end of the network of medieval trade routes could 'show a single face to the continent'. The trade of France, by contrast, was dominated by no single export commodity (not even by wine). The political and cultural regionalism of France was reinforced by forces working against economic integration; the magnetic poles of European trade and industry were just beyond French borders in the Low Countries and in northern Italy. French merchants felt the pull of the Mediterranean in the Midi and the pull of England, Flanders, and Brabant in the west and north. Being essentially a country of transit, France might be expected to have developed an effective customs system as a pillar of royal revenues; tolls on the mere passage of goods through a particular territory had been, after all, a feature of feudal and urban revenues for centuries. But on the scale of the kingdom of France the problems ballooned into an altogether different order of magnitude: a busy traffic in a variety of commodities would have to be watched over by a small army of officials operating especially along the Mediterranean coast and the long land frontier with the Empire. The French government must have been well aware of the wool custom Edward I instituted in 1275; only two years later Philip III regulated the export of wool and other goods from France and began the customs service. Yet the different roles of the customs in the two countries could scarcely be more clear. Edward I was augmenting his certain revenues by as much as one-third and, equally important, was consciously creating a base for a system of regular and systematic borrowing from the Riccardi of Lucca. Philip's motives seem to have been 'internal economic stability and political advantage';[159] only from the last year of his reign were export licences (the *haute passage*) sold and only in the difficulties of 1303–5 did Philip IV show a willingness to allow merchants to export forbidden goods regularly by paying fixed rates. Miller observes, 'it is perhaps natural that French export duties should have come into existence in this scrambling way, and that revenue from the sale of export licenses was fairly modest. . . .'[160] The significant development of the French

[158] What follows draws on Miller: 'The Economic Policies of Governments', 291, 305; Strayer, 'Pierre de Chalon'. [159] Ibid.

[160] Miller, 'The Economic Policies of Governments', 305.

customs was the work of Pierre de Chalon whose dominance in this field is clear from about 1311. After 1321 merchants could easily obtain export licences which were widely sold by the French government. But income from this source was declining at just about this time as the Italians shipped more English wool directly by sea to Mediterranean ports, bypassing France altogether. In the war with England in 1324-5, the revenue function of the customs was thus bolstered and expanded by additional duties. To the old *haute passage* Chalon added the *droit de rève* (an export duty of 1⅔ per cent, with special rates for wine and other commodities). Though this duty was cancelled in 1333, it was quickly revived after the opening of the Hundred Years War. Useful as these customs revenues were, a sense of the relatively modest place they occupied in French war finance is quickly obtained from surviving figures. At their peak the sale of export licences in 1322-3 brought 55,000*l.t.*, or about 5 per cent of treasury receipts in these years. The *haute passage* was worth only 8,000*l.p.* (6400*l.t.*) in 1331, and had fallen to 2000*l.p.* (1600*l.t.*) in 1344; the *droit de rève* brought in 60,000*l.t.* in 1332, but had slipped to 40,000*l.t.* in 1344. On the scale of French finance, the customs were not a major item and were clearly insufficient and unsuited to provide a base on which French kings could build a relationship with Italian financiers.

Philip the Fair may have toyed with the idea for a while. Ever watchful of the moves of Edward I across the Channel, he certainly recognized the advantages to be gained from working with the Italians;[161] for a number of years he relied on the Guidi brothers of the Franzesi Company, 'Biche' and 'Mouche' (Albizo and Musciatto Guidi of Florence) for financial assistance and advice. They were in the king's employ by 1289, were general receivers by 1291, and reached a peak of influence in the first great crisis of the reign in 1295 when they became treasurers of France. Their general oversight of French royal finance declined after the end of 1295, but until their deaths in 1306-7, they never lost Philip's confidence. As their fellow countrymen did in England, the Franzesi lent the crown large sums of money. At the

[161] Strayer, 'Italian Bankers and Philip the Fair'; id., *The Reign of Philip the Fair*, *passim*; Henneman, 'Taxation of Italians'.

outset of the war over Gascony in 1294-5[162] Philip felt the shock that many monarchs in our period would experience; he suddenly learned what tremendous cost ambitious war could entail. In his emergency he considered currency manipulation and massive loans. Though he soon turned to debasement, Philip at first followed a loan policy on the advice of Biche and Mouche who solidly supported their argument by lending 880,000*l.t.* over the next several years (200,000*l.t.* from their own firm and other Italians at Paris and the Champagne Fairs; 630,000*l.t.* from rich townsmen; 50,000*l.t.* from prelates and royal officials).[163] But for the remainder of the reign borrowing on this scale seemed either impossible or undesirable. The French crown repaid the loans very slowly; 'indeed, it is hard to think of any time between 1295 and 1314 when Philip had 880,000*l.t.* to spare', as J. R. Strayer noted. He concludes that 'the French financial system was not yet capable of operating with a large floating debt.'[164] Certainly the French monarchy did not continue or develop Philip's brief if close relationship with another Italian *societas*. The reasons were probably complex, and may have involved a mutual disinclination for any closer ties. French kings, especially during Philip the Fair's reign and whenever his influence was felt later, showed a special sensitivity to any dependence on quasi-independent financial agencies, especially if they were international organizations such as the Italian companies or the Order of the Temple. Philip the Fair valued Biche and Mouche as capable agents and financiers (and as the first agents he had chosen on his own), but their influence passed a peak in 1295 and Philip relied more on Frenchmen, less on Italians; he moved against the Temple in 1307.

For their part, the Italians may always have felt in France the kind of vulnerability that could impede willing entry into royal service. Foreign merchant bankers basked in no great popularity on either side of the Channel, but in England the peculiar mixture of royal power and credit finance provided both employment and

[162] By this time royal indebtedness to them may have been considerable. At Candlemas, 1291, the king paid them 264,353*l.p.* (211,282*l.t.*), possibly as repayment for loans (Strayer, *The Reign of Philip the Fair*, 147).

[163] Ibid. 150; Fryde and Fryde, 'Public Credit', 478, 481-2.

[164] Strayer, *The Reign of Philip the Fair*, 151-2. For what follows see *ibid.* 49-51, 73, 97, 116, 147-57.

protection; in France the crown rather early decided to do without large-scale Italian finance and turned to direct seizure of Italian wealth. 'The position of the more important creditors of the French Crown was always precarious under Philip the Fair and his successors in the first half of the fourteenth century', as Edmund Fryde notes. 'In no other country were lenders so frequently despoiled and ruined.'[165] Ecclesiastical legislation against usury gave French kings an excellent opportunity to combine piety and profit by arresting 'Lombard usurers' and releasing them only on payment of large fines. This process was repeated at least five times between 1277 and 1349.[166] In the last ten years of his reign Philip IV regularized the milking of the Italians by imposing the *boîte aux Lombards*, a tax on their merchandise sales (one *denier* per livre or 0.4 per cent) and on their exchange contracts (one-half *denier* per *livre* or 0.2 per cent) paid in lieu of other taxes and impositions in the Champagne Fairs, the town of Nîmes and the province of Narbonne. All Italian transactions outside these areas were to pay on a higher tariff (4 *deniers* per *livre* on sales; one *denier* per *livre* on exchange). The rates changed over the reigns of Philip's sons, but in 1317 the *boîte aux Lombards* was farmed for 11,000*l.t.* In 1315 Louis X imposed a 5 per cent property tax on all Italians not paying the *boîte aux Lombards*; that this proved a more lucrative device is evident from a farm for the tax in 1330, set at 22,500*l.t.* After 1317 the French crown required both the *boîte* and property tax from all Italians in the realm.

Such regular taxation of Italians, however, was minimal in comparison with the periodic tallages or extortions which continued across our period. Neither war nor peace brought immunity to the Italian merchants, for foreign mercantile wealth was an irresistible target in the emergency of war and a politically safe target in peacetime when the king's subjects saw no reason that they should be troubled with taxation. These periodic extortions could raise several times the annual yield of regular taxes on Italian transactions or exports, perhaps 100,000 to 200,000*l.t.* But in 1331 the French crown made a quantum leap in creative exploitation. In addition to the traditional arrest and

[165] Fryde and Fryde, 'Public Credit', 479.

[166] Ibid. 479-80; the remainder of this discussion of Italians and the French crown is based on Henneman, 'Taxation of Italians'.

fine of Italians, Philip VI ordered debtors to pay the crown immediately the principal owed on loans from the Italians; by royal grace the 'sinful interest' could be totally omitted. At a stroke the French crown was moving from an occasional raid on Italian liquid assets to a major confiscation of capital assets. The strategy was repeated in 1337 as the great war began, again in 1340, when the first serious fighting of the war broke out, and again from 1347 to 1363 in the crises of defeats at Crécy, Calais, and Poitiers. The change in scale between fines on Italians and confiscation of outstanding debts was enormous; in 1347, the debts were estimated at more than a 1,000,000*l.t.*[167]

The policy of squeezing the Italians, especially as operated after 1331, may have been short-sighted. The modest taxes collected and the occasional fines extorted from Lombards were available to the crown at virtually no political cost, brought in a small but not negligible portion of royal income, and were sustained by the trade of France without any apparent strain. But as the policy of collecting the outstanding principal of Italian loans was repeatedly followed in the opening decades of the Hundred Years War, the picture changed. The revenue realized fell disappointingly short of expectations; there was resistance to crown collection; assemblies of the era regularly opposed the policy; and the repeated expropriation of capital assets, particularly in 1347-63 added its force to the ravages of plague, war, and political instability and helped to destroy the money-lending business of most Italians in France.[168] The war finance of the French kings, like that of their English opponents and at about the same time, had disastrous effects on Italian merchant bankers operating in northern Europe. There is a certain circularity in the cause and effect of French relations with the *societates*. As Edmund Fryde suggests, 'It is probable that these repeated royal acts of violence against important financiers had the effect of gradually restricting the Crown's choice of lenders.'[169] In other words, a lack of French royal interest in an Italian credit relationship like that linking Edward I and the Riccardi, perhaps caused by the absence

167 Actual receipts, however, must have fallen disappointingly short of expectations in the chaotic situation following the plague. See Henneman, *Royal Taxation in Fourteenth-century France* (1971), 240.

168 Id., 'Taxation of Italians', 43.

169 Fryde and Fryde, 'Public Credit', 480.

of the type of trade and customs on which it could rest, led to a royal policy of extortion; in the 1330s and 1340s the crown escalated this policy into outright confiscation, possibly crippling or at least thoroughly discouraging the Italians.

Yet even if they could not, or chose not to borrow from Italian *societates* in a regular and sustained relationship, the French crown was not totally cut off from credit resources. Though borrowing on the scale of 1295, with a major role assigned to Italians was not repeated, the French crown from the late thirteenth century[170] was beginning to find some of the credit it needed in loans from its own officials and from rich townsmen. These two groups significantly overlapped. In contrast to the situation in England, the French central and territorial financial administration regularly employed businessmen who were, in effect, expected to find ready money for the crown through their private business connections.[171] The pressures of financing the Hundred Years War would greatly expand this practice. On the eve of the war the trend appears in a comparison of the estimates of revenues drawn up in 1296, during the Anglo-French war over Gascony, and in 1329, when war with England was again expected. The earlier document lists massive loans to Philip IV arranged by Biche and Mouche who together with other Italians provided nearly a quarter of the total of 880,000*l.t.* raised in loans. In 1329 the only borrowing considered important to an estimate of war revenue was a series of loans from French townsmen.[172] Such levies are often called forced loans and did involve royal pressure; but the advantages of gaining the king's gratitude may have been sufficient indirect pressure to loosen bourgeois purse strings, even though repayment was uncertain and so slow that inflation and currency changes could convert loans into virtual gifts.[173]

French coinage manipulation

As the reign of Philip the Fair had shown, coinage manipulation was a tempting alternative to borrowing as a means of securing

170 As early as 1285, in the crusade against Aragon; ibid. 481.

171 Fryde, 'Financial Policies of the Royal Governments', 826-9.

172 Fryde and Fryde, 'Public Credit', 481.

173 Ibid. 482; Strayer, *The Reign of Philip the Fair*, 151.

ready cash for war.[174] Royal mint revenues or *monnayage* (composed of *brassage*, or charges to cover mint costs, and *seigneurage*, the pure profit) was attractive because the king could alter the value of the currency by fiat, realizing massive profits speedily. Philip the Fair apparently was the first king to take this step on a significant scale. From around Easter 1295 he turned away from the advice of Biche and Mouche to the plan of Thomas Brichart, master of the royal mints, and altered the coinage which had been stable since the reign of St Louis. In 1298 and 1299 the policy brought in between 50 per cent and 64 per cent of the royal treasury receipts;[175] in the second half of 1298 alone coinage profits came to more than 555,000*l.p.* (444,000*l.t.*) or nearly two-thirds of treasury receipts.[176] But, as J. R. Strayer has observed, 'there are limits to financing a government by inflation and Philip had reached those limits by the end of 1303.'[177] The price of silver had risen 300 per cent in Philip's devaluation and in 1306 the royal government switched to a policy of deflation by ordering a return to good money.[178] The sudden shock to the poorer subjects who paid rents provoked a riot which temporarily sent Philip to refuge in the Paris Temple and sent twenty-eight men from Paris craft guilds to their executions.[179] After about two decades of stability, Charles IV returned to the resource of coinage changes and especially in 1326-7 collected large profits, 314,691*l.p.* (251,752*l.t.*) in the first ten months of 1327. Resistance to this policy forced a restoration of 'sound money' in 1329-30, but the beginning of the Hundred Years War led to new devaluations. As we have seen, Philip VI obtained a war subsidy in 1343 by promising currency reform. But the effects of a Draconian 76 per cent reduction in the price of silver 'really ended the long period of nostalgia for the coinage of St Louis.'[180] Subjects directed future criticisms less against royal debasement than against the

[174] In general see Henneman, *Royal Taxation in Fourteenth-century France* (1971) and esp. app. I; Cazelles, 'Quelques réflexions', 83-105, 251-78.

[175] Fryde, 'Financial Policies of the Royal Governments', 834.

[176] Henneman, *Royal Taxation in Fourteenth-century France* (1971), 335.

[177] Strayer, *The Reign of Philip the Fair*, 152-3.

[178] Cazelles, 'Quelques réflexions', 85-6.

[179] Fryde, 'Financial Policies of the Royal Governments', 836.

[180] Cazelles, 'Quelques réflexions', 94-95, 257-60.

disruption brought about by manipulations.[181] Under heavy pressure of war costs, Philip's sound money policy lasted only about three years. From 1346 monetary mutations went forward systematically under the direction of experts. In the second half of 1349 coinage manipulation represented nearly 70 per cent of royal receipts.[182] In the period 1346-55 Cazelles has outlined six cycles of depreciation followed by brusque returns to good currency. That monetary reform was prominent in the demands voiced in the 1356 Estates-General is hardly surprising. But the promise of reform, even when backed by the dismissal of mint officials in 1357, could not alter the administrative need for mint profits. The Dauphin, in fact, could not carry on without them; currency mutations came to a record high in 1360 with twenty official alterations, so many that not all mints could keep up with them. 'The monetary chaos became indescribable', Edmund Fryde writes, 'and the quality of the silver coinage sank lower than at any other time in the fourteenth century.'[183] Stability returned only with the new coinage of John II, based on the franc, named to honour the king's freedom from captivity. The price for this stability and loss of royal revenue was the new and heavy taxation initially imposed to secure the king's ransom.[184] As is so often true, complete documentation is lacking, but what we know of the history of French war finance in the first phase of the Hundred Years War lends credence to H. A. Miskimen's assertion that *monnayage*, the royal revenue obtained by minting money, was the largest tax paid by Frenchmen in the fourteenth century.[185]

4. COSTS OF WAR

Historians in the late twentieth century face a difficult task when they try to form an accurate impression of medieval warfare and its effects. The topic of war usually impinges on modern consciousness in terms of total conflicts which have been

181 Henneman, *Royal Taxation in Fourteenth-century France* (1971), 337.
182 Ibid. 335, 343-4; Lewis, *Later Medieval France*, 57.
183 'Financial Policies of the Royal Governments', 850.
184 Ibid.; Cazelles, 'Quelques réflexions', 105.
185 Miskimin, *Money, Prices, and Foreign Exchange*, 46.

devastatingly powerful forces in modern social, economic, and political life. By contrast the topic of medieval warfare may bring to mind images from Shakespearean stage productions with the accompaniment of half-remembered lines of martial verse. Neither image is appropriate to the task at hand. Moreover, to ask about the cost of war in any age is to enter one of the more prickly and pathless thickets historians traverse. 'The reticence of economic historians on the subject of war', J. M. Winter writes plainly, 'is surely related to the intractibility of the problems that it raises.' If historians were to turn for help to the somewhat arcane mysteries of economic theory they would 'find many observations and tangential comments on war as an "exogenous variable" but no fully worked-out analysis open to empirical testing.'[186]

Thus it is important that we pose the questions we are asking carefully. In debating the economic consequences of late medieval war historians have sometimes displayed a surprising conversion to mercantilism. The issue has been defined in terms of balance sheets that could prove whether England managed to possess an augmented stock of precious metals as a result of more than a century of taxes, military wages, ransoms, and looting. Though the debate[187] has produced much of value in fact and interpretation, the issue is quite likely beyond proof, and possibly even beyond clear definition; certainly it seems anachronistic to seek for the winner in nationalistic and mercantilistic terms and to ignore the broader implications for an economy not bounded by existing kingdoms. Even if issues of national and feudal geography were reconciled and some measurement of the inward and outward flows of bullion across accepted lines of political demarcation were achieved,[188] the result would still seem of far less significance than the issue of how war affected the development of the European economy in the late Middle Ages.

We will simplify the task somewhat if as modern historians we are willing to use the historian's vision and even the historian's

[186] Winter (ed.), *War and Economic Development*, 2.

[187] Postan, 'Some Social Consequences of the Hundred Years War'; McFarlane, 'England and the Hundred Years War'; Postan, 'The Costs of the Hundred Years War'.

[188] See the discussion of Bridbury, 'The Hundred Years War: Costs and Profits', 90-2.

hindsight in assessing consequences of actions which may have been utterly unknown to the people of late Medieval Europe, especially if we can disclaim any intent to praise or condemn their actions.[189] Much ink and no little emotion have gone into establishing the normality, inevitability, and contemporary approval of medieval warfare. Yet wars which might be thought more or less inevitable and which were supported with great contemporary enthusiasm could, of course, have disastrous long-range consequences. Moreover, these consequences may be discernible by the historian even if lost to the view of the actors themselves. That the need for some outlet for human aggressiveness, spurred on by the warrior ethos of chivalry, could produce wars in the late Middle Ages can be taken as a given. But this should not lead us to dismiss the search for the economic consequences of war as an artificial endeavour. The wars fought were not the only wars that could have been fought, on the only scale possible. The terms would change considerably if we were to imagine a persisting Anglo-French peace during which the kings of England and France might be pictured comparing notes, at some tournament, on their respective campaigns in Scotland and Flanders.[190] But in fact the warfare entangled the leading kingdoms of Western Europe for generations. Contemporary accounts and records suggest that much devastation was wrought by the warriors and that vast sums were collected by state apparatus to pay for the campaigns. A sense of the economic consequences of war thus depends on answers to three questions. First, could medieval warfare be really devastating and was it devastating in the Anglo-French conflict beginning in the 1290s? Second, was war disruptive of the economy even when and where physical devastation was slight? Third, did the vast sums spent on war by the states represent a use of wealth and a social transfer of

[189] Bridbury is particularly concerned that historians avoid slipping 'by imperceptible degrees, into the drawing up of an indictment of a way of life' based on warfare (see ibid. 80). However, he also suggests with much justification that 'The historian is notably reluctant to follow his investigations through and judges his heroes, if he must judge them at all, not so much by what they did for themselves as by the consequences of what they did for everyone else'; *Historians and the Open Society*, p. xii.

[190] On the importance of Scotland and Ireland to England and of Flanders to France see Powicke, *The Loss of Normandy*, 448 and Strayer, 'The Costs and Profits of War', 270-1, 290-1.

wealth likely to spur on the economy or to retard economic growth? Then looking beyond the issue of economic cost, we must try to gain a sense of the consequences of war in the political sphere by asking a fourth question. Did the costs of war spill over into the political and legal dimension, affecting those processes by which states were built?

Daunting obstacles stand in the way of approach to such questions. Beyond the difficulties in using evidence that is vast in quantity but randomly preserved, there is the additional problem of finding a scale for determining its significance. How can we measure and evaluate the forces at work, even where fairly good and continuous series of sources survive? Given the scope of the questions we want to ask and the nature of the evidence we are constrained to use, elaborate quantification is unlikely to prove satisfactory or even possible. Yet we can still try to understand this warfare in its context. In broadest terms the late medieval period is generally thought of as a time of contraction or economic depression, following the economic expansion of the several preceeding centuries.[191] Should late Medieval warfare be considered among the major causes of this change of economic development?

Destruction and disruption

Attempting to steer clear of points of view engendered by modern warfare, some historians—and particularly some students of English history—have raised doubts about the seriousness of medieval warfare in general and have questioned the relevance of our modern tendency to condemn war. In particular they have played down the destructive capacity of medieval war. These campaigns of armoured soldiery were, to quote the most outspoken view, 'little better than caricature: petty gang-warfare flamboyantly decked out and caparisoned, but for the most part, mere swagger and bluster, clamour and rodomontade.'[192] With small armies, crude weapons, and rudimentary tactics, the damage a medieval army could inflict on contemporary society and economy was slight; in fact, far from wasting resources, war

[191] Among a vast literature see Genicot, 'Crisis: From the Middle Ages to Modern Times' and Cipolla (ed.), *The Fontana Economic History of Europe: The Middle Ages*.

[192] Bridbury, 'Before the Black Death', 400.

used them.[193] Such destruction as occurred was quickly repaired, 'because there was so little to destroy that could not be quickly and easily rebuilt or made good.'[194] In this view the late Medieval economy was at once wealthy enough to sustain military campaigns and primitive enough not to be wrecked or even seriously disrupted by them.

We can usefully approach this complex question of the destructiveness of late Medieval warfare by looking at the opening campaign of the Hundred Years War. There was very little in the invasion of the Cambrésis and Thiérache by Edward III and his allies in the autumn and winter of 1339 to interest the historian of battles and tactics; Philip VI in fact avoided battle.[195] But the plunder and destruction of the invading forces, which left a distinct impression on contemporaries, are well worth our attention. The chronicler Geoffrey le Baker records that one night early in the campaign Geoffrey le Scrope, the English Chief Justice of King's Bench, showed one of the papal nuncios, the French Cardinal Bertrand de Montfaves, the awesome panorama visible from the top of a high tower: as far as the eye could see flames and smoke from burning villages lighted the night sky. The cardinal, as papal nuncio, had urged Edward to avoid war which, he had said, could never break the silken thread binding together the kingdom of France.[196] Against the backdrop of destruction, Scrope asked the nuncio, 'Eminence, does it not seem to you that the silken thread surrounding France is henceforth broken?' Baker writes that the cardinal fell to the tower floor, senseless.[197]

Benedict XII who had tried to prevent hostilities, sent a war relief fund once the invasion had occurred. He provided 6,000*fl.*, which were changed by his Italian bankers, the Buonaccorsi, for 9,020*l.t.* in Paris, and were distributed to war victims after a

193 See the two articles by Bridbury: 'Before the Black Death'; 'The Hundred Years War: Costs and Profits'. McFarlane similarly suggested that war could be beneficial and discounted the disruption war brought to the English economy in 'England and the Hundred Years War'.

194 Bridbury, 'The Hundred Years War: Costs and Profits', 57.

195 Henry S. Lucas provides a general description of this campaign, *The Low Countries and the Hundred Years War*, 333-9.

196 Deprez, *Les Préliminaires de la guerre de cent ans*, 253.

197 Thompson (ed.), *Chronicon Galfridi le Baker*, 65, quot.: Deprez, *Les Préliminaires de la guerre de cent ans*, 257-8.

careful investigation by Bertrand Carit, archdeacon of Eu. The record of this charitable mission, preserved in the papal archives, was studied and partially printed by Louis Carolus-Barré in 1950.[198] His analysis of the roll showed that thousands of victims received payments in no fewer than 174 parishes in four adjoining dioceses. Yet, if anything, these figures for payments and for numbers of parishes give an inadequate sense of the damage inflicted. First, it must be recognized that the devastation reached more than 174 villages, since several villages often comprised a single parish (as the thirty-two villages in the twenty-two parishes of the Deanery of Aubenton). Second, in one of the four dioceses, Cambrai, only the parishes in the realm of France were included in the investigation and relief, though many other parishes in that part of the diocese which was located within the Empire were similarly devastated. Third, the sum of 9,020*l.t.* provided was pure charity, not in any sense repayment of losses suffered by villagers. In the single parish of La Capelle-en-Thiérache in the Deanery of Aubenton (for which Carolus-Barré printed the record *in extenso*), the relief paid was £82.10*s.*; the estimated damages were nearly seven times this sum, coming to 5,4590*l.t.* War damages are seldom underestimated when charity is in the offing, but the investigation was careful and the order of magnitude is interesting. These figures at least suggest that the campaign in which no significant battles were fought produced some thousands of war victims, brought devastation to more than (perhaps many more than) 200 villages and may have wrought damages to the region in the range of 50,000*l.t.* (or £12,500 sterling). A sense of the meaning of a loss of this order of magnitude appears in a comparison of English taxation results: a standard tax of tenth and a fifteenth collected across the entire realm of England yielded about £38,000.

These estimates are reinforced and their significance clarified by Robert Fossier's study of an earlier, private war fought in this same region.[199] The villages of Busigny, Wambais, Bevillers, Erre, and Cagnocles were attacked in 1298 as part of a long-

198 Carolus-Barré, 'Benoit XII et la mission charitable de Bertrand Carit'. H. J. Hewitt discusses this information in *Organization of War*, 124-6. Philippe Contamine prints a useful map based on that which appears at the end of Carolus-Barré's art.; see his *La Guerre au moyen âge*, 372-3.

199 Fossier, 'Fortunes et infortunes paysannes au Cambrésis', 171-82.

standing dispute between the chapter of St-Géry, Cambrai, and Gilles de Busigny, 'descendant of a long line of shameless pillagers' and lord of at least three castles. Fossier concentrated his analysis on the effects of Gilles de Busigny's assault on the village of Cagnocles. The village consisted of eighty-two households, perhaps 400 to 450 people. In the raid, which lasted only a few hours, Busigny's men destroyed the grange belonging to the chapter, about half the houses (thirty-seven of eighty-two), the oven, and the forge. The total loss by fire came to 996*l.t.* and the pillaging cost the village goods worth 431*l.t.* (half in livestock). Loss by theft would have been much greater if the villagers had not used an early warning system which allowed most people to flee, taking their livestock and some goods with them. Only one man was caught and tortured until he revealed the hiding place of his money. Still, the raid cost the villagers nearly 1,500*l.t.* which, as Fossier points out, was the equivalent of 300 *muids* of grain or 40,000 man-hours of work by a roofer, mason, or harvester. The damages were, as in the 1339 instance, based on local inquest with clear motive for exaggeration: the chapter was indignantly drawing up the particulars of damages it had suffered. But Fossier thinks that though the estimates are probably high they are within reason. Where he can check particular points, such as the cost of rebuilding houses, the estimates seem to be in line with current costs of materials and labour. The effects of this raid of a few hours may have still been felt as long as six years later.

Figures from the raid on Cagnocles and other villages in 1298 thus support a view that the 1339 damages revealed by papal investigation are believable. But the nature of the loss revealed by Fossier may be equally significant. Peasant housing was no doubt cheap and easily repaired, as some scholars have suggested, but the more significant loss in an attack may have been the tools, livestock, and foodstores possessed by villagers. Possession of these goods, Fossier found, made the real difference in status among villagers: 'c'est donc le bétail ou l'outillage agraire, plus encore les réserves de vivres qui représent la vrai puissance . . .'.[200] Georges Duby likewise emphasizes the importance of livestock: 'draught stock was very expensive; the portion of capital that is represented for each family was perhaps

[200] Ibid. 177.

greater—and definitely less secure—than the portion represented by landholdings'.[201] If an army destroyed stores of foodstuffs, livestock, and agricultural implements the economic effect on a village or region can scarcely be dismissed, however we may regard their elaborate knightly costumes or deprecate the rudimentary nature of their weaponry or tactics. Fire is a terrible weapon of war in any age and should not be underestimated in an era in which campaigning 'consisted very largely of military pressure involving the destruction of the means by which life is maintained'.[202] The point is worth emphasizing, since military history can easily become an account of rapid marches and famous pitched battles. In fact battle was only a small part of warfare in the late Middle Ages. Hewitt makes the point clearly, writing of the English armies sent across the Channel:

> The men who landed in France were shortly to spend much of their time and energy in the destruction of property, in the forcible seizure of food and forage, and in plundering. These three operations were of course illegal in their own country. They were, however, normal and purposeful accompaniments of war . . . and they could be carried to lengths which exceeded military necessity, military advantage or even good sense.[203]

There is sometimes a tendency to attribute such regrettable activities solely to non-chivalric or disreputable elements in the armies.[204] But just as fourteenth-century knights thought profit in war no stain on their chivalry, so they seem to have accepted arson and pillage as normal and expected accompaniments of campaigning.[205] Most medieval warriors showed that they accepted Henry V's dictum: war without fire is like sausages without mustard.[206] They might even find such methods congruent with their notion of the highest religious criteria for

[201] Duby, 'Medieval Agriculture, 900-1500', 187.

[202] Hewitt, *Organization of War*, 93, 112-15; cf. Denifle, *La Désolation des églises, monastères, et hôpitaux*, ii. 769-70. Boutruche, 'La Dévastation des campagnes', 36 comments: 'Le feu est donc l'habituel compagnon du guerrier, son instrument préféré'.

[203] Hewitt, *Organization of War*, 93.

[204] Allmand, 'The War and the Non-combatant', 168-9; id. (ed.), *Society at War*, 16. This point of view is most strongly advocated in the popular book by Terry Jones, *Chaucer's Knight*.

[205] Hewitt, *Organization of War*, 99-101.

[206] Quot.: Gillingham, 'Richard I and the Science of War in the Middle Ages', 85.

warfare. As the *routier* captain Merigot Marches said at his trial at the Châtelet in 1391, he had 'done all those things which a man can and ought to do in a just war, [such] as taking Frenchmen and putting them to ransom, living on the country and despoiling it, and leading the company under his command about the realm of France, and burning and firing places in it'. He was executed not for these activities *per se*, but because he lacked the legitimate authority to make just war in France and was thus a traitor.[207] Writing of the *chevauchée* of the Black Prince in 1355, H. J. Hewitt notes that pillage was legitimate, honourable, and expected. He quotes the Black Prince's own description of his progress: 'We took our road through the land of Toulouse where were many goodly towns and strongholds burnt and destroyed, for the land was very rich and plenteous; and there was not a day but towns, castles and strongholds were taken. . . .'[208]

Evidence of the conduct of medieval warfare and of its results at the village level thus suggests the great potential for destruction inherent in medieval campaigning. But once the potential for destruction is established, the issue becomes one of scale. Was the destruction wrought by war so episodic and limited as to be from a general perspective economically negligible, however regrettable the losses were at the level of individual villages or even regions affected?[209] Writing at the end of the nineteenth century Father Denifle filled each page of two heavy tomes with detailed accounts of the ruin visited upon ecclesiastical establishments throughout France during the Hundred Years War.[210] Just after the Second World War Robert Boutruche wrote a short but even more sweeping survey, focused on the countryside devastation during the war. In his view the Hundred Years War had brought damage which in some regions of France reversed the great land clearance (*les défrichements*) of preceding centuries that had brought woodland or wasteland under the plough; consequences of the destruction and terror of war were depopulation and a serious loss of regions won for cultivation.[211]

207 Keen, *The Laws of War in the Later Middle Ages*, 97-100.

208 Hewitt, *The Black Prince's Expedition*, 72-3.

209 Philippe Contamine discusses the historiography of this issue in 'La Guerre de cent ans en France'. What follows draws on this useful discussion.

210 Denifle, *La Désolation des églises, monastères, et hôpitaux*.

211 Boutruche, 'La Dévastation des campagnes', 127-63.

Boutruche realized, of course, that the story had to be examined region by region across the expanse of the realm of France. He wrote one such study himself, concentrating on the Bordelais.[212] Since he wrote, the destructiveness of the Anglo-French war has been evaluated time and again at the level of regional or local study.[213] Clearly the intensity of damage varied greatly with the area and time period in question. In the period of our concern (roughly 1294–1363) the population of Languedoc endured only the destructive *chevauchée* of 1355; Burgundy suffered only in the early days of 1360. Yet Brittany, Normandy, Picardy, Flanders, the Agenais, Quercy, Saintonge, and Poitou were raided by hostile armies several times before the peace of Brétigny and would suffer again after the fragile peace agreement collapsed.[214] The diversity of the evidence and the understanding that war damage must be set carefully into the context of other social and economic changes have made generalization difficult; a general view has yet to be culled from the detailed studies so much a feature of modern French historical scholarship. Yet we can remind ourselves that an assumption of peace had long pervaded most regions of France; though private warfare was incessant, as we will see, major campaigning was not an accustomed feature of life in entire regions of France prior to 1337. Normandy, Brittany, and the Loire region had last experienced war in the reign of Philip Augustus; the most recent war in Languedoc had been the Albigensian crusade; Saintonge and Poitou had been free of war since the time of St Louis. Aquitaine and especially Flanders had, of course, suffered the military campaigns of Philip IV and Philip VI but, as Cazelles emphasizes, peace was the normal state in France, war was the exception.[215] Philippe Contamine suggests perhaps the best generalization possible: 'Pour fixer les idées, disons qu'en moyenne, entre 1337 et 1453, les destructions frappèrent une année sur quatre ou cinq, alors qu'entre 1220 et 1340 comme entre 1455 et 1570 elles ne frappèrent qu'une année sur quinze ou vingt. . . .'[216]

212 Id., *La Crise d'une société* (Paris, 1947).

213 See for example Wolff, *Commerces et marchands de Toulouse*; Fourquin, *Les Campagnes de la région parisienne*; Leguai, *De la seigneurie à l'état.*

214 Hewitt, *Organization of War*, 139.

215 Cazelles, *Société politique, noblesse et couronne*, 11.

216 'La Guerre de cent ans en France', 146.

It is a historical commonplace that England largely escaped the destruction of war. But a number of studies suggest that we must be careful not to underestimate the effects of raids by the French and the Scots. Periodic French naval raids brought devastation to the southern coast of England: in the early years of the war; again in the raid of 1360; and in the Franco-Castilian raids after 1369, especially that of 1377.[217] Scottish raids across the northern border affected an even wider region.[218] 'After Bannockburn', G. W. S. Barrow writes, 'the Scottish raids south of the Border became so regular and frequent that they amounted to the virtual subjection of England north of the Tees and involved the selective devastation of a still larger area. Northumberland suffered heavy depopulation and was reduced to a miserable anarchy.'[219] James Willard traced the effects of such raids in the reduced tax assessments on the border counties of Northumberland, Cumberland, Westmorland, and on the counties of Lancashire and Yorkshire further south.[220] H. J. Hewitt plotted on a map the location of the manors, towns, and hamlets devastated in the raid of 1345 in the Carlisle region; the map recording this single raid requires north/south and east/west axes of roughly thirty miles.[221] In the view of Jean Scammell 'the constant menace of invasion must have dominated the lives of everyone north of Humber.' To encourage willing and hasty payment of tribute the raiding Scots burned the countryside. 'Fire was a quick, easy and thorough method of creating havoc and was not really wasteful for the invaders, who could hardly have transported the clumsy domestic equipment of the Border cottages any more than the standing corn and meadow.' As a result of the raids in the opening decades of the fourteenth century rent rolls on manors in the northern counties declined—sometimes dramatically—and the region suffered a significant migration: 'In places as far apart as Carlisle, Alnwick and Cockersmouth the lesser tenantry largely disappeared.'[222] This sort of devastation crossed the Irish

[217] There is a good discussion of the coastal raids, citing numerous sources, in Searle and Burghart, 'The Defense of England and the Peasants' Revolt'.

[218] Campbell, 'England, Scotland, and the Hundred Years War; Barrow, *Robert Bruce*, esp. ch. 13; Nicholson, *Edward III and the Scots*; Hewitt, *Organization of War*, 126-30.

[219] Barrow, *Robert Bruce*, 336.

[220] Willard, 'The Scotch Raids'.

[221] Hewitt, *Organization of War*, 126-30.

[222] Scammell, 'Robert I and the North of England', 389.

Sea with Edward Bruce's invasion of Ireland in 1315. The invasion devastated eastern Ireland and led to the collapse of effective royal rule in Ireland.[223]

Though the extent of devastation is difficult to quantify, a factor of great importance to understanding the destructive consequences of fourteenth-century warfare is the changing scale on which war was conducted. Scholarly opinion, as noted above, generally supports the idea that warfare significantly expanded in the late Middle Ages, from roughly the 1290s on. As the resources of states grew, state capacity to wage war grew correspondingly and, after the atypical peace which lasted through much of the thirteenth century, states exercised this capacity with a will. It seems likely that by the fourteenth century more of the resources of society could be channelled into major wars than had been possible at any earlier stage of medieval history. 'The basic contrast', Edward Miller suggests of British history, 'would seem to lie . . . between the post 1294 period and all preceding time.'[224] Describing the 'new type of warfare that began in the 1290s' in both England and France, J. R. Strayer notes 'a temptation to raise bigger armies and to keep them in the field for longer periods than before, because the state could demand and pay for military service, unhindered by feudal restrictions on time and place.'[225] John Maddicott has similarly studied the effects in the period after 1294 of 'the inauguration of wars which were more continuous, more extensive and more costly than those of earlier days.'[226] Maurice Keen opens his survey of late Medieval English history in 1290 as the beginning point for events leading to prolonged warfare with 'consequences, both of the wars directly and of the strains and pressures that they engendered [which] were only beginning to work themselves out when the first Tudor, Henry VII, came to the throne in 1485.'[227] Philippe Contamine points to the generally expanded base for warfare utilized by Philip the Fair and specifically notes that this king's reign marked the first time in centuries that

223 Lydon, 'The Bruce Invasion of Ireland'. I am grateful to B. W. McLane for pointing out this Irish case and supplying the reference.

224 Miller 'War, Taxation, and the English Economy', 22.

225 Strayer, 'The Costs and Profits of War', 269-70, 291.

226 Maddicott, 'The English Peasantry and the Demands of the Crown', 75.

227 Keen, *England in the Later Middle Ages*, 1.

warriors from Languedoc were brought to fight on northern French battlefields.[228] The papacy, in its secular capacities, showed the same trend. Norman Housley has documented the rising war costs incurred by the papal monarchy, especially from the late thirteenth century. He suggests that the papal war effort went forward even though by this time the proceeds of papal taxation in England and France had come mainly into the hands of the kings of those realms; their war chests were now augmented with funds which would formerly have gone to pay for warfare across the Alps.[229] In the mid-thirteenth century the papacy had paid for its 'crusade' against the Hohenstaufen with funds obtained in France and England; by the late thirteenth century that situation was reversed.[230]

A recognition of the destructive capacity of late medieval warfare and a sense of its broadened scope, fuelled by the resources of the growing states, suggest that sheer physical destruction was a significant outcome of the warfare of the period and a significant force acting on the economy. We cannot attempt some graph of numbers of acts of arson and pillage per square mile per decade, region by region, for England and France, nor can we suggest the calibration or critical thresholds to apply to some scale of significance for such statistics. But we have every reason to believe that late medieval warfare could be highly destructive and that its scope broadened significantly in the fourteenth century.

Economic damage was not, of course, limited to simple physical destruction; in fact, the destructive and disruptive consequences of war can be traced even where no tell-tale records of smouldering villages point the way. We can find other results of medieval warfare by looking first at credit and coinage. To a large decree English war finance depended, as we have seen, on the credit afforded by crown use of Italian merchant-banking companies, one Lucchese or Florentine *societas* after another serving as royal banker. Though the French crown, for reasons already considered, relied less heavily on credit arranged by

228 Contamine, 'Consommation et demande militaire', 421.

229 Housley, *The Italian Crusades*, ch. 6 and 7, esp. pp. 198-201, 204-6, 221-2, 234-51.

230 See Maurice Keen's comment: *The Pelican History of Medieval Europe*, 212.

Italians, French war finance too drew heavily on money extracted in various ways from the Italian companies. On either side of the Channel, the results of the warfare beginning in the 1290s were fatal to the financiers.[231] The Italian companies had expanded their trade and money-lending and planted their partners and factors in branch offices across north-western Europe during the relative peace which characterized so much of the thirteenth century. Their credit facilities had been a factor of importance in the economic development so evident in that century. Yet these company operations were fragile, relying in some measure on the continuance of peaceful relations between the major powers of north-west Europe and their reasonably harmonious relationship with the Holy See; only under these conditions could their international trade and continuous transfers of sizeable sums by letter continue to function smoothly. The Riccardi of Lucca were ruined when the Anglo-French war of 1294 destroyed most of these necessary conditions; with much of their capital (and especially the proceeds of papal crusade taxation) tied up in investments, the company was faced with demands from Edward I to fill his war chest while Philip IV raided their coffers in France; the Riccardi lost English royal favour, suffered a run on the bank, and had slipped into bankruptcy by the opening years of the fourteenth century. Although their successors, the Frescobaldi of Florence, did not directly fall victim to the uncertainties of war finance, the problems left unsolved (and in no small degree unpaid for) after Edward I's massive war effort lay behind the political revolt of 1311 in which they were thrown out of England. In the opening phase of the Hundred Years War the Bardi and Peruzzi of Florence were strained to the limit in trying to keep Edward III supplied with cash. The king's inability to repay what he had so

[231] Fryde and Fryde provide a survey for both England and France in 'Public Credit', ch. 7, pts. iv, v. See also Kaeuper, *Bankers to the Crown*; id., 'The Frescobaldi of Florence'; Prestwich, 'Italian Merchants'. Of the major Italian financiers of the English crown, Antonio Pessagno of Genoa (who was very helpful to Edward II) managed to end up with a profit, and one of the major Riccardi partners, Baroncino Gualtieri, left the firm before its break with the king. On Pessagno and Edward II see Fryde, 'Antonio Pessagno of Genoa'; On Gualtieri see Kaeuper, *Bankers to the Crown*, 13-15. On the Bardi and Peruzzi see Fryde, 'Materials for the Study of Edward III's Credit Operations, 1327-1348' (1949); and his 'Financial Resources of Edward I in the Netherlands, 1294-1298'.

insistently borrowed compounded their financial and political problems at home and failure soon followed. Thus in three-quarters of a century the English crown, largely because of the exigencies of war, had brought down four of the leading trading and financial companies of Europe. The several collections of English merchants which followed the Italians tumbled even more swiftly.

In their heyday these companies, Italian and English alike, had drawn on the chief sources of capital available. Of course, in their constant cycle of lending money to the king while collecting his revenues the financiers in effect lent the king his own money. But the resources of the Italians also included the proceeds of papal taxation and some deposits placed with them by the great; moreover, all the financiers drew on the profits of trade and the English syndicates in particular were frequently investing the money of other English merchants who preferred some safe distance from royal finance.[232] Thus the English crown siphoned off a considerable volume of merchant capital for war and in the process brought down major merchant-bankers.

French royal demands did less spectacular work in bringing down Italian companies, as we have seen, but in time they produced results in the same vein. Through the first several decades of the fourteenth century French officials contented themselves with various taxes, fines, licences and extortions which could raise significant sums of money without apparently imposing intolerable losses on Italian companies. But after 1330 the scope changed significantly as crown extortions 'became confiscations of capital assets, a vastly more serious matter, involving (in 1347) over a million pounds'. This policy of extortion was particularly severe in the military emergencies of 1347-63; since the effects of extortion worked in tandem with the Black Death and military and political disturbances, John Henneman thinks the combination 'must have destroyed the money-lending business of most Lombards in the kingdom'.[233]

The only non-Italian agency with resources and expertise enabling it to play a role at all similar to the great Italian companies was the military order of the Temple. The suppression of the Templars by Philip the Fair is, of course, one of the most

232 Id., 'Edward III's Wool Monopoly of 1336'; id., 'The English Farmers'.
233 Henneman, 'Taxation of Italians', 42-3.

famous and controversial acts in that king's reign. Philip's motives may have been complex, but in two ways the Templars were almost bound to be targets, just as the Italians were: they were very wealthy (or were at least thought to be); and they were foreign bankers whom the king could not fully control. By the fourteenth century the great age of Templar involvement in European high finance may have passed, but it is worth noting that they fell victim, at least in part, to the financial needs of the French crown.[234]

Though we cannot quantify the consequences for credit in England and France brought about by royal crushing of Italian merchant banking, we can scarcely ignore them. John Henneman suggests that French extortion practised against the Italians 'injured the financial position of many royal subjects by seriously restricting credit at a time of declining purchasing power and economic contraction'.[235] A similar situation most likely obtained in England where many great secular and ecclesiastical lords borrowed large sums from the Italians and often relied on their financial services generally. Credit scarcely disappeared as a factor in north-west European trade as a result of royal war finance and its effects on Italian and English companies and the Order of the Temple. But the market for credit was undoubtedly sensitive to the financial measures of kings as they struggled to pay for warfare. It is not surprising that the Riccardi found it necessary to suspend private loans in England while paying heavily for Edward I's Welsh war in 1282-3.[236] When the pope granted this same king the proceeds of a sexennial crusading tenth imposed in 1274 and held in deposit by various Italian companies, a member of one company observed that ready money would be available only at higher rates, now that the crusading tenth was in royal hands.[237]

As the importance attributed to this papal tax reminds us, the availability of credit in north-western Europe cannot be fully

[234] Strayer, *The Reign of Philip the Fair*, 287-8.

[235] Henneman, 'Taxation of Italians', 42-3.

[236] Kaeuper, *Bankers to the Crown*, 187.

[237] Ibid. 211-12. The assessment was made by a member of the Cerci company. His sense of the link between the cost of money and royal financial measures is instructive, even if he failed to know that the crusade tax was simply to be concentrated in Riccardi hands, rather than actually taken out of circulation. See ibid. 218.

understood with a view bounded by the Alps. As the kings of England and France squeezed the sources of cash for their war efforts, the pope had the same end in mind. Between 1295 and 1302, as Norman Housley points out, 'the total lent to the allies of the pope which was repaid from the proceeds of the clerical tenth and the subsidy came to about a million florins.'[238] The combination of Italian crusading for papal aims and the Anglo-French war in a time of economic stress brought serious consequences for trade and credit. 'The coincidence of papal, French, and English demands', Housley writes, 'together with the general decline of trade at the close of the thirteenth century, led to falling credit and the collapse in swift succession of several banking houses, including the Buonsignori of Siena, the Ammanati of Pistoia, the Riccardi of Lucca, and the Mozzi of Florence.'[239] If we can think of a first generation of failures of Italian *societates* in the two decades after 1290, and a second generation of failures following 1340, the striking fact is the coincidence of the commercial bankruptcies with particularly active phases of Anglo-French warfare. Of course, causation was complex and involved Italian communal and papal politics and war no less than the warfare across the Channel.[240] Yet this northern warfare seems to have been one factor in the significant change away from the thirteenth century trend towards an integrated international trade in western Europe as a whole. Edward Miller, taking this larger perspective, notes that from the 1290s crown war measures in England and France imposed some check upon 'the tendency of western Europe to become more of a commercial unit and a single field of operations for international business firms'.[241]

If the French monarchy was not at the forefront in bringing down the major Italian financiers, it was pre-eminent in coinage manipulations.[242] In the crisis of the Anglo-French war of 1294,

[238] Housley, *The Italian Crusades*, 238.

[239] Ibid. 239.

[240] Renouard, *Les Rélations des papes d'Avignon*, 80-5; Bowsky, *A Medieval Italian Commune*, 246-57.

[241] Miller, 'The Economic Policies of Governments', 316.

[242] The following discussion emphasizes the fiscal motivations of coinage measures. Some scholars have argued that scarcity of precious metal forced manipulation of currency. As Leopold Genicot wrote 'Whichever happens to be the explanation we accept . . . the others should not thereby be rejected . . .';

French coinage depreciation, favoured by the master of the mint, was only delayed for a year and a half by Biche and Mouche, Philip's Italian financiers.[243] Although this devaluation of 1295 was the first major departure from the coinage of St Louis, we have already seen that it became a recurrent French practice throughout the period under study, as devaluation alternated with restoration at sometimes stunning frequencies. Devaluation could have ruinous effects on great lay and ecclesiastical landlords with fixed rent incomes, and on leading merchants with large assets of cash.[244]

Scholars have vigorously debated both the royal motivation and the economic effects of repeated coinage manipulations between 1295 and 1360.[245] Though (as we have already seen) the monetary policy of the French crown obviously yielded sizeable profits, which were obviously useful during periods of pressing war expenditure, some scholars see at least some of the recoinages aimed at protecting the supply of coin in the realm. Of course bullionism and profit could often have been compatible crown aims, but the filling of war chests seems the stronger motive when frequent coinage changes coincide with costly military activity. The economic effects of coinage measures raise even more questions. Did prices closely follow the value of silver? Could landed incomes adjust to the changes? Was an index to preserve the value of rents and debts independent of coinage mutation, though prohibited by royal edict, in widespread use? Did it prevent serious economic disruption? Such questions must largely be left in detail to the future work of economic specialists. It is at least interesting to note that Boniface VIII thought that Philip's original mutations were damaging to international

'Crisis: From the Middle Ages to Modern Times', 699. On motivation for coinage manipulation see Favier, *Philippe de Bel*, ch. 6, 7; Cazelles, 'Quelques réflexions'; Fryde, 'Financial Policies of the Royal Governments'; Henneman, *Royal Taxation in Fourteenth-century France* (1971), app. I.

243 Strayer, *The Reign of Philip the Fair*, 152-3; Fryde, 'Financial Policies of the Royal Governments', 831, 834.

244 Ibid. 834.

245 Jean Favier provides a convenient list of studies: *Philippe le Bel*, 549-50. In addition see Munro, 'Bullionism and the Bill of Exchange in England'. On indexing and incomes see Fournial, 'L'Indexation des créances et des rentes', 583-96; Cazelles, 'Quelques réflexions', 252-62; Lewis, *Later Medieval France*, 57-9.

trade;[246] it may be much more significant that resistance to coinage manipulation within France apparently built up with explosive force across the first half of the fourteenth century. It is difficult to believe, in any case, that years and even decades of rapidly fluctuating coinage values across the kingdom of France had a beneficent effect on the economic development of north-western Europe.

Although the English kings did not regularly fill war chests by means of coinage alterations,[247] their war finance may have contributed to what some economic historians consider a bullion famine in England.[248] War, hoarding, some export, and an unfavourable balance of trade seem to have reduced the stock of bullion in England well before the Hundred Years War broke out. But even earlier the warfare of the late 1290s probably caused a massive flow of bullion from England as Edward I, trying to finance continental war without a satisfactory relationship with a major Italian financier, shipped perhaps £350,000 in specie to the continent. The staggering size of such an outflow can be gauged by comparison with the issue from the mints during

246 Edward Miller cites this view: 'The Economic Policies of Governments', 315-16.

247 Michael Prestwich notes that the alteration of the English currency in the recoinage of 1279 was 'hardly sufficient to qualify as a debasement.' But, as he suggests, by charging seigniorage the crown made £35,788 in the first two years of the recoinage, at a time of heavy expenses for the Welsh wars; 'Edward I's Monetary Policies and their Consequences', esp. 407, 416. N. J. Mayhew suggested that royal confiscations of light, clipped, or foreign money in the 1290s 'may have been seen as an easy source of income, as well as a means to maintain English monetary standards'; 'Crockards and Pollards', 131. A more significant use of currency for fiscal needs accompanied the opening phase of the Hundred Years War. In a series of moves resisted by parliament, Edward II reduced the weight of the penny by 19 per cent between 1343 and 1351. See Mayhew, 'Numismatic Evidence', 13. 'If the initial debasement was certainly defensive [as a measure against foreign imitation and a loss of bullion], the subsequent ones', John Munro argues, 'were more likely aggressive measures related to the fiscal demands of his French war'; 'Bullionism and the Bill of Exchange in England', 190-1.

248 For a range of views see Miller, 'War, Taxation, and the English Economy', 24; Mavis Mate, 'High Prices in Early Fourteenth-century England'; Prestwich, 'Edward I's Monetary Policies and their Consequences'; id., 'Currency and the Economy of Early Fourteenth-century England'; Munro, 'Bullionism and the Bill of Exchange in England'; Lloyd, 'Overseas Trade and the English Money Supply'.

Edward's first recoinage in 1279, estimated at about £500,000. Some recovery came in 1300 with a coinage reform aimed at converting to sterling the notorious crockards and pollards (coins resembling sterling but with lower silver content) flowing in from the Low Countries. An end of the Anglo-French war and the revival of the wool trade helped also.[249] Yet the demands of war did cause a continuing bullion drain. Though the surviving evidence is too scanty to provide totals, considerable sums were paid out as protection money to the Scots during the reign of Edward II. The war finance of Edward III seems to have had a greater impact. Unlike his grandfather, Edward III did not ship silver across the Channel by the barrelful; but his heavy war taxation and the diversion of capital through his bankers to continental allies could well have contributed to the bullion drain already in progress. The tax of a ninth in 1341 had to be collected in kind because of the shortage of specie. Even if Englishmen were spared the fluctuations of the currency in France, the first half of the fourteenth century was for them 'a period of unusual uncertainty about the currency in England.'[250] Bullion flowing across the Channel was not lost to the economy of Europe as a whole, but the drain did produce an acute deflation in England with wide economic ramifications. Wool producers were badly hit by high taxation on wool and various embargoes and wool seizures essayed at the opening of the Hundred Years War by a government eager for cash; at the same time the currency crisis (at least intensified by war finance) reduced their purchasing power. The effects of war cannot always have reduced the supply of coin; profits of war in the form of ransoms may have helped alleviate the bullion crisis after the victories of 1346 won for the English a rich crop of captives. Moreover, factors unrelated to war—the recoinages of 1343 and 1351 and the dramatic fall in the population caused by the Black Death—seem important alleviating forces.[251] Edward Miller's general evaluation seems balanced:

[249] Prestwich, 'Edward I's Monetary Policies and their Consequences', 414-15.

[250] M. C. Prestwich, 'Currency and the Economy of Early Fourteenth-century England', 48.

[251] Ibid. and Maddicott, 'The English Peasantry and the Demands of the Crown', 48-50; Miller, 'War, Taxation, and the English Economy', 23-5.

Monetary disequilibria between nations were aggravated and more stringent exchange control became the order of the day to safeguard internal supplies of currency and bullion. The transfer of balances on which international trade depended became correspondingly more difficult. Some place must be allowed to all of this amongst the assemblage of causes of the contraction of economic activity during the later Middle Ages. . . .[252]

It is much more difficult to assess the place among causes of economic contraction for the movement of goods retarded by warfare, for migration of significant numbers of people effected by warfare, or for the numbers of men removed from production. Clearly war stimulated trade in certain goods, as any fletcher or armourer would have testified. English clothworkers likewise found their fortunes improved by the contrast between the heavy taxation of exported raw wool and extremely light taxation of exported cloth. After 1303 the higher duties paid by foreign merchants favoured English merchants who could not be convinced to pay them.[253] Just as clearly, however, the passage of armies and fleets, the breaking or burning of bridges and requisition of merchant ships disrupted trade. Bertrand de Born expressed the knightly anticipation of wartime plunder in the late twelfth century: 'And it will be good to live for one will take the property of usurers and there will no longer be a peaceful pack-horse on the roads, all the townsmen will tremble; the merchant will no longer journey in peace on the road to France. He who wishes to enrich himself will only need to steal well.'[254] Two centuries later, the veteran *routier* Merigot Marches expressed the same sentiments as he sat by the fireside in an inn talking with Froissart. Marches recalled the happy times

when . . . we could find in the fields a rich abbot or a rich prior or a rich merchant or a mule train from Montpellier, Narbonne, Limoux, Fougas, Béziers, Carcassonne or Toulouse, loaded with cloth of gold or silk, or from Brussels or Montivilliers . . . or spices coming from Bruges or other merchandise from Damascus and Alexandria. . . . All was ours, or ransomed at our will. Every day we had more money.[255]

252 Id., 'The Economic Policies of Governments', 316.
253 Id., 'War, Taxation, and the English Economy', 23-6.
254 Quot.: Painter, *French Chivalry*, 35.
255 Quot.: Lewis, *Later Medieval France*, 54.

Such attacks on trade were scarcely limited to *routiers*. Merchants shipping goods across the Channel might find the passage of war fleets an addition to the usual dangers from pirates. The English fleet which transported Edward III to Brabant in 1338 was a scourge to Channel shipping on its return; it 'plundered indiscriminately merchant ships of every nationality that it encountered'.[256] English merchants could not have felt entirely safe in their own country. The record of the royal inquest held in Lincolnshire in 1341, for example, records charges that royal purveyors extorted money for permission to trade at Boston Fair, or simply to transport goods from one point to another.[257]

Such extortion was illicit. But the crown might with complete legitimacy command a large fleet of merchant ships to transport an army and its supplies to the continent. M. M. Postan estimated that such a fleet might be collected about once in four years. The effort could require surprisingly large numbers of ships and sailors. Crown demands brought 5,800 sailors into this transport duty in 1297; 374 ships and 8,500 sailors (for differing lengths of time) in 1342 between September and December; no fewer than 738 ships and 15,000 sailors in 1346-7. Moreover, as a result of delays expected in such military operations, the ships and crews might be detained for the king's service a considerably longer time than the brief double crossing of the Channel. For the Black Prince's expedition of 1355, ships collected in Southampton and Plymouth from late April or early May did not even set sail until September.[258]

Was labour more generally withdrawn from productive employment for purposes of war? The issue is not numbers of battlefield deaths, which all agree were low in proportion to population, nor even total deaths brought by war, including non-combatants, which can have equalled only a small proportion of the mortality inflicted by the Black Death. For the years 1346-7, which saw intense military activity, Philippe Contamine estimated that the total loss of life caused among Frenchmen by

256 Fryde, 'Financial Resources of Edward I in the Netherlands, 1294-1298 (1967), 1183.

257 JUST 1/521/m 4, E 101/21/38 m.5 d. For a calendar of this document see McLane (ed.), *The 1341 Royal Inquest*, no. 87.

258 Postan, 'The Costs of the Hundred Years War', 35-9; Hewitt, *The Black Prince's Expedition*, 25, 33-9, points out that a few ships would be 'arrested' for the king's use even in peacetime (p. 34).

war stood as high as 100,000; yet soon thereafter the Plague may have carried off several million.[259] Yet some scholars argue that the reduction of the supply of labour brought about a decline in production. M. M. Postan, in fact, considered the diversion of manpower to war-making, in the form of field armies, fleets, and garrisons, the most obvious real cost of war. Philippe Contamine argued that overall mortality increased in wartime; combined with diversion of productive manpower this meant a serious check on the economy.[260] In the Crécy year Postan estimated that 60,000 to 80,000 men were either in the English army or in all the attendant logistical services; for several later expeditions total manpower requirements may have reached 40,000 to 50,000. Philippe Contamine suggests that in 1340 perhaps 50,000 men-at-arms and footmen were organized to fight for the French crown and that such a number implies a total mobilization of 100,000 men and an equal number of horses (to serve both as mounts and as transport).[261] The problems with this line of argument are, of course, to know how frequently such manpower demands were made and to determine whether all of those counted would have been productive if left totally free of the apparatus of military campaign. Contamine, however, argues that consumption has always risen in war. Armies expect to improve the quality and quantity of what they eat and drink; thus an army of only 10,000 fighting men would mean in fact 20,000 men and an equal number of horses and would consume as much as a city of 50,000 people.[262] On the other hand John Maddicott, analysing military service *per se* in the period before the dramatic population decline, considered the economic burden of supplying troops a more serious drain on English villagers than any reduction in labour supply or change in wage-rates.[263]

For France afflicted with most of the actual campaigning, the question of labour quickly becomes an issue of veritable migration. A close correlation between demographic swings and the incidence of warfare is not surprising, considering the intent

259 Contamine, 'La Guerre de cent ans en France', 143.

260 Postan, 'The Costs of the Hundred Years War'; Contamine, 'La Guerre de cent ans en France'.

261 Ibid. 133.

262 Ibid.

263 Maddicott, 'English Peasantry and the Demands of the Crown', 34-45.

and effectiveness of English *chevauchées* and the misery visited upon regions which became the scenes of chronic, if less spectacular campaigning. The dislocation brought about by such movements may have increased mortality rates, especially among the old, and the poor.[264] French local studies repeatedly find population movements which seem significant and clearly related to war, even if they generally resist quantification.[265] Even in England there may have been some dislocation of population, though on a much more limited scale than the French experienced. French naval raids do seem to have caused a drift of people away from the dangerous southern coastal areas. Major French naval raids were relatively few in number, but we cannot easily measure the fear they inspired or estimate the wartime increase in piracy and pillaging; these sea-borne threats seem for a time to have reduced agricultural production and the capacity to pay taxes in some areas.[266] As H. J. Hewitt noted, France was able 'to keep thousands of people in a state of anxiety and, in brief, to cause social and economic dislocation out of proportion to the effort she had expended.'[267] Moreover, though the issue has been little studied, the effects of extended periods of warfare on the population of the northern counties would be worth further investigation. Jean Scammell has called attention to a sizeable migration of lesser tenants away from manors in areas repeatedly ravaged by the Scots. 'Return was impossible', she suggests, 'and the refugees must have been reduced to a vagabond existence.'[268] Both Scammell and James Campbell have observed that the northern warfare produced bodies very much like the free companies which ravaged France. In general, as Campbell suggests, such a situation 'had much the same effect on the border that it did in parts of France.'[269]

More copious evidence survives concerning the effects of war on the wool trade, though a supply on medieval evidence seldom

[264] Contamine, 'La Guerre de cent ans en France', 142-5.

[265] See Fowler (ed.), *The Hundred Years War*, 12-14, and the studies he cites in n. 50, p. 26. Raymond Cazelles comments on the phenomenon of flight from France into the Empire: *Société politique, noblesse et couronne*, 566-7, 573.

[266] Searle and Burghart, 'The Defense of England and the Peasants' Revolt'.

[267] Hewitt, *Organization of War*, 15-17; cf. 20-7.

[268] Scammell, 'Robert I and the North of England', 389.

[269] Campbell, 'England, Scotland, and the Hundred Years War', 214.

insures scholarly agreement on its interpretation.[270] The trade in raw wool, England's major export, clearly declined in the late Middle Ages; by the late fourteenth century recorded wool exports were decidedly falling and the downward secular movement in wool prices was likewise clear.[271] The difficulty lies in determining how much of an effect was exercised by the twin royal policies of taxes on wool and taxes in wool. Some agreement seems to be emerging on the economic consequences of the extraordinary taxation on wool imposed by Edward I in the crisis years following 1294. The export duty on wool was raised sixfold, jumping in 1294 from the 6*s*. 8*d*, per sack of the 1275 Ancient Custom to the maltolte of 40*s*. per sack. Wool merchants apparently were unable to pass on the costs to foreign buyers; they seem to have succeeded much better with native growers. As T. H. Lloyd has shown, the prices paid for wool in England fell to their lowest level since mid-century. Some sellers could find no buyers at any price.[272] His tabulated figures on prices show that the annual mean price of wool throughout England in 1294-7 fell by nearly 24 per cent. Such a slump may, Edward Miller suggests, have clipped as much as £40,000 a year from landowners' incomes. 'This is a sufficent sum', argues Miller, 'to justify some sense of oppression. . . .' He notes that it may explain why in the *Monstraunces* presenting complaints to Edward I in 1297 the earls exaggerated the value of wool as half the total value of the land and denounced that maltote as 'too heavy a charge and a grievous burden'.[273] The king had to jettison the maltote in the crisis of 1297, but when Edward III fully renewed it in 1338 under the intense financial pressures of

270 Scammell, 'Robert I and the North of England', 388-9, 396. The most comprehensive study is that of T. H. Lloyd, *The English Wool Trade in the Middle Ages*. The classic essay of an earlier generation is Power, *The Wool Trade in English Medieval History*.

271 Lloyd, *The Movement of Wool Prices in Medieval England*; Carus-Wilson and Coleman, *England's Export Trade*.

272 This point figured in the long-standing debate between K. B. McFarlane and M. M. Postan: McFarlane, 'England and the Hundred Years War', 8; Postan, 'The Costs of the Hundred Years War', 40-1. Cf. Fryde, *The Wool Accounts of William de la Pole*, 14-15; Lloyd, *The English Wool Trade in the Middle Ages*, ch. 3; id., *The Movement of Wool Prices in Medieval England*, 16-17.

273 Miller, 'War, Taxation, and the English Economy', 12-14.

the opening campaigns of the Hundred Years War, the economic effects were again disastrous to English merchants. After examining the wool accounts of William de la Pole, Edmund Fryde concluded that 'the normal profits of the wool trade were not high enough to allow it to bear the high wartime rate of custom and subsidy. The raising of the duty payable by Englishmen . . . was likely to take away most of the normal profits of English merchants.'[274] Apparently failing in the attempt to pass on the export duty costs to foreign buyers, the only recourse was to offer lower purchase prices to wool growers in England. King and Commons struggled to find a balance between financial needs of the crown and the wool producers. The king needed profit from the export trade in wool, either through special arrangements with favoured groups of English companies or through a high level of taxation; the wool producers were convinced that high taxation or monopolies lowered their profits. Beginning in 1351 parliament agreed annually to a subsidy of 40*s*. a sack on exported wool; it thereby edged out the merchant assemblies with which Edward III had been negotiating and soon was secure in the knowledge that the English companies he had created to serve his war finance were a worry of the past.[275]

Forced loans in wool, the second English royal wool policy, also began under Edward I. The seizures of foreign merchants' wool in April 1297 and the more general seizures ordered in July and intended to raise significant sums for payments to continental allies, were quickly stopped by the resistance which Edward's policy and his collectors encountered.[276] The seizures and various embargoes ordered must have caused some disruption to wool exports in these years, but the total amount of wool seized and sold in the Low Countries in 1296-8 yielded only about £25,000 (after expenses) at a time when the annual value of exported wool may have approached £200,000.[277] Edward III was more thorough and persistent in his role as 'woolmonger

[274] Fryde, 'The Wool Accounts of William de la Pole', 14-15.

[275] Harriss, *King, Parliament, and Public Finance*, ch. 18; Lloyd, *The English Wool Trade in the Middle Ages*, ch. 5.

[276] Fryde, 'Financial Resources of Edward I in the Netherlands, 1294-1298' (1962), 1182-3; Prestwich, *War, Politics, and Finance*, 197-8.

[277] Fryde, 'Financial Resources of Edward I in the Netherlands, 1294-1298' (1962), 1185; Miller, 'War, Taxation, and the English Economy', 13.

extraordinary'.[278] The failure of his ambitious wool monopoly scheme of 1337-8 to sustain his ambitious campaigning has already been discussed. One important economic result was the royal seizure from the English merchants of roughly 10,300 sacks of wool valued at £110,000 at Dordrecht in Zeeland. Though the merchants were promised repayment, most of them were still waiting for their money in 1343 and only those willing to lend money to the crown were ever properly compensated.[279] Over the next decade Edward's complex agreements with quasi-monopolistic groups of English merchants brought considerable confusion to the wool trade and considerable risk to merchants involved in it. 'The farming of the customs and the financial schemes connected with it', Edmund Fryde writes, 'profited only a small group of businessmen at the expense of most other economic interests in England. The wool producers, the lesser merchants and the majority of the royal creditors were especially bound to suffer.'[280]

Over roughly the first half of the fourteenth century English royal action in the wool trade seems disruptive and sometimes disastrous. Yet the downward movement in wool prices cannot be simply tied to the wartime manipulations of the trade by Edward III; in fact the fall in wool prices began before his schemes to finance war with wool had been launched and may have resulted from complex deflationary trends. Population decline or a serious bullion famine, rather than the disruption of war and the pressures of war finance, may stand behind the problems in the fourteenth-century wool trade. The secular slump in wool prices, moreover, must be placed even later than this short-term decline; the long-term decline is apparent in the late 1370s. Likewise, the decline in wool exports is a feature of the second half of the century when the most ambitious wool schemes of Edward III were only troublesome memories. Thus it would be difficult to construct a convincing case for warfare as a chief cause of the long-term decline of the wool trade, although it clearly caused setbacks and even disasters over shorter spans of time, as in 1294-7, 1338-42. For longer range consequences we need to

[278] The phrase is that of Lloyd, *The English Wool Trade in the Middle Ages*; title of ch. 5.

[279] Fryde, 'Edward III's Wool Monopoly of 1336'; 'The English Farmers', 3.

[280] Ibid. 16.

consider royal exploitation of wool as one important species of the general phenomenon of war taxation.

War taxation and the transfer of wealth

The transfer of wealth via taxation is one of the crucial issues in evaluating the economic consequences of late medieval warfare. When royal governments on either side of the Channel amassed large war chests and disbursed them for the men and materials of war were they wasting precious resources or merely spending them in a fashion different from but no more wasteful than the uses to which they would otherwise have gone?

During the traditional period of the Hundred Years War direct taxation, the great bulk of it going for war, extracted vast sums of money from town and countryside in England and France. Once again the 1290s mark a significant turning-point both in England and France. In England the incidence and rate of taxation climbed. Edward I collected six levies on movables during the last fourteen years of his reign, four of them (amounting to 30 per cent of the yield of lay taxation and more then 40 per cent of the yield of clerical taxation) in the crisis years 1294-7. This sharp change points to a long-range trend. Across the major part of the thirteenth century, from 1216-90, the English crown had taken only seven levies. In the forty-one years following 1294 the crown collected sixteen levies. Moreover these more frequent taxes were collected at a higher rate, different percentages being specified for towns and countryside.[281] In France, Philip IV tried to launch general taxation in the 1290s and in fact took subsidies for war in seven of the ten years 1295-1304.[282] But, as we have seen, French monarchs after Philip encountered great resistance; direct taxation continued but remained a matter of contention and proved an inadequate source of war funds before the emergency brought about by the capture of King John II in 1356.[283] No overall estimates of the yield of French taxation have ever been attempted, but a notional sense of scale is provided by such estimates for England. K. B. McFarlane calculated the rough total

[281] Willard, *Parliamentary Taxes on Personal Property 1290-1334*; Maddicott, 'The English Peasantry and the Demands of the Crown', 6-7; Prestwich, *War, Politics, and Finance*, 179.

[282] Strayer, *The Reign of Philip the Fair*, 153.

[283] Henneman, *Royal Taxation in Fourteenth-century France* (1971).

of English taxation during the traditional period of the Hundred Years War (1337–1453) at eight and a quarter million pounds sterling.[284] While this staggering figure includes the later phases of the Hundred Years War which lie largely beyond the scope of our investigation, it does not take into account the costly warfare of the years following 1294. Michael Prestwich estimates that between the outbreak of war in the summer of 1294 and the return of Edward I from Flanders in early 1298, English military spending was in the order of £750,000.[285]

Such figures take on more meaning when closely analysed for a particular period of war. For the Anglo-French conflict of 1294–1303 (the Gascon War to the English, the War of Aquitaine to the French) J. R. Strayer has studied the sums raised by each side, the sources tapped to obtain the money, and the manner in which it was spent. Such questions are especially interesting for our purposes because 'this war which was no war' involved 'no major battles, no prolonged sieges, very few deaths in combat, and relatively little devastation of the countryside.'[286] Thus for this campaign the effects of military taxation and spending can be studied in almost total isolation from the issue of devastation. The French estimate of funds available (about 1,735,000*l.t.*) and the English record of monies spent (about £360,000 or 1,440,000*l.t.*), suggest that together the two kings spent roughly 3,000,000*l.t.* or £750,000 sterling in this war. In both kingdoms this treasure was extracted from the more productive segments of society: the clergy (who 'were not entrepreneurs, but . . . good estate managers'), wool suppliers in England, Italian merchant-bankers, native merchants, artisans and peasants in both kingdoms. The money went largely for military pay; the more complete English evidence suggests as much as 75 per cent of the war chest went for wages and bonuses paid to soldiers and sailors. Moreover, the remainder of military spending seems to have produced no boom in industry (production of armaments or ships) or in agriculture; grain prices in England actually declined during the war. Strayer's conclusion is that

[284] McFarlane, 'England and the Hundred Years War', 6; Postan, 'The Costs of the Hundred Years War', 40, agreed on this figure.

[285] Prestwich, *War, Politics, and Finance*, 175.

[286] Strayer, 'The Costs and Profits of War', 271.

The war of Aquitaine transferred money from merchants and artisans and producers of commercial crops (such as wool) to a few great lords, many middling and petty nobles, and some thousands of poor commoners. Very few of these people were in a position to invest their earnings in any productive enterprise. Most of them must have used their wages to maintain or slightly improve their level of living; that is, the money was spent on such consumption goods as food and clothing. A very large percentage of both armies came from the poorer parts of southwestern France and (for the English forces) northern Spain. Army pay doubtless relieved the poverty of these areas a little but it did not increase their productivity.[287]

Moreover, at least in England, money taken as war taxation may have reduced the amount of disposable income landlords possessed. This could have intensified the movement away from direct demesne production toward rents, thus reducing the scale of seigneurial enterprise. Lords were liable to taxation only on the produce of their manors held in demesne; if taxation cut into their incomes they were less likely to reduce their standard of living than to reduce investment and the burden of taxation by leasing out demesne manors, especially if the land was marginal.[288] In France even the rich and populous province of Normandy, studied by Strayer, was showing a decrease in seigneurial income that may have been related to the cost of warfare in 1294-8.[289]

It could be argued that not all transfers of wealth brought about by war had negative economic consequences. Were there not profits of war as well as costs of war? Did not victorious warriors at least sometimes return from campaign staggering beneath glittering loads of accumulated wages, loots, and ransoms? Two issues seem significant. In the first instance, we need to recognize that medieval war was unlikely to stimulate demand and call forth new levels of production as it has done in more modern times, enriching those fortunately placed or clever enough to take advantage of the opportunity. Manufacturers of arms and armour would do well, as would some cloth makers. But the needs of

[287] Strayer, 'The Costs and Profits of War', 290.

[288] Maddicott, 'The English Peasantry and the Demands of the Crown', 7; Miller, 'War, Taxation, and the English Economy', 26; Fryde, 'Financial Policies of the Royal Governments', 833.

[289] Strayer, 'Economic Conditions in the County of Beaumont-le-Roger; id., 'Economic Conditions in Upper Normandy'.

fourteenth-century warfare scarcely created an early military-industrial complex. Weaponry was relatively simple, ships were mainly impressed merchant vessels and the quantity of cloth going into uniforms was too small to stimulate wool growing or cloth production of any significant scale. Philippe Contamine has even argued that although war raised economic demand in some directions (arms, horses, and the general standard of living of the warriors), its main economic consequences were to intensify the demographic crisis and thus to lower both production and consumption.[290] Second, what of the fighting men themselves? The question of their profits calls for the economist's distinction between a private and a social rate of return. A positive social rate of return would obtain only if the warrior put the goods or money now in his hands to more productive uses than would their former owners. Examples could be collected to illustrate either possibility on this point.[291] But the likelihood is that on balance these so-called profits of war were dissipated in ways scarcely able to promote economic growth. The ransoms gained so spectacularly in war, for example, were often returned to war purposes. In the case of the most spectacular of all the ransoms, that for King John, as much as a third of the perhaps £250,000 received (both for John's freedom and as protection money paid to spare Burgundy from English invasion) was kept sealed up in bags first in the Tower and later in the king's chamber, as a special war fund.[292] Not all money made in war was spent on war. Yet K. B. McFarlane, who made the strongest case for war profits reaching England, concluded that the martial entrepreneurs spent their gains 'to raise their standard of living, on more personal services, more building, more ostentation, an increased expenditure on luxuries of all sorts, mostly imported. However good for trade, this may not have been the surest way to stimulate economic growth.'[293] If, as M. M.

[290] Philippe Contamine has examined the question of warfare and production in two arts.: 'La Guerre de cent ans en France'; 'Consommation et demande militaire'. Cf. the comments of J. R. Strayer in 'The Costs and Profits of War'.

[291] A good discussion with illustrative quots. is provided by H. J. Hewitt: *Organization of War*, 104-10.

[292] Tout, *Chapters in the Administrative History of Medieval England*, iii. 243 ff.; Postan, 'The Costs of the Hundred Years War', 47-8; Broome, 'The Ransom of John II', esp. pp. xxiv-xxv.

[293] McFarlane, 'England and the Hundred Years War', 11. He closes: 'But it would have been rather odd if they had cared about that.' In the present analysis we must, of course, be closely concerned with just this issue.

Postan argued, the net balance for England in the Hundred Years War was bound to be in the red,[294] then the conclusion could scarcely be more optimistic for France; and if we change the focal length to include not national economies but the economy of Europe where did the war produce a net profit? A. R. Bridbury, objecting to the suggestions that medieval warfare could enhance the productive powers of the winning side, retorted that 'we are being asked to believe that war in the Middle Ages was capable of conferring advantages which simply did not exist in the Middle Ages for anyone to enjoy.'[295]

In a broad and speculative essay on the consequences of organized violence, Frederic C. Lane provided a useful theoretical frame for the issue at hand. He suggested that throughout the millenium 700 to 1700 violence used to control violence was economically productive, but that violence used to transfer wealth from one person to another was not productive. In general, protection against such violent transfers was one of the services provided by the state or some other prior or competing enterprise. Yet the state was at the same time a violence-producing enterprise conducting external war and often far from secure in its own internal monopoly of the use of force. A high cost in producing protection could result from vigorous war and from internal competition among various agencies to control violence; either or both would reduce what he terms the surplus ('that part of the total production which did not have to be consumed in order to maintain the existing level of production').[296] Interesting results appear if we use this model for north-western Europe in roughly the mid-fourteenth century. Lane's ideas seem particularly appropriate for the region of France which produced the Jacquerie in 1358. Protection costs carried by the peasantry were certainly high; they might include seigneurial dues, ransoms for lords captured on the battlefield at Poitiers, 'protection money' to ward off bands of English, Navarese or even royal soldiery, and fines to the crown for dealing with the enemy soldiers. The 'surplus' in France was thus reduced by competition among agencies providing protection (with varying degrees of legitimacy). In England there was much less cost resulting from competition over the legitimate locus of protec-

294 Postan, 'The Costs of the Hundred Years War', 34.
295 Bridbury, 'The Hundred Years War: Costs and Profits', 93.
296 Lane, 'The Economic Consequences of Organized Violence'.

tion. Yet in England the costs of paying for ambitious warfare across the Channel could have similarly reduced the 'surplus', external violence taking the place of internal competition. So broad a construct as Lane's might be qualified in many particular ways, but his conclusion seems defensible: 'In many centuries the main way in which governments influenced growth was through decisions that determined how much should be expended on the use and control of violence.'[297]

If the effects of massive war taxation could be significant at the macro level, they could also be troublesome at the micro level of an ordinary village household. It is notoriously difficult for the historian to generalize at this level, lighted so dimly and so indirectly by surviving evidence,[298] and it is obvious that local conditions varied a good deal; but, as John Maddicott has argued, the weight of frequent levies on movables, on top of which we must figuratively pile an additional load of extortion and bribery, could represent a 'grievous imposition'. A period of bad weather, a greedy taxer, or one with a grudge could transform a merely heavy tax burden into something more severe. The men of Ottery St Mary in Devon claimed that their assessment of £15. 10*s.* 7*d.* in 1332 jumped to £20 in 1334 simply because of an assessor's grudge; 26 of 134 tenants, apparently finding this new assessment intolerable, took the desperate step of fleeing their holdings. 'Like many others,' Maddicott writes, 'they were the indirect victims of the state of war.'[299] For most peasants the weight of taxation was especially felt because unlike the more predictable payments owed landlords, the requirements of the king's wars came suddenly and relatively unexpectedly.[300] In fact this problem should be generalized beyond the peasantry. At all levels, as Edward Miller notes, men tended to live up to their incomes (whether this was noble luxury or something close to subsistence for a peasant); since royal taxation before the 1290s had been relatively

[297] Ibid. 413.

[298] Edward Miller writes: 'The economics of a peasant household are virtually unknowable. We are seldom if ever in a position to establish, at any given moment, how many mouths a holding has to feed, how much was added to it or subtracted from it by inter-peasant leases, and what ancillary sources of income were available to the family'; 'War, Taxation, and the English Economy', 17.

[299] Maddicott, 'The English Peasantry and the Demands of the Crown', 14-15.

[300] Ibid. 4.

infrequent they had yet to learn that they must keep something in reserve. War taxation thus 'affected immediately men's ability to satisfy their consumption expectations.'[301]

But another form of direct taxation often coincided with the levy on movables and seems to have brought more stress to English villagers. Purveyance, the prerogative right of the crown to compel men to sell victuals and to provide transport needed by the royal household, was ancient; the right had even been expanded to support the king's armies under Henry II. But with the financial pressures accompanying the expanded warfare of the 1290s, purveyance took on new importance and new scope. The three Edwards were using purveyance (drawing on the elastic notion of royal prerogative) to provide war funds without the bother of consultation, as King John had used the feudal incidents.[302] The volume of supplies required from specified counties and the geographical spread of purveyor's activities could be truly impressive.[303] Edward I's purveyances in the single county of Kent in 1296-7 are thought to have taken the produce of 4,900 acres.[304] As the volume of complaint rose, the crown issued regulations to protect the king's subjects; yet these may tell more about burdens and abuses suffered than about reform accomplished. In 1296, after a most thorough purveyance aimed at obtaining 13,500 quarters of wheat and 13,000 quarters of oats in twelve southern counties, the collectors were significantly ordered to see that no one was left without sufficient grain to live on.[305] Of course the vast quantities of food sought were not always obtained, and much that was purveyed was actually paid for. In some counties the burden of certain purveyances was carefully allocated among hundreds or wapentakes, then again among their constituent villages and finally was assessed on individual villagers. But this elaborate assessment seems exceptional. 'Many more frequently', John Maddicott writes, 'the sheriff's subordinant, the hundred or

301 Miller, 'War, Taxation, and the English Economy', 20.

302 Maddicott, 'The English Peasantry and the Demands of the Crown', 16. Michael Prestwich points out that after 1297 chancery clerks used the more respectable word purveyance rather than prise, but that the propaganda fooled no one; *War, Politics, and Finance*, 131.

303 Ibid., ch. 5; McLane, (ed.), *The 1341 Royal Inquest*; id., 'The Royal Courts', ch. 3; Thomson, *A Lincolnshire Assize Roll.*

304 Prestwich, *The Three Edwards*, 269.

305 Prestwich, *War, Politics, and Finance*, 120.

wapentake bailiff, simply descended on a village and took what he wanted, often quite arbitrarily, without payment (or at best with payment deferred through the giving of tallies), and in a way which bore little relation to the owner's ability to sustain the prise.'[306] Moreover, payment was often given at less than market prices, or for only a part of the goods taken. If payment was made in the form of wooden tallies, the seller might find that getting his cash was difficult and slow. Robert Hood of London was forced to provide ale in 1298 and 1300; his son received payment only in 1327.[307] Fraud and brutality seem to have been frequent companions of the purveyors. The king was sometimes cheated and his subjects more often were. Purveyors reported to the crown only a part of what they took, they imprisoned men and women or seized their house keys to force payment, they broke down doors and gates that interfered; they sometimes took recognizances from their victims designed to prevent any prosecution for their misdeeds.[308]

The argument could be made that, however regrettable the abuses, purveyance simply increased social mobility and somewhat altered the incidence of the burden of taxation; it benefited purveyors and fell heavily on some groups, but removed very little from the market. It is helpful to be reminded that goods extorted did not 'vanish into space' and that what was not consumed 'found its way back into farming or went to market, as it might have done in other circumstances anyway'.[309] Yet the economic effects of purveyance should not lightly be dismissed. The taking of livestock and especially oxen could have devastating effect. A 1332 seizure of thirty-two oxen at Sutton in Lincolnshire eliminated sixteen of the villagers plough teams for half a year. When the sheriff of Nottinghamshire purveyed twenty-four oxen in the same year, the plough teams of four men were broken up, their winter sowing was prevented, and they had to sell their land.[310] The *Monstraunces* presented to Edward I in 1297

[306] Maddicott, 'The English Peasantry and the Demands of the Crown', 26.

[307] Prestwich, *War, Politics, and Finance*, 118.

[308] Examples from E 159/116 m. 189d; E 101/21/38; E 101/22/4; JUST1/521 mm 4, 5; calendared in McLane (ed.), *The 1341 Royal Inquest*, no. 87.

[309] Bridbury, 'The Hundred Years War: Costs and Profits', 406.

[310] JUST I/521m3, calendared in McLane (ed.), *The 1341 Royal Inquest*, no. 87; Maddicott, 'The English Peasantry and the Demands of the Crown', 31.

claimed that many men had been forced below the subsistence level by royal demands for supplies and the failure to pay for them. In the Inquisitions of the Ninth in 1341, parish jurors sometimes associated royal taxation, abandoned land, and widespread poverty.[311] Moreover, purveying missions could easily become looting forays. They sometimes featured extortion plain and simple, as complaints from the inquests of 1298, and 1340-1 demonstrate.[312] Sometimes the goods purveyed were quickly resold to the owners, their price having risen in the short interval between the two transactions.[313] John de Oxenford (considered by Maddicott a good candidate for the dubious honour of being a prototype for the Sheriff of Nottingham in the Robin Hood Tales) purveyed 200 oxen and 12,000 sheep and later sold them back to their owners.[314] If we knew only the original transaction we might think that the livestock was not lost to the economy, but merely arrived in the market circuitously; the resale reveals instead a process of extortion. On occasion, communities paid fines to the purveyors 'so that they would take no more';[315] and in 1337 the people of the county of Lincolnshire collectively paid 2,000*m*. to be freed from purveyance.[316] That the people of Lincolnshire were willing to pay for relief is not surprising. Counties along the east coast and in the east Midlands were hard hit by purveyors because they were the chief grain-producing areas and were well supplied with waterways leading to convenient coastal ports.[317] But repeated purveyances in these areas fell, Maddicott argues, on a vulnerable population: at least parts of the counties most often visited by purveyors also suffered from overpopulation, serious land shortage, and rural poverty; and the absence of heavy seigneurial dues imposed by powerful local lordship may well have been countered by an absence of the pro-

[311] Prestwich, *War, Politics, and Finance*, 31.

[312] E101/21/136; E101/21/4; Prestwich, *War, Politics, and Finance*, 129-30; and McLane (ed.), *The 1341 Royal Inquest*, no. 87.

[313] JUST I/521m5, calendared in McLane (ed.), *The 1341 Royal Inquest*, no. 87; E101/21/38-9; E101/22/4.

[314] Maddicott, 'The Birth and Setting of the Ballads of Robin Hood', 290.

[315] E101/22/4, inquest at Grantham, Lincs., 1340.

[316] Prestwich, *The Three Edwards*, 269-70.

[317] See McLane, 'The Royal Courts', 144-8 for the crown's wartime demands placed on the wealthy county of Lincolnshire. Cf. McLane's discussion in the introduction to *The 1341 Royal Inquest*.

tection such lordship could provide against the worst terrors of purveyance.[318] The economic effect of purveyance on the peasantry in certain regions of England may thus have been severe. If oxen or seed corn sometimes went to the purveyors, as contemporary poems of complaint assert, the villager would be without a grain crop.[319]

It is possible, though more difficult to evaluate or document, that purveyance affected the population generally through its action on markets. Withdrawal of vast quantities of grain from local markets may have caused severe short-term fluctuations; men with friends at court could sell their produce swiftly when informed that purveyors were to be sent; ordinary villagers would face the sharp rise in prices once the grain was being carted off to the king's armies.[320]

Certainly these ordinary folk hated and resisted the purveyors. In 1338 a purveyor's deputy arrested two men at Kirkton in Lincolnshire as 'rebels against the lord king'.[321] In 1339 the commissioners in Nottinghamshire and Derbyshire could produce nothing for the king 'because the men of those regions in full county court of Nottinghamshire and Derbyshire asserted that they would not permit [the commissioners] by virtue of their commission to meddle or to take any victuals [beyond what had been purveyed already]'.[322] By the late 1330s complaint against purveyance (often linked with the tax on movables) had become so vigorous that gentry and magnates may have feared a peasant rising.[323]

French royal use of the right to seize goods and transport for war, the right of prise was apparently exercised on a much lower scale than in England and thus was less a cause for distress and outrage. Yet, though evidence is patchy, we know that the right was exercised frequently enough to cause complaint and that the

318 Maddicott, 'The English Peasantry and the Demands of the Crown', 17-19.

319 See for example the 'Song of the Husbandman', pr. Robbins, *Historical Poems*, 7-9.

320 Maddicott, 'The English Peasantry and the Demands of the Crown', 32.

321 E101/22/4.

322 E368/113mm 10d., 11, 11d. I have combined the testimony regarding the two commissioners.

323 Maddicott, 'The English Peasantry and the Demands of the Crown', 23-4; Fryde, 'Parliament and the French War'.

volume of the complaint brought royal promises of reform, as in England. As early as the mid-thirteenth century St Louis promised redress of grievances caused by prises;[324] in 1309 Philip the Fair issued an ordinance regulating prise;[325] as did his successors in 1315, 1319, and 1346.[326] In the difficult years of the mid-fourteenth century, the French government even formally abandoned the right; ordinances of 1355 and 1357 reserved prises only for the personal needs of the king and his household and promised a just price for property taken.[327] Yet the practice continued to provoke complaint and legal suit. Religious houses were especially affected and some bought exemptions.[328] To avoid 'popular commotions' kings of France prudently granted repeated exemptions to the townsmen of Paris.[329]

The kings of England and France, then, channelled vast resources in the form of money, goods, and services to the conduct of war; the campaigns which these resources sustained brought dislocations to the common economic life of north-western Europe and serious devastation to much of France, the premier kingdom of Europe. Close agreement on how each force worked and how heavily it weighs in the balance of effects on the European economy is unlikely where so much that is important remains insufficiently documented. But in general terms the direction of the effects of extended warfare and some rough, notional sense of its magnitude are not beyond reach. In some ways the costs of war seem to have acted like a catalyst, intensifying economic changes already at work. Philippe Contamine makes this sort of case for war stimulating demand in certain areas, at the same time it reduced productive capacity and lowered the purchasing power of individuals in favour of the state. 'Aggravant la crise démographique, la guerre, tout en entraînant une diminution de la

[324] Miller, 'The Economic Policies of Governments', 313.

[325] *Les Olim*, ii. 497. See J. R. Strayer's comments: *The Reign of Philip the Fair*, 235.

[326] *Ordonnances des roys de France*, i. 608, 680.

[327] Timbal *La Guerre de cent ans*, 81; Henneman, *Royal Taxation in Fourteenth-century France* (1971), 272.

[328] Timbal, *La Guerre de cent ans*, 82-103; Contamine, *Guerre, état, et société*, 125-7.

[329] Timbal, *La Guerre de cent ans*, 90, and the sources cited in n. 62.

production, entraîna aussi une diminution de la consumation.'[330] In other ways the costs of war were major reactants, forces causing changes on their own. The Hundred Years War was no controlled experiment, and even if they were somehow granted dispensation by Clio, historians could scarcely wish the war replayed time and again, each individual factor in turn removed for purposes of analysis. But on important issues historians have always had to use the evidence as best they can in realms beyond the sphere of controlled experiments. Thus after carefully studying the evidence on the effects wrought by wartime demands of the crown on the English peasantry, John Maddicott concludes that:

> we cannot assume that the Malthusian checks imposed by sporadic bouts of bad weather necessarily did most to determine the economic fortunes of the peasantry at this time. Equally significant, though less direct in its impact, was the inauguration of wars which were more continous, more extensive and more costly than those of earlier days. Turning points and watersheds are part of the historian's stock-in-trade; but it may be that in the history of rural England such terms are used less justly of the famine of 1315–1317 than of the wars of France and Scotland which had begun twenty years before.[331]

Edward Miller concluded his study of the effects of war taxation on the English economy after 1294 in similar terms. He thought that 'the long term advance of economic activity in England had been decisively checked well before 1349' and that even if the impact of fiscal causes cannot be estimated with precision, royal fiscal policies 'reinforced other influences at work making for a reduction in the scale of seigneurial enterprise.' In the final analysis 'it may well be that these measures were as significant in the economic field as they were in instigating those constitutional developments which made the reigns of the first three Edwards a watershed in English history.'[332] In his study of the Anglo-French war of 1294-1303, J. R. Strayer noted that scattered evidence suggests that the new warfare of the fourteenth century had similar economic consequences across Europe. His broad

[330] Contamine, 'La Guerre de cent ans en France'; the quot. is taken from p. 148.

[331] Maddicott, 'The English Peasantry and the Demands of the Crown', 75.

[332] Miller, 'War, Taxation, and the English Economy', 25-7.

conclusion is that 'the economic consequences of war certainly contributed to the great European depression of the later Middle Ages. There were other causes—overpopulation in some areas, inability to increase significantly the production of raw materials or manufactured goods, lack of new markets—but the costs of war may have been the determining factor.'[333] Strayer's conclusion based on a particular study is completely congruent with F. C. Lane's conclusion to his theoretical economic discussion of the link between war and the economy in the Middle Ages:

> With the longer perspective in mind I would like to suggest that the most weighty single factor in most periods of growth, if any one factor has been most important, has been a reduction in the proportion of resources devoted to war and police. Those princes or statesmen who organized government in such a way as to reduce the costs of protection contributed to economic growth just as did the industrial or agricultural innovators who reduced the costs of other products.[334]

Any broad conclusion about the role of warfare in the economic development of late medieval Europe and especially any attempt to rank the importance of war *vis-à-vis* other forces will encounter a host of objections and qualifications on every side. But to change the direction suggested for the force of war or radically to alter the sense that war was a factor of great importance in the economic problems of Europe in the late Middle Ages would require a demonstration that physical damage wrought was not significant, that disruption of trade and credit was unimportant and that the transfers of wealth caused basically by war taxation were not detrimental to productivity. Such a demonstration has yet to be made.

Objection to this line of analysis could be raised from the opposite direction. It might be argued not that the effects of fourteenth century warfare were less serious than has been suggested here, but rather that medieval campaigning always produced such effects, once the powers of the emerging state were channelled into war. Were the deleterious effects of warfare so new in the fourteenth century that they must be counted a major factor in economic change? Could similar effects not be found in, say, the twelfth century, especially as the kings of England tried

[333] Strayer, 'The Costs and Profits of War', 291.

[334] Lane, 'The Economic Consequences of Organized Violence', 413.

to maintain their hold on the continental principalities we sometimes simplify with the name Angevin Empire?

Twelfth-century warfare, especially as practised by the English crown, shows marked similarities to that of the Hundred Years War era, as we have already noted. Large amounts of wealth were extracted and used for the pay of troops; credit facilities were employed to ease problems of liquidity. There also can be little doubt that devastation formed an important element in campaigning.[335]

But two significant differences separate fourteenth-century warfare from its antecedents, and each suggests that the effects of war on the economy of north-western Europe would be much more intense in the later era. The scale of warfare, as noted above, seems to have climbed significantly in the period after 1290. Larger armies and longer campaigns could be achieved only by the commitment, through the agency of the state, of a larger share of the wealth of town and countryside than had previously been achieved. Though unarguable certainty will always remain elusive, it seems likely that the augmented forces of war achieved one of their chief aims by carrying out destruction and disruption on an even broader scale than their ancestors had managed several centuries earlier. In the second place, the broader warfare of the fourteenth century was acting on a medieval economy that had, in the opinion of most economic historians, passed its peak and was entering a perilous period of depression. If the vigour of medieval warfare expanded as the vigour of the medieval economy slumped, the role of war looms very large indeed in the constellation of late medieval problems.

5. WAR AND STATE-BUILDING

During the High Middle Ages as kings linked the growing powers of the state with the important and valued business of war,

[335] F. M. Powicke discusses these issues in *The Loss of Normandy*, ch. 8: 'We can only guess at the amount of beggary, prostitution and starvation produced by feudal warfare', he writes. 'All we can know with certainty is that those who suffered must have been very numerous.' Yet he thinks the twelfth-century warfare did not produce suffering on a fourteenth-century scale (see pp. 241-2).

both enterprises flourished and proved mutually augmentative.[336] In important ways the extended scale of warfare in the later Middle Ages furthered the growth of states on both sides of the Channel.[337] Involvement in nearly continuous warfare was bound to stimulate some aspects of the process of state-building. The heavy demands of raising troops and money, of conducting campaigns, of convincing populations of the rectitude of the fighting and the likelihood that it would be crowned with success all required great activity on the part of kings and their counsellors and agents and touched the lives and purses of a great many of the kings' subjects. Moreover, heightened crown demands entailed more of the consultation Bernard Guenée termed a dialogue between prince and community.[338] This dialogue drew upon the best formulations of political philosophy available and challenged thinkers no less than men of action to produce workable solutions to the problems posed by the exigencies of the crown.[339]

In France initial efforts to create a structure of taxation coincided with the opening of this period of heightened war and, as the work of John Henneman has shown in detail,[340] achieved real success only in the military and political crisis brought by defeat in war. The experience of the Hundred Years War was thus essential to the process by which Frenchmen became convinced of the necessity of regular taxation; the perils of war convinced them to pay even in periods of formal peace. Moreover, the fourteenth century began the significant expansion of the ranks of medieval French officialdom. In 1344 Philip VI was told that from the time of Philip IV the cost of salaries paid to officials in the household and central administration had increased by as much as 70,000*l.p.*; Edmund Fryde suggests this represented at least one-seventh of the royal revenue in 1344. Moreover France, unlike England, also developed a sizeable local bureaucracy 'or to be more precise, a whole series of local bureaucracies, attending to different types of royal business.' These were especially

336 See the comments of J. C. Holt, *Magna Carta*, 20-1.

337 Strayer, *On the Medieval Origins of the Modern State*, 58-9.

338 Guenée, *L'Occident*, bk., III, ch. 2.

339 The interaction of political thought and political action is a theme of Harriss, *King, Parliament, and Public Finance*.

340 Henneman, *Royal Taxation in Fourteenth-century France* (1971); (1976).

concerned with new branches of royal revenue which was expanding to meet the needs of war.[341]

In the case of England the persistent demands of war figure prominently among the forces producing parliament. Recent studies have, in fact, stressed the importance of the opening decades of the Hundred Years War in the consolidation of parliament as an institution.[342] Royal financial needs for war purposes in these years ensured that the Commons became an active and essential element. Parliament won virtual control over all forms of taxation, not only the direct grants of lay subsidies, but also the indirect taxes and quasi-taxes involving customs duties and wool levies. Such control of the purse strings was secured more by co-operation than by confrontation, but it served to emphasize the need for dialogue between king and community. Edmund Fryde has demonstrated for the period 1336-40 how very critical a stance the Commons took toward Edward III's war finance and how necessary concessions to blunt that criticism were.[343] As G. L. Harriss has written: 'The Crown became dependent on parliament for taxation, but this was because of the dependability of parliament when called on to meet the Crown's legitimate demands. . . . Parliamentary assent was no real barrier to continuous taxation in time of war, but it did force the Crown into a dialogue with its subjects over their respective political obligations.'[344]

Moreover, it could be argued that if the French expanded their nascent bureaucracy at least in part as a response to the demands placed on government in wartime, the English equivalent was to increase the involvement of unpaid locals in the work of governance.[345] As tax collectors, justices of the peace, and commissioners under many titles Englishmen increased their 'participation in government at the sovereign's command'.[346]

341 Fryde, 'Financial Policies', 825-8.

342 For recent writing on parliament see Fryde and Miller (eds.), *Historical Studies of the English Parliament*; Davies and Denton (eds.), *The English Parliament in the Middle Ages*.

343 Fryde, 'Parliament and the French War', i. 242-63.

344 Harriss, 'War and the Emergence of the English Parliament. The arguments presented in brief form in this art. are treated at length in the same author's *King, Parliament, and Public Finance*.

345 Strayer, *On the Medieval Origins of the Modern State*, 64, 74.

346 The phrase is that of John Roskell, quot. in the pref. to: Davies and Denton (eds.), *The English Parliament*; it recalls A. B. White's idea, embodied in his book, *Self-government at the King's Command*.

In the modern world we are accustomed to the significant increase in governmental powers (and in particular of executive authority) brought about by war. Even in the seventeenth century, as Sir George Clark noted, 'the consolidation of state sovereignty went hand-in-hand . . . with firmer state control over the beginning, prosecution and winding-up of wars'.[347] Yet the connection between fourteenth-century warfare and the emerging European states may not fit completely into the pattern made familiar to us by events in more modern settings.

In the later Middle Ages the state, like the economy, was in trouble. If viewed at close range the history of a European state may show only the expected variations of energy and achievement from one year (or even one decade) to another. But if we change the focal length of our observation and consider the major changes over a longer period of time, generalization about a decline in the creation of the state may be allowed to stand. The twelfth and thirteenth centuries had brought especially impressive growth and innovation in the creation of medieval states in England and France. The movement towards states was scarcely linear progressive, but the cumulative effect over several centuries was powerful. The expanse of territory ruled by the King of France had greatly increased; the functions of kings in both countries, and especially in England, had mounted so that royal government touched more people and affected their lives more deeply than ever before. Given the relatively feeble resources available to the crown on either side of the Channel, this growth could scarcely have been the result of simple imposition of the royal will. The government of kings was certainly read by some subjects at some times as misgovernment and tyranny, as an unthinkable innovation within a social and political pattern conceived as fixed and inalterable. Yet the states were in fact built and could only have been built if a great number of the people whose opinions counted accepted or even welcomed their work. The governance of kings was evidently providing what influential people in the realm wanted: leadership in war, protection of property, mechanisms for resolution of disputes, some minimal level of peace and personal security. In satisfying these needs royal governments went from strength to strength.

[347] Clark, *War and Society in the 17th Century*, 100.

But a change of pace, perhaps even a change of direction is apparent from the late thirteenth century. Across the later Middle Ages the legitimacy of royal families came under a shadow, as the worries of the Valois show in France and the worries of the Lancastrians show in England. Internal dissensions often seemed likely to rip apart the political fabric of the realms. The overall capacity of royal administrations and their capacity for administrative innovation declined. J. R. Strayer draws the contrast clearly, and points a finger at war:

> In the first period of state-building—roughly from the eleventh through the thirteenth centuries—rulers and their advisers had shown great ingenuity in creating new institutions of government. . . . But in the fourteenth century (with the exception of some of the Italian city-states), governments seemed less willing than before to assume new responsibilities or to develop new organs of administration. . . .
>
> War sometimes stimulates the growth of administrative institutions, but . . . [the Hundred Years War] was so exhausting for both sides that it discouraged the normal development of the apparatus of the state. There was a tendency to postpone structural reforms, to solve problems on an ad hoc basis rather than by the creation of new agencies of government, to sacrifice efficiency for immediate results. . . .
>
> By and large, if a department of government had not been set up by the end of the thirteenth century, it was not apt to appear until the sixteenth or even the seventeenth century.[348]

No doubt the advance of states in the twelfth and thirteenth centuries had been buoyed by economic conditions which, again viewed from a sufficient distance to flatten out the endless ups and downs of the curves, seem to have been positive. That the medieval state flourished in a period which, despite significant fluctuations, saw long-term demographic and economic growth and then declined during the economic and demographic troubles of the late Middle Ages is not surprising. But a rough parallelism between political and economic change, while it suggests an obviously important relationship, need not be read in terms of simple or complete causation. A certain level of economic well-being may indeed have been helpful or even necessary for the growth of states, without being at all a sufficient cause for the emergence of states or for their problems as that economic level fell. Again, as in the case of economic decline, our interest lies in

348 Strayer, *On the Medieval Origins of the Modern State*, 60, 77, 83-4.

trying to understand the role of war among a complex set of forces. To seek for the possibly negative effects of war on state building thus seems a difficult but not a senseless undertaking.

In France the evidence is only too clear. In so far as the invading English armies in the first phase of the Hundred Years War had a larger 'political' purpose (beyond the more immediate goal of plunder), their aim seems to have been a demonstration of the inability of the French king to provide the elementary duty of defence of his land.[349] The invaders succeeded in making this point repeatedly. Given the palsied hold of the Valois on the sacred crown of St Louis, and the rival quasi-claimant Charles of Navarre watching hopefully from the wings, the result could only have been a crisis of French kingship, even before the feud between the 'Burgundians' and 'Armagnacs' in the fifteenth century. Defeat on the battlefield near Poitiers in August of 1356 turned this likelihood into terrifying certainty.[350] In the middle years of the fourteenth century conditions in France resembled nothing so much as the early period of nominal Capetian rule five centuries before.[351] It seemed as if the work of rows of kings buried in the crypt of St-Denis had been swept away. In his recent book Raymond Cazelles draws parallels between conditions under the early Capetians and under the Valois:

Le royaume . . . était dans un triste état, paraissant être revenue en arrière de quatre ou cinq siècles. Les expéditions anglaises en France rappellent étrangement les invasions des Normands du IXe siècle et les Valois ont pris la place des Capétiens comme les Robertiens avaient évincé les Carolingiens au Xe siècle. De même que la tradition des successeurs de Charlemagne a longtemps gêné les premiers Capétiens, l'éviction des descendants de Philippe le Bel, issus de la souche royale par les femmes mais plus directs, pèse lourdement sur les premiers Valois qui

[349] Hewitt, *Organization of War*, 117. Cf. his comments in 'The Organization of War', in Fowler (ed.), *The Hundred Years War*, 89.

[350] Cazelles, *La Société politique et la crise de la royauté*; *Société politique, noblesse et couronne*, 577–8.

[351] After writing these words, I found the statement of Raymond Cazelles which follows in the text. It appears in *Société politique, noblesse et couronne* (pp. 577–8). A sense of the return to certain aspects of the Early Middle Ages appears in the use of the term 'danegeld' by both K. B. McFarlane and Philippe Contamine in describing the large payments intended to keep the Duke of Clarence from ravaging France: McFarlane, 'England and the Hundred Years War', 10; Contamine, 'La Guerre de cent ans en France', 139.

doivent compter avec les réclamations de Charles le Mauvais et d'Edouard III. On a vu à quel médiocre territoire a été longtemps reduit le pourvoir réel de Charles V, ce qui n'est pas sans rappeler encore le domaine étroit d'Hugues Capet et de ses successeurs immédiats. La haute féodalité des Xe et XIe siècles trouve des héritiers dans les princes apanages, pourvus de lieutenances royales, de la seconde moitié du XIVe siècle et le règne des ducs du temps de Charles VI a ses racines dans le système utilisé à partir de 1364 pour remettre l'ordre dans le royaume en décentralisant le pouvoir.

By the late thirteenth century some reality stood behind the words 'kingdom of France' and there was, in fact, more strength and resilience in the kingdom and its institutions than was apparent by the mid-fourteenth century;[352] but the process of geographical consolidation and the increase of royal authority that both caused and benefited from it were thrown into reverse gear by the troubles of the fourteenth century. Cohesive forces binding France together were too recent and too feeble to hold securely against the pressures of seemingly endless war. For a time it even looked as if the kingdom would be dismembered by the detachment of Flanders, Brittany, Gascony, and possibly even Normandy.

The disintegration was, moreover, functional as well as geographical. Across wide stretches of France in the second half of the fourteenth century and especially during the captivity of John II, effective control simply fell into the hands of those with effective force. The union of power and legitimate authority which had slowly come to characterize the rule of the Capetians, was very nearly severed. Raymond Cazelles provides a clear summary of conditions in mid-fourteenth century: 'On a insuffisamment mesuré la profondeur de l'abîme où a été plongée la France durant la captivité du roi Jean en Angleterre. Il s'agit d'une véritable désintégration. On ne donne plus d'ordres, ou on ne les accepte pas. Des autorités illegitimes surgies de la guerre se taillent des territoires particuliers, instituant des péages, levant des impôts, armant des troupes.'[353] After the recovery led by Charles V in the late fourteenth century, French political society was plunged into chaos once again by the insanity of Charles VI,

[352] Strayer, *On the Medieval Origins of the Modern State*, 89-90.

[353] Cazelles, *Société politique, noblesse et couronne*, 578.

the civil war of rival princely families, and the renewal of English invasion.

Even in areas spared by invasion or in periods of more general calm, the continued growth of the central or local bureaucracy did not necessarily entail a growth of effective royal power or create an increasingly cohesive realm. 'In fact', as J. R. Strayer writes, 'the French had increased the size of their bureaucracy enough to make the government more complicated but not enough to make it capable of dealing directly with the people. Many taxes were collected by tax-farmers and, in the case of the *gabelle* (salt tax) by merchants; such men oppressed the people without increasing the king's revenues.'[354] Strong reaction against the rapid expansion of French officialdom appeared as early as the provincial leagues formed at the end of Philip the Fair's reign, and hatred of the businessmen recruited especially into financial administration created bitter resentment throughout the fourteenth century.[355]

Of course, by its close the war had contributed powerfully to the aura of French kingship. As P. S. Lewis has suggested, 'out of the last struggles of the war was generated, in the efforts of loyalist propagandists to stress the duty of obedience to the Valois true king of France, a general theory of non-resistance well suited to the views on royalty of the *gens du roi* and to what the royalty was actually succeeding in doing to the politically important.' But this benefit was far from apparent in the dark days of the fourteenth century phase of the conflict: 'Theoretically the Valois monarchy could not lose. But it had first to win the war.'[356]

Across the Channel the problem of kingship and the state was somewhat different. Royal capacities in war and justice had each been highly developed, as we have seen; the king's government could tap a significant portion of the wealth of the realm for war and could call on the services of sizeable numbers of fighting men; it likewise offered the service and claimed the right of jurisdiction over major categories of crime and regulated the legal life of the realm through a series of statutes and ordinances. Though the

[354] Strayer, *On the Medieval Origins of the Modern State*, 73, citing Rey, *Le Domaine du roi*, 178-9, 233-44, 184-5, 195-8.

[355] Fryde, 'Financial Policies of the Royal Governments', 827.

[356] Lewis (ed.), *The Recovery of France in the Fifteenth Century*, pre., pp. 20-1.

royal bureaucracy was small, it supervised the operations of local government by means of such central institutions as the Exchequer, by periodic, general investigations of malfeasance, and by a willingness to receive complaints especially, as the century progressed, in parliament. How could the relationship between increasing capacities both in justice, broadly defined, and war work itself out in the fourteenth century? What effects would the balance between activities of war and those of law and justice have on the development of the state in England?

It might be argued that both capacities were developed. Parliament might, in fact, be taken as the very symbol and agency of the success of the paired goals of medieval government, since it both provided the funds for war and acted as a high court and clearing house for questions of justice and complaints against corrupt use of power. In the history of parliament we might thus read a story of continuing success in balancing the law-state and the war-state. In the writing of English history this outcome has had a great appeal; it may even have served as an antidote to any uneasiness historians have felt in dealing with the political, social, and economic effects of extended warfare; the devastation and misery wrought were deplorable, of course, (even if mainly inflicted in an area outside of the strictly national concern), but in the end the advance of parliament and limited government make the story cheerful. The argument that war, parliament, and limited government were linked obviously has some force and is one segment of a grand theme elaborated by generations of able historians. There can be no gainsaying the strengthening of parliament brought about by the active prosecution of war and few historians, if pressed to give an opinion, could consider steps toward constitutional government in England retrograde. Yet for all of the obvious truth contained in this theme, it neglects another dimension of the relationship between fourteenth-century war and the growth of the medieval state. As we have seen repeatedly, the English state in the fourteenth century was seriously over-extended; it could not *be*, it could not *do* all that it claimed.[357] The king's government could not advance its capacities in war and in the broad sphere of justice

[357] There are interesting comments in Keen, *England in the Later Middle Ages*, 23, 53, 88, 101; and in Harding, *The Law Courts of Medieval England*, 84, 91-2, 116.

simultaneously; the advance could not be carried forward on the trajectory or at the velocity that had characterized royal action across the twelfth and thirteenth centuries. By the fourteenth century limits inherent in the system of government were reached and although high expectations continued along both lines, one goal or the other had to receive less of the attention and resources available to government. As war took more of those resources, justice got less.

The tension between these basic goals of the medieval state is clearly evident in the policy of royal pardons for felonies.[358] Before 1294 such royal pardons were granted sparingly and, in the view of Naomi Hurnard, served the interests of justice: 'Things were moving, however fitfully and slowly, in the right direction so far as the preservation of law and order was concerned. In 1294 they were abruptly put into reverse. . . . Edward [I] . . . introduced the policy which made pardon available to every able-bodied male criminal who cared to earn it by military service.'[359] Royal pronouncements at first hid this motive, piously claiming official pity for those who could lose life or limb through judicial penalties; but before Edward's death the true motive was stated frankly: the king needed troops for his wars in Wales, Gascony, and Scotland. As the wars continued and broadened, so did this royal policy. In the last two decades of Edward I's reign alone well over 2,000 felons were pardoned as a result of war service. 'Pardoning on this scale could not fail to have deplorable results', as Hurnard observed.[360] Of course we must not anachronistically imagine an idyllically peaceful civilian population suddenly confronted, at the end of a campaign, with an influx of felons radically different in their habits and attitudes from orderly folk. But felons may have been hardened by war and they may have banded together in larger and more dangerous associations. Moreover, the real danger was that the royal policy eliminated any value of punishment as prevention or as deterrent and made a mockery of the king's justice. The force of the law was openly diminished when pardoned felons could return from

[358] What follows is based on Hurnard, *The King's Pardon*, 246-50, 311-26; Hewitt, *Organization of War*, 29-31, 132, 173-5; Nicholson, *Edward III and the Scots*, 130, 174, 197.

[359] Hurnard, *The King's Pardon*, 248.

[360] Ibid. 317.

campaign (if indeed they actually went) armed with a royal document excusing their crimes (often in the most comprehensive terms) to take up social life again as neighbours of those who had indicted them. As early as 1309 clause 9 of the Stamford Articles noted that people who indicted felons were fearful to remain in their districts because of the system of pardons for military service. In fact, one petition after another in the fourteenth century linked the general problem of disorder with this policy of pardoning.[361]

An equally clear and important instance of the shift from law to war appears in the fate of the well-known campaign against lawlessness carried out during the years 1328–32 by the regime of Isabella and Mortimer and then by that of the young Edward III.[362] 'Probably at no period in the fourteenth century', as Dorothy Hughes declared, 'were greater efforts being made by the executive to improve the state of the peace. . . .'[363] The directors of the campaign (Geoffrey le Scrope, chief justice of king's bench, most likely taking a prominent role among them) employed an impressive range of agencies against felons: a revival of the general eyre; keepers and justices of the peace, keepers of the counties, the court of king's bench, justices under general commissions of oyer and terminer. Moreover, the Mortimer regime at least recognized the problems created by some previous royal legal measures themselves: before the fall of Mortimer in 1330 there was a definite attempt to halt the rapid proliferation of the special, *ad hoc* commissions of oyer and terminer; such *ad hoc* commissions were becoming a part of the problem of order as lords and gentry used them as powerful weapons in local feuding.[364] At the start of the campaign the clauses of the statute of Northampton (1328) formulated one law and order measure after another, regulating courts and local officials, prohibiting anyone from riding armed or coming before royal officials armed, specifying relief for 'Felonies, Robberies, Manslaughters, Thefts,

361 Hewitt cites examples in *Organization of War*, 174.

362 What follows is based on Stones, 'Sir Geoffrey le Scrope', 142–78; and McLane, 'The Royal Courts', ch. 2. I am grateful to Dr McLane for our discussions on this campaign.

363 Hughes, *Social and Constitutional Tendencies*, 212; she is referring to the entire period 1327–40.

364 Kaeuper, 'Law and Order', 745–6.

Oppressions, Conspiracies, and Grievances done to the People against the Law, Statutes and Customs of the Land, as well by the King's Ministers, as by others . . . '[365]

The campaign was tough going as this list of wrongs and oppressions suggests; and early in 1332 the forces of disorder spectacularly challenged the judicial authorities by kidnapping and holding to ransom Richard Willoughby, puisne justice of king's bench and one of the justices acting under general oyer and terminer commissions in several Midland counties.[366] A few months later, in March of 1332, Geoffrey le Scrope, chief justice of king's bench, made a vigorous speech in parliament stressing the need for further action against disorder; in the discussions which followed another round of law and order measures was urgently proposed, including a plan for the king to travel through the counties, personally supervising measures to improve public order.

Yet a few months later the campaign had virtually collapsed. In his speech at the opening of parliament in September 1332, Scrope did not so much as refer to law and order. 'A new interest had occupied the attention of the magnates', as Stones observed.[367] That interest was politics and war; the focus, as B. W. McLane has shown, was momentarily on Ireland but soon shifted to Scotland (as new opportunities were opened by Balliol's victory at Dupplin Moor in August), and then quickly became fixed on France.[368] This parliament granted a tax of a tenth and a fifteenth for defence against the Scots; a month later the administration withdrew the commissions of the keepers of the counties (the chief agencies in the final phase of the law and order campaign), blandly asserting that the need for such measures had passed.

The argument is not, of course, that the interest in law and order vanished in an instant, but that the centre of gravity had clearly shifted. The nature of the shift is particularly apparent in a letter close of June, 1337, which explained why the crown was cancelling a general commission of oyer and terminer: 'the king has caused several men, both horse and foot, to be arraigned for

365 *Statutes of the Realm*, i. 259.
366 Stones, 'The Folvilles of Ashby-Folville, 117-36.
367 Id., 'Sir Geoffrey le Scrope', 171.
368 McLane, 'The Royal Courts', 76-9.

the repulse of the Scots, and for his passage toward the duchy of Gascony for the safety of his lands there, and men of the realm concerned in such charges cannot be attendant before them in all such inquisitions, and the king wishes to provide for the indemnity of his people in this matter.[369] As the trumpets sounded for war, men could not be kept at home on judicial business.

Even Geoffrey le Scrope, who had skilfully articulated and conducted so much of the campaign against disorder, shifted his personal focus to a different kind of campaign in France. 'We can hardly doubt', Stones wrote, 'that until his death he took a considerable part in planning the war with France.'[370] The chief justice became a knight banneret during the campaign in the Cambrais area. We have already seen him atop a tower showing the papal representative Cardinal Bertrand de Montfaves the scene of devastation brought by that campaign; the fires from burning villages punctuated the evening darkness as far as the eye could see.[371] The contrast between the two campaigns could scarcely be clearer.

Of course, simple alternatives of war or peace were not the realistic choices confronting kings of England and their subjects. There can be no suggestion that most Englishmen longed for peace and decried war as wasteful and immoral, nor indeed can we imagine that they *should* have embraced these modern, liberal views in the late Middle Ages. But most people in most ages have been perfectly capable of proposing contradictory goals and of feeling frustration and betrayal as the impossibility of achieving all their desires manifested itself in one particular situation after another. Englishmen wanted their kings to return victorious from battle; yet they no less expected them to settle their disputes with neighbours, and to hear their plaints against royal officers, to provide a central administration, at least to supervise a workable local administration and in the process to insure a tolerable level of public order. In fact, at the very time government attention and efficiency in these areas was slipping, the standards and expectations of Englishmen at many social levels were rising, heightened not only by the increasing expectations of a

369 Quot. ibid. 79.

370 Stones, 'Sir Geoffrey le Scrope', 228.

371 Stones discusses this incident ibid. 229.

sophisticated society but by the very claims advanced by the royal government itself.

Across the High Middle Ages the crown had responded repeatedly to the legal and governmental needs of English society, often with great creativity and initiative. Henry II and Edward I in particular had advanced the role of the crown in the broad sphere of justice at the same time as they had conducted vigorous military action, though Edward I strained the yoke linking governmental capacity in war and justice almost to the breaking point in his last decade of rule. But the cumulative additions to royal power in England across the High Middle Ages must have rested on a base of widespread support. Without any anachronistic thought of democracy, we can likewise assume that this 'popular' base broadened, especially with the expansion of royal judicial activity across the twelfth and thirteenth centuries, as the reception given the writs introduced by Henry II and the *querelae* under Edward I clearly suggest. People with well-developed notions of local privilege and the sacred right of violent self-help, and with a strong belief that taxation was perilously close to robbery, in time and in increasing numbers brought their disputes into royal courts and transferred significant amounts of coin from their purses to the royal coffers. Clearly they saw the benefits of the king's government as outpacing the costs and problems it entailed. Though they reacted vigorously whenever that balance seemed endangered, as in the classic thirteenth-century political troubles, there was never any question that the expanding role of the king's government in society should be reversed, only a demand that royal government live up to the claims and enforce the standards announced time and again in royal writs and statutes and reiterated at every political crisis.

Englishmen undoubtedly still accepted the king's government in the fourteenth century; it had become an important and accepted feature of their lives. But there does seem to be a change in attitude. Such a change would take form from more gradual and long-term notions than those apparent in the open and often violent disagreements which periodically shook the realm, though it may have fed into these and have been reinforced by them in turn. Political crisis swept quickly and with the force of tidal waves, but a change in the conception of the role of government in society would have been more like underground streams taking form slowly and largely out of sight of contemporaries. As the gap widened between what was claimed for the crown and what it could accomplish, and as the effects of crown action touched a larger proportion of the population of the realm, the volume of complaint rose and we may well suppose that widespread enthusiasm for the increasing capacity of royal government slipped. The evidence of dissatisfaction turning to disillusionment is to be found at every turn, expressed both in thought and action.[372] Surviving evidence from the fourteenth century fairly steams with complaint about the failure of royal justice, the weight of royal taxation, the misuse of governmental power in the localities. From the last decades of the thirteenth century *querelae* (complaints) began to come to justices on their rounds and to officialdom in Westminster bitterly charging that justice is denied, or swayed by money. The petitions show that royal judicial experiments in response to complaints about law and order were thought to be part of the problem of local justice rather than viable solutions. Later in the fourteenth century common petitions in parliament took up the refrain and proclaimed the failure of existing mechanisms to ensure the peace. The great inquests of 1298 and 1341 revealed a volume of complaint about local governance and justice rising to dangerous levels of pressure.[373] So soon as vernacular literature appeared, one of its themes was complaint about injustice, expressed in satire which is often powerful beyond its level of esthetic merit. Likewise this literature provides important insights into the depth of resentment felt against the heavy taxation required by seemingly endless war.

Such a body of complaint in parliament, in inquest, in literature might be thought to travel at a discount as merely timeless grumbling beginning now to survive with the more abundant historical evidence made available to the historian in part because the English government provided channels of complaint. Yet we need to ask in the first place why the means were provided. The English government can scarcely have been devoted in the abstract to receiving, let along soliciting complaint. The prior phenomenon would seem to be a rising tide of dissatisfaction for

[372] See below, ch. 4.

[373] Thompson, *A Lincolnshire Assize Roll*; McLane, 'The Royal Courts', ch. 3; id., *The 1341 Royal Inquest*.

which prudence would suggest some safe official channel. Secondly, we have to ask if the opinions expressed so vigorously in the varied forms of complaint ever reached the level of actions. The answer is clearly written in fourteenth-century events. Resistance to taxation in the form of conventional valuation, undervaluation, and corrupt practice forced the crown in 1334 to fix the assessment of the tenth and fifteenth at £37,430, lest the yield continue to plummet as it had in the decades after 1290. The fifteenth of 1290 yielded an assessed value of £116,347; by 1332 a tenth and a fifteenth yielded only £38,364.[374] In the extremely heavy war taxation of the late 1330s, as we have seen, there were in high places fears of outright rebellion which may not have been far off the mark; only timely concessions seem to have prevented a rising.[375] In 1381 a heavy and yet more unfair tax was significantly evaded and clumsy efforts to collect in full actually sparked the great revolt. However, the targets of the rebels in 1381 regularly included representatives of the judicial system and of local governance.[376]

By this time the royal government had largely given up the effort to secure public order which had so engaged its energies in the thirteenth century. Close royal attention to the interconnected issues of public order and local administration may have persisted into the early fourteenth century, but they basically faded as the Hundred Years War was vigorously prosecuted. From one point of view the triumph of the justices of the peace may appear, with appropriate ruffles and flourishes, as a triumph of constitutionalism. From our present perspective it represents the surrender, however slow and reluctant, of the significant degree of judicial initiative and control long claimed by the crown. A rising number of lawsuits in royal courts in the late Middle Ages need not be read as a contrary trend. The vast majority of these disputes were settled out of court, by compromise, or by the more direct means of violence.[377] The countryside dissatisfaction

374 Willard, *Parliamentary Taxes on Personal Property, 1290-1334*, 343-6. See also J. R. Strayer's discussion in his introd. to *The English Government at Work*, ii. 17-22.

375 Maddicott, 'The English Peasantry and the Demands of the Crown', 64-7.

376 Fryde, *The Great Revolt of 1381*.

377 The issues of litigation, compromise, and violence were the themes of Edward Powell's Alexander Prize Essay, 'Arbitration and the Law in England in

appears to have been serious; it arose from genuine causes; and it was taken seriously in Westminster. There is no compelling reason, then, to dismiss the dissatisfaction as a mere refraction of view brought about by a change in sources.

The English government in the later Middle Ages, caught between mutually reinforcing failure and failure of support, could not act as the great engine of change it had been for the several preceeding centuries. Undoubtedly, the dramatic economic and demographic changes played a part of much significance in the problems experienced by royal governments on either side of the Channel in the fourteenth century. But we may have underestimated the importance of governmental over-extension and failure in England and of consequent shifts in the level of support needed for success. Both were linked in the closest way to the new levels of warfare.

the Late Middle Ages', read at a meeting of the Royal Historical Society in June 1982. I am grateful to Dr Powell for providing me with a TS copy of that paper prior to publication.

2

Royal Justice and Public Order

1. MEDIEVAL VIOLENCE

In *The Waning of the Middle Ages* Johan Huizinga emphasized the striking contrasts in late medieval culture in north-western Europe. Striking contrasts are no less apparent when we consider historians' interpretations of life in this period. Certainly the range of opinion could scarcely be greater in historical estimates of 'the violent tenor of life', to borrow the title of the opening chapter of Huizinga's book.[1] The existence of a significant level of violence in the late Middle Ages has been, depending on the historian and the specific time and place forming his subject, emphasized, ignored, or denied. Europeans of the fourteenth century, that is, have been viewed as primitives, as forerunners of nineteenth-century gentlemen, or as happy denizens of a world we have sadly lost in achieving modernity.[2]

Despite these differences, we do in fact have good reasons for thinking that violence was an integral part of late medieval society. We have already examined the importance of persistent war as a force in this society. But even if any locality were happily spared the hand of war there were always other sources of violence in daily life. The act of governance itself was often accomplished through violence: public punishments and executions, often in terrifying form, were only the most obvious examples. Weapons, or ready substitutes for the real thing, were commonly carried; a staff would serve handily and everyone had a knife for table use which was easily put to other uses. The internalized restraints which we assume (sometimes incorrectly) in the modern era were generally missing. The stubborn persistence of

[1] Huizinga, *The Waning of the Middle Ages*.

[2] The flavour of this debate, and abundant citations, appear in Stone, 'Interpersonal Violence'.

an ancient code of vengeance could stir sudden passion at all social levels and at the top of the social pyramid violence was virtually enshrined in a code of honour. Where we have court records of specific violent offences, such as homicide, the rates seem high; when we have details, the routine brutality can be appalling.[3] Equally important, the literature of the time shows assumptions about violence which, though complex, do include a good deal of approbation of violent self-help and an absolute delight in the details of combat.[4]

But if violence in one form or another was a fact of daily life, were the level and nature of this violence important factors in public order? Was the violent tenor of late medieval life something simply shrugged off as inevitable if not embraced as desirable? Or did the violence threaten important values and endanger the stability of social and political life? If we accept the fact of violence in late medieval life and try to grasp its importance, the contrasts revealed by cross-Channel comparison raise fascinating questions.

The issues will emerge clearly if we compare the two famous efforts to secure charters of liberties. Read side by side the Great Charter of England imposed on King John in 1215 and the French provincial charters exacted at the end of the reign of Philip IV in 1314-15 reveal a contrast in the functioning of law and the responsibility for public order which has received little attention. The Magna Carta barons not only accepted the judicial system of royal writs, justices, and juries developed by Henry II and his sons, they asked for more. In fact, far from seeking to dismantle or strictly limit the king's jurisdiction, their demands may have expected more judicial service, more regular circuits of justices than the crown could provide.[5] A century later the French allies stressed the judicial competence of local seigneurs, tried to limit the intrusions of the king's justices and officers, and proclaimed

[3] Gurr, 'Historical Trends in Violent Crime'; Stone, 'Interpersonal Violence'; Given, *Society and Homicide*; Bellamy, *Crime and Public Order*; Langlois and Lanhers, *Confession et jugements*.

[4] Brandt, *The Shape of Medieval History*, 132-9; Kaeuper, 'An Historian's Reading of *The Tale of Gamelyn*'; Bloch *Medieval French Literature and Law*, *passim*.

[5] Holt, *Magna Carta*, 233 ff. Note esp. cap. 17, 18, 19 of the Great Charter; ibid. 322-3.

as a cherished heritage the rights of private warfare and judicial duel, private war's 'symbolic sister'.[6]

Several generations of historians of England have struggled with the evidence on public order in the late Middle Ages and have generally concluded that a crisis of law and order troubled England from the late thirteenth century.[7] Their conclusion is based on vast heaps of parchment records deposited in the Public Record Office like moraines left behind by a retreating glacier. Analysing these records historians have produced a vivid, if appalling, picture of violence and disorder which government efforts were powerless to remedy and may even have exacerbated. In French historiography the great crisis of order in the late Middle Ages is conspicuously absent, at least, until the outbreak of the Hundred Years War produced a crisis of a different sort. Sometimes it almost seems that to French historians the only problem of order in fourteenth-century France was the English.[8]

It is conceivable that medieval English society was simply more violent, more in need of strong law and order measures than medieval French society, that it was more likely thus to imprint its violence on the legal records and so cause historians to debate the existence, scope, and causes of a crisis in order. Such a view could find support in the late medieval English reputation for violence. Froissart thought that Englishmen in his day were 'of a haughty disposition, hot-tempered and quickly moved to anger, slow to be brought to gentleness and difficult to pacify; they take comfort in battle and slaughter'.[9] Fortescue even boasted of the numbers and toughness of English thieves, and wrote admiringly

[6] Artonne, *Le Mouvement de 1314*, *passim*. Contamine, 'De la puissance aux privilèges'. The phrase quot. is taken from Bloch, *Medieval French Literature and Law*, 119.

[7] Bellamy, *Crime and Public Order*, provides a summary and a full bibliog. to 1973. Alan Harding develops themes of particular interest in *The Law Courts of Medieval England*. More recent studies on aspects of the issue of order are provided by Hanawalt, *Crime and Conflict*; Given, *Society and Homicide*; Kaeuper, 'Law and Order'; McLane, 'The Royal Courts'.

[8] For John Langbein's comments on the relative lack of French interest in working through their enormous resources of archival material see *Prosecuting Crime*, 211. Of course, splendid exceptions can be cited, such as Bernard Guenée's *Tribunaux et gens de justice*, but the contrast between the volume of work done on English and French law and order is striking.

[9] Quot.: Coleman, *Medieval Readers and Writers*, 13.

of the 'hartes and corage wich no ffrenchman hath like unto a Englysh man'.[10] John Gower (writing with the revolt of 1381 fresh in his memory) gave the following assessment of his countrymen via a character in the *Vox Clamantis*: 'The people of this land are wild. Their way of life involves far more quarrelling than love. . . . They do not fear laws, they overthrow right by force, and justice falls in defeat because of their violent warfare. This rough, pernicious people devises more treachery, crime, fighting, uproar, and harm than laws'.[11]

The stereotype of violent medieval Englishmen is at least a useful antidote to any romanticization of village life or any notion that late medieval people were really Victorians in anticipation. Yet it would be hard to prove in a convincing way that public order was more severely threatened by violence in England than in contemporary France. Any observer of the two great risings of the fourteenth century, the Jacquerie in 1358 in France and the 1381 English rising, would in fact be struck by the savagery of the French rebels and the equal savagery of the nobles' suppression; the English rebels and the forces of suppression appear almost mild and orderly by comparison.[12] Extant English and French court records are distressingly similar in their numbing recitation of assault and ambush, robbery and murder, often accompanied by all of the cruelty men can inflict on other men. In both countries late nineteenth-century historians who first worked through large samples of the evidence registered similar shock. The picture of constitutional progress then at the forefront of historical writing did not include violence on this scale.[13] Of course it would be difficult to establish from extant court records convincing comparisons of the actual levels of crime and disorder, or to assess the disruption they created in society. Still, we have every reason to believe that the complex and interconnected

[10] Fortescue, *The Governance of England*, 141-2.

[11] 'Huius enim terre gens hec est inchola, ritus / Cuius amore procul dissona plura tenet. / . . . Non metuunt leges, sternunt sub viribus equm, / Victaque pugnaci iura sub ense cadunt: / Legibus inculta fraudes, scelus, arma, furores, / Pluraque pestifera plebs nocumenta parit:' (G. C. Macaulay (ed.), *The Complete Works of John Gower*, 4 vols. (Oxford, 1899-1902), iv. 76; Eng. trans., Coleman, *Medieval Readers and Writers*, 140.

[12] The contrast is considered in detail in ch. 5 below.

[13] Compare Hughes, 'The State of the Peace', ch. 11 of *Social and Constitutional Tendencies*, with Ducoudray, *Les Origines du Parlement de Paris*, ch. 14.

forces which might generate violence and disorder were roughly comparable in the two countries. The economic structures ordering the lives of the great mass of people in both France and England were broadly similar; as Jacques le Goff has suggested, certain time-lags and nuances, rather than fundamental differences, distinguish the seigneurial regime in France from that in England.[14] Certainly the harsh conditions of the era, which we can assume produced a favourable environment for violence, were generally present in north-western Europe: the gathering stormclouds of economic downturn and demographic crisis appeared in regions of both countries by the late thirteenth century;[15] the great famine beginning in 1315 scourged both;[16] as we have seen, the constant pressure of war levies, prise, and taxation was felt in both across the entire period. Notions either of 'Merrie Olde England' or of 'la Belle France' seem equally out of touch with what we know of English and French society in the thirteenth and fourteenth centuries.

Divisions between classes were more extreme in France than in England and the gap was keenly perceived and resented, as the Jacquerie showed unmistakably;[17] yet we might expect that this sharper social cleavage would have produced in France the sort of general, persistent disorder which has instead long exercised historians of England. Thus the contrast between England and France suggested by the movements of 1215 and 1314-15, and by the differences in historical interpretations of English and French public order, obdurately remains. It can point to several important and interlocking questions: about the nature of 'public opinion' on the question of order; about the role of kingship in the state of order; about the possibility of a late Medieval crisis of

[14] See Hilton and Le Goff, 'Féodalité et seigneurie'; the specific comment of Le Goff appears on p. 61.

[15] Historical controversy in the field has been intense, but see the general comments of Georges Duby in 'Medieval Agriculture, 900-1500', 181-2, and Miller and Thatcher, *Medieval England*, pp. xv-xvii. A survey is provided by Léopold Genicot, 'Crisis: From the Middle Ages to Modern Times'. Among more particular studies see Hallem, 'The Postan Thesis'; Strayer, 'Economic Conditions in the County of Beaumont-le-Roger'. For M. M. Postan's recent survey see *The Medieval Economy and Society*, chs. 6, 8, 9.

[16] Kershaw, 'The Great Famine'; Van Werveke, 'La Famine de l'an 1316'; Lucas, 'The Great European Famine'.

[17] See the comments of Maurice Keen, *The Pelican History of Medieval Europe*, 203-4, 235-6.

order. Not only are the questions difficult and intertwined, the approach to each must take special care about chronology. For as R. C. Van Caenegem has insisted[18] we must pay particular attention to the basic fact of the timing of changes that seem important in either country.

2. PUBLIC OPINION AND PUBLIC ORDER

Complex forces of cause and effect linked widespread opinion about public order with royal actions for the maintenance of the peace. People harboured and acted upon important general ideas about the state of the peace and the locus of responsibility for maintaining order; there were also powerful proprietary interests to be adjusted between kings on the one hand and seigneurs (of various ranks) and townsmen on the other.

Can we safely assume that the kings of France and England really cared about public order? By the early fourteenth century they certainly said so frequently and with some force; and what is more they took vigorous steps to back their statements with actions. We will examine their actions in detail shortly, but two brief examples will set the tone of the royal language. In 1316 Philip V sent a general letter to eight *baillis* informing them that he knew by the '*grant clameur*' of the people, which increased from day to day, that robbers and evildoers were causing great fear and were inhibiting trade and travel. 'Among all that touches the estate and government of the King and realm', Philip wrote, 'we desire with greatest fervour the peace and security of our subjects and of people who carry on necessary trade. . .'. He ordered the officers to take all necessary steps, in co-operation with local seigneurs, to bring the land to peace.[19] The phrases may be traditional and formulaic, but they come from a king who, as we will see, took active measures to improve public order. Moreover, from the other side of the Channel we have a most interesting statement from Edward I written not in the verbose and formulaic language of preambles to statutes and commissions, but recorded in a private government memorandum. The king characterized law and order measures he had taken in 1305 as

[18] Van Caenegem, 'L'Histoire du droit et la chronologie', 1459-65.
[19] *Ordonnances des roys de France*, i. 636-7.

efforts 'to suppress the disorders, tumults, and outrages of the past, which were like the start of war and which flouted the lordship of the king.'[20] The royal sense of responsibility for the public peace could scarcely be more plain.

We have every reason to believe that a very long tradition stood behind these fourteenth-century statements. As we have seen, the association of kingship with some responsibility for a tolerable level of internal order was already present in ancient conceptions of the kingly role; it undoubtedly took on added strength after Christian conversion and it developed considerably across the High Middle Ages. The Gregorian Reform of the late eleventh century was a factor of great importance in joining kingship with law and order. If kings were, as the reformers so adamantly insisted, no longer semi-sacral figures (not being within the clerical caste), they could buttress claims to legitimacy by stressing their position as dispensers of law and guarantors of justice. Moreover, they could do so with the full blessing of the most ardent ecclesiastical reformers who saw the clear need for a secular arm and urged upon kings the necessary if messy job of policeman. Thus at a critical stage in its origins, the Western state was associated with law in the most close and important ways.[21]

The point is not as abstract as may appear. For with royal responsibility for law and order came heightened power and considerable royal profit. Law was the tough and flexible bond joining power and authority in kingship. Royal power was expressed through jurisdiction which expanded steadily and brought the king's government 'over the horizon' into the localities. Jurisdiction also meant profit: *Justitia magnum emolumentum est*. Before the elaboration of efficient systems of taxation, the business of justice offered splendid opportunities for filling coffers emptied so quickly by ambitious kings. If the successful ruler, as Beryl Smalley has suggested, had to 'profiteer

20 PRO King's Remembrancer Memoranda Roll 79, Trinity Recorda, m. 41d; pr.: *CCR 1302-1307*, 454-5. Cf. Sayles, *Select Cases*, iv, p. lvi.

21 Strayer, *On the Medieval Origins of the Modern State*, 20-4; Kantorowicz, 'Kingship under the Impact of Scientific Jurisprudence'; id., *The King's Two Bodies*, ch. 4; Post, *Studies in Medieval Legal Thought*, *passim*. For a useful discussion of the Merovingian and Carolingian efforts with regard to public peace, see Dubois, *Les Asseurements au XIIIe siècle*, pt. I, ch. 1, 2. This work is broader than its title suggests.

justly', what better way than to provide a judicial system which was profitable.[22]

Of course, kings and their advisers did not simply absorb Gregorian ideas about right order in the world and then stumble upon justice as a source of increased power and welcomed profit. All of the forces so actively transforming High Medieval society worked their effects: the collective might of socio-economic change, demographic change, urbanization, the increase in numbers of educated men. These forces produced a society which expected more order, a society which welcomed and even demanded an increased royal role in securing order. Society had not been lawless before the royal role was elaborated and strengthened. In the sense of customary patterns of behaviour and mores, law was abundantly evident in early medieval Europe. The feud itself was a highly 'lawed' enterprise, whether in early medieval Europe or early modern Scotland, in the sense that it worked by a complex set of rules; it could serve as 'one answer to the perennial problem of crime and violence'.[23] But as R. R. Davies has aptly observed, 'feud as an organized and recognized institution is largely a phenomenon of the stateless society . . .'.[24] Over north-western Europe opinion shifted slowly from the ritual forms of feud, compromise, and arbitration to the normative justice provided by major institutions, and especially by the emerging state. Fredric Cheyette thinks the change is apparent in France only in the course of the thirteenth century.[25]

However slow it was, this groundswell of support for royal action was essential. Given its modest resources and limited capacity to command, the crown had to rely on the general support of the important layers of society. The growth of royal jurisdiction, in short, reflected a growing desire for order—or at least for increased civil litigation which might well effect improvements in order—and a feeling somewhere between willingness and eagerness (sometimes tempered by resentment) for the crown to lead and manage. In both England and France the business of royal courts increased fairly steadily across the

[22] Smalley, 'Capetian France', 64.

[23] Wallace-Hadrill, 'The Bloodfeud of the Franks'; Wormald, 'Bloodfeud, Kindred, and Government. The quot. is taken from the latter source (p. 97).

[24] Davies, 'The Survival of the Bloodfeud in Medieval Wales', 341.

[25] Cheyette, 'Suum cuique tribuere'.

High Middle Ages, leaving in witness thicker and thicker rolls or registers recording disputes entrusted to litigation before royal justices.

Thus, attitudes about justice and order and about the royal role in securing them were anything but simple or static. If subjects generally demanded more and better justice across the High Middle Ages, royal governments had, across the same period of time, developed their own traditions and a momentum of their own. It was inevitable that the balance of forces would place royal action sometimes in advance of widespread notions about public order, sometimes behind. In 1215, as we have seen, the general attitude of those whose views counted was that the English government should do more. A century later the French leagues firmly informed the royal government that its efforts had been excessive.

Attitudes toward the royal role in justice were bound to be affected by changing notions of justice and order *per se*. These notions seem to have shifted slowly, but significantly, across the twelfth and thirteenth centuries. The process is especially apparent in England, perhaps because of the nature of our sources. What these sources show is not a simple replacement of violent self-help by royal legal process, not the feud and midnight thrashing giving way directly to courtroom pleading, but instead an intermediate step involving a more complex combination of more or less extra-legal violence with vigorous lawsuits. The court rolls document at least a beginning of the transformation of the ancient impulse toward brutal self-help. Men were clearly willing to bring an increasing number of disputes into the king's courts for settlement. The reasoning could be purely pragmatic: royal courts worked and could be used to smite enemies and to acquire goods, or to block the same efforts by opponents. But the evidence of medieval English literature provides an important addition to the evidence of court records on this point.[26] Alongside the miles of parchment rolls recording lawsuits we must read the impressive body of literature satirizing the state of justice in the realm. The authors, from anonymous moralists and pamphleteers to such giants as Langland and Gower, devoted

[26] See ch. 5 below. A good survey of the social and political content of fourteenth-century English literature is provided by Coleman, *Medieval Readers and Writers*, ch. 3.

particular attention to the failures of royal justice to live up to its high promises. This satirical literature often conveys something beyond the purely pragmatic; there is often a tone of outraged idealism. This, too, is important, for it suggests the faint dawning of a widespread conception of justice extending beyond naked self-interest. Perhaps law ought to be more impartial than it was; perhaps courtroom procedure could more often replace outright seizure or ambush as a means of setting one corner of the world right. The amalgam of outraged idealism and pure pragmatism may seem strange to modern sensibilities; but it does characterize much of one strain of fourteenth-century English literature, and it does connect with other known movements of the age such as an increased interest in personal morality in the world.[27] The literature was widely read and enjoyed and can scarcely be discounted as divorced from social life.

Public opinion on questions of public order was thus complex and difficult to characterize. But we can say that kings did take their responsibility seriously, within the limits of practical politics, sometimes as an instrument of practical politics; we can also say that for their part subjects did want more order and did place much hope for improvement of the public peace in royal leadership, retaining always a belief, perhaps even a fondness, for violent self-help in circumstances of their own choosing. Further evidence on public order will appear with every inquiry we make into the vast topic of public order; but for now the link between this topic and our second issue, the role of kingship, demands attention.

3. GROWTH OF ROYAL PEACE JURISDICTION

We must probe some distance into the medieval past if we are to appreciate how the contrast revealed by the sets of English and French charters came about. For by looking back as far as the Carolingian era we come to a point at which the contrast all but disappears. The judicial institutions on either side of the Channel, no less than the basic political and ecclesiastical arrangements associated with them, appear broadly similar. In both cases a sanctified Christian Germanic monarchy, whatever its problems

[27] Ibid. 15, 170, 187.

and shortcomings, divided the realm into counties and sub-units of counties (hundreds, centenaries, or *vicariae*) and within these units maintained a system of major and minor royal courts in which awards based on customary Germanic law were handed down by supervising royal officials, assisted by a body of important lay assessors (the lawmen, *scabini*). Both the earl in England and the count in Francia took a third of the profits of justice, as James Campbell notes. He further observes that legal prescriptions entered in ninth-century Carolingian capitularies reappear in English laws of the following century.[28] Moreover, in the county courts (*malus comitatum* in Carolingian Europe, shire moot in Anglo-Saxon England) both secular and ecclesiastical authority were present, both bishop and count or sheriff, in an easy mixing of the secular and sacred realms which the Gregorian reformers were soon to combat as the central cause of a world gone wrong. The English kings of the house of Wessex were only creating their kingdom as that of Charlemagne began its severe decline; but if we can mentally freeze the action for a moment in the late ninth and tenth century, and force from our minds the future contrasts which easily take on an aspect of inevitability, it is the similarities which are striking. A freeman bringing his case in a local vicarial court or a great landlord impleading his neighbour in the *malus* of a Carolingian count would not think his world had been turned upside down if he were transferred, respectively, to the local Anglo-Saxon hundred court or the shire court of the sheriff. Far too little information is available to permit a close comparison of public order in Carolingian and Anglo-Saxon localities; but the similarity in the skeletal frames of the kingdoms, their churches, courts, and law, is noteworthy. James Campbell, in fact, has made a strong case for considering Anglo-Saxon England 'in important ways the continuation and the heir of the Carolingian state . . .'. So close is the resemblance that he suggests a knowledge of Anglo-Saxon government 'may provide our nearest approach to apprehending what the Carolingian state was like'.[29]

Yet the divergence soon becomes apparent once we restart the historical clock and pass the millenium. The first half of the

28 Campbell, 'Observations on English Government'.

29 Ibid. See also Perroy, 'Carolingian Administration'. Cf. Stubbs, *The Constitutional History of England*, i. 223-7.

eleventh century brought the series of decisive changes, stemming in post-Carolingian Francia from the sweeping social, political, and legal developments associated with the advent of feudalism. The progressive fragmentation of most of the Carolingian Empire, halted for a time before the year 1000 at the level of the county, proceeded relentlessly in the early decades of the eleventh century to the level of the castellany. The old public courts swiftly disappeared over much of what would become France as the area dominated by a castle and its *dominus* became the effective political and jurisdictional unit. Scribes in fact ceased to identify places, as they had during the tenth century, by using the terms of the Carolingian administrative geography; for the counties had broken up into larger or smaller castellanies which often absorbed the old *vicariae*.[30] Harsh justice continued to be meted out to humble folk by their new masters, and large numbers of formerly free men fell under the domination of the castellans in whose eyes they were soon equated with an already servile population. But for the emerging group of *milites* the world took on an almost Hobbesian cast; at least there was for the time no judicial institution capable of enforcing peaceful behaviour on them, no ironclad restraint on the feuding and greed of these mail-clad warriors.[31]

Faced with the prospect of a knightly war of all against all, bishops stepped into the void which resulted from enfeebled royal power and took the lead in launching the famous peace movement,[32] which began in the last quarter of the tenth century in the south and had spread northward throughout France by the first half of the eleventh century. At many church councils bishops held large, open-air meetings attended by vast throngs of laymen (in part attracted by the powerful relics brought for display by the monks). The movement was complex in its causes as well as in its results; scholars convincingly connect it not only with the turbulence of contemporary society, but with famine, epidemic, the resurgent papacy, the Gregorian reform, the policy of crusade. But we can establish several stages important for the

30 Fournier, *Le Château dans la France médiévale*, 131-2.

31 Duby, 'The Evolution of Judicial Institutions, 43 ff.

32 Hoffman, *Gottesfriede und Truga Dei*; Duby, 'Laity and the Peace of God'; Cowdrey, 'The Peace and the Truce of God'; Dubois, *Les Asseurements au XIIIe siècle*, Pt. I, ch. 3; Strubbe, 'La paix de Dieu'.

issue of public order and royal authority.[33] At first these peace councils simply established sanctions and collective agreements which limited the places and persons subject to violence; the peace of God was to protect churches, unarmed churchmen, and the poor from the violence characteristic of the age. Fighting *per se*, especially the phenomenon of private war, was not condemned, nor the repressive form of justice practised by castle owners on their dependants. Knights could legitimately fight other knights and discipline errant rustics, so long as they did not violate the 'safety zones' decreed around certain places and social categories.[34]

By the second decade of the eleventh century, as the councils took on an increasingly penitential character, and as churchmen increasingly tried to Christianize knighthood as one of the divinely ordained *ordines* of society, the attitude towards any fighting hardened. Knights were now to be denied the pleasures of running a lance through their enemy's body—a pleasure extolled tirelessly in the epics of the First Feudal Age[35]—as a form of penitent self-denial akin to the monk's renunciation of the fond touch of money or women or the pleasures of feasting in a world haunted by the spectre of starvation. Each *ordo* now had its proper ascetic discipline as well as its prerogatives. Within a gradually lengthening list of days of the week all fighting was to cease, eventually from Wednesday evening until the following Monday morning, and during Advent, Lent, Easter, and Pentecost. Thus, the concept of a truce of God was added to that of the peace of God. The logical conclusion of this line of thought produced a new stage in the peace movement. At the Council of Narbonne in 1054, all warfare between Christians was prohibited: 'Let no Christian kill another Christian, for there is no doubt that he who kills a Christian spills the blood of Christ.'[36] The safety valve for knightly violence, in theory progressively restricted over half a century, appeared at the council of Clermont in 1095, when Urban II preached a crusade. Knightly sword-

[33] Drawn from Duby, 'Laity and the Peace of God'.

[34] Ibid. 128.

[35] As Marc Bloch commented: 'The interminable accounts of single combats which fill the epics are eloquent psychological documents', *Feudal Society*, ii. 294.

[36] Cowdrey, 'The Peace and the Truce of God', 53; Duby, 'Laity and the Peace of God', 132.

strokes must be directed at the infidel by warriors who have heeded the ban on violence at home and have gone as humble penitents to the Holy Land. We need not be hardened cynics to doubt that the peace decrees informed the minds and framed the actions of all *milites*,[37] nor need we confess blind optimism if we suppose that the peace movement produced some limitation on violence and disorder by the end of the eleventh century.

But by the second half of the century, the peace movement seems to have lost its driving force; it had pressed its themes to logical conclusions and in the process had exceeded its practical capacity for any significant degree of effectiveness. It continued in areas where the feudal reconstruction of political authority was less advanced, as a measure of some utility against rampant feuding and disorder. But further progress depended on the active appropriation of the peace movement by secular authorities, a mirror image of the process by which bishops took on the role of public peacekeeping from faltering Carolingian royalty, although now the laymen involved would of necessity be great feudatories, counts or dukes, rather than kings. This last stage of the peace movement was thus up to temporal rulers who could make use of its principles as they created new and lasting political and legal structures in their domains. An early effort in Aquitaine under Duke William V proved to be something of a false start and did not long survive him.[38] But the great northern principalities of Flanders and Normandy enjoyed more success. After his decisive victory on the battlefield of Val-ès-Dunes in 1047, the young Duke William the Bastard encouraged the proclamation of the truce of God at a council meeting at Caen in which he took a prominent role. Both traditional ecclesiastical sanctions and secular sanctions were invoked, but Duke William was himself expressly excluded from the prohibition, being authorized to

[37] In the late twelfth century Bertran de Born celebrated his defiance of ecclesiastical or royal limitation on his wars: 'When peace is on all sides, / With me one thought of war remains. / A sty in his eye, whoever separates me from it. / Although I have begun to exalt myself, / Peace doesn't give me pleasure. / With war I 'reconcile' myself, / Because I neither respect nor believe / Any other law. / And I do not pay any attention to Monday or Sunday / Nor to weeks or months or years, / Nor do I leave off for April or for March / From planning how injury may come to those who do me wrong.' See Kendrick, 'Criticism of the Ruler', 167-8.

[38] Cowdrey, 'The Peace and the Truce of God', 59; Bonnaud-Delamare, 'Les Institutions de la paix'.

wage war and maintain armed forces in the public interest.[39] In 1080, at the council of Lillebonne, the Norman vicomtes were given the task of enforcing the truce of God on behalf of the Duke; and by his death in 1087 the ducal responsibility was such that the *Treuga Dei* in Normandy was scarcely distinguishable from the *Pax Ducis*, as the 1091 Norman *Consuetudines* illustrate.[40] King Henry I of England as Duke of Normandy continued his father's work and used the truce to build a criminal jurisdiction superior to all other sources of justice.[41] This same general development took place in Flanders a generation later.[42] At the end of the eleventh century the Flemish peace movement was still very much in the hands of the archbishop of Reims; the role of the count of Flanders was simply that of enforcer of a peace arranged under archiepiscopal auspices.[43] The change came only in 1111 when Count Robert (1093-1111) summoned all the lords of the county except the bishops, and declared a peace for Flanders in his own name.[44]

As the Capetian monarchy gradually found its strengths and acted upon them, the kings of France began to establish peace arrangements within the royal domain similar to those found in Normandy and Flanders. The ideological underpinnings appeared in the papal extension of the peace of God to all Christendom by Nicholas II around 1059 and in the vigorous peace legislation of general import promulgated under Urban II in the last decade of the century.[45] But the example of the great feudatories was resolutely followed only slowly across the twelfth century by Louis VI and Louis VII who created a *Pax Dei* which was essentially royal.[46] For the first third of the twelfth century, Louis

39 Douglas, *William the Conqueror*, 51-2; Yver, 'Contribution'; id., 'Le développement du pouvoir ducal'.

40 Douglas, *William the Conqueror*, 140-2, 152; Cowdrey, 'The Peace and the Truce of God', 61.

41 Ibid. 61, and the sources cited there.

42 Bonnaud-Delamare, 'La Paix en Flandre'.

43 'Le comte de Flandre s'engageait ainsi à garantir la paix sans aucun intérêt pour lui-même. Il n'était que l'agent d'exécution de l'archevêque' (ibid. 151).

44 Ibid. 152.

45 Duby, 'Laity and the Peace of God', 132; Grabois, 'De la trêve de Dieu à la paix du roi', 587.

46 Ibid. 586-7; Fawtier and Lot, *Histoire des institutions françaises*, ii. 298-300; Langmuir, 'Community and Legal Change', 278-9. What follows draws upon Grabois's article.

VI, starting from a position of weakness, found a prop to royal power in the peace legislation and ecclesiastical sanctions which could be used against his enemies. Wearing the mantle of executor of the peace of God, Louis VI could act against such troublesome lords of the domain as Thomas of Marle. The same mantle cloaked with sanctified legitimacy royal cognizance of a case brought in 1126 by the bishop of Clermont against the Count of Auvergne. In settling this latter dispute the king had moved beyond the territorial confines of his domain, and he had brought a peace case before his feudal court; his actions also had the approval of such powerful vassals as the dukes of Aquitaine and Normandy, the counts of Flanders, Anjou and Brittany. With this initiative the king had taken a significant first step toward assuming real responsibility for peace in the realm. More royal steps followed in the reign of his son. A new papal recognition of the royal role in administering justice, announced at the ecumenical council held at the Lateran Palace in 1139, provided the ecclesiastical blessing important to Louis VII. His decision to take the cross eight years later may have been even more important. During his absence on the second crusade (1147-9), the realm was in effect governed by Abbot Suger of St-Denis for whom the pope provided special authority as in some sense a papal vicar.[47] Moreover, the entire kingdom came under the protection of the church while its king was on crusade. Thus, the peace of God and the peace of the realm were seen as coincident, and Louis returned to France to discover that Suger had bequested new possibilities for royal power. The king developed these possibilities in a number of judicial interventions during the second half of his reign. The council held at Soissons in 1155 is illustrative of his position. A great assembly, including the archbishops of Reims and Sens and their suffragans, the duke of Burgundy, the counts of Flanders, Champagne, Nevers, and Soissons, promulgated decrees similar to those issued by councils prominent in the peace movement for generations; but in this assembly the phrase 'peace of the realm' significantly replaced the traditional 'peace of God'. Since the great vassals swore to maintain the peace for ten years, this pact was more a

[47] Grabois, 'De la trêve de Dieu à la paix du roi', 592. The same author examines Abbot Suger's authority more closely in 'Le Privilège de croisade et la régence de Suger'.

commitment to a truce than a true peace; yet the long-range meaning is clear. The Capetians have moved from seeking protection behind the shield of the peace movement to directing the movement themselves, and even to legislating peace measures in their own right. Perhaps this attempt to legislate a royal peace for the realm should be seen as a first Capetian ordinance of general scope;[48] in any case, the links which connect Carolingian kingship, the peace movement, feudal lordship, and emergent Capetian authority are of great interest, however slow and tentative the action of the French monarchy was in the field of public order.

A century later St Louis was the obvious heritor of these movements, as he was the exemplar of the *nova militia* which the church wished to make of knighthood, as a force to defend the church and the poor and to fight the enemies of Christ.[49] These goals were of course the themes of St Louis's life and the principles which he tried to embody in his kingship. By the time of Louis IX the French monarchy had come to the first stage of its mature involvement with public order. That involvement was, as yet, slight by English standards, but in roughly the century between the death of Louis VII (1180) and the death of St Louis (1270) the French monarchy had vastly expanded the royal domain and within it had created and firmly emplanted the administrative and judicial structure on which royal peace efforts would rest.[50] Some time before 1190, Philip II established the local royal courts known as assizes, almost certainly borrowing an institution from his rival, Henry II of England, whose success with itinerant justices holding the king's pleas and assizes must have been known at the French court. In that year as he prepared for the governance of the realm during his absence on crusade, Philip regulated the work of the *baillis*, central court justices already going out in groups to hold *assizes* in localities. The *baillis*

[48] As Grabois suggests, 'De la trêve de Dieu à la paix du roi', 596. However, Louis VII had in 1144 issued instructions ordering relapsed Jews to be banished; Hallam, *Capetian France*, 173.

[49] Duby, 'Laity and the Peace of God', 133; Ducoudray, *Les Origines du Parlement de Paris*, 327-31.

[50] For what follows, see Fesler, 'French Field Administration'; Strayer, *The Administration of Normandy under St Louis*, ch. 3; Olivier-Martin, *Histoire du droit français*. A concise summary is provided by Hallam, *Capetian France*, ch. 4 and 5.

judged not only the free man of the king's domain, but even heard the suits of great laymen and ecclesiastics within a broad radius of the place where the justices sat. By mid-thirteenth century these itinerant *baillis* in the north gave way to single *baillis* set over territorial *bailliages*; in the newly conquered regions in the south, *sénéchaux* were established with a similarly territorial charge. The courts of the *baillis* and *sénéchaux* were vastly superior to the old local royal courts within the domain, the courts of the *prévôts*, which had lacked competence over the great and even over rustics outside the domain. In addition, the French kings lowered resistance to the new courts and officials by associating leading local men with them in their assizes and by paying close attention in these sessions to financial and juridical complaints against the *prévôts*.

During this same period changes in the king's primitive court, the *curia regis*, led to the gradual emergence of the Parlement of Paris as a distinct body of legal specialists. Records of the Parlement survive from 1254. The court apparently settled in the royal palace on the Île de la Cité and no longer followed the king by the reign of Philip III (1270-85). Despite the fluidity to be expected in the early history of an institution, more form was given to Parlement during the reign of Philip IV (1285-1314).[51]

Thus, the French monarchy by the second half of the thirteenth century had transformed the ecclesiastical notion of peace into a more royal and secular form as embodied in the kingship of St Louis, and had created the courts at the local and central levels on which a system of appeals and supervision of theoretically inferior jurisdictions could be developed. We will see that by this time, taking a divergent course, the English monarchy had already reached a second stage.

The late tenth and early eleventh century form a troublesome period for historians of English monarchy and society and have occasioned scholarly battles only slightly less fierce than those conflicts which determined the fate of kings and countries in that

[51] On parlement see Shennan, *The Parlement of Paris*; Ducoudray, *Les Origines du Parlement de Paris*; Fawtier and Lot, *Histoires des institutions françaises*, vol. ii, ch. 4; Glasson, *Histoire du droit*, i. 285-313. J. R. Strayer discusses parlement under Philip IV in *The Reign of Philip the Fair* (pp. 208-36).

era. With the exception of a hard core standing firm on high ground, most historians can sheath swords and agree that England had moved some distance in the direction of the political and social changes that were transforming institutions and social relationships across the Channel. There is no need to provoke frontal assault here by assessing just how far England had moved and whether or not this position justifies the label of feudalism which is so much in contention.[52] Instead, following the wise example of Louis VI in his search for peace and justice, we might take shelter behind a venerable institution, in this case the famous paradoxes of F. W. Maitland. Not only did Maitland deliver a salutory conceptual admonition by suggesting that feudalism was actually introduced into England in the seventeenth century by Sir Henry Spelman,[53] he addressed the question as to what long-range transformations the Norman Conquest produced by suggesting that in one sense William the Conqueror introduced feudalism into England and that in another sense he saved England from feudalism.[54] For the essential difference developing between England and France in the eleventh century was the locus of power. Whatever the royal insecurities and ominous tendencies towards regional separatism or political fragmentation, England was still for its time a relatively united realm ruled by a functioning Germanic monarchy of a Carolingian type. On the continent the hammer blows of invasion and civil war had led to the collapse of such a monarchy; only a series of complex changes worked out over centuries reconstructed a French royal authority with a conception of its responsibility for public order and with some capacity to act on the theory. We have seen that in France the process could only be said to be underway in the thirteenth century, if the yardstick by which it is judged is widespread effectiveness. But in England, as Maitland's sly aside suggests, the long process of fragmentation and reconstruction did not occur. The very symbol of seigneurial independence in Francia, the private fortress, was scarcely found in England. In fact,

[52] David Douglas provides a balanced consideration of the problem in *William the Conqueror*, ch. 2. Elizabeth A. R. Brown has surveyed the entire debate over feudalism in 'The Tyranny of a Construct', 1063-88.

[53] Maitland, *The Constitutional History of England*, 142.

[54] Ibid. 143-64; Maitland and Pollock, *The History of English Law*, i. 66-7.

fortification was almost entirely a matter of public works; Offa's Dyke and the system of burhs were the products of royal initiative and a demonstration of the power of the pre-Conquest English state.[55] The peace movement in the form of the *Treuga Dei* barely put in an appearance in England and then only briefly during the anarchy of Stephen's reign.[56] England was no peaceful Eden, but already the king's peace filled major jurisdictional space. In place of fragmentation and painstaking reconstruction, England was swiftly transformed into the most royal of the feudal monarchies of north-western Europe. For the Norman kings of England and their Angevin successors developed in a small and newly conquered kingdom the strongest political and social bonds known to their age, the personal ties of feudalism, and they could infuse this source of energy into the functioning apparatus of county and hundred courts and local government created by Anglo-Saxon kings across several centuries. Thus, the English monarchy by roughly mid-twelfth century was already beyond the point the French monarchy was approaching by mid-thirteenth century.

The scope of English law in the reign of Henry II illustrates this point well, and provides a framework for a more specific cross-Channel comparison. If the basic obligations of the state in the field of law are to elaborate and enforce codes for the peaceful resolution of disputes and to repress internal violence, then in twelfth century Europe the government of Henry II earns high marks. The thrust of Henry's measures on the civil side of law was to reduce the violent self-help that, though always present in medieval society, may have become a fixed habit in the years of the anarchy. Starting from the principle enunciated in the treatise attributed to Glanville that 'no one is obliged to answer concerning his freehold in the court of his lord unless there is a writ from the king or his justiciar', Henry II generated what was in effect a royal control over the crucially important litigation concerning land holding.[57] In the assize of novel disseisin, which

[55] A survey of both Offa's Dyke and the Burhs, with illus. and ref. to the latest detailed work, is provided by James Campbell and Patrick Wormald in Campbell (ed.), *The Anglo Saxons*, 119-22, 152-4.

[56] Boussard, *Le Gouvernement d'Henri II Plantagenet*, 402-6; Grabois, 'De la trêve de Dieu à la paix du roi', 592.

[57] The comment of Glanville is quot. Warren, *Henry II*, 332. Ch. 9 of

returned lands forcefully taken from a peaceful possessor, the king and his advisers created an elegantly simple and swift procedure which would become 'the most frequently used form of action in the king's court.'[58] Other actions, to some degree modelled on novel disseisin, soon followed to deal with disputes over rights of patronage to benefices, inheritances, and the ecclesiastical or secular tenure of property held by clerics. Indeed, for the deeper right of possession standing behind the more limited or superficial seisin, the crown moved beyond extant writs of right and provided as a 'royal benefit conferred on the people by the clemency of the king' the action known as the grand assize, by which a jury of knights was substituted for the traditional trial by battle.[59] Since all of these actions, possessory and proprietary, were held before justices sent out on circuit from the central royal court, the great practical expansion of the king's justice into county society is apparent.

For the history of public order the royal innovations on the criminal side are equally important. Certain offences since the Anglo-Saxon era had been reserved for the jurisdiction of the king as pleas of the crown: breach of the king's peace, fighting at his court, obstructing his officials, corrupting legal process, neglecting military service[60]—but, in Maitland's phrase, the king's court was concerned primarily with 'the great men and the great causes'[61] so that the actual hearing of cases in the localities fell to the sheriff. It was in the shire court and under the presidency of the sheriff that crown pleas were held, along with a great mass of other litigation both civil and criminal. But until at least late in the reign of William Rufus (1087-1100) the only charges of criminal acts were those brought by private accusation. A change, begun in the late years of William Rufus and consolidated under Henry I, reveals the characteristic legal precocity of the English monarchy. By placing local justiciars in the counties, the Norman kings placed themselves among the first European rulers to institute the 'systematic prosecution of suspected criminals by

Warren's biography provides a summary of Henry's legal advances. See also Doris M. Stenton, *English Justice*, ch. 2, and Van Caenegem, *The Birth of the English Common Law*.

[58] Sutherland, *The Assize of Novel Disseisin*, 43.

[59] Glanville, quot. Warren, *Henry II*, 353; see pp. 352-4 generally.

[60] Harding, *The Law Courts of Medieval England*, 22.

[61] Maitland and Pollock, *The History of English Law*, i. 108.

individual royal officials acting on their own authority'.[62] These officials were charged with the responsibility for 'the fight against crime and for the rights arising from crown pleas'.[63] If a private accuser was unavailable, or unable or too fearful to act, the local justiciar was expected to bring charges *ex officio*.

Henry II inherited and for a time continued the system of local justiciars, but he was clearly dissatisfied with their performance in office and distrustful of justices who might put down local roots. With the Assize of Clarendon (1166) and even more with the Assize of Northampton (1176) he swept away the local justiciars, replaced them with local accusing juries and juries of presentment. Henceforth, local grand juries would present to itinerant justices (justices on eyre) accusations against all those suspected of murder, larceny, or harbouring of criminals (1166), or of forgery, or arson (1176). Guilt, determined by the archaic ordeal until the advent of the trial jury in the early thirteenth century, was punished by terrible mutilation.[64]

Whatever a modern scholar may think of ordeals and mutilations, the role of the English monarchy in public order by the second half of the twelfth century was already quite substantial across the length and breadth of the realm. Lacking detailed evidence we cannot judge its success, yet it remains significant that the king's justices attempted to supervise the settlement of the land disputes which so exercised the aristocracy, and undertook with a harsh hand to repress those accused of some crime by local juries.

This massive legal edifice of the Angevin kings, built on the solid Anglo-Saxon and Norman foundations, makes the greatest contrast to the situation across the channel where the Capetians, vigorous though they were, at the same time were only clearing a building site. At the time when Henry I was firmly establishing his local justices, Louis VI, as executor of the peace of God, was repeatedly moving to smash the fortress of some lord resisting royal power within the confines of the royal domain; the French equivalent to the Angevin local justiciars in England, the royal procurators who would initiate cases *ex officio* where no victim pressed a charge, were still nearly two centuries away.[65] By the

62 Van Caenegem, 'Public Prosecution of Crime', 51.

63 Ibid.

64 Hyams, 'Trial by Ordeal'; Brown, 'Society and the Supernatural'.

65 On the royal procurators, see below, p. 246-7.

time Henry II replaced local justices with grand juries collected to give information to royal itinerant justices, Louis VII and Abbot Suger could substitute the theory of the king's peace for the *pax dei*, but still lacked any mechanism which could begin to effect this grand vision on a day-to-day basis outside the royal domain.

The contrast seems much less severe by the mid-thirteenth century. Henry III and Louis IX register as contemporaries in our minds, and their realms seem comparable political units, in ways that Henry I and Louis VI and their realms never could; that the comparison seems more reasonable is, of course, a measure of the vast progress of French monarchical power and prestige produced by Philip II, Louis VIII, and St Louis. Conquest trebled the size of the royal domain and the creation of an effective administrative structure, patterned to some degree on that used by Plantagenet rivals in England, secured the new territory. Thus, by the middle decades of the thirteenth century kings on both sides of the Channel could occasionally take similar simultaneous steps to solve problems in law and administration which were common to both countries. In each a developing bureaucracy, the revival of classical notions of law and jurisprudence, and in general an increasing expectation of regular and peaceful procedures generated new possibilities for royal jurisdiction, even as they created problems for the administration of the realm.

The key device was the informal complaint or *querela* which the English and French governments were willing to receive and even showed some eagerness to solicit. As Alan Harding has argued, this 'influx of plaints in the thirteenth [century] . . . constitutes something of a second beginning for English law, or perhaps better the beginning of a second stream in English law. And . . . what was the second beginning for English law was the first beginning of French law as a centralized system.'[66] Merging royal and private self-interest kings encouraged complaints against their own officials by private persons. In England Henry II had characteristically played an important early role. By broad investigations in 1170 which quickly took on the name 'Inquest of Sheriffs', the king, through eyre justices armed with a special commission, asked about '[t]he whole financial exploitation of the country and the manner of it, in whosoever's interest, whether

66 'Plaints and Bills in the History of English Law', 65.

just or unjust . . .'. W. L. Warren argues that the survival of actual returns proves that the king had not asked the impossible. 'For a king of France or a king of Germany to have contemplated such an inquiry', he continues, 'would have been unthinkable'.[67] But by the time of Henry III and Louis IX the use of complaint was evident in France as well as England; thereafter the pace quickened. The inquiry into the misdeeds of Fawkes de Bréuté in 1224 provides an English example, while the 1247 *enquêtes* commissioned by St Louis, or the '*plaintes*' against the *bailli* of Vermandois twenty years later provide French cases. From 1261 the rolls of English eyre justices begin to include special sections of *querele de trangressionibus*, and from 1278 writs of summons to the eyre proclaimed that the king's justices would hear trespasses and plaints concerning ministers and bailiffs of the king or of any other lord, or indeed complaints against anyone else.[68] By this time, that is the reign of Edward I, petitions received in time of parliament opened a regular channel for complaint and an opportunity for redress. 'This was a momentous innovation', John Maddicott writes, 'for it meant that for the first time the voice of the aggrieved and of the socially insignificant could be heard at the centre of government.' Moreover, particular opportunities were provided for special and specific needs. In 1279 the king invited complaints against the unsavoury Adam of Stratton, disgraced royal chamberlain and notorious financier; the same invitation followed the fall in 1307 of the equally notorious Walter Langton, royal treasurer, and may have followed the fall in 1294 of William March (also treasurer).[69] After the three year absence of King Edward I in Gascony (1286-9) *auditores querelarum* were available at Westminster for three years, and special commissioners to hear plaints against local and royal officials were sent into the countryside in 1298.[70] From 1305 trailbaston justices took over this jurisdiction in the shires, but the parliamentary petitions, developed since the early years of

[67] The quot. is taken from Warren, *Henry II* (p. 289). Warren provides a general discussion (pp. 287-9).

[68] See Harding, 'Plaints and Bills in the History of English Law', 66-8.

[69] 'Parliament and the Constituencies, 1272-1377', in Davies and Denton (eds.), *The English Parliament in the Middle Ages*, 62, 65-6.

[70] On the 1298 inquest in England see Thomson, *A Lincolnshire Assize Roll*; on the *enquêtes* promised in the French charters see Artonne, *Le Mouvement de 1314*, 123-4.

Edward's reign, continued to provide another channel for complaint. In France there was less variety in forms but no lack of activity on the part of crown *enquêteurs*. Though the popularity of these investigators understandably waned when they began to investigate subjects' misdoings as well as official misconduct, their services in righting wrongs could be demanded as late as the fourteenth century. The demands of the leagues in 1314 produced royal promises for triennial *enquêtes* by *enquêteurs-réformateurs* who would receive plaints against oppressions and injustices.[71]

The sphere of private complaint in such processes could easily grow, especially since the royal courts in France and England took as their touchstone an allegation that illegal force had been used against the king's peace; *vi et armis et contra pacem domini regis* (by force and arms and against the king's peace) became the standard phrase in England (often abbreviated simply *vi et armis*); in France a number of phrases were used, all emphasizing force or illegal arms.[72] By encouraging and hearing a stream of complaints, which soon grew to become a veritable flood, the kings of England and France produced two significant results. On the one hand, the immense and amorphous field of trespass was brought within the scope of royal legal systems so that the endless reciprocal violence of local families could be brought before the king's justices. On the other hand, the proportion of the population of the realm actually pleading in the royal courts was greatly extended so that the king's justice now reached much further down to touch new layers in the social pyramid. This expansion in substance and clientele thus had the effect of greatly extending the king's role in keeping the peace. In fact, the process in some sense fed on itself, since the new remedies and new classes of litigants produced great pressures for still further expansion of the king's justice.[73]

The new trespass litigation in England and France and the rapid French royal progress, capped by the saintly model kingship of Louis IX might be used to argue that the vast twelfth century

71 Henneman, 'Enquêteurs-réformateurs', 309-49.

72 Harding, 'Plaints and Bills in the History of English Law', 68-71. A standard formula in French documents by the 1330s is 'per vim, violenciam et armorum potenciam', AN X2a3, *passim*.

73 Kaeuper, 'Law and Order', 734-84; McLane, 'The Royal Courts', esp. ch. 4 and id., 'Changes in the Court of King's Bench', 152-60.

gap between the English and French monarchical role in public order had been reduced. But it would be a great mistake to underestimate the continuing importance of differences which were still very much in operation and which would long make their force felt in French and English history.

The differing chronologies by which the royal judicial role developed, for one thing, largely explain why English law early adopted and retained the jury system and accusatorial process, while in France the movement from mid-thirteenth century was towards a Romano-canonical procedure based on the inquest and appeal.[74] The formative decisions of Henry II were made between 1166 and 1179, when English royal power was sufficient to compel local jury duty, but before universities and the classical legal revival had generated enough trained men and learned treatises to base the growing royal jurisdiction on Romano-canonical process.[75] But in France the crucial decisions on method of proof were made only by St Louis who in 1260 prohibited trial by battle, at least in the royal courts; by this time the elements of Romano-canonical process were all available and were relatively well known through a century of use in ecclesiastical courts. In addition, the relative weakness of the French monarchy outside of the royal domain made the examination of individual witnesses, supplied by the parties, much more attractive to the crown than trying to compel local juries to attend court sessions. Moreover, these new procedures actually facilitated the appeals on which the French royal system of justice depended. Having started judicial centralization long after the Normans and Plantagenets, the Capetians found they had no building blocks like the shire and hundred courts in England. The French local courts were largely in the hands of feudal aristocrats and the replacements created by the king would understandably come to be based on the new, professional methods and as newcomers in a crowded field of jurisdiction would of necessity rely on appeal rather than on original jurisdiction.[76] By the time

[74] Dawson, *A History of Lay Judges*, ch. 2, provides a stimulating discussion of this evolution.

[75] Warren, *Henry II*, 292-3; Van Caenegem, 'L'Histoire du droit et la chronologie'.

[76] Dawson, *A History of Lay Judges*, ch. 9; Fawtier and Lot, *Histoires des institutions françaises au moyen âge*, ii, ch. 2; Langbein, *Prosecuting Crime*, 211-22.

of St Louis royal jurisdiction can be said to have covered the realm in the limited sense that *bailliages* and *sénéchausées* constituted legal territories covering the lordships of feudal seigneurs.[77] In the king's court held by *bailli* or seneschal, or in the emerging Parlement of Paris, a vassal could appeal not only that his lord had denied him justice, but that his lord's judgment was false. The appeal procedure was completed only in the fourteenth century, however, and significant jurisdiction long remained outside of the king's cognizance.

An English historian turning from the sources of legal history familiar to him to look at the evolution of French royal jurisdiction will probably be struck by the gradual and easy-going nature of the process across the Channel, and even more by the confusing layering of courts and jurisdictions only somewhat ordered by the system of appeals. So much was left to seigneurial jurisdictions, so much authority and responsibility was shared. To the historian of English law, the picture in France can only look untidy. The impression is important and reveals much more than the idiosyncracies engendered in historians by national culture or choice of academic field. For however much the central institutions and local extensions of royal power may seem to approximate each other in England and France by the second half of the thirteenth century, the differences produced by the great contrast in the size of the kingdoms and the timetables by which royal authority developed created structures and attitudes which differed at a fundamental level. For our purposes more important than the detailed contrast between an accusatorial procedure and an inquisitorial procedure were the differing ways in which the kings' common theoretical responsibility for justice and peace was translated into practice on either side of the Channel. The impact of kingship on public order would be felt in significantly different ways in France and England. Precocious royal power acting over the much smaller English kingdom could take on a much greater and much more immediate responsibility for public order and the peaceful resolution of disputes than was possible or even considered necessary in France. For thirteenth-century France was still in many ways a federation of lordships;[78] even so royal a king as St Louis's grandson Philip the Fair saw clearly the

[77] Fawtier and Lot, *Histoires des institutions françaises au moyen âge*, ii. 321.

theoretical and practical limits to his role as final source of justice and guarantor of order. As J. R. Strayer explains:

> For Philip the Fair the basic sign of sovereignty was his right to act as the final and supreme judge in all cases (except those dealing with purely ecclesiastical matters) that arose in his kingdom. As a corollary he insisted on his right to protect anyone who had invoked his intervention in order to remedy an act of injustice. But once these principles were admitted, Philip was satisfied; he had no desire to have his officials judge every case in the first instance. Not only did he lack the resources for undertaking such a vast responsibility; it also would have offended his sense of the fitness of things to try to deprive the upper classes of their rights of justice.[79]

The point is illustrated if we compare the English pleas of the crown or the *capitula itineris*, the articles or questions asked of local juries by eyre justices, with the French *cas royaux*, the cases reserved for the crown in France. Already in the early twelfth century *Leges Henrici Primi* the list of pleas reserved to the king's justice included thirty-seven offences. These included offences against the king and his administration—a somewhat incongruous list including royal rights of treasure trove, shipwreck, and beasts of the sea stranded on the coast, insults to the royal dignity, treason, breaches of safe conduct, injury to the king's servants, encroachments on royal property, damage to the king's highway, minting false money—and also the crimes considered most serious between subjects—homicide, arson, rape, house-breaking, robbery, and harbouring outlaws.[80] Perhaps a more practical view is provided by the articles of the eyre which number only five after Henry II's Assize of Northampton (1176) but which multiplied in the next century to become 'the seventy searching questions' of the *vetera capitula*, the old set of questions, and were soon joined by the forty-one articles of the *nova capitula*, the new questions.[81] Some of these questions were more administrative than judicial, but in the trailbaston proceedings which took up the criminal jurisdiction

[78] See the comments of Strayer, *The Reign of Philip the Fair*, 196.

[79] Ibid. 191.

[80] See *Leges Henrici Primi*, x. 1, pr.: Stubbs (ed.), *Select Charters*, 125. Cf. Warren, *Henry II*, 251.

[81] Stubbs (ed.), *Select Charters*, 125, prints the list of pleas from the *Leges Henrici Primi*. Helen Cam discusses the articles of the eyre in ch. 1 of her *Studies in the Hundred Rolls*; the quot. is taken from p. 29.

of the eyre from 1305, jurors were asked to report cases of poaching, homicide, robbery, arson, assault and battery, hiring of assailants, extortion of money or tenements by threats, reception, concealment or protection of offenders by their lords or others, intimidation of jurors or royal officials, maintenance of pleas, bailiffs or other ministers allowing felons to wander at large for fear or favour, disturbance of constables in their duty, hiring of men to make forcible entry for taking seisin, armed resistance to the levy of the king's debts, and housebreaking.[82]

In contrast to this remarkable royal determination to deal directly with a wide variety of offences, the Capetians seem to have felt relief that the hundreds of seigneurial courts lifted from their shoulders the burden of hearing 'the thousands of petty cases that make up the largest part of the work of criminal courts in any society.'[83] In his study of the *cas royaux*, Ernest Perrot concluded that no broad theory concerning the maintenance of public order stood behind the few cases reserved for the exclusive jurisdiction of the French crown, though the offence of *port d'armes* forced him to some lengthy paragraphs of explanation; for, he argued, no such theory would allow all the serious offences such as murder, arson, rape, highway ambush, and even violent dispossession to remain in the hands of seigneurs.[84] We need not accept this view entirely to recognize that the fragmentation of judicial power[85] was an especially prominent feature of French criminal justice and particularly of criminal low justice, which dealt with petty offences. But even high justice with cognizance over what the English termed felonies was so widely distributed that 'there were hundreds of nonroyal courts in the country that could impose heavy fines on, or mutilate or hang convicted criminals'.[86] Even the distinction between high, middle, and low justice might vary with the locale, and as Bernard Guenée warns: 'A la fin du XIVe siècle, sous le manteau clair et abstrait des mots, la confusion des choses subsiste.'[87]

82 Ibid. 75-6. Her list is representative but not exhaustive. See PRO JUST/I/871 mm 5,6; JUST/I/396 m 15, for example.

83 Strayer, *The Reign of Philip the Fair*, 195.

84 Perrot, *Les Cas royaux*, 180, 262-5, 317-24.

85 Ducoudray provides Parisian examples of fragmentation in *Les Origines du Parlement de Paris*, 573-84.

86 Strayer, *The Reign of Philip the Fair*, 192, 194.

87 Guenée, *Tribunaux et gens de justice*, 85. Note also pp. 98-99 where he

With so many possessors of rights of justice, and an even greater number of claimants to judicial rights, conflicts over jurisdictions were frequent enough to become in themselves a source of disorder.[88] 'Ces bizarres justiciers', Ducoudray wrote, 'se faisaient la guerre pour prouver leur droit de faire justice.'[89] A case from 1317 illustrates Ducoudray's stricture. In total disregard of the royal safeguard which the monastery of Lieu-Dieu enjoyed, 500 men of the *vicomte* of Thouars invaded the monastic prison, seized a murderer held there, pillaged the monastic granges, wounded several monks, and in front of the chapel erected gallows built from wood pilfered from the monastery. To make their claim to jurisdiction quite clear the *vicomte* 's men hanged several mannequins dressed like monks on the new gallows; then they went on to hang several live monks as well. When the royal guardian continued his helpless protests in the king's name, he was shouted down with the warning, 'Be quiet. There is no king here but our *vicomte* and if you open your mouth again, we will kill your horse under you, and you surely will not leave with your head as you came with it.'[90] In another case from 1317, Jean de Levis, lord of Mirepoix, encountered heated resistance when he tried to exercise his claim to high justice at Orsans. A crowd of 200 men from Fanjoux, he claimed, destroyed and burned his gallows and forcibly entered both the house where the judicial registers of the *greffe* (i.e. the law clerk) were kept and the residence of the judicial officers.[91] A similar dispute in 1322 brought Jean de St-Symphorien, knight, at the head of 500 horse and foot, banners and pennons flying, to attack the *bastide* belonging to the prior of Montrotier.[92]

The appeals to higher courts, which might work to unify a fragmented structure of judicial power, could likewise lead to

points out that royal complaints about churchmen and other vassals constantly nibbling away at royal jurisdiction were justified by the facts.

[88] Artonne, *Le Mouvement de 1314*, 111; Strayer, *The Reign of Philip the Fair*, 193.

[89] Ducoudray, *Les Origines du Parlement de Paris*, 610.

[90] AN X1A f.24, quot.: Paul Lehugeur, *Histoire de Philippe le Long*, i. 302, partly in French tr. and partly in Latin. Ducoudray, *Les Origines du Parlement de Paris*, 361 n. 6 quotes part of the original Latin and notes that the summary in *Actes* 6021 is inadequate.

[91] *Actes* 4687.

[92] Ibid.

violence. On the one hand, those who appealed to a higher court were for the moment exempt from the jurisdiction of the seigneur justicier against whose judgment appeal was pending; for some turbulent lords this seems to have meant licence for a wave of violent acts.[93] On the other hand, those who appealed were often subjected to threats and more than threats. Aude, lady of Tirent and wife of the knight Elie de Caupene, appealed to the king of France in 1318 against a sentence of the seneschal of Gascony; in reprisal the *bayle* of Pons ordered an attack on her manor.[94] A few years later the seigneur de Reims with a force of 1,000 men fired the house of Baudoyn Boudillac, despite the royal *panonceax* affixed to it (in sign of the king's safeguard) because he had dared to appeal to the king's justices.[95] Prisoners in the jails of the archbishop of Lyon were threatened with harsher treatment if they appealed their cases to the king.[96] The *viguier* of the abbot of Montoliue hanged three men despite their appeal, and struck those who dared speak up on their behalf.[97] But the violence in jurisdictional disputes was not always seigneurial. A royal serjeant who was a justiciable of the chapter of Toul was arrested for illegally fishing in the Meuse. Though he was released because he was a royal serjeant, the outraged lieutenant of the *bailli* of Chaumont and the *prévôt* of Andelot led an armed host to Void, a possession of the chapter, ruined the tower, tore down the fortifications, broke down the public hall where markets were held, broke mills, and devastated houses at Void and Troussay, where they battered down doors and carried off personal belongings such as eating utensils and clothes.[98]

When Parlement resolved jurisdictional quarrels and punished the violent struggles they engendered, the resolutions could produce scenes remarkable in the eyes of Englishmen. An arrêt of

93 Ducoudray comments on this problem and provides examples in *Les Origines du Parlement de Paris*, 533-9.

94 *Actes* 5143. He was sentenced to imprisonment in the Châtelet for six months or more, at the King's pleasure.

95 *Actes* 6425. Large fines were imposed on the guilty.

96 Fedou, *Les Hommes de loi lyonnais à la fin du moyen âge*, 80. Other perils of appeal are illustrated by a 1320 case from the *sénéchausée* of Rouergue. A man appealed to the king but his messenger was robbed near Orléans and all documents were lost; in the mean time the unfortunate appealer suffered judicial torture; *Actes* 6060.

97 *Actes* 3784.

98 *Actes* 6687.

1271 ordered the king's men who had arrested a thief within the jurisdictional area of lady Ermine de Verderonne to restore seisin of justice to her by a bag full of hay or by some other object.[99] The Mayor of Corbie, who had hanged a man named Mort-Fouace despite the prohibition of the royal *prévôt*, not only had to pay £600 and take down and bury the body; he was also to send to Corbie a mannequin representing Mort-Fouace.[100] Again and again the Parlement ordered that true rights of justice be restored, symbolically, by royal or non-royal officials who were to cart effigies across the countryside to be hanged on the proper gallows or set at liberty; the hanged man was beyond recompense and may have been wronged merely by being executed on the wrong seigneur's gallows; but the restoration of right order by effigy illustrates, in an admittedly bizarre way, the fragmented structure of judicial power in late medieval France.[101]

The Parlement that could order effigies hanged on this or that gallows could not, however, hang a live man as late as the reign of Philip IV. Sentences might be highly imaginative, but seldom seem severe. Those who attacked priests or violated ecclesiastical rights, for example, might find themselves sentenced to provide wood or stone statues, or in one case an equestrian statue of St Martin fashioned in wax;[102] they might have to make processions in their underclothes carrying symbols of their offence.[103] There may even be a romantic novel to be written if the facts behind a 1336 sentence are discovered: a formidable woman named Aubrie de Masterose was pardoned two large fines imposed for, among other crimes, receiving banished men, incendiaries, homicides, *port d'armes*, and breaking royal safeguards in Armagnac, Astarac, Magnas, and elsewhere, on condition she marry Master Guillaume de Villiers, clerk and councillor of the king.[104] But few sentences are so interesting and none was capital. Permanent loss of jurisdiction badly enforced or oppressively exercised seems the harshest penalty imposed. In 1306 Parlement deprived the

99 *Actes* 1767.

100 *Actes* 2102.

101 *Actes* 2975 B (1298), 3063 (1300), 3958 (1312), 6409 (1321), 7037 (1323), *Actes*, 2nd ser. 2398 (1339), 2870 (1340), 3855 (1342), 7184 (1346), 4110 (1342), 7184 (1346), 8646 (1348).

102 *Actes*, 2nd ser. 7177, 7229.

103 *Actes* 5670.

104 *Actes*, 2nd ser. 1431.

Lord of Poix of his jurisdiction over the commune of Poix during his lifetime, and ordered seizure of his lands to a value of £500 in order to provide compensation for victims of his violence.[105] Collective lordships might suffer similar penalties.[106] But loss of jurisdiction was not a common sentence. Moreover, reflecting its origins as basically a court for civil cases, Parlement had no tradition of physical punishment. Though Parlement could briefly imprison men in the Châtelet,[107] the usual penalty for even the most violent acts was a fine to the king and to the injured party. The really powerful men and institutions, great lords, monasteries, towns, could not be seriously touched by fines unless the sums were enormous; yet large fines were difficult to collect and often had to be reduced. An amercement imposed on the count of Foix, for example was reduced from 30,000*l.t.* to the loss of a rent of 551*l.t.* (with capital value about 5,500*l.t.*).[108] Even lesser lords could prove troublesome at the level of the assizes. The lord of St-Sanflieu, a knight who refused to pay amends owed for offences, found that royal officials were seizing his goods. He appeared in the assize of the *bailli* of Senlis and in full audience asked insolently why his goods were being taken. On being told the reason he called the royal officers thieves and claimed to have paid all to the clerk. The royal procurator's offer to send for the clerk to settle the matter provoked a response prudently left in the scribal Latin: 'Ego non darem de te, de clerico tuo, de Rege tuo et comite, unum magnum stercus.'[109]

Banishment was sometimes used as a penalty by courts at all levels. From one point of view it was a sentence of the utmost

105 *Actes* 3339.

106 *Actes*, 2nd ser. 5160, a case involving the town of Pamiers which in 1340 lost its consuls and was fined £4,000. The charges included more than forty murders left unpunished, pillaging of homes in plain day, insults and physical assaults suffered by royal officials, royal letters torn to shreds.

107 *Actes* 5550. Judging from the harsh conditions there, even a brief incarceration might seem punishment enough. See the comments and case cited by Strayer, *The Reign of Philip the Fair*, 232, and the discussion by Monique Langlois and Yvonne Lanhers, *Confessions et jugements,* introd. All of the cases discussed by Langlois and Lanhers concern the Châtelet which is discussed in more detail below.

108 Strayer, *The Reign of Philip the Fair*, 231 n. 102.

109 *Actes* 7916 (1327). His outburst added 400*l.t.* to the sum he owed, though collecting it must have been difficult. He was in addition to declare in full assize that he had had no intention of insulting the king.

severity; from another point of view, like English outlawry, banishment simply declared the inability of the court to deal with a hardened offender. Certainly men banished for their crimes from one jurisdictional area turned up there again or in other areas committing the same violent acts for which they were banished.[110] They were often thought to form a part of the forces recruited for private wars.[111]

The persistent problems of Parlement as an agency to repress violence are summarized by J. R. Strayer:

> Although the Parlement was usually correct in deciding whether or not there had been violence, it was not very successful in decreasing acts of violence. It usually heard only those cases in which men of some standing were involved; such men could find many ways of delaying a decision. When delay became impossible, they would receive a judgment from the king's court but such a judgment did not persuade them to give up their rights (as they saw them) of vengence and private war. The penalties were almost always purely pecuniary, and they could hope, with some reason, that the full amount would never be collected. The real unfairness was in the penalties, not in the judgments. At a time when poor men were hanged for theft, when counterfeiters were quite literally boiled alive, men who were guilty of arson, looting, and homicide merely had to pay fines. The communes were treated more harshly than were the nobles, a town riot was usually more expensive than a private war . . . but even the leaders of town riots were not punished physically.[112]

Indeed, large areas of France were hardly touched by the Parlement in its role as overseer of justice in the realm. Before the death of Philip the Fair only one regular appeal had come to the Parlement from the duchy of Burgundy; and the record was not vastly different from Brittany, or Flanders.[113] Royal control over

[110] In 1317 Arnal de Roilhas, banished for wounding Grimoard de Panisols, returned to the *pays* and committed homicides, sacrileges, highway robbery; by night he invaded and pillaged the house of the *curé* of Roilhas (*Actes* 4970). By an order sent in the same year, two royal serjeants were sent to arrest two brothers and their squire, banished from the realm but known to be living in the duchy of Burgundy (*Actes* 5560). A similar order in 1320 directed four serjeants of the Châtelet to arrest two brothers banished from the realm who had obviously returned and made their presence felt (*Actes* 6152).

[111] *Actes* 379 (1259); *Actes*, 2nd ser. 2335 (1339).

[112] Strayer, *The Reign of Philip the Fair*, 232-3.

[113] Small, 'Appeals From the Duchy of Burgundy'. She cites sources for appeals from the other great fiefs.

the justice administered by barons and great prelates in thirteenth- and fourteenth-century France was always 'very spotty', and in the case of the great fiefs was 'practically nonexistent . . . even by way of appeal.'[114]

The Parlement, of course, was not the only royal court in Paris to which the king's subjects might bring cases involving violence and disorder. From 1269 the *prévôt* of Paris was considered to rank as a *bailli* and his court, taking its name from the *Châtelet* where it sat, developed a broad, if ill-defined jurisdiction which reached considerably beyond Paris.[115] The *Châtelet* involved 'a large and vigorous organization long before the time of Philip the Fair';[116] from 1320, and likely even before that date, the king thought its legal business sufficiently voluminous and important to have a royal proctor and two advocates there. The legal procedure and especially the criminal procedure was almost amoeboid in its formlessness; but the chaos of personnel and procedure did not deter suitors who wanted a court with the prestige and learning of Paris, and who were pleased with more speed and lower costs than in the Parlement itself.[117] Moreover, the *Châtelet* offered the litigant a change to put his opponent through the process of severe imprisonment, and torture, with the possibility of hanging, mutilation, or the pillory as well as banishment as sentences imposed on the guilty.[118] Parlement sometimes sent cases it received on appeal to the *Châtelet* and in the later fourteenth century shared with the *Châtelet* large numbers of cases within certain jurisdictional categories.[119] But the real growth of *Châtelet* jurisdiction was more a phenomenon of the fifteenth century than of the fourteenth century.[120]

114 Strayer, *The Reign of Philip the Fair*, 200.

115 In general, see Ducoudray, *Les Origines du Parlement de Paris*, 703-10, 954-6; Fawtier and Lot, *Histoires des institutions francaises au moyen âge*, ii. 372-85; Coupland, 'Crime and Punishment in Paris'; *Registre criminel du Châtelet de Paris*; Cohen, 'Patterns of Crime in Fourteenth-century Paris'; Langlois and Lanhers, *Confessions et jugements*.

116 Strayer, *The Reign of Philip the Fair*, 123.

117 Guenée, *Tribunaux et gens du justice*, 250, 255, 452-71.

118 Ducoudray provides examples of process at the Châtelet in 1332, *Les Origines du Parlement de Paris*, 500-4; Langlois and Lanhers print numerous confessions with informative discussions of the cases in *Confessions et jugements*.

119 Cohen, 'Patterns of Crime in Fourteenth-century Paris', 308-9.

120 Guenée, *Tribunaux et gens de justice*, 468-70.

Equally important for questions of law and order was the large force of royal serjeants: those on foot acted within the city of Paris; the mounted serjeants could be sent anywhere. In 1302 the number in each group stood at eighty, but it rose steadily across the early fourteenth century to reach a total of 700 in 1327, before being reduced because of public outcry.[121] The serjeants had a reputation for high-handedness[122] and extortion which often led the crown to promise reductions in their numbers and even sometimes to carry them out.[123] Yet a force of police agents on this order of magnitude was highly useful to the crown. On occasion, rather than exhorting local officials once again to do their duty the king could send out mounted serjeants; in February 1318, for example, seven mounted serjeants were ordered to arrest eight named men and their accomplices who were guilty of an attack on a knight, and to deliver the guilty for judgment to the *bailli* of Rouen.[124] Yet the serjeants, even when their numbers were rising to a peak, were an inadequate force to supplement the local officers across the vastness of France. In about 1308 there were roughly thirty *bailliages* and *sénéchausées*, with more than 300 subordinate courts of *prévôts* (in the north), *viguiers* or *bayles* (in the south) coexisting with the thousands of feudal justices.[125] Vigorous kings like Philip IV and Philip V found it necessary to commission special agents to arrest particular offenders or whole classes of evildoers;[126] in December

[121] *Ordonnances des roys de France*, ii. 7, 131-2, 199-200, 239, 262, 519; iii. 31, 439, 680; iv. 190, 194, 410; Ducoudray, *Les Origines du Parlement de Paris*, 707.

[122] In 1318 three serjeants of the Châtelet were removed from office for having violated the immunities of the cathedral chapter of Paris by entering the cloister of Notre Dame to seize an offender and, in the process, striking a serjeant of the chapter (*Actes* 5406).

[123] *Ordonnances des roys de France*, ii. 7, 131-2, 199-200, 239, 262, 519; iii. 31, 439, 680; iv. 190, 194, 410; Ducoudray, *Les Origines du Parlement de Paris*, 707.

[124] *Actes* 5220. In 1344 a sizeable force of Châtelet serjeants arrested and disarmed a force of horse and foot intent on private war (*Actes*, 2nd ser. 5786).

[125] Ducoudray, *Les Origines du Parlement de Paris*, 585-6. Bronislaw Geremek notes that the Châtelet serjeants were a more numerous force than was available in other European cities, but concludes that they were unable to maintain even public security in Paris itself: 'La Lutte contre le vagabondage à Paris', ii. 229.

[126] *Actes* 4329, 5134, 6798.

1318, Philip V even ordered the seneschal of Lyon to raise a troop of twelve to twenty knights at the king's expense in order to find and punish the sons of iniquity who were desolating the *sénéchausée* by their violence.[127] The comment of Lot and Fawtier on *Châtelet* jurisdiction seems true of French royal criminal justice in general, whether the agents acting for the crown were the serjeants of a *bailli* or seneschal, a force of *serjeants à cheval* from Paris, or specially commissioned agents: 'On a le sentiment que les délits et crimes jugés au Châtelet frappent seulement une partie infime des coupables. Ceux qui sont pris sont jugés et condamnés pour l'exemple. On sait le peu d'efficacité du procédé.'[128]

4. THE LATE MEDIEVAL CRISIS OF ORDER

By the late years of the thirteenth century and the early years of the fourteenth century, the kings of England and France were seriously involved (with very mixed success) in measures designed to secure public order. As we noted at the outset of this chapter, historians writing about England in this period have asserted that a crisis of order troubled the realm; historians of France, by contrast, have seldom suggested that such a crisis existed in France. Could this historiographical contrast merely reflect the directions in which French and English historical study have moved over the last hundred years or is it reflective of different historical experience? We need to consider if there is any merit in the concept of a late medieval crisis of order and whether the formulation, if it is granted validity, should be applied to England alone, as present historical writing suggests.

The political, economic, and demographic setting could easily suggest a medium in which serious problems of justice and order would flourish. Although Plague and War, the two dread horsemen of the Apocalypse which would ravage Europe, appeared in

[127] *Actes* 5617.

[128] *Histoire des institutions francaises*, ii. 383. The jurisdiction of the Châtelet itself extended over more than 100,000 people; in the nearly three years covered by the sole surviving *registre criminel* of the Châtelet, 107 trials involving 128 people are recorded; Cohen, 'Patterns of Crime in Fourteenth-century Paris', 309.

extreme form only from the mid-fourteenth century, the demographic crisis may well have been felt over much of north-west Europe by the late thirteenth century;[129] moreover, the villager whose cart was requisitioned or whose seed crop went to pay the king's war taxes in the 1290s would have found cold comfort could he have been assured he was not yet supporting the cost of the Hundred Years War.[130] With maximum population pressure on the land, rising prices, falling agricultural wages, guild restrictions, and urban unrest, mounting costs of extended warfare financed by general taxation, hordes of rapacious officials (in the eyes of those fleeced and in the tracts of all moralists), public order was certain to be an issue of more than usual concern and importance.[131] The long list of troubles was common to England and France. Why should a crisis of order figure only in English historical study?

We can approach the question first by looking at some quite specific evidence. In England concern for problems arising from war and the unfavourable socio-economic setting appeared in measures taken late in the reign of Edward I. In the spring of 1305 general commissions empowered panels of justices to visit the whole of England, which was divided into five circuits; the justices were to hear and determine a list of serious offences committed since 1297. The particular target seems to have been the violences of 'trailbastons', clubmen or hired assailants, many of whom were veterans of the king's wars. It was from them that the popular name of trailbaston was borrowed and applied to the inquiries themselves. The justices heard thousands of cases of 'bizarre and methodical brutality', protection rackets, and conspiracy committed both by officials and private persons.[132] At intervals across the first half of the fourteenth century the crown sent out new commissions of trailbaston and other itinerant commissions, such as those of 1341. In one direction all of these commissions provide a link with the stresses of war: the original

129 See n. 14 above.

130 Maddicott, 'The English Peasantry and the Demands of the Crown'; Miller, 'War, Taxation, and the English Economy', 11-31; Strayer, 'The Costs and Profits of War', 269-91.

131 In addition to the sources cited in n. 129 and 130, see Hibbert, 'The Economic Policies of Towns'; Miller, 'The Economic Policies of Governments', 316-39; Fryde and Fryde, 'Public Credit', 454-85, 527-40.

132 Harding, 'Early Trailbaston Proceedings', 147.

commission of 1305 looks like an emergency wartime measure; the problems of violent land seizures may have been especially severe in wartime; and the practice of wartime purveyance caused endless disruption and dispute.[133]

Viewed from another perspective the trailbastons also reflect the results of long-range economic and social dislocations as rising population pressed against the ceiling imposed by available land and fairly primitive agricultural technology. Medieval agrarian society had undoubtedly long generated a floating population of vagabonds who attracted the suspicions of those in authority,[134] but the problem apparently intensified in the early fourteenth century and it attracted major governmental action. Scholars once mistakenly located the original trailbastons in a commission to arrest vagabonds issued in 1304.[135] But this vagabond commission lacked determining power and was only the last in a series of more than thirty such commissions which extends across the reign of Edward I. Yet the evidence of these vagabond commissions is important for they empowered justices either to inquire or to do justice concerning 'vagabonds and their receivors', 'malefactors wandering at large who, through the absence of nobles and others in the Welsh war, are growing bold', 'vagabonds who commit homicides and other crimes . . . so that certain of the king's loyal subjects dare not leave their houses without escorts of armed men', 'vagabonds in league within the liberty of the town of Newcastle-on-Tyne [who] commit depredations by night and refuse to submit to justice . . . the king reflecting that it may go from bad to worse and desiring that the peace be firmly observed while he is in Scotland . . . '.[136] The inter-

133 Ibid. 146-7.

134 Suspicion of vagabonds appears as early as the reign of Henry II: see Assize of Clarendon, cc. 9-10, 15; Assize of Northampton, c. 2. I owe these ref. to John Maddicott.

135 See for example Foss, *The Judges of England*, iii. 28. For the writ of 23 Nov. 1304, see *CPR 1301-7*, 343, *CFR 1272-1307*, 504.

136 *CPR 1272-81*, 137 (Mar. 1276), 178 (July 1276), 181 (Sept. 1276); *CPR 1281-92*, 66 (June 1283), 256 (Feb. 1286), *CPR 1292-1301*, 44 (Jan. 1293), 45 (Apr. 1293), 108 (Dec. 1293), 109 (Feb. 1294), 110 (Feb. 1294), 111 (Feb. 1294), 303 (Sept. 1297), 472 (Aug. 1299); *CPR 1301-7*, 89 (Aug. 1302), 186 (Feb. 1303), 187 (Feb. 1303), 194 (July 1303), 193 (Aug. 1303), 194 (Aug. 1294—2 commissions), 197 (Oct. 1303), 271 (Nov. 1303), 272 (Jan. 1304), 277 (June 1304), 285 (Sept. 1309), 284 (Sept. 1304), 284 (Oct. 1304), 284 (Nov. 1304), 343 (Nov. 1304), 504 (Jan. 1305), 504 (Mar. 1305).

connections between the pressures of wartime, the vagabondage resulting from over-population, and serious fears for public order are striking; and equally striking is the grim determination and vigour with which the government of Edward I announced its measures to deal with the problem.

Vagabondage presented similar problems in French society,[137] but royal legislation dealt with it as a labour problem, rather than an issue of law and order as in England, and took steps only in the wake of the Plague. The first repressive measures appeared in ordinances issued by Jean II in 1351 and 1354. The first of these measures is mainly concerned with Paris and its region, while the second prescribes action 'en toutes villes, par les justiciers d'icelles'. In both ordinances the remedy is to expel from within town walls the unemployed, the vagabonds, the idle who were thought to spend their time in drinking, debauchery, and in seeking alms. If these idlers would not work they were given three days to remove themselves; those remaining were to be imprisoned on bread and water.[138] Clearly these measures are comparable with the contemporary English labour legislation following the Black Death rather than with the long series of vagabond commissions of the reign of Edward I culminating in the great criminal inquests known as trailbastons. In France the shock of the Black Death, the problems of the appalling mortality registered within the labour force, the description of the problem perceived, and the measures prescribed, all point to emergency labour legislation similar to the English statute of Labourers of 1351 rather than to the type of campaign against crime carried out in England three-quarters of a century earlier.[139] We may doubt the efficiency with which the measures were carried out in French cities. But in any case the contrasting reaction to problems of vagabondage is instructive. Characteristically the English king divided the realm into circuits and sent out his justices; in France the linked problems of vagabondage and lawlessness were largely left in the hands of the *seigneurs*

137 Guenée, *Tribunaux et gens de justice*, 213, 307.

138 Geremek, 'La Lutte contre le vagabondage à Paris', 213-36; id., *Les Marginaux parisiens*, 29-32.

139 Id., 'La Lutte contre le vagabondage à Paris', 216. The document he prints in app. VI showing the initial link with crime *per se* dates only from 1395. See pp. 222-3 for evidence of a continuation of the effort in the fifteenth century (the document misdated 1322 on that page is dated 1422 in app. X).

justiciers. Royal reaction to the perceived lawlessness of a floating population of unemployed men and women illustrates the basic contrast between the direct criminal jurisdiction of the kings of England and the large measure of seigneurial jurisdiction in France.

This striking difference in the level of royal capacity and the nature of the royal response to a perceived problem of order can provide a key to the vexed concept of crisis. The issue is not the absolute level of violence. Violence and disorder may have been greater on one side of the Channel or the other; but we will probably never know and we do not need to know in evaluating the notion of crisis. A crisis, after all, is more a matter of widespread perception than of objective fact; if large numbers of influential people believed their society was in crisis, the crisis existed.

In France of the late thirteenth and early fourteenth century public order was a problem that evidently concerned the last Capetian kings. But we have seen that in these matters of internal order the Capetians were latecomers compared to their royal English cousins and that their influential subjects were more concerned to protect noble and provincial rights than to encourage further royal responsibility for public order. They made such views clear in the provincial leagues of 1314–15. A real sense of crisis in France came later, not from an over-extended legal apparatus unable to make good its promises, but from the stark fact of protracted war. The ravages of English, Navarrese and Norman forces, and of the Free Companies brought the virtual disintegration of France. We need not search diligently to find a sense of crisis in France crumbling under the hammer blows of war. In the writing of French history of this period the all-embracing war has understandably subsumed the issue of public order.

Yet England, which more nearly escaped the devastation of war, suffered a genuine though more insensible crisis of order. There is much evidence for a contemporary English perception of crisis and for a series of actions based on that belief. The precocious nature of English royal power is critically important. For it seems that the very development of the machinery of government, a process itself intimately linked with crown war policy, could have counter-productive effects on the state of peace. This ironic turn by which the growth of royal power contributed to disorder appears to some degree in France, but much more strikingly in England. For the broad claims of the English crown in the field of public order and the vigorous measures taken by the king's agents to effect those claims unwittingly contributed to the problems they were intended to solve.[140] The kings of England had in fact accepted and even generated a volume of judicial business and encouraged a level of expectation of order which were finally beyond their capacity. Perhaps a government which relied on the unpaid service of local men supervised by a small corps of bureaucrats, without anything approximating a standing army or a police force, facing slowly building resistance to taxation, had come to the limits of its effective action. To extract the funds necessary to provide a major expansion of royal courts, paid professional judges, and officials would have fractured the very foundations on which the king's government had rested for centuries. Yet the king claimed a near monopoly of jurisdiction over the serious violence and major property disputes critical to public order; his officials vigorously acted against law breakers and encouraged the flood of lawsuits coming before the king's justices. The very capacity of high medieval English government, puny though it may seem by modern standards, may have lowered the social threshold for the perception of unacceptable violence and disorder. What is at issue, then, is a contemporary English perception of crisis and a series of actions based on that belief.

At least from the last quarter of the thirteenth century preambles to government documents such as statutes and commissions denounce the deterioration in the state of public order in England.[141] Though such statements can be exaggerated and do become formulaic, they are seconded by chroniclers and polemicists of the period, and even by the opinion of Edward I in a private memorandum already quoted.[142] Contemporary literature complements the evidence from government documents and private commentators. The failure or perversion of justice is one of the most common themes of fourteenth-century satiric writing; and the failure of the judicial system to satisfy expectations is often

[140] Kaeuper, 'Law and Order'.

[141] For examples and refs. see ibid. 735-7.

[142] See n. 20.

explicitly linked to predictions of revolt or memories of the events of 1381.[143]

Such evidence of a contemporary sense of crisis takes on all the more significance when we find opinion resulting in action. From the late thirteenth century the king of England and his officials persistently worked with the forms and agencies responsible for public order in obvious response to the continuing pressure of litigation and the increasing perception of violence and disorder. As successive means of control proved inadequate, new experiments were launched. Since the crown by this time had developed an advanced structure of taxation, the motivation cannot be set down to simple fiscality.

The strains are evident in the slow demise of the general eyre.[144] This great workhorse of English government, which had served for generations, was moribund by the end of the thirteenth century. Since the reign of Henry II panels of justices had visited the shires, bearing the civil pleas of subject against subject, taking from local juries accusations against those who had committed the serious crimes reserved for crown judgement, inquiring into royal rights, receiving accusations of misdeeds committed by the king's local officials. Such usefulness ironically killed the eyre by overwork; successive kings had piled one administrative and judicial task after another upon the eyre and from the mid-thirteenth century, as noted above, the immense new jurisdiction over trespass was added to the load. The eyre moved more and more slowly and then ceased to move at all, except for attempts at revival scattered both in time and geographical scope. By 1294 the eyre was finished and Edward I was deeply involved in the warfare in Wales, Scotland, and Gascony which would occupy his attention for the remainder of the reign; yet the tasks of the eyre remained to be done, more numerous and more pressing than ever. Thus the first half of the fourteenth century witnessed a series of judicial experiments as the central government sought to devise adequate institutions to replace the eyre. The late medieval outcome of this process would be the virtual delivery of much local jurisdiction into the hands of local gentlemen serving as

[143] Discussed in detail in ch. 4, p. 2.

[144] For what follows, see Harding, *The Law Courts of Medieval England*, 52-92; Cam, *Studies in the Hundred Rolls*, ch. 1; Crook, 'The Later Eyres'; McLane, 'The Royal Courts', ch. 1.

justices of the peace. The change from a system based on the eyre to one in large measure based on the justice of the peace is a striking reversal of the thrust of the English royal centralization which had been carried forward at least since the work of Henry II and it clearly illustrates the impossible strains created by that thrust.[145]

But in the half-century before the triumph of the JPs was an accomplished fact, several experiments had produced equally illuminating results. As the eyre faltered, some of the pressure of trespass litigation was diverted to special commissions delegated to 'hear' (oyer) the evidence on a charge (usually regarding trespass) provided by an inquest, and to 'determine' (terminer) the case by taking a jury verdict.[146] As the general eyre slowly ground to a halt, the crown willingly granted large numbers of these special commissions to deal with the pressing volume of trespass litigation. As many as 100 commissions a year issued from chancery late in the reign of Edward I, and more than 200 in some active years of Edward II. Since the number of these special commissions rose when a general eyre was not in progress and fell during an eyre, their initial usefulness as a safety valve against a potentially dangerous build-up of litigation is apparent. But the crown quickly came to see that the new device created more problems than it solved. Speed, efficiency, and awards of heavy damages recommended oyer and terminer to plaintiffs. Within a matter of months their complaint might be heard in their own locality by justices who kept at the tasks of collecting jurors, securing verdicts, and imposing fines. Though the crown originally saw in oyer and terminer a substitute for some of the work of the eyre and a useful device for settling disputes and repressing local feuding, in 1285 (within a decade after the oyer and terminer experiment was begun) legislation against abuses was clearly necessary; it began to be uncertain on which side of the balance of public order their weight fell. Across the reigns of the three Edwards an unending stream of complaint to the crown shows that the oyer and terminer produced consequences which must have been unexpected in their scale if not in their very nature. In their *querelae* some petitioners recited doleful or

[145] Harding, *The Law Courts of Medieval England*, 86, 116, 119.

[146] For a more detailed account of oyer and terminer commissions see Kaeuper, 'Law and Order'.

outraged accounts of violences and injustices suffered and prayed that the king grant an oyer and terminer as the sole effective remedy. But others bitterly charged that the special commissions were used for malicious prosecution in which the plaintiff's wrong was imaginary or his damages were awarded out of all proportion to the real injury he had sustained. A schizophrenic attitude toward oyer and terminer is thus evident; the commissions were bitterly denounced in petitions by the same groups in society which sought them eagerly and used them vigorously against their opponents. The key to this love-hate relationship is to be found in the unusual degree of influence to which these powerful commissions were susceptible. Even in the easy-going world of medieval English justice 'where bribery and corruption merged imperceptibly with back-stairs influence and the traditional exercise of patronage'[147] oyer and terminer seemed unfair. For petitioners regularly expected to name the men who would be commissioned as justices in their case, the men who would set the date and locations of all sessions, empanel and instruct jurors, and set damages. The crown regularly seems to have granted the plaintiff's request, with results recorded in the smouldering Latin and old French phrases of private and common petitions: defendants claim that they have not been informed of the sessions or that they have feared bodily injury if they appeared; the local officials and jurors have been intimidated or corrupted; the justices are relatives, friends, lords, or retainers of the plaintiff. Throughout the period, clauses in one statute or another promised strict regulation over the granting of commissions, the types of offences in their cognizance, the personnel who may sit as justices. But a continuing, parallel stream of complaint to king and council, often in time of parliament, shows how little effect the pious statutory clauses had on practice. A device intended to promote order has in effect been given over into the control of local lords and gentry who used it as a new and powerful weapon in their countryside feuding. Handing over a generous measure of royal judicial control to local lords and gentlemen did not prove to be a successful formula for securing countryside peace. From this point of view we might read royal reluctance to yield to Commons' pressure for the appointment of justices of the peace with full determining power

147 Maddicott, 'Law and Lordship', 2.

not as monarchical resistance to the inevitable march of constitutional government, but as a realistic reaction to the oyer and terminer experiment.

The troubles with oyer and terminer, recognized as early as 1285, point towards the central difficulties confounding the English efforts to secure public order across the late middle ages. The crown had established not only a clear judicial supremacy but a veritable monopoly over major property disputes, serious crime, and breaches of the peace. This jurisdiction had been expanded from the second half of the thirteenth century to include the enormous judicial territory of trespass. The flow of judicial business into royal courts was a widening stream, swelled by the plaints and suits brought by an expanding clientele.[148] The harsh economic and demographic pressures can only have increased the litigiousness of an already contentious society in which lawsuits were at best a partial replacement for violence. Crown claims, announced in the preamble to every statute dealing with the peace, every writ and commission, and crown actions carried out in every shire served as a powerful catalyst to intensify the desire for order also present in a violent society; however, for enforcing his regulations the king's government had to rely on the very groups in society most likely to deform or disregard them whenever it was convenient. There was no massive expansion of personnel of central government to match the massive increase in jurisdiction and judicial business; in fact, it is difficult to imagine how the king and his advisers could have accomplished such an increase. The traditions of reliance on local notables certainly stood directly in the way, and the revenues available through taxation were seemingly all committed to war; even war taxes had generated resistance, and additional tax burdens were unthinkable to maintain an expanded administration in peacetime. Contemporary criticism of war taxation took the line that the burden was simply too heavy, or that the results were incommensurate with the cost; moralists might associate the absence of the king or the return of veteran soldiers to England with violence in some general way, but they did not complain that the money was being diverted from the bench of justice to the battlefield, nor did they urge the king to provide the needed corps

[148] Harding, 'Plaints and Bills in the History of English Law'. Cf. his *Law Courts*, 84, 86-7.

of paid justices or the even larger and even more urgently needed corps of armed officers to enforce judicial decisions.[149] Yet they expected the crown to carry out its claims to secure an acceptable level of public order, and noted bitterly how often it failed, using the resources available.

The English kings continued to rely on a small corps of central government judges and officials whose responsibility was in part to supervise the work of unpaid local notables. Especially after the reign of Edward I it is difficult to escape the conclusion that at both levels the negative influence of lords and gentlemen made itself felt with increasing force. As K. B. McFarlane has noted, 'by the time of Edward I disorder was obliged to assume subtler forms. . . . Men in fact found it safer to pervert the law than to break it. The result was the outcry for legislation on the evils of maintenance, champerty, conspiracy and embracery.'[150] Justices, who were now usually laymen rather than ecclesiastics, put down roots in the localities and strove to become territorial magnates; they could scarcely remain independent of those social relationships and assumptions historians have called bastard feudalism. In one of the oldest Robin Hood ballads the virtuous knight in conflict with a wicked abbot appeals for mercy to the 'hye iustyce of Englonde' only to learn from the justice that he is retained by the abbot: 'I am holde with the abbot . . . both with cloth [*i.e. robes*] and fee'.[151] In fact, in the first half of the fourteenth century the practice by which lords retained the king's justices was more prevalent than it had been earlier or would be again; the justices 'became part of the fabric of the countryside, often implicated in local feuds and quarrels'.[152] But to quote Maddicott:

> The enforcement of the law depended not only on the execution of impartial justice in the central courts but on the still more difficult task of preventing great men from retaining malefactors in their company and

[149] See the comments of Barnie, *War in Medieval English Society*, 30 ff.

[150] McFarlane, *The Nobility of Later Medieval England*, 115. Maintenance involved the corrupt support of friends in lawsuits; champerty was more specifically the maintenance of a suit in return for a share in the proceeds; embracery meant tampering with a jury.

[151] Maddicott, 'Law and Lordship', 34. Cf. his 'The Birth and Setting of the Ballads of Robin Hood', 276-99.

[152] Id., 'Law and Lordship', 17-18, 22-5.

of supervising the provincial justices of assize, gaol delivery and oyer and terminer, many of whom were country gentry rather than 'career' justices and men with even stronger roots in the localities than their professional superiors. These large questions occupied the government persistently in the fourteenth century. . . .[153]

During the same half century when the king's justices were most likely to be found receiving lords' robes and fees, the crown reluctantly yielded to pressure from the social levels represented in the parliamentary Commons and handed over to the gentry acting as justices of the peace a generous degree of judicial control in the localities.[154] The gentry and leading burgesses wanted positions which would place the royal stamp of legitimacy on an authority in the counties and boroughs which they saw as their natural right. Whatever the evident doubts on the part of the king and his advisers, which led the government now to give peace officers determining power (as in 1316, 1329, 1332, 1338, 1350, 1361, 1368), now to withdraw it (as in 1327-8, 1330, 1332, 1344, 1364), the drift toward true justices of the peace was clear. Edward III overcame the traditional royal reservations about justices of the peace by a prudent assessment of the support he needed to fight the war in France. He could scarcely call on the county leaders to pay war taxes or lead warrior contingents to the continent while denying them their ideal of local justice and administration at home. Certainly the statute of 1361, once thought to be the virtual creator of the office, simply sanctioned a transformation which had long been coming. The stream of judicial authority which 'for the whole of the period from c.1160 to c.1290 . . . was flowing strongly to . . . the king's "central" courts', Alan Harding writes, 'reversed itself once more, flowing back to the localities and to the landlord who found himself again keeping a "peace"—though this time it was in theory the king's and not . . . his own'.[155]

But since the number of ambitious and contentious gentlemen greatly exceeded the number of offices, chance would

[153] Ibid. 41-2. Cf. McFarlane, *The Nobility of Later Medieval England*, ch. 6.

[154] On the early history of the JPs, see Harding, 'The Origins and Early History of the Keeper of the Peace'; Putnam, 'The Transformation of the Keepers of the Peace'; ead., 'The Keepers and Justices of the Peace'.

[155] Harding, *The Law Courts of Medieval England*, 84, 116. Cf. McLane, 'The Royal Courts', 36-40.

inconveniently place one's enemies occasionally in a position of power as justice under one sort of commission or another. If all the means to sway sheriffs or their subordinates, to bribe or intimidate inquest or trial jurors failed—or if they simply felt haste or hot temper—the gentlemen of England turned to force. Amid the dry records of court proceedings any researcher finds striking accounts of the murder or maiming of opponents, the pillaging of his house or devastation of his fields or flocks.[156] Even more striking are the descriptions of actual court sessions disrupted by force, sometimes ending in the killing of the judge.

Not only were such scenes played out in life, they were celebrated in literature. The popular mid-fourteenth century 'Tale of Gamelyn' ends with an unforgettable scene in which a wronged hero surrounds a court held by a corrupt justice procured by his brother (who is sheriff), assaults the justice and hangs him along with the sheriff and jurors 'To waiven with ropes and with the wind drie.' This scene from literature can be all but reproduced from extant court records. The feelings ascribed to the crowd witnessing the scene—an uneasy compound of admiration and fear—seems very close to what we know of widespread attitudes toward violence and justice.[157]

The evidence on contemporary opinion and that on contemporary action are thus entirely congruent. A large number of people were discontented. Perhaps like Gamelyn in the tale they had felt with bitterness the effects of a system of law which was easily swayed by money or force. Perhaps like the courtroom audience watching Gamelyn they were caught between an emerging belief in legal process supervised by the crown and an ancient admiration for hot-blooded vengeance. Perhaps they could see (what is more visible to historians) that measures taken by the crown, in response to demands for justice and order which it had encouraged if not generated, might more readily compound problems than solve them. It is little wonder that they complained with great feeling about justice and the state of the peace and patronized a literature which poured an acid bath of satire and complaint over crown efforts which inevitably failed to achieve the high claims repeatedly made by officialdom.

156 For many examples, with refs. to more see Bellamy, *Crime and Public Order*, *passim*.

157 Kaeuper, 'An Historian's Reading of *The Tale of Gamelyn*'.

On both sides of the Channel, then, the crisis of order was real; but it took particular form in each realm from the long process by which the crown had acted to secure internal peace and from the specific impact of Anglo-French warfare. An analysis of public opinion about the role of the state will provide further comparative evidence on the sense of crisis in England and France; this will be the concern of the final chapter. But we must first look more closely into the question of public order itself.

3

Chivalry, the State, and Public Order

The subtle bias of modern views creates a danger of misinterpreting the medieval problem of order. In the modern world many people tend to associate in some loose formula public order, the control of violent crime, strict action against criminals by police and judges. In our world, in contrast to the medieval world, violence is often seen as by and large a phenomenon of the people in the bottom layers of society; violence thus appears as a regrettable concomitant of poverty, lack of opportunity, or the downward spiral of drug addiction. Such crime as is found, and found abundantly, in the upper ranges of modern society seems to many not to pose a direct threat to public order; tax evasion, bribery, business fraud, while regrettable, do not disturb the citizen in his day-to-day life beyond the furrowing of a brow as he reads his newspaper.

Thus, the attempt, often made with considerable labour, to transport our modern sociological and criminological concerns and methodology back across the medieval centuries, while it has produced some results of great interest, cannot be the master key to the problem of public order.[1] Exactly how much any particular length of computer printout can tell us about any particular category of crime may be debated, but we must not confuse the sum total of these printouts with even the raw material from which an analysis of public order could be redefined.

If we think of medieval public order simply in terms of crime (currently of great interest to historians) or of periodic rebellion

[1] See the discussions of Bronislaw Geremek, *Les Marginaux parisiens*, ch. 1. Victor Bailey states the problem concisely in his bibliographical essay, 'Crime, Criminal Justice, and Authority in England', 36: 'The essential dilemma is whether the criminal indictments . . . should be taken as a measure of the changes which occurred in criminal behaviour over time, or as an indicator of the contours of the system of criminal justice.' B. W. McLane usefully distinguishes patterns of crime and patterns of prosecution in Lincolnshire in 'The Royal Courts', 79-103.

(long studied) we will ignore half of the picture. For in the Middle Ages one of the greatest threats to the peace of the realm came from the day-to-day conduct of the knightly classes whose tendency to violent self-help was often proudly proclaimed and recognized as a right, rather than condemned as a crime, and whose excesses in any case were for a very long time not prosecuted rigorously by the same mechanisms employed against the misdeeds of lower social orders. In fact, these lords and gentlemen who were especially in France possessors of extensive rights of justice, and who even in England exercised wide authority either in their own name or as agents of the king, were all too frequently themselves plunderers, bandits, arsonists, slayers. The interminable warfare between the houses of Foix and Armagnac in the south-west of France provides a good example. In 1339 the Parlement of Paris partially confirmed the sentence of the seneschal of Toulouse against a long list of nobles entangled in this feud. Despite all royal checks, the guilty had troubled the peace of the realm by, among much else, assaults on houses and mills, arson, murder, attempts to burn people in their houses, devastation of forests, and support of banished men collected in their houses. The nobles' reply to these charges was that they had simply met force with force and had fought against their enemies by virtue of a right sanctioned by the custom of Armagnac and Foix. The royal safeguards were dismissed as contrary to the liberties and franchises of the region; moreover, the accused claimed, they had not been properly informed. Though they had obtained letters of grace from the king and from his representative in Gascony, the bishop of Beauvais, covering murders and excesses committed, the seneschal had unsportingly condemned them on charges of *port d'armes* and of violating royal safeguards.[2] On such men fell much of the task of maintaining order since they had extensive rights of jurisdiction within their lands. In a letter to several *baillis* in 1316, Philip V urged all action necessary to preserve peace; the *bailli* and his men were to take vigorous steps, as were 'those who hold the land (*ceus qui ont les terres*)'. Yet these lords over widespread domains were often the problem rather than any support towards solutions.

Though the English crown reduced private jurisdiction on the French scale, it too had to rely on local notables as occasional

[2] *Actes*, 2nd ser. 2335.

agents of royal justice, and it had to contend with and rely on men no less ferocious than their French counterparts. When Robert de Vere, constable of Rockingham Castle and keeper of Rockingham Forest, was charged in two cases of official misconduct in 1332, he discouraged the suit of one plaintiff, the abbot of Pipewell, by ambushing him. Then he openly confronted the justice coming to hear the charges. These were his wrathful words to the royal judge: 'You wish to destroy me, but before I am destroyed I shall destroy all those who intend to destroy me, whatever their rank or estate may be.'[3] A little earlier the knight Henry de Staunton caught a Lincoln burgess who with other jurors had indicted him before royal justices. The knight robbed and beat the juror, and held him for ransom; before releasing him, Staunton gave a message to be spread among the other jurors: any caught outside the safety of Lincoln city walls would be killed, or at least would lose a limb.[4]

Clearly our view of public order must extend far enough to include activities that only rarely or only very slowly came into the cognizance of courts of law. In short, as we try to understand the problem of internal peace we must consider not only crime, but also a host of issues linked with or at least symbolized by the code of the knightly classes, the code of chivalry. A conscious effort is required to bracket chivalry and the problem of order. As moderns we have tended either to dismiss chivalry as silly, employing varying degrees of cynicism to explain if or why medieval men thought it important, or we have romanticized chivalry, preferring to think it made men more noble and gentle, a little more like the knights in a Burne-Jones painting.[5] Cynicism has generally outpaced romanticism in our age, but neither view ultimately takes chivalry seriously. This is unfortunate, since, as Johan Huizinga pointed out, 'next to religion, chivalry was the strongest of the ideas that filled the minds and the hearts of those men of another age'.[6] If anything, Huizinga may have somewhat underplayed its importance, for in many aristocratic minds

[3] PRO SC8/130/6498.

[4] PRO JUST 1/1411B m. 3 d., and *CPR 1330-1334*, 235.

[5] There is a useful discussion of the entire topic in Barnie, *War in Medieval English Society*, ch. 3. The most recent study of all aspects of chivalry is Keen, *Chivalry*.

[6] Huizinga, 'Political and Military Significance', 197.

chivalry did not rank second to religion but was fused with it. The point has been made most convincingly in the recent study of Maurice Keen.[7] Keen has no doubts that ecclesiastics tried to influence, channel, and control chivalry from the latter part of the eleventh century; but he thinks their success was extremely limited. The chivalric code was indeed deeply religious; the strand of piety ran so deeply in knights that it is useful to consider chivalry the aristocratic form of lay piety. But though its practitioners were religious, by and large they did not accept the framework proposed for their lives by churchmen. Knights went on crusades, because this was an enterprise in accord with their own independent ideas of longstanding, but they felt little desire to accept sacerdotal control over knightly activity *per se*. In fact, they showed a strong belief that 'the knightly life, with all its violence and with the richness and decor of its aristocratic trappings, [was] within its own terms a road to salvation'. Geoffrey de Charny, one of the model knights of his age, who died on the field of Poitiers in 1356 as standard-bearer of the king of France, wrote for King John's Order of the Star a *Livre de Chivalerie*; the winning of salvation through proficient exercise of arms is the dominant theme of the book. 'Appositely', Keen observes, 'it concludes with a combination of a prayer and war cry: "Pray for him who made this book: Charny! Charny!" '[8]

So powerful a force inevitably attracted the efforts of various groups in society—not only ecclesiastics, but women, and as we will see, royalty—to channel the energy of the warriors in particular directions. In trying to mould knightly conduct, each attempt produced what was, in effect, a heightened justification of chivalry. The process, as we have seen, was as old as the peace movement and was a continuation of that same impulse, in so far as the church and kingship were concerned.

For the complex code of chivalry contained a basic contradiction when considered in relationship to issues of public order. Chivalry has often been interpreted as a restraining force on the

[7] Keen, *Chivalry*, *passim*.

[8] Id., 'Chivalry, Nobility, and the Man-at-Arms', 36-7, quot. from *Œuvres de Froissart*, i. 533, which prints part of Charny's book. Froissart praised Charny as 'le plus prudomme et le plus vaillant de tous les autres', ibid., v. 412. Raymond Cazelles discusses Charny's career in his *La Société politique et la crise de la royauté*, 60-1. Malcolm Vale comments on the fusion of religion and chivalry, *War and Chivalry*, 91.

admittedly violent tendencies of the social ranks which embraced it. As a code of restraint and honour it could mitigate the violence so close to the surface of late medieval life. But the contradiction appears if we consider that honour can be a very aggressive force: in the words of the anthropologist Julian Pitt-Rivers, 'the ultimate vindication of honour lies in physical violence'.[9] As Malcolm Vale has commented, if this is true 'then one cannot argue (as Huizinga did) that chivalry promoted moderation.'[10] A concern for honour could lead proud men to warfare on any scale they could manage, from duel or judicial combat to private wars involving veritable armies. Vale sets out the problem clearly:

> On the one hand, chivalry is seen by Huizinga as a means whereby limiting rules were imposed on later medieval warfare; on the other, it permitted and justified the exercise of violence in the prosecution and avenging of essentially private quarrels. Such quarrels could lead to wars between both nobles and sovereign princes and the difficulty of drawing a line between a private quarrel and a public war was an acute one.[11]

What Maurice Keen has suggested regarding the problem of medieval warfare can likewise be applied to the problem of order, to the prevalence of wars within realms:

> . . . one reason for the failure of this age to keep the social problem of war within bounds lay, ironically, in the idealism of its attitude to war and the soldier, in what we may call the ethic of chivalry.
>
> Because of its underlying religious and idealistic justifications, it made it difficult for men to look squarely at the parasitic activities of soldiers and to recognize them for what they were.[12]

Maintaining the peace in the emerging medieval state was a problem of significant dimensions because of the existence and the idealization of a noble code of violence; it is the violence of the powerful and privileged classes which so sharply differentiates the medieval from the modern problem of order. We need to think of the deterrence of crime, violence, and disorder at roughly two social levels. Although historians have barely launched a comparative study of the phenomenon of crime and public order, we can assume a certain level of police court crime as the

9 Pitt-Rivers, 'Honour and Social Status', 29.
10 Vale, *War and Chivalry*, 9.
11 Ibid. 9-10.
12 Keen, 'Chivalry, Nobility, and the Man-at-Arms', 44-5.

common liability of all societies and a threat to the social order. This violence of the great masses of men in the lower ranks of society may well have been increasing under the pressure of the social, economic, and religious crises from the late thirteenth century on. Though we can never accurately measure medieval crime of this sort by totting up offences in court records, we have already noted the increased concern over a perceived problem in the forms and levels of crime, especially in England. Officials and subjects were concerned about order, and they were willing to take steps to secure peace by changing their institutions.

But whether or not crime at this level was increasing the threat may not have been more disruptive of order in England than in France. Perhaps French lords hanged thieves and murderers just as high as the justices of the English kings. Who hangs thieves is surely important to the development of government and over the course of centuries may be important to the issue of order. But in the short run the particular agency which represses crime may not be vastly important to the state of the peace. If the repressive action taken is efficient, whether the judge is the king's man or some lord's man is not significant; if, as many believe, deterrence of crime by harsh punishment is a myth, then the question of who hangs thieves and how well he catches them becomes irrelevant. In other words, the precocious power of the English government in police court jurisdiction may have had more effect on the growth of the English government than on the deterrence of crime or the achievement of order; likewise, in France the development of royal government rather than the level of ordinary crime may have been affected by the seigneurial role in policing much of the countryside. But in dealing with the violence of the chivalric groups in society the difference in English and French royal capacities may be more important. Whether or not some agency can stop or mitigate the reciprocal violence of the vendetta or prevent private war is a question of importance not only for the development of central authority, but also for the state of the peace.

In considering the problem of order as a function of the privileged layers of society our attention will focus on the knightly classes, revelling in proud violence. But by extending our gaze only slightly we can see how often the upper ranks of townsmen aped the chivalric code and followed the example of lords and knights. This bourgeois knightliness was largely limited to the French sphere, for English towns were (with the obvious exception of London) much weaker than their French counterparts and much more closely controlled by the crown which granted them their fundamental charters, demanded urban 'farms' paid into the exchequer and expected town representatives to appear in parliament.[13] But on the Continent a greater measure of independence on the part of towns and a bourgeois interest in chivalry went hand in hand. At the conclusion to her analysis of the *feste du roy Gallehault* held in Tournai in 1331, Juliet Vale argues that the whole town was seized by a jousting 'craze'. Her broad conclusion is important:

> It is clear that distinctions in the social hierarchy based on juridical status were becoming increasingly eroded. The *bourgeois* of Tournai doubtless considered themselves 'hommes d'honneur' and they assumed without hesitation facets of the noble life-style, such as the right to carry arms and to armorial bearings, that were traditionally regarded as the exclusive prerogatives of the noble class. At the same time the notion of the individual chivalric ideal, with its associated Arthurian and other literature, increasingly permeated this section of society. The civic *festes* themselves were very similar to those held in distinctly knightly milieux and it is evident that some nobles of the region involved themselves actively in civic *festes* in the late thirteenth and early fourteenth centuries.[14]

Maurice Keen likewise comments on the growing popularity of tournament among the rich town patriciate as a reflection of 'the eagerness of the leaders of a rising bourgeoisie to demonstrate that they were not incapable of the knightly virtues or of appreciating the refinements of chivalry.'[15] Along with the virtues and refinements they also claimed, at least in France, the rights of the chivalric classes to wage private war and they certainly possessed urban if not castle walls. The collective lordship behind these walls, in other words, often acted very much like the feudal lords usually found beyond town walls. 'Les guerres entre habitants roturiers des villes', Pierre Dubois insisted, 'ont été aussi fréquentes, aussi durables, aussi légales

[13] I am indebted to John Maddicott who reminded me of the important differences between English and French towns.

[14] Vale, *Edward III and Chivalry*, 40.

[15] Keen, *Chivalry*, 90.

que les guerres entre possesseurs de fiefs.' He noted the bellicose municipal device of the town of St-Quentin: 'tot cives, tot milites'.[16] Noting the similarity of spirit between the French nobility and the upper bourgois ranks, the author of the *Chronographia regum Francorum*, wrote, 'Potentes, tam nobiles quam burgenses, sine lege crudeliter tractabant subjectos suos.'[17] In 1307 the commune of Corbie was fined for carrying illegal arms within the land and justice of the abbey of Corbie 'by manner of vengeance'.[18] In 1318 Parlement confirmed a sentence of the seneschal of Carcassonne against the inhabitants of Bordes who 'au son des cloches, précédés d'un étendard et en armes' attacked the inhabitants of Mas d'Azil.[19] In 1323 Parlement confirmed a sentence of the *bailli* of Mâcon (increasing the fine he had levied) against the Sire de Beaujeu and the men of Villefranche who had joined in a war against the dean and chapter of Lyons.[20] Feudal lords sometimes formally began wars against communes with the defiance (*diffidatio*) used by one lord against another; the knight Richard d'Autigny, for example, defied the inhabitants of Langres to begin his war in 1317.[21]

In fact, the mixture of policies pursued by these towns shows the medieval problem of order with particular force.[22] As miniature realms within the realm of France, towns struggled with the necessity of maintaining a tolerable level of peace within their walls. In the writings of French historians communes have thus often appeared as institutions of the peace and adjuncts to the peace movement.[23] They took many of the steps to suppress violence and disorder that we will associate with the French monarchy at a later stage: They prohibited the carrying of arms for offensive purposes within their jurisdiction; they imposed a waiting period at the onset of private quarrels; they recognized or

[16] Dubois, *Les Asseurements au XIIIe siècle*, 45, 119. See his general discussion, pp. 45-53, 102-13.

[17] Quot.: Raymond Cazelles, *Société politique, noblesse et couronne*, 573.

[18] *Actes* 3407.

[19] *Actes* 5869.

[20] *Actes* 7169.

[21] *Actes* 4698.

[22] What follows is based on Dubois, *Les Asseurements au XIIIe siècle*, *passim*. An excellent first-hand account revealing these themes is Galbert of Bruges, *The Murder of Charles the Good*.

[23] Vermeesch, *Essai*, 135-48.

imposed assurances of non-violence between enemies; they punished great offenders by removing the doors of their houses or even by demolishing the dwellings. Yet these towns were also collective lordships which entered into private war and took vengeance in the best style of the day. Knightly society often wished to increase its social distance from the bourgeoisie and chose to measure and emphasize that distance by elaborations of the code of chivalry. Yet the distance can be easily exaggerated and the important point for thinking about the issue of public order is that a code of honour recognizable to all stretched across the ranks of privileged society; whatever refinements ambitious townsmen might lack in the eyes of their knightly betters, they shared with them a keen appreciation of the defence of honour through prowess.

This tension between a sense of responsibility for an ordered life and a delight in the colourful violence extolled by chivalry operated on a larger scale within kingship. Such inherent tensions, moreover, make it difficult for us to see kings whole. It would be much easier, though obviously incorrect, to picture Edward I as a good Victorian statesman forced by the fashion of his time to wear inconvenient suits of mail and occasionally relying on a tournament or Round Table to humour along his less far-sighted contemporaries. How convenient it long proved to be for historians to picture a crafty, essentially modern Philip the Fair surrounded by even craftier legists who were devoted to helping him destroy all that smacked of reactionary feudalism in France.[24] We must in fact recognize the existence of what seem to us to be contradictory qualities in the minds of fourteenth-century kings. The knight and the king existed in the same man, each dimension real and important. A fourteenth-century ruler could love tournaments, and fight in them himself, he could listen with rapt attention to romances and use chivalry as a 'form for . . . political thought' which reduced 'the appalling complexity of events' to 'a grave spectacle of honor and virtue . . . a noble game with edifying and heroic rules'.[25] Yet he could also bend every effort to ensure that his co-operation with the manifestations of the chivalric code was of the most masterful and regal sort. This

[24] Templeman, 'Edward I and the Historians'; Pegues, *The Lawyers of the Last Capetians*, 1-35; Strayer, *The Reign of Philip the Fair*, ch. 2.

[25] Huizinga, 'Political and Military Significance', 199.

sense of mastery, of kingly control, explains the apparent contradictions in the stance kings adopted towards chivalry. They encouraged chivalry so long as they could lead, and they tried to regulate or prohibit when they could not, or at least when they thought it timely to remind lords and gentlemen of their mastery.

Edward I provides an excellent example. Here is the towering state-builder revered, especially by nineteenth-century historians of law and administration, as the English Justinian. Even after passing through the acid bath of more modern criticism he emerges in the tradition of William I, Henry I, Henry II, who 'had a passion for order, or at least a dislike for disorder as an insult to their kingship, which amounted, in practice, to the same thing.'[26] Yet to the poets of the Midi, Edward was a model of chivalry, 'the best lance in the world'.[27] As an Arthurian enthusiast he patronized Round Tables and opened the tomb which the monks of Glastonbury assured him held the bones of King Arthur and Queen Guinevere.[28] Late in his reign he enacted a scene that could have been written by Chrétien de Troyes; in the famous Feast of the Swans in the banquet hall at Westminster he led the assembled knights in the swearing of chivalric and pious oaths before God and the gilded swans ceremoniously presented.[29] It is even possible to speculate that had he lived a little longer Edward I might have created some royal chivalric order; an Order of Swans would not be impossible to imagine, especially since his grandson (who took him as a model) apparently toyed with the idea of an order linked with the popular swan-knight romance before he created the Order of the Garter.[30]

By mid-fourteenth century the potentiality of royal chivalric orders has been transformed into actuality.[31] Edward III's Order

[26] Warren, *Henry II*, 323.

[27] Powicke, 'King Edward I in Fact and Fiction', 132-3. Cf. id., *The Thirteenth Century*, 515-16.

[28] Loomis, 'Edward I, Arthurian Enthusiast', 114-27; Vale, *Edward III and Chivalry*, 16-24.

[29] Powicke, *The Thirteenth Century*, 514-15; Wagner, 'The Swan Badge and the Swan Knight'; Vale, *Edward III and Chivalry*, 16-24.

[30] Denholm-Young, *The Country Gentry in the Fourteenth Century*, 147; Wagner, 'The Swan Badge and the Swan Knight'.

[31] Keen, *Chivalry*, ch. 10; Vale, *Edward III and Chivalry*, ch. 5. Renouard points out that the earliest royal chivalric order was founded by Alphonse XI of

of the Garter, in preparation since 1344, was fully developed before 1349; John II's Order of the Star, also planned in 1344, was established in 1351.[32] That the Order of the Star was dimmed by diverted royal attention and then in effect was extinguished by the French defeat at Poitiers[33] does not detract from the similar royal impulse in both countries. King Edward and King John wanted to associate the glory of chivalry with their own person and dynasty; the king was the founder and chief of each order, and the site for the rich religious ceremonial of each was chosen to reinforce the royal link: for the Garter, Windsor, the birthplace of Edward III; for the Star the Noble House of St-Ouen, a property of Charles of Valois, who founded the dynasty, and a favourite family estate. In creating his own order each king clearly hoped, as Powicke said of Edward I at the Feast of the Swans, 'to divert this undisciplined energy into the channels cut by his own wrath.'[34] Sidney Painter wrote engagingly on three types of chivalry which he distinguished as feudal, religious, and courtly love.[35] If we accept Painter's three categories of chivalry we can add a fourth; for by the mid-fourteenth century there seemed to be emerging a distinctly royal chivalry.

Yet we have good reasons for thinking that the union of chivalry and kingship was a marriage of convenience rather like the earlier link between feudalism and Carolingian kingship. Where the functions claimed for lords in chivalrous thought were not incompatible with the powers of kingly government, they tended to become competitive. Kingship and chivalry were moving on divergent courses which only for a time appeared to be parallel. The list of ideal virtues extolled by almost all writers on chivalry might seem fully compatible with kingship, even an aid to its tasks. Kings could easily praise and adopt as their own the

Castile in 1330, that Louis of Bavaria created an order about the same time, and that Humbert II played a major role in an order established a little later in the Dauphiné; all of these efforts thus preceded the creations of the kings of England and France; 'L'Ordre de la jarretière', 281.

32 Ibid.; Cazelles, *Société politique, noblesse et couronne*, 144-5.

33 Some of the revenue earmarked for the king's chivalric order had to be diverted to help pay the king's ransom after the French defeat at Poitiers, ibid. 298. John II may have hoped to revive the order in 1363 (see ibid. 442).

34 Powicke, *The Thirteenth Century*, 516.

35 Painter, *French Chivalry*.

chivalric virtues of loyalty, generosity, prowess, largesse. Yet the catalogue of ideal chivalric virtues by no means adequately describes the broader role chivalry played in social and political life. The desire for an orderly solution to disputes must occasionally have appealed to lords even more than polishing swords and sounding the trumpets for war. They might have courts of their own and they did bring cases into the king's courts. But did chivalry reinforce such desires? The code which summed up the knightly conception of the good and the true glorified proud sword strokes in defence of honour and buttressed a sense of the knightly right to decisive, independent action. Kings would increasingly have second thoughts about this glorification of lordly freedom of action and knightly independence; and though (as knights) they generally loved violent action more than ecclesiastics, they shared with churchmen the desire to channel the potentially destructive energy of knights in directions they approved. Thus, the obvious royal sense of responsibility for public order would be troubled when kings observed the chivalric code of honour (which found, as Pitt-Rivers suggested, its ultimate vindication in violence) glorifying private war in France or encouraging the blatant overawing of royal judicial agencies in England.

Moreover, many chivalric writers assumed the virtual absence of effective royal power and urged its exercise in the name of chivalry by the knightly classes. The chivalric ethos easily made kinglets of knights. Chivalric writers never tired of urging knights to be the policemen of Christian society, the protectors of the weak, the righters of wrongs.[36] Yet over the high medieval centuries kings increasingly claimed these functions as aspects of their sovereign rights and responsibilities. In short, chivalry by and large represented a countercurrent to the movement toward the Western form of state which was so evident across the twelfth and thirteenth centuries in France and especially in England. The movement of kingship and the state was toward public authority vested in a sovereign and exercised theoretically for the common good. Chivalry was rooted in the intensely personal and private world of ancient Germanic custom, modified by the whole host of changes seen in almost every aspect of life, which shaped the

[36] For an informative discussion of medieval writings on chivalry see Keen, *Chivalry*, 1-17.

Europe of the High Middle Ages.[37] In fact, chivalry was taking form and force at roughly the same time as the state and was coming to its prime in the fourteenth century. We can easily be misled by older notions of the decline of chivalry in the later Middle Ages.[38] As is true with most ideal codes, its practitioners and even more its theoreticians viewed practice in their day as an intolerable slippage from the golden age. But perhaps they decried the more vigorously what they saw as slippage as the ideal actually took on more importance in life and thought all around them.

The chronology seems important. Chivalry came to the peak of its influence in the late Middle Ages. This was, significantly, a time when the drive for increased royal power and for an increased role of kingship in social life (at least in all areas not related to war) had already come to the end of the active, High Medieval phase.[39] Chivalry had, moreover, developed at a time and in a region of Europe in which kingship was weak: it germinated in late eleventh- and twelfth-century France; significantly, its early centres of patronage were noble courts rather than the Capetian royal court. Chivalry was noticeably weak or even absent in contemporary England where kingship was particularly strong. In life as in literature the young Englishman who wanted to lead the life of knight errant, to enjoy the tournament cycle, had to cross the Channel. In the late twelfth century William Marshal and his patron Henry (son of Henry II) found England deadly dull. 'The comparatively quiet life in England soon palled upon young Henry and his household', Sidney Painter wrote, 'and their adventurous spirits longed for the land of knightly deeds.'[40] The 'semi-historical Romance of Fulk Fitzwarin' tells that so soon as they had been knighted Fulk and his brothers 'crossed the sea to seek honour and distinction; and never did they hear of a tourney or joust at which they did not wish to be present.'[41] In

[37] This is a theme of Keen's *Chivalry*.

[38] Id., 'Huizinga, Kilgour, and the Decline of Chivalry'.

[39] Strayer, *On the Medieval Origins of the Modern State*, 57 ff.; see also the conclusion to Guenée, *L'Occident*.

[40] *William Marshal*, 37. R. W. Southern states concisely: 'there were no tournaments and there was no chivalry in England'; *Medieval Humanism and Other Studies*, 143. Juliet Vale insists that by the late thirteenth century the English had a pre-eminent reputation in the tournament (*Edward III and Chivalry*, 15-16).

[41] Keen, *Chivalry*, 89.

much of chivalric literature, in fact, kingship wears a decidedly antique air, perhaps reflecting nostalgia for an age when kings led their warriors in battle but operated without bureaucratic encumbrance or overmuch mastery. As William Brandt aptly observed, in English aristocratic chronicles 'a fourteenth-century king and his barons are frequently described as though they were a war band left over from *Beowulf*'.[42] Of course, this point of view also appears in such classics of chivalric literature as *Roland* (several centuries earlier) and Malory's *Le Morte D'Arthur* (a century later).

If it is useful to consider the chivalric ethos as only a temporary and somewhat uneasy ally of kingship taking on sovereign power (with which chivalry would ultimately be incompatible), a qualification is important. We must keep in mind the complexity of motives and allegiances on the part of all involved. To acknowledge the pull of contradictory or even opposing ideas within royal and knightly minds is not to try to pin the label schizophrenic to crowns or iron helms, but simply to acknowledge the complex motives involved in the creation of states, in the achievement of a tolerable level of public order, and in the protection of aristocratic privilege. The sides do not divide neatly along class lines in a simplistic nineteenth-century sense, with kings and progressive bourgeoisie joining together to secure public order against reactionary feudal lords who practiced a decadent chivalry. In fact, the men who tried to order their lives by the code of chivalry were essential supporters of the emerging state; they had long appreciated its benefits, even when they resented its intrusiveness. Yet by the late Middle Ages these men were suffering troubling thoughts about the complex balance of costs and benefits associated with the state in comparison with the assertions of noble pride and privilege embodied in chivalry. Kings for their part were equally troubled by contradictory impulses. If the knightly layers of society helped make the state and simultaneously resisted some of its emerging claims, kings tried to restrain disorder and illegality and at the same time practised extra-legal violence on their own. In other words, there can be no thought that kings wearing white hats daily restrained feudal lords wearing black hats. Kings might look aside while their friends settled affairs in their own way. The popular mid-fourteenth

[42] Brandt, *The Shape of Medieval History*, 82.

century *Tale of Gamelyn* shows this expectation even on the part of the lesser gentry.[43] A king who would understand the hot-blooded settling of scores by proud men could act outside the law himself. J. E. A. Jolliffe argued at length that this was the very basis of strength for the Angevin kings of England in the twelfth century.[44] A similar combination of a prudent disregard for the violence of powerful supporters and a powerful use of violence (or at least a perversion of legal safeguards) against opponents is clearly in evidence in the later Middle Ages. Edward II not only did not take official notice of the outrageous behaviour of the Despensers, father and son, he also arranged 'stacked' commissions of oyer and terminer against his hated enemy Walter Langton, bishop of Coventry and Litchfield. He ordered his people to devise 'all the ways and means by which one can trouble the said bishop by the law and custom of our realm'. The phrase 'by the law and custom of our realm' could come easily to his mind, for it was used in a wide range of legal documents as the standard royal guarantee of fair practice: a matter was to be settled in accordance with the time-honoured practices of the common law. But here the meaning was inverted: do all possible damage under cover of law.[45]

As Alan Harding has argued in a broader vein, the by-products of more government and more law may not be internal peace and order but more disputes and violence.[46] Michael Clanchy, moreover, asserted that 'it might even be argued that royal power contributed to disorder and that the judicial authority of the crown was a public nuisance.'[47] Such warnings are salutary and remind us that royal actions might be as mixed in their results as royal impulses were mixed in their motivation. The attempt to impose order in a violent age would certainly be accompanied by violence; and if subjects put some specific royal programme to unexpected uses the disorder might be doubled. The oyer and terminer experiment carried out in England across the late thirteenth century and first half of the fourteenth century is a sobering case in point.

43 Kaeuper, 'Law and Order', 780-1.

44 Jolliffe, *Angevin Kingship*.

45 Discussed in Kaeuper, 'Law and Order', 780-1.

46 Harding, 'Plaints and Bills in the History of English Law', 69.

47 Clanchy, 'Law, Government, and Society', 78.

Yet Clanchy's comment that royal action could be a source of disorder need not be distorted into an assertion that it always was. On both sides of the Channel royal action for public order took two forms: the crown provided courts and procedures to secure justice and order; and, with varying degress of vigour, it prosecuted those who acted with extra-legal violence. Royal provision of courts and judicial mechanisms for the resolution of disputes seems important, even if we realize that such agencies long supplemented rather than replaced violent self-help, and sometimes contributed to the problem itself. These agencies were much used and they have been much studied. But what demands our attention is the other side of the royal effort, the suppression of knightly violence. This has received much less attention and almost none in a comparative vein.

How well English or French kings could control the violent tendencies of the privileged ranks of society turned not merely on a set of specific late thirteenth- and fourteenth-century judicial measures, but on the overall capacity attained by the crown in either country, the support it enjoyed, the resources it commanded, the effectiveness with which these elements were combined in the formula of governance. Since the English crown enjoyed a distinct head start in securing effective royal power, the formula might be expected to produce more royal action and a concomitant increase in the benefits of public order in England. Three related topics—tournament, private fortifications, and private war—will provide the basis for a specific comparison of English and French royal policies and their results.

1. TOURNAMENTS

A sense of tournament as a substitute for real warfare, and thus as a harmless sport, even as a helpful cathartic for knightly energy, might be suggested by the greater store of information available for fifteenth-century tournaments and perhaps especially by the many contemporary illustrations which present them to us in vivid form. But in the late thirteenth and early fourteenth centuries the tournament was probably much closer to its primitive form than to this fifteenth-century ritual. And in its primitive form the twelfth-century tournament had differed little from actual warfare; it particularly resembled the private wars so prevalent among the lords of France.[48] As Noel Denholm-Young stated, the tournament 'from A.D. 1150 to 1350 . . . is for the most part not a matter of individual jousting, but a mass-meeting of side against side, resulting in a *mêlée* which differed little from real war.' Baronial households were put on a war footing for tournaments, with different numbers of retainers specified 'in time of peace' and 'in times of War and for Tourney'. Moreover, early tourneys employed footsoldiers and even archers (although this was considered to be in poor taste) and the combatants roamed over the countryside, heightening the parallel with war. In England tournaments seem less mobile by the reign of Edward I and were less likely to be held in open countryside between two towns, but even in England the *mêlée* lasted well into the fourteenth century.[49]

That the church frequently condemned tournament will cause little surprise. Bishops and popes denounced the sport as wanton violence, as a diversion from crusading zeal, as a source of immorality (once ladies began to attend and the element of pageant and party increased). But even kings who saw themselves as leaders of chivalric society showed mixed reactions, mirroring their ambiguities about the chivalric code in general. Tournaments could be defended as useful practice for war and even for the specific warfare of crusade urged by churchmen. Pierre du Bois's treatise defending chivalry, written at the behest of Philip IV, used that approach, among others.[50] But as faithful sons of Mother Church, kings could take the opposite line, usually pressed vigorously by ecclesiastics, and argue that tournament was an immoral sport and a diversion from the proper high

[48] See Dubois, *Les Asseurements au XIIIe siècle*, 54-5. Malcolm Vale cites the example of a tournament held on the frontier between the counties of Burgundy and Nevers in 1172, which substituted for private war, *War and Chivalry*, 68. In the tournament at Chalons in 1273 the participants got so badly out of hand that the affair became known as 'the little war of Chalons'. Juliet Vale cites sources in *Edward III and Chivalry* (p. 104 n. 152) and analyses the north-western European setting for tournaments and chivalric *festes* in ch. 1 and 2 of this book. Maurice Keen discusses the tournament in detail in *Chivalry* (ch. 5).

[49] Denholm-Young, 'The Tournament in the Thirteenth Century', 260, 263.

[50] Langlois, 'Un mémoire inédit de Pierre du Bois'.

function of the knightly *ordo*. Some royal prohibitions might be motivated by more pragmatic considerations; kings stated that tournaments too often wasted in sport the men and even more often the horses needed for the serious business of warfare directed by the crown. In a tournament prohibition issued in 1314 Philip IV stated that he was acting 'considerans la grant destruction et mortalité de chevaux, et accunes fois de personnes, qui par les tournoyemens et les joustes sont avenuz souvent en notre Royaume . . .'.[51]

But the concern for public order was an important motive standing behind both ecclesiastical and royal condemnation and prohibition. 'The real bedrock basis of the church's condemnations . . . and the original mainspring of the papal prohibitions, was the encouragement that they gave to the turbulent spirit of secular knighthood in which the ecclesiastical authorities had long seen a direct threat to the good ordering of Christendom, and which led to homicide, destruction, and disorder. . . . The same objection . . . underlay the objection to tournaments of secular royal authorities.'[52] Like the military manœuvres of nineteenth-century nation-states, medieval tournaments could easily take on great political significance as a cover for anti-royal activity. In England, movements against John, Henry III, and Edward II all worked behind the rich and opaque screen of the tournament.[53] Even the young Edward III, who would become their great patron, issued a 1329 tournament prohibition 'as the king, who is going to parts beyond sea, wishes his peace to be firmly observed in his absence, and he considers that his peace may easily be broken by assemblies of men-at-arms during his absence.'[54] In short, as much as kings loved them, tournaments too easily tended to reverse the balance kings wanted between internal peace and the vigorous smiting of enemies beyond the borders of a peaceful realm, whether these enemies were pagans or merely misguided Christians.

But the problem was not simply that rulers were caught between the occasional demands of kingship and a personal love of tournaments. The relationship between kingship and

[51] *Ordonnances des roys de France*, i. 529.

[52] Keen, *Chivalry*, 96.

[53] Denholm-Young, 'The Tournament in the Thirteenth Century', 240-68.

[54] *CCR 1327-1330*, 544-5.

tournament reveals something very close to a contradiction in the expectations which both rulers and subjects focused on medieval governments. For medieval kings ruled kingdoms which were at once law states and war states, and the force required for the latter vastly complicated the task of securing the former. The chivalric classes who formed the army and followed the king's banners in war were much more reluctant to follow his precepts about order at home. The chivalric code reinforced other realities of political life. Taxation at a level which would have supported a paid force was a thought almost as offensive to lords and knights as any thought that a monopoly of the means of violence belonged of right to the king. English tournament prohibitions show the problem with particular force. On 18 June 1320, Edward II by his letters close ordered all sheriffs of England:

to cause proclamation to be made forbidding any earl, baron, knight, or other from tourneying, etc. or making assemblies in breach of the peace at present, whilst the king is absent from the realm, and to attach by their bodies any persons doing so, so that he have them before the king in fifteen days from Michaelmas to answer to the king, certifying the king of those thus attached and the circumstances of such attachment. The king has ordered his justices who hold pleas before him to proceed against and punish the persons so attached according to the sheriffs' certificate.[55]

On the same date, and entered just above this mandate on the close roll, is the following order, sent to the justices to take assizes, juries, and certificates in all counties of England:

Order to cause proclamation to be made at each of their sessions prohibiting anyone from presuming to come armed before them, or from inflicting damage or hindrance upon the parties, jurors, or others there or coming to the place of their sessions or returning thence, under pain of forfeiting all that they may forfeit, and to punish any persons doing so, as the king is given to understand that many persons come armed before his justices, and so threaten the king's ministers, the parties suing, jurors, and others, both in the presence of the justices and on their way to the sessions, that the parties, juries, and others desist from the execution of their office. The king has ordered the sheriff of that county to be intendent to them in executing the premises and to cause like proclamation to be made in such places as he shall think fit, and to attach by their bodies all persons whom he shall find out of the presence of the

[55] *CCR 1318-1323*, 243.

justices contravening the proclamation, so that he have them before the king in fifteen days from Michaelmas to be punished according to law and custom. The king wills that they shall enquire at the beginning of their sessions of the sheriff if he have executed the premises, and that they shall give their counsel to the sheriff if he need it.[56]

A similarly informative conjuncture of letters appears ten years later. On 12 July 1330, Edward III sent his letters close to all sheriffs, ordering them:

to cause proclamation to be made prohibiting anyone, under pain of forfeiture, from making proclamations of tournaments, etc., or from tourneying, jousting, seeking adventures, etc., or doing any feat of arms without the king's special licence, and to arrest and imprison any found doing so, with their horses, arms, and equipments, certifying the king of their names, as the king is given to understand that certain persons make proclamation of tournaments, etc., notwithstanding the king's preceding proclamation for knights and men to arm themselves.[57]

The 'preceding proclamation' on the roll, likewise sent to all sheriffs, takes a very different tone:

Order to cause proclamation to be made that all knights and others able to bear arms shall prepare themselves with horses and arms as speedily as possible, each according to his estate and the quantity and value of his lands, goods, and chattels, so that they shall be ready to come to the king or to those whom he shall appoint with all their power summoned, to set out against certain contrariants and rebels who lately withdrew secretly from the realm, and who have assembled a multitude of armed men in parts beyond the sea and have prepared ships of war and many other things, and who propose entering the realm to aggrieve the king and his people[58]

In 1348 the two concerns, and the two sets of letters, were joined in a single directive to all sheriffs:

Order, upon sight of these presents, to cause proclamation to be made that no one shall tourney, joust, or seek adventures or do other deeds of arms upon pain of imprisonment and the forfeiture of his horses, arms, and all other things, but that everyone of that bailiwick shall provide himself with arms befitting his estate and prepare himself for the defence of the realm against the malice of the king's adversaries of France, as the

56 Ibid. 242.
57 *CCR 1330-1333*, 147.
58 Ibid.

truce between the king and those adversaries has recently expired, and the king wishes to provide for the defence of the realm. If the sheriff finds any disobeying the proclamation, he shall take and imprison them and take their horses, armour, equipments, and other things into the king's hands, as forfeit to him, to be kept until further order, certifying the king of the names of those arrested, of the value of the horses etc. and of all his action in the matter.[59]

Read alongside the preambles to statutes and the clauses of the coronation oath in which the king promises to provide peace and justice, these prohibitions go a long way toward explaining the king's seemingly shifting views on the score of the chivalric code in general and on tournament in particular. Kings walked a tightrope in trying to require the privileged classes to maintain arms, to keep up skill in using them, and to stand ready to smite enemies foreign or domestic, while simultaneously insisting they not use those arms in ways appealing to haughty men with a fistful of private feuds easily remembered while riding armed to a tournament.

From the beginning the English crown had set itself the task of regulating the tournament in the linked interests of royal authority and public order. Though no specific edict survives from his reign, Henry II may have banned tournaments as part of a more general programme to restore order after the troubles of Stephen's reign.[60] For Henry's son, Richard I, an ordinance of 1194 has survived. Characteristically, Richard found a means to make a profit, and sold licences at hefty fees to knights wishing to tourney; but the public order concern is also present, for pairs of knights and clerks were detailed not only to collect the licence fees, but to administer an oath to keep the peace and not to pursue feuds in the lists.[61] 'The reduction of bloodshed and restraint

[59] *CCR 1346-1349*, 549.

[60] R. H. C. Davis notes that in 1142 King Stephen had to turn aside from a planned course of action 'to prevent a tournament (which could early have become a war) between William d'Aumale Earl of York and Count Alan of Brittany . . .'; *King Stephen*, 70. See Richard Barber's comment on Henry II, *The Knight and Chivalry*, p. 183.

[61] *Foedera*, i. 65; Barber, *The Knight and Chivalry*, 183-4. Charles R. Young gives a fascinating account of the troubles Abbot Samson of Bury St Edmunds had with a band of about eighty young men who had a royal licence but who were none the less forbidden by Samson from holding their tournament near Bury St Edmunds (*Hubert Walter*, 124).

upon the rancours which were so easily engendered in the heat of affray', Maurice Keen notes, 'were clearly among the principal objects of the rules of tournaments which were drawn up by the English kings Richard I and Edward I.'[62] Across the thirteenth century scores, perhaps hundreds[63] of formal prohibitions of tournaments, couched either in specific or general terms, are recorded on the rolls of chancery. A king like Henry III who was not a knight by temperament may have prohibited more regularly than his son, and in times of great political stress even a patron of tournaments could issue a flurry of prohibitions. But though the personalities of the king changed from reign to reign, and the political temperature rose and fell dramatically, the basic English royal policy was consistent. Kings assumed the role of patron of chivalry when they could, prohibited tournaments when they appeared in any sense dangerous, and always reminded their subjects that they did hold superior rights in the matter.

Obviously the many prohibitions were far from universally obeyed. But the policy may not have been quite so toothless as is sometimes assumed. Fierce language about forfeiture cannot be itself entered as proof, since tough talk in medieval edicts often stands in inverse proportion to actual enforcement; repeated prohibitions can themselves be evidence of a lack of compliance. But equally interesting are the administrative orders which sometimes follow a prohibition of some planned tournament and empower king's serjeants at arms to arrest offenders and to supervise the sheriffs, who had proved unreliable. Moreover, at least some men thought it wise to obtain licences to hold tournaments, and there are records of a few other men, who did not, buying pardons or going to prison.[64]

Royal policy in England was not all prohibition and threat, even before the open campaign by which English and French kings founded royal orders. Not only did Edward I apparently toy

[62] Keen, *Chivalry*, 86.

[63] Denholm-Young counted about 100 in 1216-74, 'The Tournament in the Thirteenth Century', 245-6, and I have read at least another hundred in the following three reigns.

[64] Id., *The Country Gentry in the Fourteenth Century*, 155. For licences see *CPR 1323-1327*, 133, 136; *CFR 1343-1345*, 196. For pardons, see *CPR 1317-1321*, 437 (2 instances). For the action of royal sergeants at arms see *CPR 1307-1313*, 139, 521; *CPR 1313-1317*, 16, 67, 604; *CPR 1317-1321*, 258, 410; *CPR 1327-1330*, 93; *CPR 1330-1334*, 138.

with the idea of a distinctly royal chivalry half a century before his grandson created the Garter, even earlier he seems to have provided an essentially royal, if rudimentary, organization for tournament in England. Probably in 1267, at a time when the Barons War had ended and the role of the lord Edward increased in his father's regime, a royal provision in answer to a petition of earls, barons, and knights established rules for tournaments, penalties for violators, and a supervising committee of four (the Lord Edward, his brother Edmund of Lancaster, and two earls, Gilbert de Clare and William de Valence). In Edward's advanced age, a request to revive this degree of organization and regulation produced the statute of 1292, known as the *Statuta Armorum*; it aimed especially at controlling the violence of squires who attended tournaments in their lord's train, and it specified the blunted weapons of the tournament *à plaisance*, rather than the true weapons of war used in the tournament *à outrance*. Although the workings of this regulation remain vague and uncertain, to Denholm-Young what mattered was the royal role: 'it is impossible to doubt that the patronage and presence of the king, no less than the rules with which he was associated, had a moderating influence on later thirteenth-century tournaments . . . .'[65] F. M. Powicke's view was more gloomy. He thought Edward:

> was conscious of the danger latent in the mingling of the passion for tournaments with the disorderly impulses to self-help, for in his time he had drunk the heady mixture himself. In his later years the danger was serious. . . . Edward had done his best to regulate tournaments and to put down illicit assemblies of men in arms, but without much success. They could not be civilized by order. Indeed, closer scrutiny might well establish the fact that in the younger generation which came to power in political immaturity after his death, the seeds of later evils were sown; and that the Scottish wars had hastened their growth.[66]

Whatever the effectiveness of royal regulation, the stream of English prohibitions dried to a trickle and disappeared by the mid-fourteenth century. In Denholm-Young's view 'especially during the years between Crécy and Poitiers (1346-56), with the founding of the Order of the Garter, tournaments became,

[65] Denholm-Young, 'The Tournament in the Thirteenth Century', 252, 257-64.

[66] Powicke, *The Thirteenth Century*, 516.

particularly in the form of the Round Table, a function of the monarchy. . . . The tournament was in fact one of the more obvious and important ways in which Edward III co-operated with his magnates. If they wanted tournaments, so did the king. . . .'[67]

Had the dangers to public order disappeared? An argument could be made that tournaments had become less disruptive occasions. Though changing forms are often difficult to date with precision, the mid-fourteenth century tournament seems more a decorative social occasion than a substitute for war. At the same time, according to Denholm-Young, successful English tactics on the battlefield, combining archers with knights who often fought on foot, were much less an extension of the tournament and its lessons than was true even half a century earlier. 'To levy war against the king, a few hundred lances would no longer suffice', as Denholm-Young observes. 'Archers, light cavalry and siege engines would be required and for them the tournament provided no scope.'[68] There is considerable force in this argument, yet it should not be pressed too far. If tournaments had been called 'schools of prowess' in the twelfth century they were even in the late fourteenth century still thought to be 'where the school and study of arms is.' There men learned not only the specific techniques of fighting (which over time did become more distant from battlefield practice), but also developed the co-operation of a group of warriors in action; indeed, at tournaments they learned the whole range of attitudes essential to the chivalric life.[69] A king who wished to keep a hand on the reins of power would still do well to watch tournaments closely. If he could not prohibit, he had better play the role of patron.

The fact seems to be that Edward III knew he could not prohibit and prudently gave up the effort. However much we may admire the skill and political realism which allowed Edward to die peacefully in his own bed, in contrast to his father's fate, we must recognize that his kingship was of a less vigorous and forceful sort than that of Edward I, more compromising and accommodating

[67] Denholm-Young, *The Country Gentry in the Fourteenth Century*, ch. 6; see esp. 140-1.

[68] Ibid.

[69] Keen, *Chivalry*, 99, quot. a statement made by Ralph Ferrers in the Court of the Constable of England. See also the comments of Vale, *Edward III and Chivalry*, 59 and Vale, *War and Chivalry*, 63-87.

with the chivalric classes of the realm. In short, if the tournament seems to have become more civilized, even more removed from the warfare of the day, it remains equally important that English kingship eased the kinds of pressures which had led to past confrontations, and the seeming royal ambivalence over tournament vanished.

French royal policy regarding tournaments, as we have seen, involved the same ambivalences as the English, but the French government was even less able to act on its regulatory impulses; in fact, it seems longer and more completely to have followed the alterations of royal personality, rather than firm policy. Regulation apparently begins with St Louis. Information is sparse, but a chronicler relates that on learning of Christian reverses in the Holy Land, Louis prohibited tournaments for two years in 1260.[70] Even earlier, as shown by the fragment of an *enquête*, St Louis had accused the sire de Nesle of summoning the men of the chapter of Noyen for a *chevauchée* and forcing them to go to a place near Beulieu to make lists and dig ditches in preparation for a tournament.[71] But St Louis's son loved tournament and wavered between official toleration and condemnation. Chroniclers depict Philip III encouraging his knights, galloping across the field of action, showing his largesse by gifts of horses to his unhorsed followers.[72] His father's example and the urging of churchmen led to a prohibition in 1278 intended to aid preparations for crusade. As Juliet Vale has argued, this prohibition apparently produced some effects. Chivalric festivities held that year at Lettem (in Picardy near the Artois border) were limited to activities which could not technically be called tournament: there was jousting with blunted lances but no mêlée.[73] However, when the crusade which occasioned the ban was not launched, the volume of knightly grumbling rose. Three tournaments a year were authorized and then complete licence was given. Only after a great tournament in 1279 in which his

[70] Du Cange, *Glossarium*, x. 127. General background is provided by Jordan, *Louis IX and the Challenge of the Crusade*, 203-4.

[71] *Actes* 233A; Ducoudray, *Les Origines du Parlement de Paris*, 376-7.

[72] Langlois, *Le Règne de Philippe III le Hardi*, 196.

[73] Vale, *Edward III and Chivalry*, 12-13. She even suggests that the proliferation of alternative terms for knightly sport so apparent in the documents of the period, reflects a care formally to avoid violation of the prohibitions.

son was so battered on his helmet as to remain an imbecile for life did Philip III return to prohibition; in the Pentecost parlement of 1280 all tournaments were prohibited until the following Easter.[74] But in the following year even the pope, Martin IV, had to recognize that customs were stronger than laws and the strict royal policy seems to have been relaxed.[75]

A consistent policy of prohibition appears only with Philip the Fair, although the justification for such a poiicy shifted frequently. Eight general or specific prohibitions or supplementary directives appear in the *ordonnances* from his reign. In the early years Philip justified prohibitions by the need to concentrate warlike energy in the current royal campaign; though the enemy is not specified, the message in the ordinance of Tousaint (1296) sent to the *bailli* of Auvergne, the order of 5 October 1304 to all *baillis*, that of 13 April 1304 sent to the *bailli* of Sens, and that sent to the *bailli* of Vermandois in 1305 is that the king's war against the English or the Flemish takes precedent over sport.[76] At the end of his reign in an ordinance of 5 October 1314, Philip returned to this theme and grandly combined the requirements of his wars with reminders that Holy Church prohibited tournaments.[77] An order (12 December 1312) to the guardians of Lyon was based on Philip's desire to make the knighting of his sons a great occasion; all other tournaments throughout the realm, at which men might steal the king's thunder by knighting eligible young men and especially the king's wards, were prohibited.[78] Even more interesting is the 30 December 1311 general prohibition. The king states that his reasons for outlawing tournaments, assemblies in arms, and the carrying of offensive arms are to ensure the peace of his kingdom: 'Periculum et incommodis quae ex torneamentis, congretationibus armatorum, et armorum portationibus in diversis regni nostri partibus hactenus provenisse noscuntur, obviare volentes, ac super hoc prorsus nostro tempore prout ex offici nostri debito tenemur, salubriter

[74] *Les Olim*, ii. 161; *Actes* 2292; Ducoudray, *Les Origines du Parlement de Paris* 377; Langlois, *Le Règne de Philippe III le Hardi*, 199.

[75] Ibid.

[76] *Ordonnances des roys de France*, i. 329 (1296); 420 (gen. prohibition, 1304); 421-2 (Sens, 1304); 426 (Auvergne, 1304); 434-5 (Vermandois, 1305).

[77] *Ordonnances des roys de France*, i. 539-40.

[78] *Ibid*. 509-10.

providere. . . .' This prohibition, which significantly links tournament with the offence of *port d'armes* (discussed below), was to last at the king's will.[79]

As is true in other matters affecting public order, Philip the Fair's policy on tournaments was carried on by his second son, Philip V. In an elaborate order sent to twelve *baillis* on 1 April 1316, he prohibited tournaments throughout the realm during his pleasure; he legitimized this order by combining the need to guard the peace and security of the realm, to provide better justice, with the argument based on crusade.[80] Philip's nineteenth-century biographer thought that the order must have been observed because it was not repeated and since the chroniclers, fond of writing about tournaments, mention none later in the reign.[81] Although the series of frequent French regulations does stop with this order,[82] explanations other than the disappearance of tournament may stand behind the change. A suggestion that royal vigour and interest in public order waned in this reign will not be convincing in view of Philip's other policies. In fact, the very energy of Philip's engagement with measures to secure order could explain the end of the tournament regulation. Governmental energies may simply have been channelled in other directions as the king and his advisers acted against *chevauchée* and *port d'armes* (mentioned with tournament in Philip the Fair's ordinance of 1316) and against much else relating to private war.

Were the prohibitions promulgated by Philip IV and Philip V in stern and sweeping phrases at all effective? One indication that they were not comes from the *ordonnances* and *mandements* themselves, which often mention in outraged tones the violations that occasioned the present orders. Even more significant is the lack of any cases concerning violations of the regulations brought before the Parlement of Paris. 'Les registres du Parlement', Ducoudray observed concisely, 'ne mentionnent les tournois que

[79] Printed in Du Cange, *Glossarium*, x. 180-1.

[80] *Ordonnances des roys de France*, i. 643-4.

[81] Lehuguer, *Histoire de Philippe le Long*, ii. 310-11.

[82] Elizabeth A. R. Brown cites a prohibition of 30 Sept. 1334, issued when Philip VI wanted no interference with his planned crusade: 'Customary Aids and Royal Fiscal Policy', 244 n. 180.

par les Ordonnances qui les interdisent.'[83] That the crown repeatedly condemned tournaments may have had some dampening effect on knightly enthusiasm, but against this likelihood must be set the apparent lack of vigorous enforcement of the regulation policy. The English kings tried earlier than the French to regulate tournament, and their precocious administrative capacity working in a relatively small land allowed them to act more often and apparently with occasional vigour which may have been marginally effective. But Pope Martin IV seems to have been correct; on both sides of the Channel one could apply his dictum that customs were stronger than laws.[84]

2. PRIVATE FORTIFICATION

At first glance the same point seems applicable to royal regulation of castle-building in both England and France. The existence of private fortifications, which could act as bases for feuding, disorder, and brigandage, was clearly not closely controlled by the royal licences granted by the king in England or by the king and great feudatories in France. Some licences were granted after the fact, and seem to describe standing structures rather than a master mason's plan; some castles were obviously built without any authorization by king or duke or other superior authority. But perhaps the most telling fact is the absence of any evidence of licence requests denied. Regulation which misses many castles, licenses others only after they are built, and never says no cannot be considered a model of stern efficiency. The verdict seems to hold true for either side of the Channel. But in fact the relationship between kings and their subjects' fortifications is a good deal more complex than such a hasty analysis would indicate, and a closer look may reveal significant differences between English and French royal policies.[85] The obviously close

[83] Ducoudray, *Les Origines du Parlement de Paris*, 378. I found only one case, an *arrêt* of 4 Dec. 1305, giving the king cognizance over a mêlée fought in a grange of the Abbey of St-Victor of Paris at Attainville in the *bailliage* of Senlis; *Actes* 3265.

[84] Langlois, *Le Règne de Philippe III le Hardi*, 199.

[85] I am indebted to Dr Charles L. H. Coulson who provided me with a copy of his unpublished Ph.D. diss.: 'Seignorial Fortresses'. The arguments and

interrelationship of castles, the growth of royal power, and the evolution of feudal relationships—complex processes following divergent courses and timetables in England and France—might lead us to expect differences in crown policy towards fortification.

As Carolingian power collapsed under the pressure of foreign invasion and civil war, the royal monopoly on fortification disappeared; along with other regalian rights, this power passed first into the hands of counts, bishops, and abbots,[86] and finally came down to the yet rougher hands of the *seigneurs chatelains* of the eleventh century. Although the Edict of Pistes, 864, still claimed central government initiative in fortification, the actual situation was changing so rapidly that by the end of the century Carolingian kings had to accept private fortification and even came to praise the public spirit of lords who undertook fortification projects. In fact they needed little encouragement. The result of royal weakness and the fragmentation of political authority was a new type of fortress no less than a new scheme of defence. Across what would become France the new motte and bailey castles, built simply but effectively of wood and earth, combining residence, fort, and centre of seigneurial administration, sprouted like mushrooms.[87]

What Marc Bloch might have termed one of the 'paper wars of historians' has been fought over the relationship of these early French castles to the origins of Capetian kingship. Nineteenth-century historians and their predecessors emphasized the private initiative of the castle-builders, their absolute independence from any royal or even ducal or comital authorization. In fact, they saw the castles as anti-royal and as a major cause of the 'feudal anarchy' which so troubled the early Capetian reigns. Some recent scholarship has emphasized instead the continuity of a theory of fortification linked with a conception of public power or at least of regalian right legitimately exercised by kings or

references of this work have been most helpful. He has published some of his findings in 'Rendability and Castellation in Medieval France'. For another broad survey of French castles see Fournier, *Le Château dans la France médiévale*. The basic work for England is Colvin (ed.), *The History of the King's Works*.

86 Fournier, *Le Château dans la France médiévale* 53-9; Coulson, 'Seignorial Fortresses', 7-10.

87 Fournier, *Le Château dans la France médiévale* 65-149; Coulson, 'Seignorial Fortresses', 4-86.

territorial princes of some sort—dukes, counts, bishops, or abbots.[88] A picture of fortifications on the whole authorized by some legitimate power as an aspect of a scheme of public defence is thus substituted for the picture of feudal anarchy manifested in a rash of private castles.

To debate the issue of public power and castles in extreme terms comes perilously close to arguing whether a glass is half full or half empty. Castles, like feudalism, were a result of the collapse of Carolingian royal authority and yet became an important structural element in the new political units built first at the ducal or comital and then at the royal level. The early Capetians maintained an inherited ideal of royal initiative in fortifying for the public benefit, but they neither inherited nor quickly acquired the power to translate the ideal into reality. 'D'une manière générale', Gabriel Fournier observes, 'les souverains, les princes, les seigneurs désireux d'imposer leurs droits en matière de fortification ne réussirent à les faire respecter qu'en recourant à la force.'[89] Across the entire eleventh century the early Capetians had to struggle with the unauthorized and hostile castles raised by even petty lords in the royal domain. The struggles of Louis le Gros with such lords as Hugh de Puiset or Thomas de Marle are cases in point.[90] Eleventh- and twelfth-century dukes of Normandy and counts of Anjou did better, both in building their own fortifications and in smashing those of their opponents, but even in these feudal mini-states the determination of duke or count was sometimes matched by a sense of independence on the part of seigneurs. In a minority or civil war, a crop of illicit or adulterine castles quickly germinated. These fortresses were the bane of rulers building political units. Fortresses held by vassals with a recognized place in an emerging pattern of feudal relationships were one thing; a lord might have to restrain a vassal and keep a close watch against his tendency to claim complete independence, but a vassal had an accepted place and role. Independent newcomers trying to carve out new jurisdictions based on new fortifications were another thing altogether.[91]

[88] Discussed by Fournier, *Le Château dans la France médiévale* 100-8; Coulson, 'Seignorial Fortresses', *passim*; see esp., 360 n. 1.

[89] Fournier, *Le Château dans la France médiévale* 104.

[90] Luchaire, *Louis VI le Gros*, lxv ff.

[91] See for example the comments of Douglas on eleventh-century Normandy, *William the Conqueror*, 42, 141-2. For gen. discussion, see Fournier, *Le*

To emphasize the dependent status of a vassal and to remind him of the ultimate control of superior lordship over castles, French lords often required vassals to declare castles under their control 'jurable and rendable.[92] The first term refers to an oath assuring a lord that the castle would not be used to his harm; the second to an understanding that he could take the castle into his temporary control whenever he required it, whether he came with a great host or a token force to demand his right. Charles Coulson has argued that kings and great feudatories showed no principled animosity to castles, but rather accepted them as a part of a scheme of delegated responsibilities, provided that the fortresses were rendable and jurable. Thus, in his view, there was 'virtually no difference between a fortress in domain and one alienated rendably in fief.'[93] As the Capetians built their power and expanded their domain they insured royal control over castles by the inexpensive but efficient device of rendability. Philip Augustus followed this policy after his conquest of Normandy and Touraine; Louis VIII followed the same policy as he conquered the Poitou. 'The Capetian monarchy was well-served by fortress customs', Coulson concludes, 'which had played some part in the reconstruction of monarchic power on feudal bases at every stage. . . .'[94]

By the second half of the thirteenth century the French crown, acting through the emerging Parlement, expanded its castle policy in a significant direction. Castles were important not only as fortifications but as highly visible symbols of power and noble status. Thus, the Parlement not only continued enforcing the royal policy of prohibiting building at certain sites[95] it also frequently punished a lord guilty of some offence by dismantling some part of his castle.[96] From St Louis to the opening years of

Château dans la France médiévale 101-8, and Coulson, 'Seignorial Fortresses', 83-4.

[92] The following draws on Coulson, 'Seignorial Fortresses' and id., 'Rendability and Castellation in Medieval France'.

[93] Coulson, 'Seignorial Fortresses', 326.

[94] Ibid. 358.

[95] See ibid., app. C. For an example of an order to raze a *maison forte* erected without permission of the seigneur of the chatellany of Brussiere, see *Actes* 3730.

[96] Many of the following cases are discussed in Coulson, 'Seignorial Fortresses', 431-6.

the Hundred Years War a series of *arrêts* illustrates this simultaneous assertion of royal supremacy over fortification and punishment of erring lords. Under Louis IX, Guillaume Purnele, a knight who had built a fortified dwelling without licence of his feudal superior, the lord of Méréville, was sentenced to have the *maison forte* demolished; when a first order in 1266 was not sufficient, a second order instructed the bailli to 'slight' the two remaining towers (i.e. to render them indefensible) in order to demonstrate to all the execution of the verdict.[97] In 1271 a bailiff of the count of Rhodez and some accomplices attacked a priest and others; they killed the priest as he said mass (the host rolled on the ground), and then took refuge in the castle of Torsac where they withstood a siege by the king's men. Parlement ordered the castle to be razed.[98] In 1283 the levelling of the castle of Chaumontet, held of the archbishop of Lyons, was ordered as punishment for its lord's crimes which the archbishop had failed to check.[99] In 1306 the castle of Aurose was to be destroyed to punish its lord's invasion of a priory.[100] In the same year a knight who had attacked a royal serjeant suffered the destruction of the fortified portion of his manor.[101] Three judgements against the violence of Geoffrey de Paris in 1309 progressed from fines to the razing of his castle of Montfort.[102] On the eve of the Hundred Years War, Parlement (confirming a sentence of the seneschal of Toulouse) ordered the destruction of the fortress of Stilhano as further punishment of men already banished for murdering a king's *bayle*.[103]

Parlement also could make its point by sentences short of total demolition. Removal of castle gates would symbolically destroy a castle, and the lesson could be made even more clear if the unhinged gates were burned in a public place.[104] This was part of the sentence handed down against the sire de Mailly in 1290, for

[97] *Actes* 1032.

[98] *Actes* 1786.

[99] *Actes*, *Essai de restitution*, 523.

[100] *Actes* 3351. Coulson, 'Seignorial Fortresses', 432 notes he was pardoned in 1310 and allowed to rebuild.

[101] *Actes* 3338.

[102] *Actes* 3564, 3607, 3608.

[103] *Actes*, 2nd ser. 1397 (Dec. 1335).

[104] The policy was also followed in the courts of *baillis* and *sénéchaux*. See for example *Actes* 6985 (1322).

making a *chevauchée*;[105] it was the punishment imposed on the *coseigneurs* and inhabitants of the castle of Capdenac in 1321, for 'rebellions, injuries, violences, and excesses' against the *viguier* (the subordinate of the seneschal) and royal judge of Figeac.[106] Sometimes the length of time the gateway was to remain without gates was specified,[107] sometimes they were not to be replaced without royal permission, as was ordered in a judgement against the count of Hainaut in 1292;[108] in the judgement against the coseigneurs of Capdenac the main gate was ordered to be destroyed forever.[109]

The exigencies of the Hundred Years War quickly forced the French crown to a new level of action regarding fortresses and changed the focus from internal order to security against the threat from abroad.[110] The new sense of urgency is indirectly reflected in clauses of two ordinances issued at the beginning of the war. Philip VI assured the nobles of Aquitaine that their fortresses would remain safely in their own hands, unless seized or slighted as part of a proper judicial sentence.[111] In a long ordinance of about the same time the king promised that he would acquire noble fortresses only as required 'pro securitate regni nostri et tuitione ipsius' and that he would pay a suitable compensation for any fortresses thus taken for defence of the realm.[112]

In the great crisis after the defeat at Poitiers, the regent ordered his regional captains to inspect all fortresses to ensure their readiness; they were to replace any owners who refused to put their fortresses in a state of defence with local royal commanders; they were to provision and guard the fortress at the owner's expense; but if the cost of the work could not be recovered, they were to demolish the fortress lest it fall into enemy hands and

105 *Actes* 2674.

106 *Actes* 6291.

107 *Actes* 3149.

108 *Actes* 2813. Coulson notes similar royal treatment of gallows and dovecotes, which also had symbolic importance, 'Seignorial Fortresses', 338, 423, 435.

109 *Actes* 6291.

110 Coulson, 'Seignorial Fortresses', 449-50.

111 *Ordonnances des roys de France*, ii. 62, art. 2. The date of this ordinance has been corrected by Raymond Cazelles, 'La Réglementation royale'.

112 *Ordonnances des roys de France*, ii. 128, art. 33.

become a base for hostile operations.[113] This monarchical control was not a merely theoretical scheme.[114] Surviving evidence from an inquest held in the *bailliage* of Melun shows that in one area of 1,200 square kilometres there were six castles, four fortified houses, five towers, twelve forts, and twenty-eight fortified churches; there was a fortification, on average, for every 20-5 square kilometres. Four of these, two forts and two fortified churches, were considered untenable and were destroyed by order of royal agents.[115] Four years later the statement of royal policy was unambiguous:

> Ad nos qui regnum nostrum pure a Deo sine alio superiore tenemus solus et insolidus super omnes alios pertinet protectio et defensio regni nostri et habitantium in eodum, modus etiam resistendi et ordinatio querriandi seu guerram inimicis nostris et regni nostri faciendi; ad nos etiam per consequens pertinet constructio et defensio fortaliciorum in regno nostro solus et insolidus.[116]

But these ringing assertions cannot be taken at face value. Royal initiative of this sort was limited by the competence of regular officials and wartime commanders. A great deal still depended on seigneurs and towns; Brittany and Flanders in the north, and most of the great lords of the south, were left to their own initiatives, and at least some level of resistance to crown action may have been general.[117] Even where kings put in their own castellans they had to face the problem of ensuring their loyalty; in a time of general insecurity the most vigorous castellans might come to view the fortresses in their guard as truly their own and force the royal council to consider some 'delicate political options.'[118]

Thus, French castle policy can be seen as an integrated aspect of the gradual achievement of royal power over a broad spectrum, showing something like the same accomplishment and limitation, and often working through the same channels. Once the early

113 *Ordonnances des roys de France*, iii. 219-32.

114 Contamine, *Guerre, état, et société*, 6-11; Timbal, *La Guerre de cent ans*, 144-9, 297.

115 Contamine, *Guerre, état, et société*, 9-10.

116 Quot.: Contamine in French, with Latin in n.; ibid. 8.

117 Ibid. 10-11.

118 Timbal, *La Guerre de cent ans*, 119-27; the quot. is taken from p. 127. Similar problems were experienced by seigneurial chatelains, *ibid.* 131-40.

Capetians could count themselves truly masters of their own small domain, having reduced the independence and the fortresses of resisting lords, they began to expand that domain dramatically. But to keep in repair and garrison the hundreds of fortresses great and small that passed into their hands would have been as impossible as ruling all of their territories directly from Paris.[119] The revenues and the bureaucracy were lacking and provincial sensibilities would have been outraged had the crown made the attempt. Yet guard of castles represented the extreme instance of the king's constant problem, that of delegating authority without losing control. Over the vastness of France the Capetians followed the prudent policy of granting the castles by rendable and jurable tenure. Only by the late thirteenth century did the crown smite castles in judicial punishment and begin the policy of direct mastery over fortification that was to blossom in the Hundred Years War, though even then with limited results.

What, then, of the licences to fortify, issued under royal, ducal, and comital seals? The question is important for England as well as for France since castellation licences were a common feature on both sides of the Channel. They cannot have been unimportant to men of the period; hundreds of licences were sought and granted by superior authorities, and the practice certainly reveals important aspects of the attitudes of these authorities towards castles. The mistake easily made is to assume that a policy of control and a system of licences are synonymous, to think that if control existed it was exercised through licences. Such was clearly not the case. In fact, the licence policy may have operated more in the interests of the recipient than in the interests of the crown; or rather 'this process of mutual compliment', in the apt phrase of Charles Coulson,[120] reflected both the theory of royal control and the vassal's acknowledged right to fortify. Since in France even a show of fortification connoted nobility, the right to fortify granted by king, duke, or count was equivalent to a certification of noble status. The connection between new *châteaux* and new seigneuries was very close and could cause great friction between the new seigneur and his neighbours; even the owner of a *maison*

[119] Strayer notes that the costs of 'works' was not a large charge on the budget of Philip the Fair; even the small sum spent included work on mills and other minor buildings, as well as on castles; *The Reign of Philip the Fair*, 143.

[120] Coulson, 'Seignorial Fortresses', 385.

forte might claim rights of high justice.[121] A royal letter authorizing construction would be highly useful if another lord or a commune were unsympathetic to one's pretentions to noble status or to specific dues and rights of justice claimed; a licence could also ward off or win a lawsuit contesting the right to build a *maison forte* or even a good stone house, let alone a castle. Viewed from this perspective, castle licences show an interesting similarity to royal protections and safeguards, rather than to any measures of official vigilance against wrongdoers of knightly rank. Many petitioners were of just the social level to benefit from the recognition of an official letter; in Gascony in the 1280s, for example, they were minor nobles or bourgeois creditors of the duke building on sites near the major cities of the duchy; they enjoyed ease of access to the ducal court and were confident of ducal favour.[122] Moreover, in troubled times the fortified houses they often built, though of very limited military value, were comforting defences against feuding neighbours or brigands.[123]

Although a noble class was less sharply defined in England, the argument loses little of its force when applied to the English county gentry. No less than their French counterparts, the arbiters of English county society could appreciate the advantages of royal sanction for an architectural display of their local importance and for some material defence against their neighbours' envy or malice. The same impulse which led a man to accept jury duty or service on a local committee could lead him to apply for a royal licence to 'fortify and crenelate his dwelling place with a wall of stone and lime', in each case the crown recognized his importance in a highly visible way.[124]

From the English king's point of view the licences may have reminded men of royal superiority in matters of fortification, but the crown's effort to control castles rested on much broader bases. As in France, castle policy in England reflects the essential

[121] Fournier, *Le Château dans la France médiévale* 238.

[122] Gardelles, *Les Châteaux du moyen âge*, 32, 38.

[123] Fournier, *Le Château dans la France médiévale* 238.

[124] R. A. Brown reproduces one of these licences in *English Castles*, pl. 46, and shows the architectural result in pl. 47 (Allington Castle, Kent). Perhaps it is not necessary to explain the eleven licences granted within the county of Devon, 1260-1377 by postulating disturbances by smugglers and pirates, as did Denholm-Young, *The Country Gentry in the Fourteenth Century*, 37: Local rivalries or local display might be sufficient reason.

quality of kingship. The situation after the Norman Conquest bears superficial resemblances to contemporary France. Scores of new motte and bailey castles were planted by the conquerors in strategic locations. Few were retained personally by William I; most were entrusted to men of importance whose loyalty was beyond question and each could be requisitioned by the crown if need arose, even though it was held in fee.[125] But the English kings did not continue to rely on castles which were in some sense rendable to the crown in an emergency. For, on the one hand, they were by and large able to insist on royal permission for castle-building and, on the other hand, they built and maintained a great number of castles themselves.

Once the threat of rebellion by the native English against Norman intruders had passed, the distinction between royal and baronial castles became increasingly important. By the early twelfth century the *Leges Henrici Primi* listed 'castle-building without permission' as one of the crimes which placed a man in the king's mercy.[126] During the reign of Stephen the rush to create these adulterine castles and the effect they had on the state of the peace, is well known. As the Anglo-Saxon chronicle relates in vivid and famous words:

> For every man built him castles and held them against the king; and they filled the land with these castles. They sorely burdened the unhappy people of the country with forced labour on these castles; and when the castles were built they filled them with devils and wicked men. By night and day they seized those whom they believed to have any wealth, whether they were men or women; and in order to get their gold and silver they put them into prison and tortured them with unspeakable tortures. . . . At regular intervals they levied a tax called 'tenserie' upon the villages. When the wretched people had no more to give, they plundered and burnt all the villages, so that you could easily go a day's journey without ever finding a village inhabited or field cultivated . . . and men said openly that Christ and his saints slept.[127]

Another chronicler estimated the number of illicit castles in England in 1153 at more than a thousand.[128] As a part of their

125 Colvin (ed.), *The History of the King's Works*, i. 33; Douglas, *William the Conqueror*, 216-17.

126 Colvin (ed.), *The History of the King's Works*, i. 33 and n. 1.

127 Quot.: Davis, *King Stephen*, 83-4.

128 Warren, *Henry II*, 39.

agreement on the succession made at Winchester in that year, King Stephen and the future Henry II agreed to work together to destroy castles erected since the death of Henry I in 1135. The larger share of the task seems to have fallen on Henry's shoulders; not only did he destroy adulterine castles, but in a bold gamble he commanded that the barons relinquish custody of castles which belonged to the crown, and struck vigorously even against offenders of status such as William le Gros, count of Aumale and earl of York, Roger, earl of Hereford, Hugh Mortimer, lord of Cleobury and Wigmore, and the bishop of Winchester.[129] After the great rebellion of 1173-4, the castles of rebel barons were again systematically destroyed, the itinerant justices being instructed to ensure that the work was indeed done, and a complete change of royal castellans was effected to ensure the royal control over castles in their keeping.[130] The series of royal licences began only in the thirteenth century with the reign of Henry III, but *licentia* in the sense of crown permission was obviously required long before formal licences were issued and enrolled by chancery; and even after the licensing system was in operation, royal control over castellation was not limited to those instances in which a builder had sought and been given a formal licence.

By this time the results of impressive royal castle-building projects were very much in evidence. From the Conquest into the Hundred Years War the English monarchy continuously built castles which were among the most sophisticated fortresses of their day. Henry II kept ninety or more castles in good repair. During his reign and the reigns of his sons, castle-building was by far the largest single charge on the royal revenues, probably reaching almost 10 per cent of total basic revenues between 1155 and 1215. Moreover, for the theme of public order it is significant that the emphasis fell on castles in the interior, rather than on frontier bastions against external enemies.[131] Given the increasing complexity of castle architecture and the great costs

129 Ibid. 39-40, 52-3, 59-61.

130 Ibid. 140-2.

131 Colvin (ed.), *The History of the King's Works*, i. 67-9. The building of the new castle at Orford by Henry II provides a good case in point. The authors quote the opinion of the chronicler William of Newburgh, that such royal castles were 'the bones of the kingdom'.

associated with building castles and keeping them in repair, a drop in the number of English royal castles in the thirteenth century is not surprising. In the long reign of Henry III the number fell from fifty-eight to forty-seven; but in the view of R. A. Brown and H. M. Colvin, the kingdom was adequately provided with castles both for administrative and military needs. Advances in the plans and materials of castle-building and changes in the strategic role of castles eliminated the usefulness of some lesser fortresses inherited from earlier kings.[132] Moreover, the climax of royal castle-building would appear in the next reign. To ensure his conquest of Wales, Edward I carried out one of the most remarkable projects of castellation in medieval history. In mid-Wales and north Wales a work force which was sometimes as large as 4,000 men built eight massive castles, five of which were integrated with fortified towns. The castles arose in five to seven building seasons (weather being suitable from roughly April to November), with three or four of them going up simultaneously in and after 1277 and again in and after 1283. This major enterprise was accomplished only by 'tapping the labour-market over the greater part of England' and by investing as much as £80,000 in building supplies and wages. As J. G. Edwards suggested, the project represents the 'medieval state-enterprise' of a king 'wielding in his iron hand the whole resources of the most compactly centralized dominion of that day.' Perhaps as no other sovereign of the time, Edward I was able to command the men and resources to carry out this project without crippling financial or political strain.[133]

Thus, the contrasts between English and French kingship, the power each possessed, and the ways in which it could be used, were writ large in the area of castle policy. From the very beginning of the age of castles the English kings could act directly, by reducing any fortress which threatened the integrity of royal power anywhere in the realm, by building fortresses of impressive strength on an impressive scale wherever they were needed. The French kings worked no less skilfully, but characteristically acted

[132] Ibid. 113, 118-19. They note that crown military needs were not yet met in Wales; but the work of Edward I changed that situation.

[133] Edwards, 'Edward I's Castle-building in Wales', 17-81; Colvin (ed.), *The History of the King's Works*, i, chs. 5, 6; ii, ch. 13, and apps. C, I, II, III; Kaeuper, 'Royal Finance and the Crisis of 1297'. The Edwards quots. are taken from pp. 16, 61, 65.

indirectly, through the network of feudal relationships, and of necessity left much action regarding castles and their control across the relative vastness of France to the great feudatories. Given the resources they could command (without causing strains that could mean political difficulties), their policies based on feudal overlordship were wise. The more rapid and substantial progress of urbanization in France and the good relations between townsmen and the Capetian monarchy may also have provided French kings with sources of support which could to some degree substitute for a network of numerous royal castles. Yet in comparison with their English rivals the French kings seem to have been forced to follow a policy which was distinctly second best. Even if they could assume that in an emergency every castle held by rendable tenure would be promptly turned over to royal agents, and that townsmen would loyally man the town walls for the king's cause, such important aid was not available on a day-to-day basis for the needs of administering an always turbulent realm. To have direct control over large numbers of important fortresses strategically located throughout the realm meant not only denying them to potential troublemakers or enemies, but also using them as command centres for a government trying to check lordly violence. For the great emergencies on the level of major rebellion or foreign invasion, French fortress policy could be made to work with some degree of success; for the less spectacular but ever-present problems of private warfare, the policy was much less effective.

The contrast between the relative success of the royal castle policy in England and the complete failure of the very different strategy followed by the English kings as dukes of Gascony is instructive.[134] From the rough attempts of Simon de Montfort as royal lieutenant in the duchy (1248-52) to the outbreak of the War of Aquitaine in 1294, only Edward I made any tentative effort to provide the castellar base for an effective policy of central control. The problem was ducal resources in Gascony which were insufficient for a policy like that carried out in England, even if Gascon revenues had not often been diverted to projects in the British Isles. As duke, Edward I had to govern a duchy studded with perhaps a thousand fortresses; he may have controlled at

[134] The following is based on the first ch. of Gardelles, *Les Châteaux du moyen âge*.

best one in six. Edward built some castles, purchased some, gained control of others by entering into *pareages*; and he insisted that vassals' fortresses were rendable to him on demand. But he could not indefinitely keep all the castles seized by Montfort, and he could not forcefully purchase castles for fear of appeals to the superior justice of the French king exercised by the Parlement of Paris, especially after the accession of Philip IV. Following the confiscation of the duchy between 1294 and 1303, a lengthening queue of creditors forced Edward to abandon ducal rights which only further reduced revenues already diminished by wartime damage and strained by the cost of defence. Likewise from 1303, Edward largely abandoned the limitations on new castle-building which had applied in theory to all parts of the duchy except the Agenais. By the reign of Edward II the situation quickly approached anarchy, with private war and brigandage especially troublesome in the south and in Agenais. An effort to remedy the deficiencies of ducal fortifications between 1323 and 1331 seems to have been too little too late. From the beginning of the fourteenth century, Jacques Gardelles suggests, the multiplication of seigneurial castles, the acquisition of regalian rights, and the imposition of new levies and dues on the peasantry led to the creation of new castellanies or the consolidation of those already extant. The result was a Gascon feudality that resembled not so much other provinces of contemporary France as the France of the eleventh or twelfth century. Thus, the situation in Gascony can hardly be taken as typical of France, but it illustrates the importance of some sound castle policy in securing not only defence against invasion, but support for an administrative structure that could ensure some measure of internal peace. The contrast between Gascony and England likewise emphasizes the long cadences of historical change: how deeply the Gascon problems were rooted in the turbulent history of the duchy and how much the successful royal policy in England rested on the cumulative power of a kingship developed over centuries, rather than on the wisdom or virtue of a particular king and his advisers. The same Edward was king in England and king-duke in Gascony.[135]

135 Colvin suggest that in the fifteenth century the English kings experienced within their own realm the problems that had plagued them as dukes of Gascony two centuries earlier. In the reign of Henry VI 'for the first time in English

By the fourteenth century kings in both England and France claimed a superior right in matters of fortification and tied this right to their responsibilities for public order. But the route by which theory came to application seems in France to have been longer and to have wound around more obstacles. If we had a map showing French royal castles to place beside the maps Colvin and Brown have published for English royal castles, the point might be shown dramatically.[136] It might be objected that plotting castles on a map could only with great difficulty be made to show the French royal power over castles. Certainly a complex set of symbols in technicolor would be required to indicate the varying degrees of royal control: these symbols would have to distinguish royal castles within the domain, fortresses shared by the crown and some lord in *pareage*, castles held in chief by rendable fee in duchies or counties closely tied to the crown, as opposed to those in areas virtually independent of the crown, infeudated castles held of great feudatories fully loyal to the crown, as opposed to those in areas virtually independent of the crown, infeudated castles held of great feudatories of more doubtful loyalty, fortified towns of unquestioned loyalty, fortified towns of more uncertain loyalty, and the like. Of course, the very difficulty of drawing up the French castle map demonstrates the contrast with England where the task was so much simpler and not merely because of the smaller size of England. In whatever measure control of castles and castle-building affected public order, the involvement of the crown was felt with greater and more direct impact in England than in France.

3. PRIVATE WAR

Kings of England and France could try to co-opt chivalry for crown purposes, they could claim to possess and sometimes could exercise superior rights over tournaments and fortification. But

history the royal castles no longer constituted the most powerful and effective group of fortresses in the Kingdom' (*The History of the King's Works*, i. 240).

[136] Ibid. 22, 112, 239. For France see the following two massive atlases: *L'Atlas des châteaux forts en France*; *L'Atlas des villes et villages fortifiés en France (moyen âge)*. The maps provided in these atlases are not intended to show royal or seigneurial control, nor do they distinguish the pattern of castles and other fortifications at any one particular period.

the heart of the problem which the chivalric classes posed to public order went beyond the mock war of tournament, and even the warrior's fortified residence; the most basic issue was the practice of private warfare. When lords at all levels, and townsmen as well, sallied forth in arms to settle their own grievances, a long tradition of private rights buttressed by the ethos of chivalry ran headlong against a developing theory of public authority vested in kingship for the common weal.

Of course, kings did not invariably and faithfully represent this theory in practice nor were they immune from the common tendencies toward violent self-help. But with their crowns kings inherited a cumulative tradition of rights and duties towards peace and justice which formed a significant part of their sense of the proper kingly role. Monarchs who thought they knew the will of the Lord God and who were quite sure of the rights of the lord king held convictions which easily ran counter to the lordly conviction, rooted in immemorial practice and glorified by chivalric theory, that warriors had the right to settle disputes in their own way.

Something of the mental framework surrounding the right of private war, and something of its consequences, can be learned from the execution scene of a French lord in 1323.[137] Jourdain de l'Isle Jourdain, lord of Casaubon, 'very noble in lineage but ignoble in deed', had capped a long list of depredations by hanging two men who had been under royal safeguard with appeals pending before the king, and by killing a royal sergeant. In answer to the king's summons he came to Paris in the spring of 1323 'with a great array and with great pride'. He was none the less condemned to death. As he was drawn to the gallows, Jourdain confessed crimes for which he admitted he deserved to die. Among these wrongs were the killing of many women and children and other people by his men and their burning of various places; Jourdain had been informed and had approved, 'but he said that it was in war'. Likewise, he confessed, his men had frequently robbed churches, abbeys, and priories; 'but he said that it was to sustain himself and his people in his war and that thus he had done it in his *pays*'. As he went to execution

[137] The confession is printed and analysed in Langlois and Lanhers, *Confessions et jugements*, 37-9; S. H. Cutler also discusses this case and provides additional information, *The Law of Treason*, 46, 144-5.

Jourdain was found to carry on his body a little purse containing a piece of the true cross ('as he says'), some relics of that most chivalric saint, George, and writings of the names of Christ and the Evangelists. Jourdain was an extreme case; yet his violent actions and his justification for them were not totally divorced from the lives of most knights. Maurice Keen puts his finger on the broad problem which Jourdain represents: 'The school of arms and errantry could, it is clear, become all too easily a school of banditry.'[138] And as Jourdain's confession *en route* to the gallows makes clear, the worst excesses could be cloaked in the noble right of private war. A few years earlier (1319) Philip the Tall as king-count of the county of Burgundy had prohibited what he termed the excesses of private war in that region: burning houses or castles, cutting down or uprooting vineyards or orchards, seizing draft animals or ploughs. These practices had all been common up to that time. Although Philip announced that they were henceforth forbidden, we may suspect that such excesses continued. For normal operations in private war involved expeditions into enemy territory to capture (or more rarely to kill) villagers, to burn dwellings, and especially to seize valuable livestock.[139]

The lineage of this private war went back to the ancient practice of feud. In France of the first feudal age it was transformed for the noble classes into a recognized *droit de guerre*. By the thirteenth and fourteenth centuries theoreticians, accepting war as 'the endemic condition of West European society' classified four possible conditions or states of war: war to the death (*guerre mortelle*) in which a beaten opponent could be slain or enslaved; public or open war (*bellum hostile*) or the war of one sovereign Christian prince against another, in which spoil could be taken, but prisoners had the right to expect to be ransomed; feudal or covered war (*guerre couverte*) with licence for the warring parties to wound, and kill, but not to burn or take spoil or prisoners; and truce, which was not true peace, but merely a pause before the continuation of war. Most of the theorists, specialists in canon or civil law and apologists either for exalted notions of papal supremacy or for the authority of rising

138 Keen, *Chivalry*, 228.

139 Richard, 'Le droit de guerre'. Robert Fossier makes similar observations for the Cambrésis in 'Fortunes et infortunes paysannes au Cambrésis', 171-82.

secular states, were uncomfortable with any war other than a crusade or a conflict fought by recognized sovereigns. 'In the last resort', Maurice Keen writes, 'the lawyers were very unwilling to admit that any war other than one levied on the authority of a prince was a war in the true sense of the word.'[140]

The *guerre couverte* fought under traditional feudal *droit de guerre* might be handled gingerly and with evident distaste by theoreticians, but the point of view common to French chivalry appears in the treatise of Beaumanoir who devoted two chapters to private war and the elaborate protocols by which it was initiated, fought, and terminated.[141] His discussion of feudal war is similar to what the more theoretical specialists say about public war:

> The difference is however seen clearly when he talks of a 'quivetaine de guerre', which the lawyers would render in Latin 'dux belli'. Such leaders have the same kind of rights according to both parties, but whereas the canonists and civilians intend by their phrase a sovereign or his lieutenant, Beaumanoir clearly means the principal or the head of the family engaged in war.[142]

Thus, the difference lies in the view of sovereign power competent to make war. Beaumanoir not only considered every baron as sovereign in his barony,[143] he granted every noble his right of war: 'gentil home puissent guerreier solonc nostre coustume'. To the extent that feudal lords are sovereigns, the second and third categories of the theoreticians collapse into one. Yet Beaumanoir was also a royal official, a *bailli* under Philip III and Philip IV; he shows not only the cherished feudal conception of private war, but the emerging concept of public weal:

> Although gentlemen may war according to our custom, the justice must no less act by his office to mete out punishment against the first misdeeds; because if one gentleman kill or wound another, when there is not open war between them (*sans guerre qui fust aouverte entre eus*) and the lineage of both parties wish to put the matter to the test of war without carrying the matter to the justice, the justice should none the

[140] Keen, *The Laws of War in the Late Middle Ages*, 64, 68, 104.

[141] Philippe de Beaumanoir, *Coutumes de Beauvaisis*, i, chs. 59, 60.

[142] Keen, *The Laws of War in the Late Middle Ages*, 72-3.

[143] Philippe de Beaumanoir, *Coutumes de Beauvaisis*, i, ch. 34, no. 1043; 59, no. 1673.

less use all his power to seize the evildoers and do justice concerning the misdeeds; because the evildoers have not only done offence to the adverse party, but also to the lord who has the duty to guard and to judge them.[144]

Any sense of the precedence of public weal over private right developed very slowly in medieval France; in the charters to the nobles of Burgundy and Picardy granted during the troubles beginning in 1314, Louis X had to confirm to these lords the right of private war.[145] To the end of the Middle Ages feudal lords claimed and exercised the right to defy their enemies and to war against them. The change away from a right of private war towards an idea of a monopoly of the right of war vested in the king as sovereign seems to move at glacial speed; but even glaciers do move and with great effect; the shift across the late medieval period is unmistakable.[146]

One of the clearest and most interesting signs of change appears in evolving royal reaction to the most spectacular form of private war, taking up arms against the king himself. Fighting the king was not treason in earlier medieval centuries, provided only that the lord or knight issued a formal defiance (*diffidatio*) to break the reciprocal bond linking him to the king as overlord. But as kingship moved toward sovereignty and as Roman law theories of public authority exercised in the interests of the common good entered the mainstream of European political thought, fighting against the king increasingly appeared as an offence against the symbol and guarantor of public peace. In both England and France the late Middle Ages thus brought dramatic development in the definition and punishment of treason. More than waging war against the king was involved in the concept of treason, of course, but since 'treason was . . . an injury against public authority as represented by the person of the king and as symbolized by the crown', war against the king would necessarily cease to be a licit private right. In fact, as S. H. Cutler has

[144] Ibid., 59 no. 1673.

[145] Artonne, *Le Mouvement de 1314*, 115.

[146] Keen, *The Laws of War in the Late Middle Ages*, 237, writes of the fifteenth century that 'the principle which then for the first time was being urged with force in actual disputes, that any sort of hostile act requires sovereign authority, was an important one. It indicates a shift of attitude on the question of war's legitimacy. The crucial question is no longer the justice of the cause, but the authority on which war is levied.'

insisted, notions of sovereignty, obedience, and war were closely interlinked in the early development of treason.[147]

In England war against the king became treason in the reign of the imperious Edward I. Between the execution of the Welsh leader David ap Gruffydd in 1282 and the end of the reign in 1307, Edward executed more than a score of important political opponents (Scots rebels in particular), the majority of them for levying war against the crown. Though the political cauldron of Edward II's reign produced a wider variety of treason charges, both Gilbert de Middleton (1318) and Thomas of Lancaster (1322) were convicted on charges including fighting against the king with banners unfurled. But the connections between public order, royal authority, and the law of treason became even more interesting in the reign of Edward III. Before the great statute of treason was enacted in 1352, the king was trying, through his judges, to extend the common law of treason as a law-and-order measure. For certain offences, such as riding armed to rob, slay, or capture, royal judges were ready to impose the horrifying physical penalties of a traitor's death (and sometimes the forfeitures of property to the crown as well). Though the judges did not turn felony into treason by the claim that these crimes usurped royal power, their movement in this direction was troublesome to English lords and knights, some of whom were known to indulge in activities of just the sort the judges had in mind, and to the parliamentary Commons as well, who were fearful of what seemed too powerful a tool in royal hands. Prudent in this case, as in all others involving his essential supporters, Edward III defined treason in the 1352 statute as a set of crimes against the king's person and regality; armed robbery, slaughter, and kidnapping remained felonies. The extension of the concept of treason in one law and order direction was curtailed; but the levying of war against the king remained a treasonable offence.

In France war against the crown gradually became treason during the early decades of the fourteenth century. The last Capetian kings generally dealt with rebellious nobles by simple military force or by skilful diplomacy, and seldom brought

[147] Cutler provides a much needed review, *The Law of Treason*. For England the standard work is Bellamy, *The Law of Treason*. What follows draws on these two works. The closely related topic of martial law in England is discussed in: Capua, 'The Early History of Martial Law'.

charges of treason. Guy de Dampierre, the rebellious count of Flanders, was not treated as a traitor by Philip IV in 1300; when the next count of Flanders, Robert of Bethune, rebelled, he was twice tried for treason, in 1312 and 1315. The changing royal attitude is even more clear by the reign of the first Valois king. Philip VI dealt with Flemish rebels as Edward I had dealt with his Welsh and Scottish opponents. After his victory at Cassel (1328), Philip executed rebels as traitors (with special refinements practised on their leader Guillaume de Deken) and confiscated the property of all who had fought against him. Across the next half century the form of rebellion most likely to incur treason charges seems to have been urban risings, especially the Flemish rising quashed at the battle of Roosebeke (1382) and the revolts in several French towns provoked by impositions of new royal taxes.

Though warfare against the crown was the most blatant offence to royal majesty, any private war would indirectly offend kings whose sovereignty entailed responsibility for public order. In France the gap between this theory and actual practice was gaping. French kings of this period could hardly eradicate by fiat the practice of private war, so deeply rooted in the social landscape, but from the time of Philip the Fair they regularly enacted legislation prohibiting the wars of individual lords during the king's war. Was this series of *ordonnances* simply a pragmatic regulation in the hope of channelling all violence against the enemy[148] or can it be taken in a broader sense as a flank attack on the private war kings considered an impediment to the internal peace they were sworn to defend?

The work of Louis IX

The problem has not been made any easier by the conflicting views scholars have advanced on the role of St Louis in royal peace measures. To Gustave Ducoudray, as to many historians of France, St Louis was 'le roi de la paix' whose conception of Christian kingship led to his struggle against private war, tournament and judicial duel.[149] More recently Robert Fawtier

[148] This concern lest private wars draw strength from the king's wars is illustrated by a 1348 case in which an esquire left the royal forces to join his father, brother, and friends in a private war. He was arrested by a relative of the family enemy (*Actes*, 2nd ser. 8558).

[149] Ducoudray, *Les Origines du Parlement de Paris,* 329-32.

and others have played down considerably the importance of St Louis's prohibition of private war in 1258, noting that the initiative rested with Guy Foucois, bishop-elect of Puy, a former royal *enquêteur* and future pope (as Clement IV), and suggesting that the prohibition applied only to his diocese of Le Puy.[150] Moreover, Cazelles has argued that the ordinance had so little import that a knight claiming he was wounded in a private war had his case thrown out of Parlement in 1260.[151]

Evidence to support the traditional view of Louis's concerns for peace is indirect and sometimes problematical, but *in toto* the evidence is of great interest. In 1239 Louis re-established peace in the diocese of Mende by an accord between the bishop of Mende and the seneschal of Beaucaire; the document refers to the action as 'secundum statuta auctoritate domini pape et domini regis Francorum in Tholosano consilio promulgata' which Perrot took to refer to the Council of Toulouse in 1229.[152] A return to the kinds of peace measures prominent in the peace of God movement is certainly not surprising, given the continuing turbulence in Occitania following the war against Raymond of Toulouse and the heretics, and considering the close co-operation between the papal legate and the young Louis IX. Such legislation could easily serve as a precedent and spur to further royal action. Apparently in 1245 Louis reissued the so-called Quarantaine-le-Roy which from the reign of Philip Augustus had in theory imposed a forty-day truce protecting friends or relatives of warring parties who might be drawn into the conflict.[153] Perhaps as early as 1254 in civil cases and by 1258 or 1259 for criminal cases Louis acted against the procedure of judicial combat, at least

150 Fawtier and Lot, *Histoires des institutions françaises*, ii. 425-6.

151 Cazelles, 'La Réglementation royale', 539. His comments on p. 541 might, however, be interpreted in a different vein.

152 Michel, *L'Administration royale*, 384; Perrot, *Les Cas royaux*, 150-1 n. 1. For the text, see Mansi (ed.), *Sacrorum Conciliorum Collectia*, xxiii. 191.

153 No text of St Louis's regulation survives. Historians have used the text in a 1353 ordinance (*Ordonnances des roys de France*, ii. 552-3), and have debated the role of Philip II and Louis IX in establishing the Quarantaine. See ibid., i, pp. xxx-xxxi, 56; Philippe de Beaumanoir, *Coutumes de Beauvaisis*, ii. 372 n. 1; Perrot, *Les Cas royaux*, 150 n. 1. John II in his 1353 ordinance linked the Quarantaine le Roy with St Louis. It is less often recognized that his father, Philip VI, did likewise. A case in Parlement in 1341 refers to St Louis's ordinance which prohibits the defier from taking vengence on friends and relatives of his enemy within forty days of the declaration of war (*Actes*, 2nd ser. 3186).

in the royal courts.[154] In January 1258 he issued the famous edict against private war from his castle at St-Germain-en-Laye, condemning even arson and the disturbing of peasants. As noted above, historians debate how widely the measure applied in the realm. But the following year two *arrêts* show an active enforcement outside the lands of the bishop of Le Puy on whose initiative the legislation had been enacted. In one case the bishop of Albi, who had disregarded formal prohibitions made by the seneschal of Carcassonne and had made *chevauchée*, including in his force men banished by the king, found his case brought before the king's court.[155] In a second case two brothers were condemned for their *chevauchée* against each other after an *enquête* had been taken by the *bailli* of Mantes and the *prévôt* of Beaumont-sur-Oise.[156] The theory behind these cases seems to have owed much to the views of Guy Fucois and connect with the development of theory and enforcement by which the offence of *port d'armes* would become the very type of *cas royaux* (offence reserved for crown jurisdiction) in the fourteenth century. As was common with royal edicts in this reign, *port d'armes* legislation was enforced by the barons within their own lands.[157] An *arrêt* of 1265 declared that the men who were fined by the count of Soissons for violences committed in his territory need not, as the zealous *bailli* of Vermandois had claimed, pay a second amend to the king for *port d'armes*.[158] A few years after Louis's death an *arrêt* ordered the *bailli* of Bourges not to impede the count of Sancerre from judging men guilty of *port d'armes* violations on his land.[159] In 1277 the mayor and *jurés* of Senlis were ruled to have cognizance over *port d'armes* offences committed by inhabitants of the commune, but not over strangers.[160]

[154] The nineteenth-century opinions of the date and character of Louis's prohibition are surveyed by Fontaine, 'Revue des recueils périodiques'. Cf. Fawtier and Lot, *Histoire des institutions francaises*, ii. 425-6; Carbasse, 'Le Duel judiciaire'; Mortet, 'Le Livre des constitutions démenées'. These refs. are supplied by Jordan, *Louis IX and the Challenge of the Crusade* 204 nn. 120-2.

[155] *Actes* 379.

[156] *Actes* 393.

[157] Fawtier and Lot, *Histoire des institutions françaises*, 289 ff., Perrot, *Les Cas royaux*, 158-9.

[158] *Actes* 980.

[159] *Actes* 1926 (1273).

[160] *Actes* 2109.

Thus, it would be a mistake to focus attention too narrowly on the edict of St-Germain-en-Laye, for the measures which seem to have preceded it and the later actions of St Louis appear to form a consistent pattern in the interests of peace. As noted above, the king circumscribed the rights of tournament in 1260, or even earlier, fearing tournament was 'the seedbed of many a private war'.[161] His court certainly encouraged the *asseurements* by which one individual swore not to war against another. Beaumanoir, in the next reign, considered such assurances much more valuable than truces, 'car trives se durent a terme et assuremens dure a tous jours'.[162] Whether or not all of these measures against *chevauchée, port d'armes*, tournament, as well as the Quarantaine legislation, originated in edicts now lost, antedating the 1258 edict,[163] or emerged piecemeal and in less formal fashion, may never be known. Obviously the sum total of these measures did not vastly reduce private warfare, which Beaumanoir considered quite normal in the 1280s, albeit regulated by an elaborate code and occasionally obviated by *asseurements*.[164] Although some peace offences continued to be tried in royal courts,[165] both Beaumanoir and the anonymous compiler of the *Établissements* of St Louis assume that cognizance over offences relating to private wars belongs to the lord on whose lands the acts occurred.[166]

That the good king Louis set his face against private warfare, however, could have been more important in the long run than in the short run. The case allowed by extant evidence is not ironclad, but it does at least suggest that the elements used by the late Capetian and early Valois kings in an effort to contain private war were nearly all present under Louis IX; and just as important as any single edict or step towards creating new *cas royaux* was the example of St Louis's efforts to reduce violence in the settling of quarrels. By his stature and moral precedent no less than in his legislation and judgements, Louis IX was a critical link between the earlier Capetian association with the peace of God measures

161 Jordan, *Louis IX and the Challenge of the Crusade*, 204.

162 Philippe de Beaumanoir, *Coutumes de Beauvaisis*, lx, no. 1694.

163 Perrot, *Les Cas royaux*, 150-2 and n.

164 Philippe de Beaumanoir, *Coutumes de Beauvaisis*, lix, lx, nos. 1667-708. Cf. Fawtier and Lot, *Histoire des institutions françaises*, 427-8.

165 Perrot, *Les Cas royaux*, 152, n. cont. from p. 151, and n. 1.

166 Ibid. 164-6.

and the more developed, more judicial, more purely royal action of St Louis's grandson.[167]

The work of Philip IV

The series of frequent regulations of private warfare really begins during Philip the Fair's reign. In 1296 a prohibition of all private wars was joined to a prohibition against judicial duels and tournaments; the prohibitions were to last during the war in Gascony.[168] Although a 1304 ordinance seems at first glance much more sweeping, since it prohibits private wars at any time and forbids judicial duels in wartime, Cazelles thinks the measure was in fact much more specific than that of 1296. It was sent to the seneschal of Toulouse, apparently in response to the requests of the inhabitants of Toulouse, and was linked as well to measures directed against the war being waged by the powerful houses of Foix and Armagnac in Gascony. Likewise, he sees the 1311 ordinance, which in sweeping terms prohibits private war throughout the realm, even where ancient custom allowed the practice, as in fact a measure designed to win support in Flemish cities.[169] In the last year of his reign Philip IV, once more at war in Flanders, prohibited the wars of his nobles.[170] Philip VI would issue a similar ordinance after the outbreak of the Hundred Years War as did John II in 1352.[171] In 1361 a bold attempt to prohibit all private wars in peacetime (promoted by a rash of struggles between nobles eager to get on with their private quarrels after the Peace of Brétigny legitimized private wars by ending the king's war) was followed by two backward steps towards the old policy: an ordinance of 1363 accepted the nobles' view that only in wartime could their private quarrels be forbidden; and in 1378 Charles V recognized private wars when the adversaries agreed and followed proper form.[172] From one point of view, the war over the succession in Brittany in the early phase of the Hundred Years War and the war between Orléans and Burgundy in the later stages of the Hundred Years War were simply private wars

[167] Fawtier and Lot, *Histoire des institutions françaises*, 429, suggest that Philip III took no stronger measures than his father.

[168] *Ordonnances des roys de France*, i. 328.

[169] Ibid. 390 ff., 492-3; Cazelles, 'La Réglementation royale', 539-40.

[170] *Ordonnances des roys de France*, i. 538-9.

[171] Ibid., ii. 511.

[172] Ibid., iii. 646-9; Cazelles, 'La Réglementation royale', 544.

writ large; Gustave Ducoudray devoted some interesting pages to developing this theme and Maurice Keen notes a long argument in the Parlement in 1433 as to the proper classification of the great conflict between the French and English kings: private war of *bellum hostile*?[173]

The persistence of violence over decades and across a wide scale of political and military power, and the persistence of views identifying every nobleman's right with sovereign power to make war should nevertheless not blind us to the real efforts of French kings. Solemn pronouncements against private war may have been intended to reinforce a wide range of steps against disorder which did not solely depend for their validity on the *ordonnances*. Offenders were brought into royal courts for offences specifically stated to be violations of the king's ordinances against private war,[174] but whether or not such legislation had been recently enacted, the king's officers could bring charges of *port d'armes*, *chevauchée*, and ambush;[175] and cognizance of violations of the king's safeguard given to an individual or institution, or of violation of a peace or assurement sworn before a king's justice were independent of any ordinance on private war. Yet the very specific actions and the broad statements seem complementary; the sweeping nature of some of the ordinances against private war (those of 1304 and 1311, for example) would well serve the purposes of publicizing and reinforcing efforts to reduce the worst disorders produced by a custom which could not be eradicated, even though they did not provide the only legal bases for action in royal courts. Though most of these measures had probably been available since the time St Louis, a significant level of royal activism invested in public order and indeed a royal capacity to enforce public order measures hardly appeared before the later years of Philip IV.

Ducoudray, who held a very low estimate of the character of Philip the Fair, thought the incidence of disorder greatly

[173] Ducoudray, *Les Origines du Parlement*, 366-74; Keen, *The Laws of War in the Late Middle Ages*, 104.

[174] e.g. *Actes* 3855, 3957, 4771.

[175] For a *chevauchée* the sire de Mailly was condemned in 1290 to a 500*l*. fine, his accomplices were fined a similar sum, and his castle doors were burned, *Actes* 2674. The last royal *ordonnance* against *chevauchée* could only be that of St Louis, thirty-two years earlier. Even if Philip III's instructions to three seneschals in 1275 had more general scope (which Fawtier and Lot doubt; *Histoire des Institutions françaises*, 429), fifteen years had elapsed.

increased in that king's reign and attributed the formation of the leagues of 1314 to exasperation with the anarchic condition of the realm. His evidence was the sharp rise in the number of cases involving private war brought before the Parlement:

> Il n'est point d'année sans que des arrêts ou des enquêtes signalent soit des émeutes comme à Arras, au Puy, ou perissent les gens de la cour de l'évêque (1285), soit des chevauchées et les ravages comme ceux dont se rend coupable le comte de Bar, guerroyant contre les religieuses de Beaulieu en Argonne.
>
> . . . le comte de la Marche et le vicomte de Limoges se font une guerre acharnée avec incendies, ravages de territoire. Renaud de Pens, sire de Bergerac, dont le nom revient, à plusieurs reprises, dans les registres, se signale par une invasion de la ville d'Issigeac (1301) à la tête de six cents hommes criant: 'Bergerac! à mort! à feu!'[176]

Ducoudray thought that in the last decade of Philip's life, evidence from the registers of Parlement showed that the increasing disorder became extreme.[177]

This argument based on good sources should actually be stood on its head. An increase in cases of private warfare heard in royal courts, given what we know of Philip's high sense of kingship and the growth of royal jurisdiction, should be read as evidence of a heightened tempo of royal action rather than as a passive record of increasing seigneurial violence. We cannot know abstractly if there were more instances of disorder, but we do know that more of them were coming before the king's justices in his Parlement.[178] The increase in royal activism is indirectly measured by the outcries on behalf of seigneurial independence and the sanctity of the right of private warfare directed at Louis X after 1314. Obviously the royal efforts at restraining private warfare were not as ineffectual as might appear from an overview of *ordonnances* which periodically prohibited and regulated them.

As Ducoudray noted, cases involving public order increase significantly in the registers of the Parlement from the latter half

176 Ducoudray, *Les Origines du Parlement de Paris*, 338-9.

177 Ibid. 340, 343.

178 Following the evidence of the criminal registers of the Parlement, Ducoudray thought that the private wars, while increasing in number, were becoming smaller affairs than previously, involving knights and their vassals. But it is more likely that wars continued on the same scale and that the King and his agents directed their prosecutions against those lords who might possibly be brought to court and punished. Ducoudray's comment is ibid. 352.

of the reign of Philip the Fair. The king clearly recognized the impossibility of eliminating the custom of private war, even though it tended to spread and to draw in increasing numbers of combatants; he said as much in a confidential letter to Pope Clement V in 1308 in relation to a particular quarrel between the count of Soissons and the Hangest family: 'Nam cum de regni consuetudine que commode tolli non potest, nobilibus viris et precipue illis qui sunt de Remensi provincia liceat guerram ad invicem facere tam ex sibi attinentibus consanguinitatis vel affinitatis vinculo quam ex aliis sibi confederatis, quosque confederates undecumque fuerint in regnum adducere. . . .'[179] But royal sovereignty and the king's dignity were affected by an attack on someone enjoying the king's protection, by a violation of an *asseurement* given in a royal court, or by the open carrying of arms for offensive purposes. Moreover, the king as final and supreme judge was offended by flagrant abuses of power or the equally damaging neglect of duty on the part of seigneurial or local royal judges. The heritage of St Louis's concern for peace, the extreme royalism of Philip the Fair, and the growth of a royal bureaucracy all combine to increase the intervention of Parlement in public order generally and in private war in particular.[180]

This intervention increased across the late years of Philip the Fair's reign.[181] An *arrêt* of 1294 ordered the seigneur de la Veute to reconstruct a castle of the bishop of Valence and Die which he had burned during a truce between them and to pay fines of 2,000*m* to the bishop and 2,000*l.t.* to the king.[182] Two years later the sire d'Harcourt and his accomplices, who had ambushed Chambellan de Tancarville, were sent on pilgrimages to various churches in France; however, the attacker who had struck the first blow and gouged one of the victim's eyes was sent on pilgrimage to Cyprus.[183] In 1298 the *vicomte* of Limoges and the count of March were both condemned for violences 'cum gravibus portamentes armorum'; the court imposed fines of 10,000*l.t.* on the former, 5,000*l.t.* on the latter, plus amends to

179 Quot.: Boutaric, *La France sous Philippe le Bel*, 48 n. 1.

180 See Strayer, *The Reign of Philip the Fair*, 191-236.

181 The following cases are intended as only a sample, not an exhaustive list.

182 *Actes* 2859D; cf. *Actes* 2859E which orders an inquest to determine if the king should not receive part of the 2,000*m* paid to the bishop.

183 *Actes* 2922.

the victims. The disputed places over which the war had been fought were taken into the king's hands until the rights in dispute could be sorted out in Parlement.[184] In 1302 the sentence of the seneschal of Gascony imposing amends on the noble and non-noble inhabitants of numerous villages in the country of Foix and the inhabitants of the Vallée of Andorre was confirmed in Parlement; they were guilty of *port d'armes* in the fief of the sire de Mirepoix.[185] After a private war fought with veritable armies by Erard de St-Veran and Oudard de Montaigu in 1308, a chronicler relates that Erard 'and many others' were seized and imprisoned by the king.[186] The dispute between the houses of Foix and Armagnac, fought on an even grander scale, had already brought royal intervention; in 1309 the Parlement ordered heavy fines and the temporary imprisonment of the count of Foix.[187]

The pace quickened in the king's last years. In 1310 Pierre d'Avene was fined 700*l.* damages and interest plus 500*l. amend* and was deprived of the justice of his castle of Avene: he had lured his enemy, Raemond de Sine-gradu, into his castle after a peace had been concluded between them, embraced him, and attacked him so that he was left for dead.[188] For a private war fought despite the royal prohibition in 1311, Guillaume de Dampierre, lord of St-Dizier, and Gaucher de Châtillon the Younger, lord of Dampierre, were ordered to pay mutual damages.[189] For the same offence an *arrêt* in the following year reveals the *vicomte* of Polignac and the knight Bertrand de St-Izaire imprisoned in the Châtelet.[190] Much of the king's attention seems to have been focused on the south where private wars were especially troublesome.[191] Another case from 1311, for example, presents a picture of the public crier of Gignac making proclamation on the king's behalf that certain knights abstain from the carrying of arms; unfortunately one of the knights named was on the spot and

184 *Actes*, *Essai de restitution*, 927.

185 *Actes* 3185.

186 Continuator of Nagis, quot.: Ducoudray, *Les Origines du Parlement de Paris*, 340.

187 *Les Olim* iii. 328-87, *Actes* 3619, 3621; Ducoudray, *Les Origines du Parlement de Paris*, 341-2.

188 *Actes* 3894.

189 *Actes* 3855.

190 *Actes* 3957.

191 See the comment of Strayer, *The Reign of Philip the Fair*, 194-5.

ordered the crier to stop; when he refused, the knight struck him with his fist 'subtus gulam'.[192] But most of the king's officers were not so easily silenced as the public crier of Gignac. In the same year Philip ordered the seneschal of Toulouse to prohibit the count of Comminges and the other barons of that region from hearing cases of the offence of *port d'armes*, since that offence was the king's to punish.[193] In the following year the same point was reinforced in the north; in conformity with the general prohibition issued for the whole realm the *bailli* of Orléans was ordered to prohibit the carrying of arms in his *bailliage*, and he was to see that the bishop made the same prohibition to his clerics.[194] Those who carried arms legally, however, were protected. Royal letters of 1304 in favour of the nobles of Auvergne confirmed the right of nobles with high justice to carry arms in its exercise, even in some other lord's territory.[195] Likewise an *arrêt* of 1312 fined Roger de Castelnau 500*l.* for imprisoning Bernard Civade who had entered his domains with a mandate and who carried a royal baton (*bacula regis*) as a sign of his right to bear arms.[196]

In 1313 and 1314 particular royal attention focused on private wars in Vermandois. More than a score of knights and squires were fined in one case for making *chevauchée* against each other. Moreover, the separate criminal registers of the Parlement, begun in 1313, contain an interesting list of knights from Vermandois imprisoned for offences against the *port d'armes* prohibition: 'Ce sunt les nons des chevaliers qui sunt à present à Paris en prison pour le port d'armes quil ont fait en Vermandois sus les deffenses le Roy meseigneur. . . .' The lord of Pinon and four other knights on one side and Johan de Monceaus and five knights and squires on the other were imprisoned and there were 'bien XL autres escuiers qui encore ne pevent mie estre plain venuz a la congnoissance dudit ballif et chevaucherent avec ledit seigneur de Pinon'. The list shows that fifty-one knights and

[192] *Actes* 3766. Parlement, however, quashed the judgment of the Seneschal of Carcassonne against the knight, at the request of the king's procurator.

[193] *Actes* 3862.

[194] *Actes* 4113.

[195] *Ordonnances des roys de France*, i. 410. Note the elaborate conditions for legal bearing of arms laid down by Beaumanoir, Philippe de Beaumanoir, *Coutumes de Beauvaisis*, lviii, no. 1653.

[196] *Actes* 4015.

squires were involved, that the sire de Pinon, *chef de guerre* on one side, did not deny that he 'had made *chevauchée* with uncovered arms and unfurled banners', that Johan de Monceaus, and the other men on his side had equally ridden across the *bailliage* 'with trumpet calls and uncovered arms, making open war' against their enemies.[197]

In other parts of the realm the royal pressure was also maintained. A knight who sent his men to invade the house and mill of a Poitiers bourgeois and who replaced a royal grain measure with the lord's measure, was fined £1500.[198] A commission to the archdeacon of Bourbon to investigate a private war between a knight and another man was renewed.[199] Armed attacks on houses and mills brought fines levied on lords and knights.[200] New *enquêtes* were ordered concerning the violences charged against the countess of Foix and the vicomte of Bern by Amanieu d'Albret.[201]

Even this somewhat impressionistic survey of important cases from the registers of the Parlement gives evidence of the increased royal activity in public order under Philip the Fair. The impression is confirmed by other evidence. Certain categories of offence were increasingly prosecuted. Although royal safeguards were known under St Louis, the number of cases brought before Parlement because of violations of safeguards swells across the fourteenth century. Before the end of the century the French chancery had developed elaborate standard forms for granting the royal safeguard to various types of persons under various conditions.[202] Moreover, the device of the royal *panonceaux* even earlier came into widespread use as a visible sign of the king's safeguard. These *panonceaux* (batons embellished with the fleur-de-lis)[203] seem to appear everywhere in the reign of Philip the

[197] *Actes* 4183 gives the latter case, 4285 the former.

[198] *Actes* 4033.

[199] *Actes* 4043.

[200] *Actes* 4122, 4124, 4168 4176, 4194, 4220, 4262.

[201] *Actes* 4133-5, 4160.

[202] The indexes to *Les Olim* and *Actes* provide a rough guide to the increase. Late fourteenth-century chancery models for letters of safe conduct and safeguard, written in Latin and French, are given in Bibliothèque Nationale MS 4641, ff. 5, 8, 9, 10, 11, 14, 22-4, 26, 42. I wish to thank Fredric Cheyette who called these documents to my attention and kindly supplied a microfilm copy.

[203] e.g. *Actes* 3109, *Actes*, 2nd ser. 4995.

Fair and later. In the early fourteenth century these signs were affixed to castles,[204] churches and abbeys, [205] manor houses,[206] farmsteads,[207] mills,[208] ships,[209] forests,[210] and gallows.[211] Their presence by no means always deterred attackers. In fact, cases in the registers show that the *panonceaux* were sometimes treated by the offender with contempt as a visible reminder of the king's interfering jurisdiction. They were ripped off walls and hurled in the mud,[212] chopped with axes,[213] and shot with crossbow bolts.[214] One attacker threatened even worse. Étienne d'Anglure assaulted Jean de Vlandes in his house in 1341, struck him on the head with a lance and nearly choked the man with his own hood; when the desperate Jean pointed out the royal *panonceaux* prominently affixed at the top of his house, Étienne contemptuously replied 'quod super ipsis stercararet.'[215] Sentences handed down by the Parlement against such offenders might show an equal sensitivity to symbolism; the miscreant who fired his crossbow at the royal *panonceaux*, for example, found that in addition to fines and imprisonment, he had to stand in the pillory of the local market town on two market days wearing a parchment notice painted with a crossbow and the royal *panonceaux*. But the significant point is that the widespread grants of royal protection often witnessed by the *panonceaux* increased royal jurisdiction in matters of public order;[216] the numerous violations did come into the king's courts.

204 e.g. *Actes* 4821.

205 *Actes*, 2nd ser. 2370. This practice was abused. An ordinance of Philip VI in 1338 (*Ordonnances des roys de France*, ii. 124, art. 4) promised that the *panonceaux* would be placed only on possessions enjoyed peacefully by churches, not on those in dispute. Art. 5 promised, in more general terms, restraint in granting the king's safeguard.

206 e.g. *Actes* 6722, *Actes*, 2nd ser. 3026.

207 e.g. *Actes*, 2nd ser, 4883.

208 e.g. *Actes*, 2nd ser, 7286.

209 e.g. *Actes*, 2nd ser, 2159.

210 e.g. *Actes* 4644.

211 e.g. *Actes* 5426, *Actes*, 2nd ser. 4603.

212 e.g. *Actes* 6722.

213 e.g. *Actes*, 2nd ser. 4267.

214 e.g. *Actes*, 2nd ser, 7286. The guilty man had previously shouted down the crier making public proclamation of the safeguard. Royal letters of safeguard might also be viewed with wrath: one set shown to an assailant in 1322 was ripped to shreds *Actes* 6903.

215 *Actes*, 2nd ser. 3676.

216 Literally hundreds of cases involving violation of royal safeguard can be read in a volume of the calendared *Actes*. The index to the second series, covering 1328-50, for example, lists nearly 400 cases.

Jurisdiction based on *asseurements*[217] (assurances of peaceful behaviour between specified parties) also seems to increase in the late years of Philip IV and represent another royal device for reducing private war. These assurances could be arranged by mutual agreement or imposed under crown pressure; they were often preventive, but could be arranged after violence had occurred. They were, of course, often broken, but the royal courts could than prosecute the violators. The number of *asseurement* cases coming before Parlement in roughly the first half century of its life, before 1300, was small, perhaps a few score; in the next half century the number probably increased on the order of tenfold.[218] That lords had felt the beginnings of the change before the death of Philip IV, and resented the effort, is registered in the demands of the leagues of 1314. The second charter to the Burgundians granted them freedom from having to give *asseurements* or make truces unless there was clear or known menace or grave suspicion.[219]

The pattern of *port d'armes* prosecution is more difficult to assess. Even a precise definition is hard to construct and to integrate with the acknowledged rights of private warfare. The open carrying of arms with offensive intent may have numbered among the peace violations that were the targets of St Louis's measures. According to Perrot, from about the death of St Louis to about 1310 the crown reserved judgment of *port d'armes* infractions to royal justices only in the south, the *pays du droit écrit*, and even there encountered some resistance. Only in the last few years of Philip's reign did the royal government begin to make and act on the same claim in the north, the *pays du droit coutumier*.[220] The sense conveyed by most of the relevant cases before the Parlement is an armed breach of the peace, rather than a mere bearing of arms;[221] usually some violent assault has

217 There is a good discussion in Dubois, *Les Asseurements au XIIIe siècle*. For a summary account, see Luchaire, *Manuel des institutions françaises*, 233-4. Chancery forms for letters of accord, peace, or asseurement are given in MS Bibliothèque Nationale 4641, ff. 39, 47.

218 The indexes to the *Actes*, though they cannot be considered exhaustive, show the trend.

219 Artonne, *Le Mouvement de 1314*, 52, 116.

220 Perrot, *Le Cas royaux*, 158-66. The claim was consolidated only in the reign of Philip V.

221 In 1326, for example, an *arrêt* of Parlement returned to the Archbishop of Reims a case prosecuted before the *bailli* of Vermandois. Though violence had

occurred and the incident is brought within the cognizance of royal courts by a charge using the *port d'armes* formula. The injuries, damages, violences, arsons, and excesses committed in the conflict between the vicomte of Limoges and the count of March were said in 1298 to have been carried out 'cum gravibus portamentis armorum;'[222] likewise, those who attacked the consuls of Cahors in 1322 were said to have acted 'cum armis prohibitis et more hostili'.[223] A lord's pillaging raid into the lands of a knight in 1321 was described as carried out 'cum armis prohibitis et apparentibus'.[224] These key elements of serious armed foray, prohibited weapons, and open display of these weapons are repeated time and again in one combination or another. Occasionally the carrying of arms is said to be against the peace and public security.[225] In all these cases *port d'armes* appears quite similar to the English *vi et armis* formula which similarly brought cases before royal justices. As we have noted, a sense that wrongful force could bring a case into royal courts had emerged at about the same time in the England of Henry III and the France of St Louis. Though an effective jurisdiction based on *port d'armes* developed much more slowly in France than the *vi et armis* jurisdiction in England, both could have sprung from a shared stage in legal developments otherwise often divergent.

However, alongside the many French cases which deal essentially with armed breach of the peace, there are ordinances and some court cases which turn specifically on the carrying of prohibited weapons, regardless of whether or not they were used in violent fashion. The crown exercised the right both to license and to prohibit. By the late fourteenth century the existence of standard chancery forms granting permission to carry arms suggests a significant traffic in licences; men fearing violence

been proved, it did not involve the sort of violation of the public peace which characterized *cas royaux* (*Actes* 7781). Royal officials who arrested knights carrying arms without committing any acts of violence were the subject of complaints to the crown; see Langlois, 'Doléances', 10-11, 33.

[222] *Actes*, *Essai de restitution*, 927.

[223] *Actes* 6987.

[224] *Actes* 6385. Boutaric prints the Latin text. The brief French calendars usually given in the *Actes* provide no guide to language about *port d'armes*, although the original Latin terminology may have charged a specific violation of arms prohibitions.

[225] *Actes* 7917.

were allowed to go armed 'pro sui corporis tuicione'.[226] Selective permissions could give the king additional leverage in control of private wars. But specific prohibitions also appear. Parisians were prohibited from carrying even pointed daggers by an ordinance of 1288, for example,[227] and a royal serjeant in 1321 arrested a stranger who was carrying only a misericord.[228] An ordinance of Charles V in 1371 seems to define the matter clearly, referring to 'port d'armes notables, qui est à entendre quand ils auront compagnie de gens armez, garniz d'autres armes que epées, cousteaux ou bastons'.[229] This exclusion of such common weapons as swords, daggers, and cudgels would on the one hand leave to seigneurs a large measure of peace jurisdiction, since a band of determined men with clubs or swords could surely break the peace in striking fashion; on the other hand excluding common weapons which might with great hopefulness be classed as defensive would seem only reasonable if the lord king or any lord really intended to make the legislation work on a population which must in large part have put aside one or another of these weapons only while sleeping. Moreover, a prohibition directed mainly against the obviously offensive weapons (presumably lances, bills, bows and arrows, etc.) would accord well with the traditions of the ecclesiastical peace legislation which were the forerunners of the king's peace.[230] Even swords, however, might be prohibited on occasion: an *arrêt* of 1264 fined the mayor and *jures* of St-Riquier for guarding their fair 'with swords and other arms'; and an order of 1312 to the bailli of Orléans specified that even carrying swords was prohibited, except when on a journey.[231]

Perrot suggested that two distinct offences could be intended by the term *port d'armes*. One was simply an arms prohibition established within his jurisdiction by some possessor of high

226 For examples of the formulas, see Bibliotèque Nationale MS 4641, ff. 18-19; for examples of specific permissions granted see *Actes* 4934, 5267, 2nd ser. 7560, 8624; for legislation, see *Ordonnances des roys de France*, 509-10; iv. 523. The English kings as Dukes of Gascony followed a similar policy; see Chaplais, La Souveraineté du roi de France', 462 n. 45 and the sources cited.

227 *Actes* 2645.

228 *Actes* 6493.

229 *Ordonnances des roys de France*, v, 429-30.

230 See R. Bonnaud-Delamare, 'La paix en Flandre', 147.

231 *Actes* 862 and 4113 respectively.

justice; in this case the king was only one of many lords who prohibited and punished. By far the more serious and important was the *cas royal* by which French kings punished offences against private war regulations.[232] Popular riots pure and simple were not included, though they might resemble private war,[233] but ambush committed on a highway was included, though it might involve only a single assailant. To kill by ambush was considered especially hateful and likely was seen as a cause for setting one lineage against another.[234] Though Beaumanoir and royal ordinances specify that private war applies only to noble quarrels, the wars of nobles and towns were brought easily under the rubric.[235]

Despite all the blurred definitions and the confusions, the aim of the crown is clear. The *cas royal* of *port d'armes* gave the crown a significant jurisdiction whenever it chose to act against the private wars that so troubled the peace of the realm.[236]

Closely connected with the enforcement of *port d'armes* was the increasing role assumed by the royal procurators who could prosecute a case either by themselves on the king's behalf or in co-operation with a plaintiff. They seem to be in place in the *bailliages* and *sénéchausées* under Philip III but their early history in this reign is still obscure and their role was probably still quite limited. An active role in prosecuting cases involving *port*

232 Perrot, *Les Cas royaux*, 149 ff.

233 *Actes* 6570; Perrot, *Les Cas royaux*, 155-6 n. 5.

234 *Actes* 2922 (1296), 4172 (1313), 4585 (1317), 4812 (1317), 5205 (1317), 4944 (1317), 5735 (1319), 5736 (1319), 6187 (1320).

235 Beaumanoir is quot.: Dubois, *Les Asseurements au XIIIe siècle*, 45; for royal ordinances, see *Ordonnances des roys de France*, ii. 395, art. 17.

236 Distinctions sometimes blurred and exceptions had to be made, but the Parlement followed its own rules and sometimes returned to lower jurisdictions cases which did not qualify as *cas royaux*. See, for example, *Actes* 7781 (1326). In 1313 an *arrêt* of the seneschal of Carcassonne condemning the prior of Cambon for *port d'armes* was annulled by Parlement on grounds that he had convoked armed men in his house only for personal defence, *Actes* 4036. Nobles with rights of high justice could carry arms in its exercise. A set of letters in favour of the nobles of Auvergne in 1304, for example, granted this right even when the *seigneurs justiciers* were acting on the land of some other lord; *Ordonnances des roys de France*, i. 410. Royal serjeants could, of course, carry arms in the lands of lords; see *Actes* 4015 (1312) for an *arrêt* against a lord who arrested a royal serjeant on a charge of *port d'armes* within his jurisdiction, though the serjeant bore a royal baton to attest his official duty.

d'armes, *chevauchée*, breaking *asseurements*, and the like begins to be prominent only at the end of Philip's reign.[237] By this time the procurators have become sufficiently active for their role to be regulated in some of the provincial charters granted after Philip's death.[238]

Thus despite their obvious limitations, Philip the Fair's peace efforts appear significant when measured against the past royal record. Near the end of his reign in 1313 Parlement opened a separate register for criminal cases. The innovation is a clear witness of increasing judicial activity on the criminal side; more intense royal intervention had produced enough cases to warrant special procedures and records.[239] But Philip the Fair's efforts also provoked the reaction which followed his death. In charters granted to the nobles of Burgundy and Picardy, Louis X had to deal with requests for a restoration of judicial duel and private warfare to full legality, and for limitations on *asseurements*; in general he had to contend with a great touchiness where issues of crown and baronial or ecclesiastical jurisdiction were concerned. A sense of nobles who feel themselves pushed too far appears in every province.[240] This reaction raises a basic question about the action of the crown in the sphere of public order. Were Philip the Fair's active measures simply a late development in the reign of an unusually hard-driving king? Was the reaction at the end of his reign directed against a unique royal initiative? The storm-clouds of the Hundred Years War are so close to Philip the Fair's reign that their shadow can easily obscure any royal efforts to advance internal peace in the decades before private wars merged with national war,[241] and public peace became an issue of the defence of the realm.

[237] Aubert, *Le Parlement de Paris*, 201-8; Glasson, *Histoire du droit*, iii. 343-5; *Ordonnances des roys de France*, 360; Ducoudray states that the royal procurators had an active role in criminal prosecution from the early thirteenth century, but clearly intended the early fourteenth century—he cites *Les Olim*, iii. 104 (1301), 129 (1304); *Actes* 4126 (1313), 4375 (1315). Cf. *Actes* 3902 (1311), 4015 (1312), 4036 (1313), 4266 (1314). The case in no. 4036 involves a plea *a minima* by the procurator. Fawtier and Lot comment on procurators in *Histoire des institutions françaises*, ii. 364-7.

[238] Artonne, *Le Mouvement de 1314*, 47-9, 194.

[239] Strayer, *The Reign of Philip the Fair*, 196.

[240] Artonne, *Le Mouvement de 1314*, *passim*, esp. ch. 6.

[241] A phrase adapted from Fawtier and Lot, *Histoires des institutions françaises*, 430.

The work of Philip V

The reign of Philip V, short though it was, is ample proof that the increased role of the crown in public order was not simply a side-effect of the personality of Philip the Fair brought to an abrupt end by the king's death and the movement of 1314. Once Louis X had survived the crisis of these years of reaction, a king with the ability and temperament of Philip V[242] could act again along lines which seem a characteristic development of high medieval French monarchy. Shortly after his coronation Philip V sent a letter to eight *baillis* noting the 'grant clameur' against disorder, and urging the *baillis* to take all steps possible to remedy the troubled state of the peace, co-operating with the lords possessed of judicial rights.[243] In his ordinance establishing town captains in the second year of his reign, Philip stated his desire 'to protect right and justice and to keep the people in tranquility and peace as in the time of St Louis.'[244] A letter to the *bailli* of Meaux of about the same date notes that 'among all that which touches the estate and government of the king and the realm we desire with the greatest affection the peace and security of our subjects' whose great and increasing clamour against evildoers has prompted the king to take action to bring peace to the land.[245] In a commission issued to several serjeants the king again stated his motives: 'Nous . . . sommes desirans que li mauvais soient puni, si que le bon puissent paisiblement vivre et demorer en pais.'[246] An echo of his father's iron will appears in the characteristic expression 'We wish to be obeyed by all.'[247] Such statements could be dismissed if they were not accompanied by vigorous action. In

[242] This is, of course, no suggestion that Philip V was a rational bureaucrat or a nineteenth-century reformer before his time. Lehugeur, his nineteenth-century biographer who greatly admired him, recognized that he could be superstitious and fanatical. But Lehugeur stressed his vigour, perseverance, and practical intelligence. See esp. pp. 460-6 of his *Histoire de Philippe le Long*.

[243] *Ordonnances des roys de France*, i. 636-67 (20 Mar. 1316).

[244] Ibid.

[245] Ibid. Cf. Lehugeur, *Histoire de Philippe le Long*, 315-16 who cites sources in which Philip justifies his intervention on grounds of his duty to peace, stating that he prefers 'la pez, l'accord et le tranquillité des dites parties que leur plez et descors', and 'pour qu'ils puissent vivre en paix en droiture et en justice'.

[246] Artonne, *Le Mouvement de 1314*, app. 4, p. 339.

[247] Lehugeur, *Histoire de Philippe le Long*, 118, citing *Actes* 4827 as an example.

fact, the reign of Philip V may represent a peak in the public order efforts of the monarchy, at least before the reconstruction following the Hundred Years War.[248] Philip V was not reckless or fanatical in this cause; he seems to have had as good a sense of what was possible as of what was desirable.

Public order was, of course, disturbed by discords ranging from villagers' quarrels with some petty squire to veritable civil wars. Philip the Fair had shown his determination at the upper end of this scale by his efforts to quell the private war between the houses of Foix and Armagnac which so troubled the south-west of France.[249] The challenge to Philip V in Artois may have been even greater, and was met with equal determination and with even greater success. The gentlemen of Artois who claimed a right to 'chevaucher' according to ancient custom were met with a statement of the Parlement 'que armes sont defendus de droit, et par tout le royaume de France'; this declaration was moreover backed with sufficient force.[250] Likewise, the quarrel between the count of Comminges and the countess of Vendôme was settled by a sufficient show of force, in this case the armed force of the seneschal of Carcassonne.[251] But even more impressive are the efforts of Philip V, following his father's example, to move beyond a few spectacular efforts against these upper ranks of society and to take action regarding the ceaseless occurrence of private war, riot, and reciprocal manslaughter among lesser nobles. Philip V won Lehugeur's praise for tailoring his policy to the particular requirements of each province of France. In regions such as the *bailliage* of the Auvergne mountains he prudently reserved for the king's courts only cases touching the royal safeguard. While vigorously enforcing royal safeguards he took the conciliatory step of removing from the doors of abbeys any royal *panonceaux* illegally placed there, at least in provinces where the state of the peace would not be adversely affected.[252] But, overall, the vigour of the king's policy was unmistakable.

[248] See the comments of Lehugeur, *Histoire de Philippe le Long*, 330, 460 ff.

[249] Ducoudray, *Les Origines du Parlement de Paris*, 342, 347-8.

[250] Lehugeur, *Histoire de Philippe le Long*, ch. 3; Artonne, *Le Mouvement de 1314*, ch. 8.

[251] Lehugeur, *Histoire de Philippe le Long*, 305-6.

[252] Ibid. 301. Some allies had demanded this step in 1314; see Artonne, *Le Mouvement de 1314*, 113.

The point is made by an examination of the registers of Parlement for this reign in comparison with others. From each of the Parlements of Philip III a few significant cases relating to the peace of the realm could be extracted. As we have seen this level of royal intervention basically continued during much of the next reign and changed only in the late years of Philip IV; even in these years the number of cases which seem important to public order is small enough for a survey and summary of each. The number of such entries during the entire reign of Philip V becomes simply unmanageable; in fact, even the cases from any single Parlement are beyond case-by-case summary. A few months from a single Parlement can serve to illustrate the king's policy and the volume of judicial business it entailed. Moreover, the active crown intervention is emphasized by the number of *mandements* recorded in parlementary registers; a steady stream of these orders flowed to *baillis*, seneschals, and special agents, instructing them to do justice, to prosecute some case, to seize evildoers, etc.

The following table summarizes the orders and *arrêts* from only the first several months of the Tousaint Parlement of 1316-17.[253]

Royal Mandements, *December 1316 - February 1317*

Sent to:	*Action Ordered:*
Seneschal of Toulouse	Do prompt justice to Fortenier de Cirac, convicted of killing Callard de Cirac after provoking him into a judicial duel.
Seneschal of Périgord	Force former seneschal of Gascony to return what he had taken from abbey of Sauve-Majeure, Bordeaux diocese.
Baillis of duchy of Burgundy	Present king's letters, addressed to duke, to three knights charged with pursuit and arrest 'by force or otherwise', of lord of Rougemont because of his misdeeds against Jean d'Is.

[253] Relevant cases drawn from *Actes* 4491-664.

Royal guardian of county of Burgundy, *baillis* of Macon, Sens, Chaumont, Troyes, and other justiciars of realm	Find and take into king's hands goods of Jean d'Is and his children which have been seized by the lord of Rougement.
Bailli of Caen	Arrest and punish two clerks and two laymen accused of attacking and horribly wounding a royal sergeant and subordinate on royal service.
Bailli of Vitry and Chaumont	Pursue and punish those who abducted an esquire, taking him out of the realm.
Bailli of Amiens	Pursue men who pillaged the house of a knight.
Baillis of Auvergne and Auvergne Mountains	Pursue former *bailli* of Auvergne Mountains for abuse of power while in office.
Bailli of Rouen	Make *enquête* secretly concerning 'schedules' distributed in streets of Rouen against two citizens. Arrest authors of the libels.
Bailli of Caen	Judge without delay case of a man suspected of mutilating another; assailant has been let out of prison by gaoler, his relative.
Seneschal of Carcassonne	Send before next Parlement a knight who cut off the hand of a cleric; royal procurator to come and attend to king's right.
Seneschal of Carcassonne	Punish those who attacked and severed the hand of R. Raynal.
Bailli of Vitry	Punish Marie La Ferrière, accused of burning the grange of Brandis.
Arrêt	Partial confirmation of sentence of seneschal of Périgord against man accused of an attack with prohibited arms, against the king's edict.

Arrêt	Confirmation of sentence of lieutenant of seneschal of Périgord against four men who attacked two artisans who had insulted them.
Bailli of Amiens	Investigate accusations of injustice against the serjeant and receiver of Jeanne, Lady of Creseque.
Bailli of Vitry	Pursue a murder left unpunished because of official corruption.
Bailli of Troyes and Jacques de laNoue, advocate	Make inquest on the misdeeds committed against a former *enquêteur* in Champagne.
Bailli of Caen	Judge without delay the former serjeant of Thorigny accused by a widow of death of her husband, a charge he claims is made in vengeance for his official actions.
Seneschal of Lyon	Find by *enquête* which citizens of Condrieux cut the vines of *prévôt* of Lyon. Punish them in such a way as to make an example.
Seneschal of Périgord	Proceed to *enquête* concerning violences and criminal excesses of people of Périgueux against the mayor, consuls, and certain bourgeois of the city.
Seneschal of Carcassonne	Punish the consuls and inhabitants of Castres in Albigerois who made a conspiracy against their lords the count of Cominges and Gui de Cominges and took arms against Gui and his men.
Seneschal of Toulouse	Do justice for Alvard Vivat who claims that because of his suits against the violences of the men of Jourdain de l'Isle and the bishop of Toulouse he was arrested by Jourdain and brought before the bishop's temporal court.
Pons d'Omelas, king's	Inquire into the wrongs and

knight, and Master Bernard Gervais, *docteur es lois* and *juge mage* of of Périgord and Quercy	excesses charged by the count of Cominges and his brother against the countess of Vendôme.
Bailli of Auvergne	Pursue a knight and esquire who ambushed and abducted beyond the realm a *damoiseau*.
Bailli of Auvergne	Pursue a knight and his accomplices who attacked and pillaged a house, seeking to kill its owner.
Bailli of Senlis	Pursue Eustace, called 'le de Boves de Fresnes', who led a dawn attack by men armed with lances and other weapons, and left their enemy for dead in front of his house; they had attacked without the customary defiance required in noble quarrels and thus the attack was treason.
Bailli of Auvergne	Place under king's special guard Jean Aymes de Clermont whose enemies had not appeared in court at the session agreed on for swearing an *asseurement*.
Baillis of Tours and Orléans	Proceed to *enquête* sought by the heirs of man murdered on his way to prosecute his case appealed to Parlement; local justice had left the crime unpunished.
Bailli of Vermandois	Make *enquête* and rule on plea of the chapter of Noyen concerning the violence of a troop of armed men who invaded a canon's house; *bailli* is to make a terrible example of the guilty.
Bailli ot Caux	Pursue Jean called 'Beaufils' who attacked a man to whom he had sworn *asseurement* before *bailli* at assize of Arques.

Juge Mage of *sénéchausée* of Rouergue and judge of Millau	Prosecute *enquête*, begun by order of Louis X, against Gui, seigneur and baron of Sevrace, under suspicion of criminal excess and disobedience.
Seneschal and *juge mage* of Toulouse	Do not prosecute or molest Pierre Rubei, criminal clerk of Toulouse, the object of noble hatreds because of official prosecution brought by the former seneschal.
Bailli of Vermandois	Determine who broke the truce between Jacques de Frechancourt and Jean de Caux; Jacques claimed that though his enemy had resumed the violence, his goods had been seized by the crown as if he were the aggressor.
Seneschal of Beaucaire	Punish the bourgeois of Montpellier who had attacked a serjeant of king of Majorca and freed a townsman he was conducting to Parlement.
Seneschal of Rouergue	Punish those guilty of criminal violences against the king's protection.
Bailli of Macon	Punish the townsmen of Macon who threatened the royal *prévôt* as he made his nightly rounds with the watch; they had invaded his house two days later and smashed his wine barrels.
Seneschal of Toulouse	Find by *enquête* if Arnaud de Blancafort, who had taken part in a war between Othon de Temda and the abbot of Belleperche, had been included in a truce concluded between the parties by the efforts of the seneschal.
Seneschal of Rouergue	Prosecute those who by night destroyed a woods under the king's protection, as a royal baton attested.

The registers time and again present ugly vignettes of the local quarrels which so easily became minor wars. After a dispute between his nephew and a brother of Gilbert de St-Brie in 1320, Guillaume de Brae, knight, called together his friends, tenants, and subordinates and seems to have issued a general invitation to join in the action by making proclamations in several towns, urging a rendezvous at St-Ouen on St Madeleine's day. The knight led a score of men backed up by a 'great crowd of men at arms' and Gilbert was attacked and killed.[254] The abbot of St-Nicholas-au-Bois led a troop of armed men against the town of Crespy in Laonnais. After wounding some unfortunate shepherds and a man tending partridge traps, they sighted more men from Crespy on a nearby height and attacked them with cries of 'Kill, kill. Death to the louts from Crespy!' The abbot wounded one man with his own hand and then trampled him beneath his horse's hooves. The Crespy men raised the cry 'harou' and a serjeant sent by the *prévôt* brought out a sworn body of men from Crespy to rescue their fellow townsmen; but the serjeant was himself thrown from his horse and beaten.[255] Even more blatant was the attack of the knight Jean de St-Symphorien who led 500 men with banners and penons flying against a *bastide* (a fortified administrative centre) belonging to the prior of Montrotier. Though the *bastide* was under royal safeguard this veritable army broke in, tore down gallows, smashed wine barrels and measures, attacked and wounded some of the inhabitants, carried off others to be ransomed, etc.[256]

Parlement handed down judgments in hundreds of cases like these, sometimes involving men of higher status and damages on a vaster scale. But the reign of Philip V is distinguished by more than numbers of cases brought to Parlement. A series of measures undertaken in the first two or three years of the reign created or continued institutional changes affecting the peace. An ordinance of 1318 commanded all seneschals, *baillis*, and other officers to remain at their posts 'continuellement et personnellement'; they were not to serve by lieutenants without royal licence.[257] In the same year and with the same

[254] *Actes* 6038.
[255] *Actes* 6147.
[256] *Actes* 6745.
[257] *Ordonnances des roys de France*, i. 671, art. 8.

improvement in mind an ordinance ended the practice of farming the *prévôtés*, the local judicial and administrative sub-units of the *bailliages*.[258] A close study of the effects of this change (reversed by a return to farming in 1357) might prove interesting; the *prévôts* had a police jurisdiction and a police function of no small importance to public order.

The royal initiative is seen more specifically in orders to make terrible examples of evildoers[259] or to do justice where local justice has failed.[260] The concern is equally apparent in a series of more general commissions for the pursuit of groups or types of offenders troubling entire regions of France; sometimes these orders urge vigorous action on established local officials, but in other cases they commission action by *ad hoc* royal agents. In fact, we can find such commissions in the last years of Philip IV. In June 1314, for example, all justices of the realm were ordered to allow Jean Bardeau, *prévôt* of Montargis, to exercise freely his commission from the king to find and arrest evildoers in the *bailliages* of Sens, Orléans, and Nevers.[261] This type of commission became more common under Philip V. The seneschals of Poitou and Limousin and the viguier of St-Yrieix received orders in July 1317 to punish evildoers who were going about armed night and day, carrying off and violating women, pillaging homes, and committing other outrages.[262] In January 1318 orders to the seneschals of Périgord and Poitou instructed them to pursue and arrest evildoers, murderers, brigands on highways, and the banished men troubling their *sénéchausées* by enormous misdeeds.[263] Another order in the same month commissioned Jean Payen, *auditeur* at the Châtelet, to pursue anywhere in the realm (ubilibet in regno nostro Francie) counterfeiters of royal or other coin, or other offenders against monetary regulations, and 'abusers of our people'.[264] The

[258] Ducoudray, *Les Origines du Parlement de Paris*, 676. Some of the allies in 1314-15 had sought an end to forming of various offices: *prévôtés* in the North, the offices of *viguiers*, *bailles* and *notaires* in the South; Artonne, *Le Mouvement de 1314*, 109.

[259] *Actes* 4600, 5592, 5593, 5597, etc.

[260] *Actes* 4598, 5644, 5656, etc.

[261] *Actes* 4329.

[262] *Actes* 4949.

[263] *Actes* 5156.

[264] A N MS X2a 2 f. 210v, pr. Artonne, *Le Mouvement de 1314*, app. II, no. 5, p. 341. Cf. *Actes* 5171.

seneschals of Périgord and Poitiers were ordered in January 1318 to pursue and punish masked thieves and evildoers who were desolating the region with their intolerable crimes. The king believed that barons and prelates were aiding the evildoers by giving them asylum. The royal officials were to proclaim the prohibition against carrying arms, against going about masked and against receiving evildoers; they were to urge barons and prelates to aid royal efforts; and they were to provide them with a copy of the order under the king's seal, so that they could not pretend ignorance.[265] In the following month the king ordered Pons de Mortagne to pursue evildoers, arsonists, and thieves who committed ravages in the realm and troubled the public peace.[266] A few days later the *baillis* of Sens and Burgundy were ordered to correct an outrageous situation which had come to the king's attention 'par la clameur de pleseurs': armed men of various ranks were coming in parties of horse and foot from the 'pais d'Auceurroys' (the region around Auxerre and the nearby borderlands) secretly and in disguise to ambush rich and loyal subjects, merchants, and others, and carry them by force to cruel imprisonment and torture outside of the realm where they were kept until ransom had been paid.[267] Within the year Philip ordered the seneschal of Lyons to raise a troop of twelve to twenty knights at the king's cost as a force to find and punish the 'sons of iniquity' who were desolating the region by their armed violences.[268]

The creation of town captains was closely related to the public order campaign evident in the registers of Parlement.[269] On 27 January 1317 Philip V convoked the proctors of the *bonnes villes* to deliberate on the common profit of the realm. The result of the deliberations was a request from the towns to 'faire exercer bon droit et bonne justice dans le royaume, de maintenir le peuple en paix en la manière quil fut maintenu au temps de monseigneur Saint Louis et de leur fournir le moyen de repousser la force par la force'. Philip V responded in the ordinance of 12 March 1317

265 *Actes* 5169. Boutaric provides a Latin text.

266 *Actes* 5193.

267 *Actes* 5207.

268 *Actes* 5617.

269 The following is based on *Ordonnances des roys de France*, i. 635-6; Lehugeur, *Histoire de Philippe le Long*, 112-14.

which established captains to whom the townsmen would swear obedience in matters of defence. These captains would supervise the selection of suitable people with horses and arms and those who would be foot-soldiers. They were to keep the arms in a secure place, lest the needy sell them or pledge them and 'to avoid all other perils', which hints at a prudent concern over civil strife. In each *bailliage* a superior level of command was vested in a captain general, also to be installed at the king's cost. It remains uncertain how fully this plan was implemented. If the captains were implanted in the twelve *bailliages* to which the king's letters were sent their number would have reached several hundred. Lehugeur cited some archival evidence to show instances in which captains were actually chosen and he states vaguely that town militias were created 'where it was useful.' Timbal cited evidence of captains being paid (at widely varying rates), but observed that the king never agreed to assume the cost of captains' wages as the towns had requested; the difficulties and legal actions over wages noted by Timbal suggest something less than a settled, functioning system.[270] In the absence of a careful study the degree of implementation and the effectiveness of the plan cannot be assessed. However, the attempt at co-operation between townsmen and the crown in the area of public order remains significant.

Overall, the policy of Philip V meant a more active crown effort in peace measures than at any previous time.[271] But his death at an early age in 1322, followed by his brother's early death and the shift to a collateral line of kings in 1328 reduced this role considerably, even before the Hundred Years War radically changed the nature of the problem of maintaining the peace in France. Charles IV did not suddenly abandon the policy of his father and brother. From the end of July to the opening week of November 1322, for example, an almost continuous stream of executive orders recall the long series of *mandements* for the peace issued by Philip V,[272] and significant judgments against the

270 Timbal, *La Guerre de Cent Ans*, 172-4.

271 Lehugeur saw in this reign in general 'non ce qu'on appelle souvent avec dédain une période de transition, mais au contraire une sorte d'apogée'; *Histoire de Philippe le Long*, p. ix. Cf. ch. 3. He considered the restoration of justice in particular to have been one of the major accomplishments to the credit of Philip's government.

272 *Actes* 6896-940. A similar, but shorter run of orders is found in nos. 7536-46.

private warfare and excesses of lords and townsmen can be found in the registers from his later Parlements. After an armed invasion of the land of the sire de Tetancourt by the inhabitants of St-Dizier, acting with the blessing of the sire of St-Dizier in 1324, the *bailli* of Vitry was ordered to make an *enquête* and do justice; the crown, in fact, marvelled that he had been thus far negligent.[273] Of even more interest is the order of the same year instructing all *baillis* to send to Parlement a list of all individuals banished from their *bailliages*, the criminal *enquêtes* begun, and the letters of remission and other royal letters received; the order was issued because of the great number of crimes committed in the realm and the forged royal letters which were being used.[274] But the momentum of Philip V was not maintained, especially in the last two or three years of Charles IV's reign. The uncertainties caused by the end of the Capetian dynasty and accession of the Valois, together with the awful certainties brought to many parts of France by the great Anglo-French war, clearly lowered the level of royal activity in public order attempted by Philip IV and Philip V.[275]

Yet it seems important that by the end of Philip the Fair's reign the French crown had begun to use its judicial procedures and officers, on the whole long available, against private warfare. Almost any private quarrel of nobles pursued with violence could in theory be brought into a royal court on one charge or another. A seigneur would have to fight his *guerra* with sword in one hand and rule book in the other to avoid violating a general *ordonnance* or a specific prohibition, a royal safeguard or an *asseurement* imposed by the crown; he must remember to restrain his impulse to ambush the enemy, and at the same time he had to count out the days of the *Quarantaine le Roy* before acting. Obviously, many lords threw away the rulebook and attacked with vigour, and just as obviously the number of cases brought before the king's judges represented only a portion of all the private wars fought in early fourteenth-century France. Moreover, entire

[273] *Actes* 7410.

[274] *Actes* 7317. Cases involving royal letters surreptitiously obtained are mentioned in 1317 and 1319. See nos. 5024, 5026, 5865.

[275] This conclusion was reinforced by an examination of the unpublished registers of the Parlement for this period. To sample this voluminous evidence the registers for 1334-5, 1345-6 were searched (A N MS X2a3, X2a5). I wish to thank Miss Kathleen Parrow who made the initial search for me and Mr David Kaeuper who secured the microfilm from the Archives nationales.

regions of France completely escaped the king's jurisdiction over private warfare.[276] Even outside the great fiefs, the king's courts could have brought only a few of the warring nobles into court for their actions. Lacking detailed regional studies and full records it is difficult to know on what basis particular quarrels came into the royal courts or to estimate what effect royal action had on the state of the peace across the expanse of the kingdom. That a start was made seems significant. That this beginning did not produce a sustained expansion of the royal role in public order is not surprising.

Private war in England

The contrast between the resolution of the problem of private warfare and associated disorders in England and France is evident from a comparison of the treatises of Bracton and Beaumanoir. Whereas Beaumanoir, as noted above, devotes two full chapters to the elaborate code by which the legitimate right of private war was to be conducted, Bracton's commentary is limited to an ambiguous assertion that a tenant must stand with his liege lord in the case of quarrels among his several lords. As Maitland commented, 'The ordinary English criminal law is strong enough to suppress anything that we could fairly call private war . . . .'[277] In other words, the early growth of royal jurisdiction over serious breaches of the peace, and the actual power of the crown to enforce this jurisdiction, prevented any growth of a right of private war in England.

276 The lord of Mont-Saint-Jean, convicted of violence and waging private war in Burgundy by the ducal court was sentenced in 1323 to a loss of several castles. His appeal to the king of France disputed not the justice of this conviction but the duke's right to jurisdiction. This case might have opened the entire question of judicial competences at a time when the royal control over private war was expanding. But as Carolla Small explains, 'in the end the lord of Mont-Saint-Jean, considering as he put it, the peril which might arise in the duchy from such an appeal, withdrew it. It would be interesting to know what means the duke employed to induce him to do so.' 'Appeals from the Duchy of Burgundy', 363. Cf. the letters of non-prejudice given to the Duke of Brittany on the subject of *port d'armes* jurisdiction in 1326 that are printed in Artonne, *Le Mouvement de 1314* (p. 346).

277 Philippe de Beaumanoir, *Coutumes de Beauvaisis*, chs. 59, 60; Bracton's views are cited by Maitland and Pollock, *History of English Law*, i. 302; the quot. from Maitland is taken from pp. 302-3 n. 3.

The comparison between England and France is illuminated by the striking contrast suggested by J. G. Edwards between England on the one hand and Wales and the Welsh Marches on the other.[278] In the relatively small area of the Welsh March, lords built castles when and where they liked within their lands and fought wars among themselves at will; the crown accepted the situation. But in England itself, several times larger than the March, the crown insisted on control over the rights both of fortification and of war. Edwards argued that the Norman lords penetrated into Wales and created the March of Wales not simply by conquering Welsh lands but by taking over the existing Welsh commotes (the units of lordship). A Norman lord who acquired one or more commotes acquired not merely the land, but the traditional rights of the Welsh lord (called variously lord or prince or king) within the commote. Welsh lordship was royal in character; it entailed comprehensive jurisdiction, high and low; and it gave to its possessor the right of making war. This right of war, recognized by English kings as late as 1241, was the crucial aspect of lordship in the Welsh March, for legitimate private war differentiated Marcher lordship from the realm of England. Edwards points to developments in kingship as the cause:

> Regarded from the constitutional point of view, the contrast between Anglo-Saxon England and Welsh Wales had been this: that whereas both countries had started with kingship that was multiple, in England multiple kingship had by the time of the Norman Conquest developed into a single kingship, while in Wales it had remained multiple, diffused among the 'lords' or 'princes' or 'kings' whose number varied but whose status remained royal. Moreover in attaining singleness, kingship in Anglo-Saxon England attained also a surprising degree of institutional development.[279]

In an important rethinking of the issues Edwards raised, R. R. Davies has proposed that the military realities of Wales and the Welsh border were, in fact, more important than the constitutional framework later created to order them in men's minds.[280] Given the fluid situation as the Normans pressed their conquests, any definition of the March of Wales in geographical terms, let alone in legal or constitutional terms, would be premature; we must

278 Edwards, 'The Normans and the Welsh March'.

279 Ibid. 175.

280 'Kings, Lords, and Liberties'.

think in terms of marches of Wales, rather than *a* March of Wales. And above all we must think in terms of war:

> Wales throughout this period was a land of war; peace there was brittle and short-lived. In such a society the liberty to wage war was no constitutional right but the primary rule of survival and the only sure means to lordship. It is only in a society which assumes peace as the norm, and the king's peace as the universal exclusive guarantor of man's rights, that war becomes a transgression and that a distinction can be drawn between 'public' and 'private' war. The March of Wales was as yet innocent of both assumptions.[281]

Professor Davies's comment suggests, from a new perspective, the parallel between conditions which obtained over much of the continent and those which interest him in Wales. As in post-Carolingian France, ambitious lords in Wales and the marches planted motte and bailey castles in their territories and exercised rough rights of justice over the common people of the region. The emerging lordships must have seemed to them more than a little like the castellanies into which so much of contemporary France was being divided. Of course, there was a king of France and there was not a king of Wales, but the effects of that difference lay some distance in the future. In the English realm built by Norman and Angevin kings on solid Anglo-Saxon foundations, the continental *droit de guerre* was not welcomed. According to the chronicler Ordericus Vitalis, this absence of private war was a noteworthy difference between England and Normandy in the reign of Henry I.[282]

By the late thirteenth century Edward I considered the right of war, even in the March, a dangerous anachronism. In 'the most spectacular incident of the first half of his reign'[283] Edward brought two of the greatest magnates of the realm, Humphrey de Bohun, earl of Hereford and lord of Brecknock, and Gilbert de Clare, earl of Gloucester and lord of Glamorgan, to trial in 1291 for waging private warfare in the March against his prohibition.[284] Defiant raids by the quarrelling lords had brought

281 'Kings, Lords, and Liberties', 45-6.

282 Maitland and Pollock, *The History of English Law*, i. 302-3 n. 3.

283 Altschul, *A Baronial Family in Medieval England*, 146.

284 See *Rotuli Parliamentorum*, i. 70-7; *Calendar of Various Chancery Rolls, Welsh Rolls*, 334-49, and Morris, *The Welsh Wars*, 224-39; Altschul, *A Baronial Family in Medieval England*, 145-56. As Edwards points out, Maitland and Pollock (*The History of English Law*, i. 302) omit the vital point that the private war was fought in the marches and thus was not subject to common law rules, *The Welsh Wars*, 173 n. 1.

a harsh reaction from Edward. At one point in the process Edward's judges pointedly reminded the marcher lords that their liberties could not exclude the lord king 'qui, pro communi utilitate, per prerogativam suam in multis casibus est supra leges et consuetudines in regno suo usitatas'.[285] The sentences against both Hereford and Gloucester contain a statement that the earls thought that they could do under cover of custom of the March what they would not dare to do elsewhere—'credentes quod per liberatatem suam marchie possent evadere a pena et periculo que merito incurisse debuissent si extra marcham alibi in regno talem excessum perpetrassent.'[286] Both earls were committed to prison, their Welsh lordships were seized into the king's hands and declared forfeit. Although the earls were soon allowed to redeem their bodies (Gloucester for 10,000*m*, Hereford for 1,000*m*) and in a matter of months had their Welsh lordships returned, the earls had suffered a major disgrace and the rights of private war in the March had suffered likewise. In Michael Altschul's view: 'The drama was completed. The dignity of the Crown had been fully asserted at the expense of the mightiest lords of the march. The king . . . had successfully appealed to concepts of public welfare and the supremacy of royal prerogative to eliminate the best known feature of marcher custom.'[287] In fact, although this spectacular case was followed by others of lesser note, the custom of the March was not permanently eliminated by Edward I.[288] But even if the achievement of the first Edward was not maintained by his successors, crown suppression of the right of private war in England was sufficiently established that the imperious Edward could temporarily suppress the custom even on the Welsh March; this situation presents a distinct contrast to that which obtained in France.

We need not believe that English lords and gentry behaved in decent and orderly fashion or that they settled in a court of law all of the squabbles that a sporting sense of fair play could not resolve. The privileged ranks of English society did bring a large and increasing number of their quarrels into the king's courts, as

[285] *Rotuli Parliamentorum* i. 71, quot.: Altschul, *A Baronial Family in Medieval England*, 150-1.

[286] Quot.: Morris, *The Welsh Wars*, 233-5.

[287] Altschul, *A Baronial Family in Medieval England*, 153.

[288] Morris, *The Welsh Wars*, 237-9.

the growing bulk of court records testifies. They seem likewise to have combined their litigation quite comfortably with a propensity for violence and self-help similar to that found among the nobility and townsmen of France. The absence of a recognized right of private war probably had a restraining effect in England, somewhat lowering the scale of quarrels if not their emotional temperature. What a French lord might claim as his right was prohibited to any Englishman by law, though of course he might try anything in a fit of passion or an act of calculated violence. After reading some portion of the surviving court records for each country one is left with a distinct impression that in his lifetime an ordinary English villager or merchant would be less likely than his French counterpart to see veritable armies clanking off to smite a foe, that he would be less likely to witness castle ramparts scaled by an assault force, or to be present in a village, small town, or abbey that had been sacked and left smouldering. But at the level of gentry or minor noble feuding, of attacks on fortified manor houses, armed encounters over rights to arable or pasture, town riots, personal assault, there is a wealth of evidence on either side of the Channel. The difference lies in the locus of jurisdiction rather than in the likely incidence of outbreaks of violence on this scale. In England the entire responsibility was shouldered by the king's government. As we have already noted, the fragmentation of justice which complicated efforts at maintaining order in France, was much less of an issue in England where possession of noble status and a castle, or even a good manor house, did not allow a man to claim rights of high justice over lesser mortals in the vicinity.

Having long denied the right of private war, English kings did not need to build a jurisdiction on specific royal safeguards, or on the violation of assurances made in royal courts before the king's officials; violation of the encompassing king's peace was the snare in which all manner of violators were caught. The charge that your enemy came *vi et armis*, by force and arms, was sufficient to bring your case into the royal court. So popular was this device, as we have noted, that the sheer volume of business was a major factor in the demise of the general eyre which had for more than a century brought the justice of the king's court into the counties and which had, in theory, repressed crime and punished the king's errant officials.

The dilemma of a medieval government trying with its limited resources to maintain a war policy and at the same time preserve internal peace is almost painfully illustrated in the efforts of English kings in the late thirteenth and fourteenth century; they tried within a matter of a generation or two to smite the Welsh who refused to believe in the permanence of English conquest, to carry out the conquest of Scotland after a client king proved intractable, and then to conquer France, the premier kingdom of Western Europe, while at home they experimented with replacements for the eyre and tried to prevent lords animated by a code of violence, on whom the war effort depended, from tearing apart the fragile structure of the peace in the counties. The fact of their failure is less surprising than the dogged vigour with which they worked.[289]

Thus, repressing the right of private war certainly did not relieve the English crown of the problem of open violence by lords and gentry. In a curious way the long-standing English prohibition against private warfare may have increased the business of outlaw gangs like the Folvilles and Coterels, the outstanding examples that have attracted careful study.[290] These gangs were available for hire and so were useful agents in local feuding. They could, as it were, carry out extra-legal services for those who wished to remain, or at least to appear to remain, technically within the law. Either the evidence on similar groups in France has not been brought to light or the different status of private warfare in France made them unnecessary.

Of course, many Englishmen liked to carry out their feuding personally. As a result Edward I,[291] Edward II, [292] Edward III,[293] no less than their French cousins thought it wise to supplement

[289] See the comments of J. R. Strayer, 'The Promise of the Fourteenth Century'. G. W. S. Barrow writes of the 'calm ambitiousness and the extraordinary thoroughness of the thirteenth-century English monarchy' under Edward I: 'Here was a feudal king, peripatetic and personally attentive to all the details of administration, ruling an empire and fighting a complex war by means of a handful of hard-working officials. It is staggering to think of the weight of responsibility that rested on such men. . . .' (*Robert Bruce*, 107).

[290] Stones, 'The Folvilles of Ashby-Folville'; Bellamy, 'The Coterel Gang'; id., *Crime and Public Order*, ch. 2.

[291] *Foedera*, i. 709, 711; *CCR 1296-1302*, 373, 408, 588.

[292] *CCR 1318-1323*, 293.

[293] *CPR 1334-1338*, 200.

extant peace regulations with prohibitions against armed assemblies, riding armed, going 'with armed force and banners flying as in war',[294] or appearing with horses and arms in fairs and markets or at court sessions.[295] As John Bellamy has suggested, one source of pressure leading to the conservative definition of treason in the great statute of 1351 was the lord's concern that an accusation of riding armed to rob, slay, or capture might be treated as treason. Not only did lords fear a loss of their forfeitures in the event their vassals were convicted of felony (since a traitor's goods were forfeit to the king rather than to the traitor's lord), they may have been uneasy over a policy which threatened tough reprisal for an activity that on occasion had some appeal for them.[296]

The problems confounding English governmental efforts to secure some level of public order thus read as a homily on the perils of over-extension both at home and abroad. A machinery of governance with high claims to political and social control and some significant capacity to act on those claims was worth fighting over. That medieval Englishmen did indeed fight over royal government is writ large in the famous struggles of the twelfth and thirteenth centuries. The issue for public order is not merely the obvious problems of civil war and its close cousins, but the uncertainties generated by a control of judicial machinery somewhat short of the impartial. For a medieval realm England was a much-governed country,[297] but more laws do not automatically make a realm more lawful. We have only to consider the effect on public order of the agonizing political upheavals which followed the death of Edward I. With so much authority cumulatively invested in the monarchy, a capable regime generally acceptable to the politically potent was essential to the maintenance of confidence in royal justice. The results of royal incapacity or a great reliance on favourites are clearly outlined by Natalie Fryde:

The personal nightmare of any medieval landowner, whether a great magnate at court or a substantial knight in a far-flung part of England,

[294] *CPR 1334-1338*, 204.

[295] Statute of Northampton, 2 Edw. III, c. 3, *Statutes of the Realm*, i. 258.

[296] Bellamy, *The Law of Treason*, ch. 4, esp., 74-8.

[297] See the comment of Maitland and Pollock, *The History of English Law*, i. 688.

was that one of his neighbours should become so powerful that he would be able to ride with armed men into his ancestral lands and disseize him of them. This could happen in one of two circumstances. The first was that the neighbour became a royal favourite so that nobody dared challenge him. The second was that the character of the king had so diminished the royal authority that the neighbour no longer feared the king's wrath or that of his ministers. Both nightmares became a reality under Edward II . . .[298]

Parts of this nightmare would trouble the sleep of a good many Englishmen across much of the late Middle Ages.

England had been a tight little island for a long time in the reign of Edward II. In contrast, the political atmosphere in France seems to have been much more relaxed, the actors seem to have worked under pressure much less intense than that in England. The combination of the sheer size of France and the degree of pure chance in royal genetics might be advanced in explanation, and would contain much truth: the expanse and regional diversity of France dictated a royal policy which differed from that pursued by kings in England; and the steady production of reasonably competent heirs by the Capetians is a well-known factor in their success. How well any of the late Capetians would have managed the problems of rule across the Channel fog is obviously beyond our knowing. But that does not rule out the likelihood that the early success of the kings of England, operative by fits and starts from the ninth to the thirteenth centuries, had paradoxically led to problems of law and justice which by the late thirteenth and fourteenth centuries were beyond the human and material resources available.

4. CONCLUSION

In both kingdoms royal administrations attempted to expand the control they could exercise over the violence of the privileged in society, the violence closely related to a chivalric code of honour. This effort reached its apogee in the late thirteenth and early fourteenth century, but faltered across the remainder of the century.

The differences between England and France are as important as this common decline of royal efforts to control chivalric

[298] Fryde, *The Tyranny and Fall of Edward II*, 14.

violence within the realms. This decline stemmed from quite distinct historical processes on either side of the Channel. In England an over-extended crown, unable to provide the order it promised, especially while it fought the wars which held out the lure of loot and glory, backed away from confrontations with the men whose support provided the military campaigns. At the same time, taking the path of least resistance in a difficult time, the crown increasingly enlisted the arbiters of local society in the ranks of those enforcing the law, with perhaps predictable results. Thus English lords saw no need to confront royal jurisdiction directly; they clearly were acquiring a large share in its control and operation. The king's justice was a fact in their lives, but they lived all the more comfortably with this fact when they, their friends, relatives, or retainers were the king's justices, or at least chose them.[299] But in fourteenth-century France the royal effort to effect public peace was only in its infancy in contrast to seigneurial rights entrenched behind ramparts of usage three centuries old, exercised by lords in possession of ramparts more concrete still. Royal efforts were easily associated with the problems of demographic and economic crisis, of extended warfare financed by prise and taxation.[300] The degree of French noble resistance and the demand for independence thus come as no surprise. As Lehugeur suggested, royal institutions were outpacing social customs.[301] Although the efforts of the crown may have come to a peak under Philip V, the programme could not be sustained at full vigour, especially after the change of dynasty in 1328 and the outbreak of war in 1337. French kings were given very little choice between the war and peace goals of the medieval state for the next century.

Thus the decline of royal efforts to expand kingly controls over chivalric violence took different forms in England and France and stemmed from different historical processes. Quite different historical results also emerged, as will be apparent when we turn to evidence on public opinion.

[299] Kaeuper, 'Law and Order'; Harding, *The Law Courts of Medieval England,* 94-5; Maddicott, 'Law and Lordship'.

[300] Contamine points out the connection between the impulse toward reform and the hard times of the early fourteenth century; 'De la puissance aux privilèges', 248-9.

[301] Lehugeur, *Histoire de Philippe le Long*, p. ix: '. . . les mœurs sont en retard sur les institutions'.

4

Vox Populi

At the start of the fourteenth century, though in somewhat different ways and degrees, royal government in England and France had become the authority finally responsible for the provision of justice and the supervision of public order. The king's government not only pursued the most extensive and energetic warfare Europe had yet seen, it also affected the state of justice and order within the realm in complex and sometimes even contradictory ways. The crown did not simply repress internal disorder and provide alternatives to violence. By the sheer exercise of administrative power in demanding the service and wealth of subjects, especially for the inexorable demands of war, it provoked loud cries of resentment and bitter charges of injustice. Political resistance, vitriolic complaint, and major risings mark the fourteenth century and suggest important questions about responses to the action of the emerging state in England and France. Such issues are as difficult as they are important for they take us into the perilous realm of public opinion. 'Little is known about anybody's opinion for the larger part of recorded history', as J. R. Strayer has noted, and when medieval historians in particular have tried to gauge popular opinion they have 'had to deduce its existence, its weight and its direction from political perturbations, much like astronomers trying to prove the existence of a new heavenly body which they have not yet seen.'[1] Squinting into the night sky may seem an appropriate image whenever a medievalist tries to take from his fragmentary sources a coherent reading of some layer of popular opinion on the emerging state. Not only are the sources painfully inadequate, the very abstraction, state, was scarcely conceived by men who saw, experienced, and wrote about only particular rulers, officials, and courts, and whose critical acumen ran more

[1] Strayer, 'The Historian's Concept of Public Opinion', 263.

along the lines of moral denunciations of particular orders in society, rather than analyses of institutions which were often thought to be immutable, even while they were changing rapidly and with powerful effect. Yet the sources which seem so inadequate in bulk are at the same time frustratingly diffuse; almost any aspect of medieval culture in our period could yield its bit of useful information on widespread attitudes towards the governance of kings, royal policies, and the conduct of officers, especially as the scope of royal government broadened to touch so many aspects of life.

Three approaches, however, seem particularly fruitful for trying to understand popular opinion about the actions of the royal governments in war, justice, and public order. We will turn first to the dialogue between prince and subjects that is so evident in the attempts from each side to reform the working of the institutions of governance. Secondly, we will look for reflections of the state in works of literature on either side of the Channel. Finally, we will compare the great fourteenth-century risings that, momentarily at least, shook the English and French realms to their foundations. On the basis of these efforts, which can only be exploratory, given the complexity of evidence and interpretations, we can again raise the general question of a widespread view of the state as it was developing its powers in each country.

1. THE DIALOGUE OF SECULAR REFORM

Ideas of reform in one sense or another have been hardy perennials in Western history. But in the High Middle Ages, when so many lasting European institutions began their life, reform was often used in an institutional sense, especially with regard to the major institutions that ordered life—the institutional church and the emerging state. In this institutional or even constitutional sense reform meant the process of continuing adjustment in the frame of governance conceived in legal terms.

The conceptual atmosphere was probably influenced by the Gregorian Reform of the late eleventh and twelfth centuries.[2] For whatever the purely spiritual dimensions in their concept, the church reformers came to see that they could only effect their programme by constructing effective, centralized institutions. Among the most significant outcomes of the reform movement in the church, after all, was the creation of the papal monarchy which registered its triumph in the growing body of canon law. Historians often label this papal monarchy the first Western state. Without accepting that designation we can note the close association of a High Medieval reform impulse with the elaboration of a great machinery of governance and a body of law. We might think of a reform movement in the emerging state as a 'secular' parallel to the reform of the institutional church—secular, that is, only in the sense of non-ecclesiastical, for the state always claimed its own sacred status. The state drew upon the church for that sacral quality, but it also drew upon its own expanding role in law. In each case reform involved a major institution of governance and voiced its hopes in the language of law.

Across the late eleventh, twelfth, and thirteenth centuries the socio-economic foundations for the growth of the European state came into being as population, arable land, towns, and commerce expanded.[3] Moreover, the great revival of jurisprudence which was so prominent a feature of Western European society gave the emerging state its characteristic form as a law state.[4] Under the circumstances kings and subjects could carry on a dialogue about respective rights and obligations within an institutional and legal framework. All acknowledged that this framework was enduring; but all, in practice, considered it to be subject to continuing change. Reform was not simply created by kings, neither was it always forced down royal throats by subjects zealously defending their rights; it was instead (to borrow for this context the words of Bernard Guenée) the result of a dialogue between prince and *pays*.[5] We can thus consider the secular reform movement not as a static attempt to effect some fixed list of specific goals and

[2] Tellenbach, *Church, State, and Christian Society*; Fliche, *La Réforme grégorienne*; Chenu, *Nature, Man, and Society*; Cowdrey, 'The Peace and the Truce of God'; Duby, 'Laity and the Peace of God'. For the somewhat different Early Medieval notions of reform, see Gerhardt Ladner, *The Idea of Reform*.

[3] Classic accounts are given by Charles Homer Haskins, *The Renaissance of the Twelfth Century*; Marc Bloch, *Feudal Society*, i, pts. I, II.

[4] Haskins, *The Renaissance of the Twelfth Century*, ch. 7; Post, *Studies in Medieval Legal Thought*, pt. II; Kantorowicz, 'Kingship under the Impact of Scientific Jurisprudence'.

[5] *L'Occident*, 245.

behaviours but as a dynamic and essential aspect of the growth of the western state, as the continuing effort of kings and a growing body of important subjects to come to terms with the state they were jointly creating. Far from being static, reform meant law in action, 'a process of allocating rights and duties and thereby resolving conflicts and creating channels of cooperation.'[6]

This conception of a constantly evolving reform can modify, if not completely replace, the view, often expressed, that to medieval men reform was conservative rather than progressive or revolutionary. It is true that they formulated their plans with eyes on an ideal past: the golden age of St Louis in France;[7] in England, lacking so obvious a choice, a shifting succession of eras just far enough in the past to be viewed through a mist of romanticism—the good old days of Edward the Confessor in the coronation charter of Henry I, the good old days before Henry II in the Magna Carta.[8] But belief in the better times past simply steadied them in their purpose of solving present problems and hardly kept them from attempting fresh and creative solutions to problems which struck them as new in their intensity if not in their very nature.

The legal renaissance of the twelfth century, then, given impetus by the Church reform and the war of propaganda which accompanied it, could only intensify the mental set favouring notions of secular reform. Kings who had been clearly notified by Gregorians that they were laymen, not semi-sacral priestly rulers (*reges et sacerdoti*), quickly developed new sources of legitimacy and profit as guarantors of justice. In the process they were, of course, becoming increasingly enmeshed in a more political society. As they made rules for others, they came to be bound by rules themselves.[9] 'Scientific jurisprudence gradually began to change the vocabulary of statecraft', as Ernst Kantorowicz observed, 'and the new vocabulary began to influence statecraft itself.'[10] In the concise formulation of R. W. Southern, by the

[6] Berman, *Law and Revolution*, 6.

[7] Cazelles, 'Une exigence de l'opinion depuis Saint Louis; Jordan, *Louis IX and the Challenge of the Crusade*, 181; Artonne, *Le Mouvement de 1314, passim*.

[8] Holt, *Magna Carta*, 96, 98-9.

[9] Strayer, *On the Medieval Origins of the Modern State*, 23; Holt, *Magna Carta*, 30.

[10] Kantorowicz, 'Kingship under the Impact of Scientific Jurisprudence', 99.

twelfth century 'government by ritual came to an end, and government by administration began. . . . We hear much of oaths and fealty and homage, and later of the common good and the rule of law . . .'.[11] Medieval legists loved the substance (as well as the dialectics) of the formula for sound rule which opened the *prooemium* of Justinian's Institutes: *armis decorata—legibus armata* (decorated with arms—armed with laws).[12] The close connection between law and the emerging state is evident. In the very closeness of the link between law and political systems we can recognize a peculiarly important feature of Western European states at their origins.

To think of the Western state as, from the beginning, a law-state is not to cover harsh realities of medieval life with romantic mist. The bonds linking kingship, the state, and law were important, but they were not realized in any ideal way and certainly entailed conflict as well as harmony. Powerful interests were at work.

The crown component in reform is clear and quite practical. Across the twelfth and thirteenth centuries the sheer increase in the capacity of government, especially in the spheres of finance and law, generated a need for more sophisticated judicial and accounting procedures; these readily led to changes at the centre of government which kings would be eager to cloak in the virtuous notion of reform. For there was a danger that, as J. C. Holt has written, 'these same actions whereby kings overhauled and improved the government of their realms were often regarded by their subjects as tyrannous invasions of ancient right and custom.'[13] In fact, these central government reforms could have significant effects on local government and the behaviour of local agents since they might well require more vigorous administrative effort and especially more revenue. Within a period of seventeen months in 1332-4, the sheriff of Bedfordshire received nearly 2,000 writs and was required to take 'about 2400 separate and definite steps'.[14] During the reign of Henry II Alan of Singleton, hereditary bailiff of Amounderness in Lancashire, did the necessary administrative work by himself and at his own

[11] Southern, *Medieval Humanism and Other Studies*, 51.

[12] Kantorowicz, 'Kingship under the Impact of Scientific Jurisprudence', 98.

[13] Holt, *Magna Carta*, 22.

[14] Fowler (ed.), *Quarto Memoirs*, iii. 12, 27.

expense; his son did the same. But his grandson needed a full-time subordinate and by 1334 his great great grandson had let the office to a man who employed five others. The local men who complained had to admit that four of these assistants were needed.[15] At the local level government expansion translated into rising revenue farms, the cost of which was passed on to subjects with vigour. In the conclusion to his perceptive study of the 1298 inquest in Lincolnshire, W. S. Thomson pointed an accusing finger at rising farms as 'one of the main causes, if not indeed *the* main cause, of local misgovernment in England'.[16] The point is applicable to France as well. The widow of Guillaume Dollé of La Flêche told St Louis's investigators in 1247 that the *prévôt* Mocart had informed her husband: 'You must pay the price of my *prévôté*.' Likewise, Raoul de St-Quentin, *viguier* of Beaucaire, was reported to have told a local man: 'My friend, the *viguerie* has cost me dearly and I want to have something from you.'[17] Even some Norman *prévôts* themselves complained to the *enquêteurs* about the high levels of their farms.[18]

Yet complaint was, of course, far more likely to come from aggrieved subjects. The need and desire for reform, as seen from the subject's point of view, fill the surviving parchment records from almost any English or French commission. The initial impression gained by reading the endless lists of charges still in manuscript or the analyses of these charges by modern historians is that common abuses of power troubled local society on either side of the Channel. Almost at random one could pick the following examples:

Petronilla de Assildeham complains that Richard le Brun and Richard le Bel of Haniggefeld and their followers came to the house of the said P. in the village of Assildeham on the night of Monday after the feast of St Martin three years ago, while the husband of the said P. was living, entered the dwelling, and said, 'Rustics, where is your money? Give it to us or you will die.' And they answered 'We have no money.' Then they wounded P. and her husband and bound them with cords so that blood flowed and stole from them [a long list of goods of small value] and other

15 Cam, *The Hundred and the Hundred Rolls*, 6-7.

16 Thomson, *A Lincolnshire Assize Roll*, p. cxxiii.

17 Langlois, 'Doléances', 26. Cf. the comments of Charles Petit-Dutaillis, 'Querimoniae Normanorum', 111-12.

18 Ibid. 113.

small things to a total value of 4*l*. and carried off those goods and they left P. and her husband tied thus until they were freed by their neighbours.[19]

William Haucet complains that . . . Martin Clark arrested him although he had taken the cross, and held him captive for several days in the king's prison, and would not release him even on letters from the official; and while he was captive, Martin extorted from him 5 measures of rye worth 16*s*.[20]

Only the place names reveal that the first charge comes from an English source (a complaint against a hundred bailiff in Essex, 1272) while the second is French (a complaint from one of St Louis's famous *enquêtes* of 1247, in this case from the investigation in Maine and Anjou). Though the cases are separated by several score miles and a quarter of a century, the legal formulary followed is remarkably similar: 'Petronilla de Assildeham queritur de . . .'; Guillelmus Haucet conqueritur quod . . .'.

In general, the complaints of official misconduct heard by itinerant panels in both England and France seem to be drawn from a common and deep well of experience. Helen Cam's commentary on the misdeeds revealed by the inquests of Edward I in 1274-5 reads very much like that of C. V. Langlois on the abuses revealed by the *enquêtes* of St Louis and his successors.[21] Detailed analyses of many of the inquests carried out in each country have yet to be made. Given the bulk of the records for even a single inquest, the task would represent a formidable undertaking.[22] Until a full range of particular studies is available for both countries, it would be foolhardy to attempt to compare types of offences or offenders and the punishments meted out to them. Yet we have every reason to predict that such studies will

[19] Pr. in Latin in Cam, *Studies in the Hundred Rolls*, 185-6.

[20] Pr.: Harding, 'Plaints and Bills in the History of English Law', 67.

[21] Cam, *Studies in the Hundred Rolls*, ch. 3; Langlois, 'Doléances', 19-41.

[22] Of the 1298 inquest in England, for example, only the rolls for Lincolnshire have been published and analysed, yet these alone fill a volume of several hundred pages; Thomson, *A Lincolnshire Assize Roll*. Although the surviving records of the 1247 *enquêtes* of St Louis have been printed, Jean Glénnison comments that 'en dépit d'un bon nombre de commentaires, on ne saurait dire que les enquêtes de saint Louis qui laissèrent chez les contemporains un si vif souvenir, soient aujourd'hui parfaitement connues. La liste des enquêteurs demeure incomplète. L'étude institutionnelle reste presque entièrement à faire.' ('Les Enquêtes administratives', 19).

reveal similarities in the pattern of charges against local officials. The hundred bailiffs and serjeants in England, the *prévôts*, *viguiers*, *bayles* in France (the common class of official against whom so many complaints were lodged) shared common perspectives on the world and their tasks; they were all revenue farmers, frequently pressured by their superiors to pay higher farms;[23] yet in trying to collect the required sums they were periodically denied the harsh means routinely practised by local officials for generations. In financial matters 'there must have been many . . . harassed officials who found it more expedient simply to take what the king wanted without payment, rather than risk his displeasure by excusing themselves.'[24] In judicial matters, lacking better means of enforcing compliance, local officials in either country relied on distraint, the temporary seizing of goods; in the evocative phrase of Simon de Montfort the practice of distraint was 'the beginning of all wars.'[25] The wrongs most commonly charged against officials, as Alan Harding has suggested, 'were the by-product of more government and of more law, which brought much arbitrary as well as much judicial distraint and arrest.'[26] Clearly the line separating legitimate distraint or purveyance from simple extortion and robbery could easily blur in the eyes of either local officers or subjects; and the crown, desperately scraping together a war chest, could at times appear to erase the line altogether. The infamous financial mission (or 'raid' as J. R. Strayer frankly labelled it)[27] through Languedoc carried out by Pierre de Latilly and Raoul de Breuilli in 1297, often described by historians,[28] used methods of extortion outrageous to modern sensibilities, and produced a great howl of protest from the countryside. But at the subsequent investigation into their activities, the two commissioners made no attempt to deny charges; they had merely acted in the accepted manner in

23 See the comments in Petit-Dutaillis, 'Querimoniae Normanorum', 111-12, and Thomson, *A Lincolnshire Assize Roll*, pp. cxxiii-cxxvii.

24 Maddicott, 'The English Peasantry and the Demands of the Crown', 29.

25 Quot.: Harding, *A Social History of English Law*, 251.

26 Id., 'Plaints and Bills in the History of English Law', 69.

27 Strayer, *The Reign of Philip the Fair*, 404. Maddicott notes that the activities of English purveyors often became mere plundering expeditions. 'The English Peasantry and the Demands of the Crown', 56.

28 Accounts of the Latilly-Breuilli mission are given in Langlois, 'Les doléances des communautés'; Henneman, 'Enquêteurs-réformateurs', 314-15; Pegues, *The Lawyers of the Last Capetians*, 113-16.

securing money for the crown. That the king shared this point of view is indicated by the continued royal favour in which Latilly and Breuilli stood.

The body of evidence for which the Latilly-Breuilli mission is only a famous example suggests an important perspective on local administration. Most historians who have read through the accounts of official misdeeds (and have been appalled by them) hasten to remind themselves and their readers that courts are not concerned with good deeds, that the bad news is most often printed in the newspapers. Many local officials must have laboured faithfully, serving king and community without outrage, never appearing in a plaint or the *veredictum* of a dutiful jury. Even those accused, the argument runs, often stand mute in the records we have, since only charges, not the officials' defences, may be on the rolls that survive.[29] For all of the obvious merit in such a line of argument, a different line is also possible. The abuses distilled into formal Latin phrases on one roll after another may have been more common than any counting of complaints would ever indicate. It seems likely that these recorded cases are the tip of an iceberg submerged beneath fear of reprisal and lack of confidence in the efficacy of complaint. There is ample evidence, both French and English, of attempts by local officials to discourage complaints about their conduct.[30] Since violence and threats were the frequent accompaniments to ordinary lawsuits, we have every reason to suspect their presence, even where it cannot be proved, in suits where one party controlled a sphere of legitimate violence easily enlarged to meet new requirements. While many subjects boldly and confidently brought their complaints, we have no way of knowing how many were too fearful nor how many simply thought redress unlikely. Painful lessons might have been learned in Gloucestershire villages while those who had complained against local officials in 1274-5 waited until 1287 for the king's justices to appear and act on their charges. Even some complaints of official retribution against

[29] Templeman, 'The Sheriffs of Warwickshire', 15-16, 50; Cam, *Studies in the Hundred Rolls*, 142; Jones, '*Rex et ministri*', *passim*.

[30] Cam, *The Hundred and the Hundred Rolls*, 43-4; ead., *Studies in the Hundred Rolls*, 146, 191; Jordan, *Louis IX and the Challenge of the Crusade*, 55-8, 61; Strayer, 'La Conscience du roi, 733; Fryde, 'Edward III's Removal of his Ministers and Judges', 148; Maddicott, 'Parliament and the Constituencies', 66-7.

those who had brought charges had to wait six years, as in one case involving a Lincolnshire jury.[31] Edward III, soliciting complaints against his officials in 1340, suggested that aggrieved subjects 'bring written bills and present them in London, secretly if there was a danger to them from officials still in office.'[32] Within the year he felt the need to reassure his subjects that the inquest was genuine. He had learned, he announced, that 'many men of our realm greatly fear that . . . wrongdoers will be reconciled with us and will escape lightly . . . and will afterwards be as great masters and maintainers as they have previously been.'[33] Similar evidence is available across the Channel. In letters to his agents in Carcassonne in March 1303, Philip IV admitted that royal inquests produced the most ingenious attempts on the part of local officials to escape unscathed. Subjects had been pointedly reminded that dismissed officials were often reinstated, that earlier reform efforts had produced no results. Bribes were offered to some potential accusers; others were simply threatened.[34]

To suggest a common pattern of official misconduct revealed by the complaints delivered to itinerant commissioners is not, of course, to suggest that the French and English panels were themselves identical. As essential agencies of governments which had followed quite different courses of development, the commissioners would obviously have different overall powers and tasks in the two countries, though they shared the responsibility for the correction of local officers. Given the much vaster jurisdiction, and particularly the criminal jurisdiction of the English crown, itinerant justices or trailbaston justices would inevitably hear a great many suits between private parties and charges of wrongdoing brought against private persons by juries of presentment. A panel of *enquêteurs* in the French countryside, by contrast, would likely hear relatively few private suits, but

31 Cam, *Studies in the Hundred Rolls*, 191.

32 Fryde, 'Edward III's Removal of his Ministers and Judges', 148-9.

33 Maddicott, 'Parliament and the Constituencies', 85, quot. PRO SC1/62/85; he notes that such fears 'in the event were well justified'.

34 *Ordonnances des roys de France*, i. 361, cl. 22, discussed by Elizabeth A. R. Brown: 'Corruption, Finance, and Reform', ch. 2, p. 5. The parallel with violence to suppress legal appeals to the crown is instructive; see above, ch. 3.

might concern itself with a wider range of administrative problems.[35]

Likewise, there is no claim that the eyres, trailbastons, inquests, *enquêtes* of the mid-fourteenth century will show the same pattern of complaint and reform produced by similar investigations a century or more earlier. Changes in the administrative structure or the demands of the crown, the political sophistication or co-operativeness of the population, the economy, the pressure of population on food resources, even the weather, could affect the flow and content of complaint and thus the pattern of reform. Helen Cam's study of Essex complaints in the 1270s showed a typical thirteenth-century concern with sheriffs and their underlings in local administration.[36] The work of W. S. Thomson and B. W. McLane on Lincolnshire in 1298, 1328, and 1341 shows a growing popular concern over the measures taken by a wartime government; in 1298 complaint reflects the demands of war but it was still focused on the traditional local administrators; by 1341 the storm was directed against 'a relatively new type of official who collected either victuals or wool, the two main sources of complaint.'[37] These men roamed over one or more counties armed with a commission which placed them beyond the reach of the ordinary shire officialdom; as events proved, they were in effect beyond the control of the central government as well. Such evidence usefully reminds us that reform was a process of reaction and adjustment to a changing set of problems.

If ordinary Englishmen and Frenchmen had good reason to be watchful and resentful whenever they had to deal with royal officials in their localities, another brand of watchfulness motivated central government officials as they surveyed the conduct of local officials. In fact, the view from Westminster or Paris focused on two potential troubles: local officials might, in the first place, be so rapacious as to strike dangerous sparks of local resistance, with the danger of lighting the fires of rebellion; secondly, they might be slipping much of what they collected into their own pockets rather than into the royal coffers, or they might more generally usurp royal rights as their own. The king wanted

35 The range of work done by a French reform mission appears clearly, ibid.

36 Cam, *Studies in the Hundred Rolls*, ch. 3.

37 Thomson, *A Lincolnshire Assize Roll*, *passim*; McLane, 'The Royal Courts and Disorder', ch. 2, 3; the quot. is taken from the latter source, p. 174.

his rights preserved and his revenues collected, especially for the emergency of war; he might look aside when his men used efficient methods which strayed from the ideals of official pronouncements; but he had to sense when vigorous methods crossed a critical threshold, and he would not abide private profiteering on the grand scale by his own local agents. Obviously there was some common ground between the king's unwritten bill of complaint against local royal officialdom and the thousands of actual complaints penned by outraged subjects: both the king as superior and the subject as justiciable of the official wanted his actions watched and certain excesses restrained; the crown's interest was to maintain (sometimes to establish) central control over its men and its revenue; subjects wanted protection from petty tyranny. In disciplining sheriffs, undersheriffs, serjeants in England, or *baillis*, sénéschaux, *viguiers*, *bayles* in France, the crown not only protected itself against malpractice by its own agents, but also satisfied a need strongly felt by local populations which had suffered oppressions and exactions practised almost routinely by local crown agents.

Kings and subjects might agree in principle, yet capable men were hard to find in sufficient numbers and even harder to reward in a way acceptable to all concerned. The obvious solution was to spread the effectiveness of a corps of trusted and rewarded men by occasionally sending them around the localities as inspectors and agents of central power. A veritable hallmark of reform was the use of such itinerant agents: in England the eyre justices (especially from the second half of the twelfth century), trailbaston justices and justices on special inquest (such as those in 1298 and 1341); in France the earliest *baillis* (before they acquired territorial circumscriptions by the end of the reign of Philip II) and the *enquêteurs* from the second half of the thirteenth century. Though such commissions in England and France do not represent the entire arch of reform they at least formed the keystone.[38]

In administrative history the secular reform movement thus ended the era of government in the localities more or less left to local strongmen who were largely unsupervised. Through his commissioners the king could keep a tighter rein on local

[38] See the comments of Jean Glennisson, 'Les Enquêtes administrative', 19.

officialdom, prevent the real and present danger of usurpation of crown rights, hear pleas reserved to the crown (in England) or carry out sensitive local tax negotiations (in France). There is a basic similarity in the use of itinerant commissions of central court personnel as agents of government reform in both countries at one stage in their development. Before they could send out the full complement of trained agents needed for local governance, kings relied on the expedient of itinerant commissioners.

Moreover, from roughly the mid-thirteenth century royal governments on either side of the Channel found it advisable and useful to invite complaints against their own agents; English and French kings solicited informal plaints, *querelae*, from their subjects, provided justices to hear them, tried the officers charged and punished those found guilty.[39] Even before baronial movements established or demanded circuits of commissioners, as in 1258 in England[40] or 1314-15[41] in France, kings understood the need for avoiding trouble by taking action against the most spectacular offenders among local officials and by correcting outstanding problems in law and administration.

If itinerant commissioners under one title or another were a primary feature of the opening phase of secular reform, a second feature can be identified as the demand for grants of charters of liberties. Behind such demands there often stretched a long period of intense governmental pressure, usually associated with the heavy demands of war. An early example in England is evident in the coronation charter of Henry I, issued in 1100, and intended to separate the new king from the oppressive policies of William Rufus and his chief minister, Ranulf Flambard. King Stephen found it prudent to issue not only a coronation charter in 1135, but a second charter (especially in favour of the church) in 1136. After losing Normandy in 1204 and failing to recoup his loss by the ambitious campaign of 1214, John was forced to issue the Great Charter in 1215. Its periodic reissues became a feature of political life in thirteenth-century England.[42]

[39] The importance of this procedure is discussed by W. S. Thomson, in *A Lincolnshire Assize Roll*, cxiii-cxx; Harding, 'Plaints and Bills in the History of English Law'; Richardson and Sayles, *Select Cases of Procedure*; Proctor, *The Judicial Use of the Pesquisa*.

[40] Powicke, *The Thirteenth Century*, 147-51.

[41] Artonne, *Le Mouvement de 1314*, *passim*, esp. 123-4.

[42] Holt, *Magna Carta*, *passim*; Southern, 'Ranulf Flambard', and 'King

Across the Channel charters of liberties appeared at the provincial level in the twelfth and thirteenth centuries, but the Capetians were successful enough (and slow enough to develop capacities liable to provoke massive response) so that the line of royal charters with broad application—or the reform ordinances that could substitute for them—began only in mid-thirteenth century. On his return from crusade, Louis IX issued the first of the great reform *ordonnances* in 1254. His grandson Philip IV issued another in 1303, just following the defeat of French arms at Courtrai. Philip's son Louis X agreed to an entire set of provincial charters in 1315, an act often compared to the granting of Magna Carta in England a century earlier.[43]

By this time, as J. C. Holt noted, an observer could scarcely have been surprised by charters of liberties extracted from monarchs whose coffers had been depleted by war. 'If he were a royal servant of a cynical bent', Holt suggests of this imagined observer, 'he might have reflected that they were one of the probable costs of administrative inventiveness and efficiency.'[44]

England and France, then, saw broadly common methods emerge for mediating the interests of king and subjects as government became a pervasive rather than an occasional force in the localities. Yet we can also see the characteristic differences in the two states and in the chronologies by which they developed their capacities. Not only did the English government develop its power much earlier, it rested this power on foundations completely different from the early civil service in France; through their reliance on unsalaried local men the rulers of England in effect created a centralized government before they produced a bureaucracy.[45] Self-government at the king's command in England quite rightly stands in sharp contrast to the French bureaucratic tradition in historical writing on medieval administration. This peculiar administrative structure acted as a catalyst intensifying the reaction which produced governmental

Henry I' in: *Medieval Humanism and Other Studies*; Davis, *From Domesday Book to Magna Carta*, 114-15, 133-4, 190.

[43] Holt, *Magna Carta*, 21; Carolus-Barré, 'La Grande ordonnance de réformation de 1254', 181-6; id., 'l'administration et la police du royaume', 85-96.

[44] Holt, *Magna Carta*, 22.

[45] Strayer, *On the Medieval Origins of the Modern State*, 35-49.

reform in England. Local officials such as sheriffs were local men of some importance who had interests and loyalties rooted in the communities they governed; they were landowners and they lived within the nexus of feudal ties and the patronage of magnates. In the opinion of those whose views carried weight, the sheriffs' roots in local society were highly desirable; demands that sheriffs be local men appear in the Provision of Oxford of 1258, and in the fourteenth-century rolls of parliament.[46] As we will see, reform statutes in France took exactly the opposite line: the royal *baillis* were to be thoroughly cut off from the locality in which they served; above all, they could not be local landowners. The English arrangements surely intensified pressure for reform by strengthening the voice of subjects in their dialogue with kings who were rapidly expanding their power and authority. That the political temperature of England seems to have been decidedly warmer than that in France comes as no surprise: a precocious government vigorously developing its capacities (often without scruples about its methods) within a relatively restricted geographical space was at most times encouraged but at all times closely watched by subjects who staffed local government and who most likely held local interests uppermost. The formula produced political explosions with some regularity across our period—1215, 1232, 1258-67, 1297, 1311, 1327, 1341—and both the number and the duration of these periods of crisis make a sharp contrast to conditions in France where governmental crises appear later, less frequently and for shorter periods—in 1314-15, 1346-7, 1356.

We will see these contrasts and their results clearly if we survey the course of governmental reform in England and in France. In England the era of secular reform began in the reign of Henry I. As R. W. Southern argues, by the reign of Henry I 'the heroic age of government' seems to have passed, government was just becoming 'entangled in its own precedents' and instinct was soon to become 'cooled into calculation.'[47] If the government of Henry I was still predatory in the primitive Norman tradition, it was coming to be respectable.[48] If the famous coronation charter

[46] Stubbs, *Select Charters*, 382. John Maddicott cites numerous petitions seeking local men as local officials in 'Parliament and the Constituencies', 71-2.

[47] Southern, *Medieval Humanism and other Studies*, 205.

[48] Ibid. 231.

of Henry I was an election manifesto rather than a guide to constitutional principles actually effected,[49] still it showed how early constitutional issues were in men's minds.[50] More important, the exchequer was established at the centre of administration and the barons of the exchequer together with the itinerant justices[51] began their work of supervision over local officialdom.

The work went forward under Henry I's grandson. Henry II restored the exchequer in 'an unhurried act of fresh creation'; he revived the general eyre and 'it surged forward to take on a larger share of the work of actually administering the country than any previous government had thought possible.'[52] After the massive Inquest of Sheriffs launched in 1170, all the sheriffs of England, largely drawn from the ranks of local magnates, were dismissed and replaced by men of lesser status who made a profession of royal service.[53] The co-operation between king and community appears in a particularly happy light in the legal reforms of Henry II, with pride of place going to the assize of novel disseisin; much desired and regularly used by subjects, the king's new writs and process likewise augmented royal power, prestige, and revenue.[54] The movement leading to Magna Carta leaves no doubt that conflict could be no less the result of the vigorous kingship of Henry II and his sons. By 1215 reforms often granted, or sold, piecemeal to particular groups or communities, were demanded on the grand scale of the realm by the politically powerful non-royal elements of English society just learning the difficult lesson of the need for common action based on a conception of corporate rights.[55] Across the thirteenth century the lesson was learned well in the political crises which punctuated the long reign of Henry III. Magna Carta was repeatedly confirmed and soon began to take on the mythical aura so important for its later life.[56] At the end of the thirteenth century, in the great crisis of Edward I's

[49] Sayles, *The Medieval Foundations of England*, 296.

[50] Holt, *Magna Carta*, 30-2.

[51] But note the qualifications of William T. Reedy, jun., 'The Origins of the General Eyre'.

[52] Warren, *Henry II*, 291-2.

[53] Ibid. 287-91.

[54] Sutherland, *The Assize of Novel Disseisin*.

[55] Holt, *Magna Carta*, ch. 3.

[56] Ibid, ch. 10.

reign, the settlement which prevented open conflict was embodied in the classic form of a *Confirmatio Cartarum* in 1297; as discontent continued to simmer, there was a further confirmation, and further articles added to the charters, in 1300.[57]

The century which had opened with Magna Carta was rich with further reform initiatives, both in Westminster and in the shires and towns. During the long minority of Henry III successive powers behind the young king's throne altered the relationship between the central government and the sheriffs in the name of reform, but the crucial steps were taken as a result of the crisis and civil war which began in 1258.[58] Although the king's government had listened to the plaints of subjects before, by means of the eyre and by other special investigations, the eyre of the justiciar carried out under the supervision of the barons who took control of Henry's government represents a turning-point. The policy of soliciting complaints became a fixed practice of government to be put into operation whenever necessary or convenient. Special sections of the eyre rolls recorded *querelae* concerning trespasses from 1261.[59] The massive inquest of 1274-5, which produced the famous Hundred Rolls collected a veritable encyclopaedia of misdeeds of local officers.[60] From 1278 writs of summons to the eyre informed Englishmen that the justices would hear trespasses and plaints concerning local royal officials or anyone else.[61] After Edward I returned from a long absence in Gascony in 1289, the level of complaint prompted him to conduct a showy series of state trials and to name *auditores querelarum* to sit at Westminster and receive complaints against royal judges and officials.[62] In 1298 the crisis brought on by warfare in Wales, Scotland, and Gascony led to the classic device of itinerant commissioners sent round the country to hear

[57] Powicke, *The Thirteenth Century*, ch. 14; Prestwich (ed.), *Documents Illustrating the Crisis of 1297-1298 in England*.

[58] A general survey is provided by F. M. Powicke, *King Henry III and the Lord Edward*.

[59] Richardson and Sayles, *Select Cases of Procedure*, 114. This and the following four sources are cited and discussed by Harding, 'Plaints and Bills in the History of English Law', 68.

[60] Cam, *The Hundred and the Hundred Rolls*, 43.

[61] Harding, 'Plaints and Bills in the History of English Law', 68.

[62] Tout and Johnstone, *State Trials*.

querelae.[63] Panels of commissioners investigating vagabonds late in the reign produced such a picture of violence and illegality and stuffed the gaols so full of suspects that trailbaston commissions were launched in 1305. Although their major task was to carry on the criminal work of the defunct eyre, they also heard charges of oppressive local officials.[64] Of course, complaints were not solicited and heard only during the periodic circuits of eyre justices or the visitations of panels on special inquests. In the reign of Edward I the volume of petitions received during time of parliament became so great that restrictions were twice ordered, lest the business of dealing with petitions choke all other business.[65] In the strongly stated views of H. G. Richardson and G. O. Sayles, disputed by others, parliament was much less a political institution deciding great causes than a court of last resort where justice might be done not only to the great but to lesser men bringing in their plaints.[66]

Across the thirteenth century the grievances of a growing number of people had got a hearing. By the reign of Edward I, in fact, such complaints were not only solicited by the crown, they also formed the basis of reform legislation enacted in great statutes whose utility was recognized both by king and subjects. The progression toward this accepted procedure is fascinating: in 1215 barons in arms forced King John to issue reform guidelines in the Great Charter; after the eyres conducted by the barons who temporarily controlled Henry III's government, the crown acted on its own restored authority to promulgate the reforms so evidently desired by many of its subjects in the Statute of Marlborough (1267); in 1275 Edward I's Hundred Roll commissioners collected widespread complaints which became the basis of the important Statute of Westminster I.

Across the first half of the fourteenth century—as Englishmen suffered the capricious rule of Edward II, the movement to restrain his actions in the Ordinances of 1311, his deposition of 1327, the temporary regime of Isabella and Mortimer in 1327-30, the

[63] *CPR 1292-1301*, 338; Thomson, *A Lincolnshire Assize Roll*, *passim*.

[64] Harding, 'Early Trailbaston Proceedings', 144-51; McLane, 'The Royal Courts', ch. 3.

[65] See the regulations of 1280 and 1293 found on the Close Roll and pr. in Ludwik Ehrlich, *Proceedings Against the Crown*, 90, 235.

[66] The views of Richardson and Sayles are summed up in Sayles, *The King's Parliament of England*, with a select bibliog. on the vast literature on parliament.

personal assertion of control by the young Edward III in 1330, and the opening campaigns of the Hundred Years War after 1337—governmental reform was much in men's minds. In fact, scholars once interpreted the movement leading to the Ordinances of 1311 as essentially a struggle between competing principles of government, Edward's 'household system' being opposed by the baronial reformers' high-minded conception of properly constituted 'offices of state' more responsible to the political nation.[67] In more recent accounts this view has been discounted; instead, the clear personal element involved in ridding the realm of a list of offenders headed by Piers Gaveston has received greater emphasis, along with the financial grievances imposed by Edward II, particularly via the prerogative of prise.[68] Although the movement of 1311 bears obvious resemblances to that of 1258, it seems less concerned with reform measures at the local level. Only clause 40 addresses this level of officialdom forcefully by ordaining that in each parliament a committee of a bishop, two earls, and two barons will hear and determine all complaints against king's officers who contravene the ordinances.[69] The desperate needs of high politics seem to have precluded more local concerns among the temporarily united baronage. But when these concerns came to the surface later, predictable solutions were proposed. In 1329-30 officials close to the crown planned to revive the general eyre (defunct since the 1290s) and actually launched eyres in some counties,[70] but for *ad hoc* measures the crown usually turned to itinerant commissions with more specific charges, such as those in 1314-16, 1328, and 1341.[71] As a sweeping investigation of local justice and administration the 1341 commissions in particular stand in the tradition of great inquests stretching back to 1298, 1274-5, 1259, and even 1170. Edward III's commissions of December 1340, granted his

[67] Tout, *The Place of the Reign of Edward II in English History*; Davies, *The Baronial Opposition to Edward II*.

[68] Maddicott, *Thomas of Lancaster*. Though dealing with a later period of the reign, Natalie Fryde takes a similar view of the politics of early fourteenth-century England in *The Tyranny and Fall of Edward II*.

[69] *Statutes of the Realm*, i. 167.

[70] Cam, 'The General Eyres'.

[71] For the commissions, see *CPR 1313-1317*, 122-4, 129, 242-4, *CPR 1327-1330*, 297 (which must be supplemented by PRO C66/169, as B. W. McLane notes in 'The Royal Courts', 125, n. 23); *CPR 1340-43*, 106-8, 111-13, 202, 204, 328, 336.

agents oyer and terminer power 'touching any oppressions by ministers of the king and of Edward, duke of Cornwall, late Keeper of the realm, and of the bearing of the justices, and all other ministers, from the time the king assumed the governance of the realm both towards the people and towards the king.'[72]

Yet this comprehensive and searching investigation also represents the swan-song of itinerant commissions in medieval England. It is the last in the series; by this time the eyre had practically ceased,[73] and no other broad commissions were issued to panels of justices. It seems likewise important that from the end of the reign of Edward I the Charters (Magna Carta and the Forest Charter) no longer occupied the central position on the political stage. As Harry Rothwell wrote of Edward's last years, 'the organic history of the Charters ends here and English liberties have not in fact been developed by a development of the charters. . . .'[74]

In the first half of the fourteenth century, then, the initial phase of governmental reform, characterized by the regular work of itinerant commissions and the use of reform charters ended. Yet by the mid-fourteenth century the impulse for governmental reform was taking on a different character and was finding its expression primarily through institutional channels new in their scope if not in their basic form.

The institutional change marking the new era is evident in the growing role of parliament as the agency for reform. Behind this change, as is so often the case, we can see the impact of war. Though the origins of parliament can be sought far back in the thirteenth century, the parliamentary role in the dialogue between crown and subject began to take shape in the late thirteenth and early fourteenth centuries, the opening of an age of more extensive warfare as we have seen.[75] As early as the 1270s aggrieved subjects were encouraged by the crown to bring their

[72] *CPR 1340-1343*, 106. The commission is recorded in McLane (ed.), *The 1341 Royal Inquest*, 1.

[73] Putnam, *Proceedings*, pp. lvii-lxiii.

[74] Rothwell, 'Edward I and the Struggle for the Charters'.

[75] See the following essays in Davies and Denton (eds.), *The English Parliament in the Middle Ages*; Holt, 'The Prehistory of Parliament'; Harriss, 'The Formation of Parliament'; Maddicott, 'Parliament and the Constituencies'. See also the two-volume collection of essays ed., with introd. essays by E. B. Fryde and Edward Miller, *Historical Studies of the English Parliament*.

complaints against royal officials. At first the eyres were 'the *parlemenz* of the real commons of England', but since parliament was 'a final resort of complainants',[76] the number of petitions received in time of parliament grew considerably. The evidence suggests that a broadening social stratum was responding to the opportunity to bring charges of official oppression and malfeisance and that they chose to do so in time of parliament. The volume of complaint may have surprised and even somewhat troubled the crown. In 1280 the government tried to deflect this flood of petitions away from king and council to other central officials and agencies (chancellor, exchequer, justice of Jews); only in this way, the king claimed, could he prosecute 'the great business of his kingdom and of his foreign lands.'[77] By the early fourteenth century the possibilities of complaint seem to have been realized even by the very humble. After reading many such *querelae*, John Maddicott concluded that 'we are listening to men of no great importance and men whose complaints would have gone unheard a hundred years earlier.' Moreover, he points out that petitions presented by shire communities, rare in the 1270s, became common by the end of Edward I's reign, and numerous from the middle years of Edward II. Often these sought influence on appointments, the removal of men thought unsuited and their replacement by others named. During these same years the common petition emerged, submitted formally in the name of the entire parliamentary commons. These developments suggest that 'men did not go to parliament merely to treat the matters put before them by the king. They went also (perhaps mainly) to defend the affairs of their communities and their constituents and to do local business.'[78]

Parliament was thus assuming a more central role in the process of reform. The crown voice in parliament remained predominant and could claim to speak for reform. But reform required dialogue and the answering voice began to be heard with rather more strength and clarity. From the 1290s G. L. Harriss finds in parliament 'the aspect of a place of confrontation between

[76] The two quot. phrases are taken from Harding, *The Law Courts of Medieval England*, 87.

[77] Quot. and discussed by Edwards, *Historians and the Medieval English Parliament*, 18-19.

[78] Maddicott, 'Parliament and the Constituencies'. The quots. are from pp. 69-70.

king and subjects' and he notes that the reign of the second Edward 'accentuated rather than reversed this trend.' The deposition of Edward II in 1327 'divides as accurately as any single date can the phase when parliament was still essentially a royal tool from that when it developed a political momentum of its own.'[79]

The reign of Edward III, however, brought a change in the scope and direction of royal governance. Acting in concert with parliamentary change, this significant shift in the enterprise of governance helps to explain the appearance of new characteristics of secular reform in England. The essential factor was the agreement of king and lords to pursue a war policy with great single-mindedness. The role of parliament in this business was to authorize and to pay. 'For the greater part', G. L. Harriss writes of Edward III, 'he was able to impose his consistent view of parliament as the place where the support of the realm could be authoritatively secured for the policies of the crown and the nobility, these being essentially the furtherance of their military ambitions.'[80] Edward III could avoid the nasty problems that had so troubled his grandfather's late reign and the yet nastier end to his father's reign by leading his warrior lords into the rich French countryside on expeditions financed by parliamentary taxation. That Edward III won famous victories in France and died peacefully in his bed in England might be taken to constitute an argument for the correctness of his policy, at the immediate level.[81]

What becomes apparent only with longer perspective is how much the sights and sounds of war can mask the levelling off or even the reduction in royal activism and initiative in so many other areas of kingship, a reduction which was necessary as a part of the price-tag attached, however indirectly, to the prosecution of war. Measurement of royal activism is a tricky matter, but it would be difficult to argue that from the mid-fourteenth century the crown was the most active and experimental force in English society as one might plausibly argue it had been in the age of Magna Carta[82] or indeed across the twelfth and thirteenth centuries.

[79] Harriss, 'The Formation of Parliament'. The quots. are from pp. 29-31.

[80] Ibid. 32.

[81] McKisack, 'Edward III and the Historians', 1-15.

[82] Holt, *Magna Carta*, 29-30.

Edward III secured support for the war he and his nobles wanted so much at least in part by giving the parliamentary commons so much of what they wanted locally. The triumph of the justices of the peace makes the point most clearly. The graph of their rise to power traces an erratic curve across the first half of the fourteenth century, with sudden rises followed by equally swift falls. The men at the helm of government were clearly reluctant to loosen their hold by sharing the judicial and administrative powers they and their predecessors had long collected with the gentry and leading townsmen who claimed a share as their natural right. But across the century the strains of governing England while fighting France and Scotland were too great; the efforts to control public order from Westminster were largely given up and the keepers of the peace became true justices in their localities. A parallel course was followed in the important business of taxation. After 1334 the crown accepted a conventional figure as an assessment of the movable wealth of the realm and collected from each community a lump sum whose burdens were distributed in the population by leading local men.[83] The same trend is evident in legislation, which came to be based on petitions from the commons.[84]

The point is not to award praise or blame to Edward III, but to recognize that, however skilful and perceptive he may have been, English kingship of necessity took on a different role by the mid-fourteenth century. Compromise and a scaling-down of efforts other than the war effort were the concomitants of relatively peaceful politics within the realm. As county leaders secured a generous share in local taxation and judicial power, the lords of England were reassured by the definition given to treason in the famous statute of 1352. Any thought of making the penalties of treason a deterrence to open acts of disorder, by including within the conception of treason such acts of violence as 'riding armed to rob or slay', fell away before lordly objections. Warriors who accompanied the king with just such violent objectives in mind in France wanted no talk of treason if they lapsed a bit and pursued their quarrels with equal vigour at home. Treason was narrowly defined.[85]

[83] Putnam, 'The Transformation of the Keepers of the Peace'; Maddicott, 'The English Peasantry and the Demands of the Crown', 50 ff.

[84] Harriss, 'The Formation of Parliament', 45-8, and the sources cited there.

[85] Bellamy, *The Law of Treason*, 59-101, 207.

Compromise on virtually all matters other than the financing of the war was all the more effective because of the dramatic change brought about by the Plague which struck at mid-century. With the balance of supply and demand in human labour suddenly upset by massive mortality, landlords of all ranks had to join in a policy of wage restriction. 'Almost overnight', G. L. Harriss argues, 'the Commons became the allies of King and Lords and their necessary agents for the enforcement of this policy in the shires.' The social ranks making up the Commons thus joined the establishment—as the king's comrades in arms in France, as the king's loyal commons approving war taxation in parliament, as true justices of the peace in the counties, as justices of labourers, as local agents of tax collection. That political society which would ensure the stability of political life in England up to the seventeenth century was thus taking shape by the mid-fourteenth century.[86] It might be objected that, in view of the internecine strife so prevalent in later medieval English society, the political life of the realm was anything but stable. Yet the point seems well taken that something like a lasting framework for political life had been achieved, however frequent and spectacular might be the quarrels over who should operate the machinery and to whose benefit it should run.

We can thus establish a contrast between two ages of reform in England. The earlier era encompassed roughly the twelfth and thirteenth centuries, though it drew upon the solid work of Anglo-Saxon and Norman kings. Across this initial period of reform both the body of those who counted politically and the claims of the royal administration were expanding dramatically. Reform meant the complex process and the ideas by which the claims of this broadening political community could be accommodated with the powers of the crown so actively at work in important dimensions of life. In courts, councils, and inquests, in the shires and in Westminster, through charters, statutes, and responses to individual *querelae*, acceptable limitations on royal jurisdiction, royal taxation, were worked out. In short, in the first era the dialogue (sometimes the clash) of crown and subject created the framework of the state in its most basic sense:

[86] Harriss, *King, Parliament, and Public Finance*, 516. See also his 'War and the Emergence of the English Parliament. A theme basically in agreement with that of Dr Harriss is presented in Anthony Goodman, *A History of England*.

Englishmen whose views counted accepted the assumption of major responsibility for public order by the crown; they accepted and even encouraged its jurisdiction over major categories of crime and over the important if amorphous category of trespass; they willingly accepted royal protection of their property; they grudgingly accepted royal taxation as an unpleasant necessity.

The second era began in the 1290s, under the driving pressures of more extended war. In this era the rapid development of the role of the state in basic categories of political, social, and economic life slowed and changed direction.[87] There was a marked falling off of that rapid expansion of royal governance which had made reform so lively an issue. The emphasis shifted more exclusively to war and war finance. Conflicts turned less on the basic competance of governmental action in some sphere than on questions of who should rule or receive royal patronage. Parliament was the great development of the second era and was, of course, immensely important then and for the future. But the history of parliament has so long been associated with whiggish notions of the grand struggle for freedom and progress that it is useful to remind ourselves how well an unwhiggish notion of parliamentary history fits the characterization of the second era of reform presented above. Parliament had grown rapidly in the late thirteenth and early fourteenth centuries. But the similarities of structure and methods between fourteenth- and seventeenth-century parliaments suggest that parliament was a part of that relatively stable political order lasting from the mid-fourteenth until the seventeenth century. In fact, with telescope to his eye the medieval historian might see in the upheavals of the seventeenth century a third era of governmental reform in England. For in Jacobean and Stuart England the expanding role and capacity of government was very much in the forefront of men's minds, as it had been during the High Middle Ages. As D. H. Pennington suggests of the seventeenth century, 'parliament was now made up of men deeply involved in a state whose impact on the subject was vastly greater than it had been.[88] The dialogue between king and subject, mediated through parliament

[87] See the comment of Strayer, *On the Medieval Origins of the Modern State*, 57-8.

[88] Pennington, 'A Seventeenth-century Perspective', in: Davies and Denton (eds.), *The English Parliament in the Middle Ages*, 197

across the long second era of reform, would become a civil war in the seventeenth century as the crown attempted to expand the place of government in English society at a time of dangerous polarization between Court and Country within the body politic.[89]

In France the chronology of the reform movement is nearly a century later than that in England. If the beginning of reform appeared with the opening of the twelfth century in England, the end of this century brought first signs of reform in France. The first efforts resulted from royal initiative and seem to reflect an awareness of the administrative innovations of the English kings. Philip II (1180–1220) began to use itinerant commissioners known as *baillis* early in his reign. The 'testament' of Philip Augustus, written on the eve of the Third Crusade, shows that before 1190 the French crown had attempted to establish itinerant panels of central court personnel in immitation of the eyre justices either in England or in the duchy of Normandy (which also had the English system of itinerant justices.) These *baillis* of Philip II were originally members of the royal court charged with *ad hoc* missions to hold the periodic courts known as assizes from town to town; they took complaints about injustice and financial oppression of *prévôts* and in general watched over local administration. Supervision of the *prévôts* may have been the chief motive of the crown in creating the *baillis*. Clearly the local administration of the *prévôts*, which may have sufficed for the small royal domain before Philip II, was hardly adequate after the fourfold expansion produced by Philip's conquests, even when supervised occasionally by itinerant *baillis*; a layer of officials with fixed territories was needed between king and *prévôts* and was gradually created, apparently in the 1220s and 1230s, by assigning each *bailli* a territorial charge and stationing him within it as the superior of the numerous *prévôts*. Within less than a half century, in other words, the French crown had learned that its local administration was inadequate (whether viewed from Paris or from the localities) and had planted the initially itinerant *baillis* as a more effective intermediate layer of administration.[90]

[89] See Zagorin, *The Court and the Country*.

[90] Fawtier and Lot, *Histoire des institutions francaises*, 144 ff.; Fesler, 'French Field Administration.'

But the need for supervision of a territorial administration by prestigious itinerant commissioners was then simply moved one rung up the ladder of command; the work done by the eyre and inquests in England still needed doing in France. In short, the English, with a local royal administration long in place, had added itinerant panels as a new administrative layer in the twelfth century; for the French the *baillis* had to become, in effect, a first effective layer in the following century. The administrative timing in England and France parallels the differential jurisdictional growth in the two countries by which informal complaints vastly expanded the business and clientele of royal courts. As Alan Harding has noted, this addition of complaint litigation, mainly about trespasses, meant a significant first stage in French royal legal history, but represented a second stage in England.[91]

Thus, we might say that the real beginning of reform (or at least of successful reform) in France came not so much with the *baillis* of Philip II as with the *enquêteurs* of St Louis.[92] In 1247 Louis IX, on the eve of his crusade to Egypt, sent out teams of *enquêteurs* to investigate local royal officials and correct abuses.[93] The effort qualifies as reform by the most exacting of definitions and set a high standard for later French rulers. Philip II's ambitious initial attempt at supervision by itinerant agents had been premature in that the crown had not prepared an adequate base of local officials; there were simply too many *prévôts* for the commissioners to supervise, and the *prévôts* held their office too often as a species of real property (as revenue farmers) rather than as an administrative post. Crown control over their activities can never have been very effective and over serjeants it was nearly non-existent.[94]

Certainly the Franciscan and Dominican friars chosen by St Louis to fill most of the *enquêteur* positions found much to correct at all levels of local administration.[95] In the south and south-west of France subjects complained about undue severity of

[91] Harding, 'Plaints and Bills in the History of English Law', 65.

[92] See the comments of Cazelles: 'Une exigence de l'opinion depuis Saint Louis', 91-9.

[93] Jordan, *Louis IX and the Challenge of the Crusade*, ch. 3.

[94] Ibid. 46-7, 55 ff.

[95] The records are printed by Léopold Delisle in Bouguet (ed.), *Recueil des historiens des Gaules*, xxiv.

officials in the aftermath of rebellion; in other parts of France the complaints show the common pattern of petty official corruption and abuse.[96] Their findings were not without result. Many officials were fined and the entire upper level of the field administration was shaken up by new appointments in the years immediately following the inquest. Moreover, the important series of reform ordinances issued by St Louis in 1254 and the following years drew on the information collected by the *enquêteurs* on their circuits.[97] Nearly thirty articles in the original ordinance were aimed at reforming administration in the *bailliages*: even after the *baillis* left office they were liable for a specified period of time to charges of misconduct; they were forbidden to hold property, marry their older children to local people, or enroll their younger children in abbeys or priories; judges were not to accept gifts, sell offices, delay justice, or make it expensive. The list should not be thought merely pious wishing on the part of a saintly king; Louis IX bent every effort to make his regulations work, possibly, as W. C. Jordan argues,[98] with considerable success:

> The *baillis* and *sénéchaux* were appointed by a carefully selective king: this was the first check. Their accounts would be audited two or three times a year at the Exchequer for Normandy or at Paris. They submitted themselves after 1254 both to cyclical investigations of their conduct in office by the *enquêteurs* and, except in the south, to the inquiries of an almost constantly mobile king. . . . The likelihood of their succumbing to local pressures was reduced by the frequency of transfer after 1254; and every such transfer was probably accompanied by at least a cursory inventory of possessions in the *bailliage* and *sénéschaussée*.

After the work of St Louis the idea of reform became in the phrase of Raymond Cazelles 'a required opinion (une exigence de l'opinion)'.[99] Especially across the first half of the fourteenth century the twin engines of reform, *enquêteurs* and royal reform

[96] Langlois, 'Doléances'; Jordan, *Louis IX and the Challenge of the Crusade*, 55 ff.

[97] Carolus-Barré, 'l'administration et la police du royaume', 90-4. Cf. his 'La Grande ordonnance de réformation de 1254'.

[98] The preceding analysis and the quot. which follows are drawn from Jordan, *Louis IX and the Challenge of the Crusade*, 158, 170-1.

[99] In the title of his art. on reform, 'Une exigence de l'opinion depuis Saint Louis: la réformation du royaume.'

ordonnances, are much in evidence; reform ordinances or confirmations, for example, appeared in 1303, 1309, 1315-17 and *enquêteurs* visited all of the *bailliages* of the realm in 1302-3, 1315-17, 1325-6. The great reform ordinance of 1303 (termed *Magna Statuta* by the clerks of the royal chancery) was confirmed no fewer than twenty-four times between Philip IV and Charles V.[100] Though it dealt with some purely administrative problems and protected ecclesiastical rights against harsh action by royal officials, the greatest number of its clauses were drafted to meet the complaints of laymen against the king's agents.[101] When the leagues of Philip IV's subjects formed in opposition to his policies in 1314, and demanded charters from his son, the two guarantees of good faith on the part of the king and of some minimal enforcement of good behaviour on the part of his officials were oaths administered to officials and a promise of triennial tours of *enquêteurs*.[102] The crisis which followed the defeat of French arms at Crécy in 1346 showed that, as in England, subjects demanded reforms, yet also resented some crown action carried forward in the name of reform. An assembly of the Estates in Languedoc in June 1346 voiced so many complaints that Duke John of Normandy (the heir to the throne) issued a reform ordinance which included articles on oppressions caused not only by royal sergeants, but by the *réformateurs* themselves. After the disastrous defeat at Poitiers in 1356, another reform ordinance was necessary; but even the radical leaders of the Estates General who demanded the reforms turned to the traditional mechanism of enforcement: commissions toured France, supervised by a board of *généraux réformateurs*.[103] This French action after the capture of John II in 1356 bears obvious similarities to the English action a century earlier when impossible schemes (the 'Sicilian business') had captured the imagination of Henry III.

A general comparison of the timing of reform in the two countries is, in fact, enlightening. At least the opening scene was enacted in England at the beginning of the twelfth century in the reign of Henry I; by the third quarter of that century, in the reign

[100] Ibid. 92-3; Glénisson, 'Les Enquêteurs-réformateurs', 82.

[101] Strayer, *The Reign of Philip the Fair*, 414-15.

[102] Artonne, *Le Mouvement de 1314*, 121-4.

[103] *Ordonnances des roys de France*, iii. 124-46; Henneman, 'Enquêteurs-réformateurs', 346.

of Henry II, the impulse is clear. In France the earliest efforts (the creation of the *baillis*) began only late in the twelfth century; the *enquêteurs* appeared only around mid-thirteenth century; the reform ordinances became prominent (after a start under St Louis) in the fourteenth century. The time-lag is just what the general histories of the two monarchies would lead us to expect. But it is more difficult to compare second phases. Indeed, France did not experience a second phase in the manner England did. In England a movement closely associated with charters and itinerant panels of commissioners had come to an end by the middle of the fourteenth century; the focus had narrowed to the cost of the French war, and reform became domiciled in parliament. In France the reform movement seems to wane at about the same time, or slightly later; 'the last years of John II's reign . . .', as John Henneman has suggested, 'represent the end of an era in the history of French reform commissions'.[104] Raymond Cazelles, following the evidence of reform ordinances rather than *enquêteurs-réformateurs*, saw 'le coeur de ce mouvement' ending with Charles V in the 1370s; the early fifteenth-century Cabocian movement was 'au contraire un épilogue òu l'exigence des réformes sert surtout de prétexte à l'assouvissement des rancunes des partis.'[105] Yet the reliance on *commissaires* in government continued in France for several centuries,[106] in contrast to the disappearance of the eyre justices and all of their continuators in England. Why did the English experiment in government by commissioners end, while it continued in France? Why did the impulse for reform in France not produce the second phase characteristics evident in England?

Close agreement on answers to such large questions cannot be expected, but several factors seem clear. If the French longer retained their commissioners, one reason may be found in the return of these agents in the second half of the fourteenth century to something like their original role. As John Henneman has argued, the *enquêteurs-réformateurs* came full circle between their establishment by St Louis and the later fourteenth century. Conceived in mid-thirteenth century as watch-dogs over royal fiscal officers, they themselves took on fiscal responsibilities

104 Hennemann, 'Enquêteurs réformateurs', 346.

105 Cazelles, 'Une exigence de l'opinion depuis Saint Louis', 4-45.

106 Gustave Dupont-Ferrier, 'Le Rôle des commissaires royaux'.

under Philip IV and saw the beginnings of a decline in popularity. But once a system of royal taxation was in place with negotiations in assemblies and localities, the frankly extortive role of the commissioners could fade, and their use in the process of reform could resume.[107]

Yet even as they reluctantly adjusted thought and action to the distasteful necessity of recurrent taxation, the French never found it necessary to develop central assemblies with the capacity or permanence found in the English parliament. The difference is a major feature of the history of the two countries and some of the classic explanations still have much merit. The sheer size of the kingdom of France, both in geographical area and population, created problems of scale and transportation. To bring together in one place all of the notables and representatives of those not quite so notable, yet important, was onerous and costly. As Robert Fawtier pointed out, the king would have encountered great difficulty in finding a building of sufficient size for a common meeting. Moreover, there was the further obstacle of language; the people of the north and the south did not, in fact, speak the same language.[108]

However, as P. S. Lewis has suggested, such 'mechanical difficulties' need not have blocked the development of assemblies in France. Town governments showed themselves prepared to send representatives long distances on business they considered important; committee systems devised *ad hoc* in 1356 and 1484 smoothed over the organizational difficulties of assemblies for the whole kingdom; the linguistic problem, though serious, was not an insuperable obstacle.[109] Moreover, as John Henneman has stressed, around the middle of the fourteenth century major steps seemed to be leading to a greater role for central assemblies in French political life. In the quarter century beginning in 1343, 'the most important period in the history of the French Estates General', such assemblies were instrumental in the process by which the French crown bargained for its military needs with guarantees of governmental reform. Vast sums might have been collected in this way through the work of the assemblies of 1347 and those of 1355-6. But the Plague swept away all such hopes in

107 Henneman, 'Enquêteurs-réformateurs', 309-11, 345-9.

108 Fawtier, 'Parlement d'Angleterre'.

109 Lewis, 'The Failure of the French Medieval Estates', 9-10.

the former case and popular resistance to taxation negated the latter effort; most Frenchmen did not consider the action of the assembly as binding on them. In the latter half of the fourteenth century though assemblies would proliferate at the level of the *bailliage* or the region, consent to taxation remained basically local.[110]

Thus, the differences in the course of reform in England and France reflect not only the greater size and linguistic diversity of France in comparison with England, but also the particular modes of governance which created the movements for reform on either side of the Channel. In England the precocious development of royal power not only meant a capacity to compel subjects to attend central assemblies, it also created in subjects an acute awareness of the need to be watchful and, in time, resistant. Parliamentary taxation is the chief, though not the sole, case in point. In general, the rapid expansion of the crown's role in English society was slowed or halted in the fourteenth century, the focus of chief concern turned to the finance of the French war, and a single 'national' assembly became the agency for reform in this second phase. In France not only was the crown less likely than in England to collect central assemblies, its historically weaker powers were less likely to compel that common restraining action so evident in England at least from the early thirteenth century; when necessary the French crown defused potential difficulties by allowing major tax exemptions to the privileged, especially the noble segments of society.[111] In a double sense, then, several centuries of strong monarchy in England stand behind the growth of parliament. In France, with a different timetable for the development of royal power, these two compelling forces (the strength to compel attendance, the strength which provoked restraints) were felt with much less force; localism, in fact, seems to have been the most powerful reagent in the chemistry of French politics. But it is striking that in both countries the late thirteenth century and early fourteenth century seem to mark a critical stage in the history of secular reform.

110 These themes are developed in John Henneman's two books: *Royal Taxation in Fourteenth-century France* (1971) and *Royal Taxation in Fourteenth-century France* (1976); the quot. appears in the latter (p. 14).

111 This complex topic is surveyed by Henneman, 'Nobility, Privilege, and Fiscal Politics'.

The motives of kings and their subjects in seeking governmental reform have been the subject of considerable discussion.[112] Royal purity of heart has been especially called into question by the suspicion that mere love of power and money was at the root of the matter, rather than 'true reform'. Certainly thirteenth- and fourteenth-century people were sensitive to the kingly acquisitiveness inevitably associated with reform. Matthew Paris denounced the 'infinite sums' of money culled by the general eyre in thirteenth-century England and later chroniclers commented on the trailbaston inquests of 1305 and on the 1341 inquests in a similar vein.[113] An even clearer instance of popular suspicion is provided by the reaction to an initiative of Philip V of France. By the 'Grand Design of 1321' (the phrase of Charles Taylor) 'Philip V was going to the country for money in time of peace and for support of a programme in the public interest, with only ultimate suggestions of helping toward a crusade.'[114] The public interest was to be served by three specific reforms: unification and reform of the coinage; introduction of a unified system of weights and measures; and the recovery of wrongly alienated domain lands.[115] But his subjects remained unconvinced that the reforms were indispensable either for the crusade or for the profit of the whole kingdom; the king could judge whether or not domain alienations had been wise; they thought that the coinage was really royal business; and for their part they were happy with existing money, weights, and measures. The chroniclers reported a fear that the king intended to introduce reforms on his own authority and to support them by a large exaction imposed on the country. The opinion was widespread enough for the king explicitly to deny the charge when writing to his officials and to emphasize his concern for the common profit.[116] Even where such contemporary medieval

112 Elizabeth A. R. Brown surveys the debate in French historiography in the introd. to 'Corruption, Finance, and Reform'. Comments presenting the narrower range of opinion over English reform appear in Cam, *Studies in the Hundred Rolls*, 39, 191-2; ead., *The Hundred and the Hundred Rolls* 34-5; 223, 225, 229, 240-7; Plucknett, *The Legislation of Edward I*, 1; Prestwich, *War, Politics, and Finance*, 281; Jones, '*Rex et ministri*', 5.

113 Cam, *Studies in the Hundred Rolls*, 29, 73, 145.

114 Taylor, 'French Assemblies', 230, 237.

115 Ibid. 229-30; Brown, 'Subsidy and Reform in 1321'.

116 Ibid. 417-21.

denunciation or suspicion of royal motive is lacking, historians have been able to demonstrate inherent fiscal interest by means of royal instructions to commissioners, institutional changes, or financial accounts. In a study tracing the changes in the royal *enquêteurs* in the century after St Louis, John Henneman concluded that even by the time of Louis's grandson 'perverting the function envisioned by St Louis, they now sought to remedy abuses by the king's subjects as well as those by royal officials. They became another arm of the fiscal administration, searching for new or neglected sources of revenue for the crown.'[117] This state of affairs persisted until the second half of the fourteenth century when elaboration of better mechanisms for taxation virtually eliminated the need for the fiscal functions which had been grafted on to the original reform stock.[118] Reaction to the financial motive is also apparent when English shires offered the king a lump sum to be spared the visit of his justices and the fines and amercements such visitation inevitably brought.[119]

'*Nolo contendere*' might be the royal response to the charge that fiscality underlay many reform initiatives. But a potentially more serious charge would hold that the shallowness of the kingly interest is apparent in the abuses allowed at the very heart of government, in the inner circle of royal advisers. Though the evidence is understandably scarce, it is highly revealing, as appears from the case of Walter Langton, bishop of Coventry and Lichfield, treasurer and chief minister of Edward I in the last decade of his reign.[120] Had he died about the same time as his royal master, Langton's reputation might be simply that of a hard-driving, efficient administrator to his king and his church, and the author of certain reforms in exchequer and wardrobe. Since he outlived the royal favour of Edward I and was the object of Edward II's hate and wrath, Langton was instead brought to trial and his activities minutely scrutinized. Reading the records of his trial the historian may feel as if he has lifted a stone in a field and is watching low forms of life scurry out of the bright light suddenly thrown on them. Was Edward II's prosecution of

117 Henneman, 'Enquêteurs-réformateurs', 310. For a similar view, see Fournial, 'Enquêteurs, réformateurs, et visiteurs généraux', 35.

118 Henneman, 'Enquêteurs-réformateurs', 346-9.

119 A number of examples are given in Putnam, *Proceedings*, p. xlvii.

120 For what follows see Beardwood, 'The Trial of Walter Langton'. She also published *Records of the Trial of Walter Langton*.

Langton a reform measure? Was he settling scores with an old personal enemy? Are the processes separable in Edward's mind or our own? Langton had apparently committed the linked offences of champerty and maintenance[121] (offences at that time the object of parliamentary attention); as treasurer he bent sheriffs to his will and broke those who resisted; he used statute merchants (designed for speedy debt collection) as unscrupulous means of securing non-prosecution of lawsuits, or conveyance of land he wanted. Langton was, as Alice Beardwood described him, the knave in Edward's hand of cards, and 'it would seem that Langton was not unique, except in his opportunities and in the trust and support of the crown. . . . the king, aging and ill and beset with problems of war and finance, was no doubt content to rely unquestioningly on a faithful treasurer, who made a show of enforcing economies, even against the Prince of Wales, while feathering his own nest by taking advantage of his official position'.[122]

Yet the evidence of corruption more or less tolerated in the highest circles does not empty the notion of reform of all meaningful content. Itinerant commissioners were regularly sent into the English and French countryside and clearly accomplished work appreciated by subjects; in some measure these commissioners fulfilled the high aims of reform and common profit which in sonorous Latin phrases adorned the preambles to their commissions and the reform statutes associated with their work. Time and again when kings offered the opportunity Englishmen and Frenchmen took advantage of the chance to bring charges against royal officials. Kings were surely not mistaken in their belief that a flurry of reform activity, and especially the perambulations of commissioners, could act as a safety valve for popular discontent, as in Edward's inquests of 1298 or Philip IV's inquests of 1302-3; if they seemed in danger of forgetting this fact, subjects might well remind them, as witness the French leagues of 1314-15. The sentiment was not found solely in the privileged upper stratum of society: between 1340 and 1355

[121] Champerty (support of a plea in consideration for a share in the spoils) and maintenance (support of another's plea) were not clearly distinguished as offenses, but punishment of champerty belonged only to the king, who chose to pardon his minister. See Beardwood, 'The Trial of Walter Langton', 14, 19, and Sayles, *Select Cases in the Court of King's Bench Under Edward III*, x, p. liv.

[122] This and the preceding quot. are taken from Beardwood, 'The Trial of Walter Langton', 37-8.

when Bertrand de Ribérac served as *réformateur général* in the Midi, the lower classes of Béziers formed a *réformateur's* party;[123] in England, many of the accusations brought before trailbaston justices in Lincolnshire came from men who seem to be simple villagers.[124]

If evidence on royal motive and popular response presents a dilemma it may be largely of our own making. Too close a distinction between profit and reform would have little meaning to the men of the thirteenth or fourteenth centuries; they would be as puzzled by our discomfort at the link between fiscality and reform as by our uneasiness with the clear medieval fusion between profit and chivalry or profit and piety.[125] A search for 'pure reform', without a fiscal component may edge close to anachronism, as does discussion of pure chivalry, unstained by brutality or profit. Reform was a function of government and the operation of government had always meant a profit; indeed, taking the long view, it was only recently that government had come significantly to involve much else. As Beryl Smalley has suggested, 'The most admired and most successful ruler . . . would be he who combined the maximum exploitation of his subjects from a financial point of view, since this constituted government by definition, with the minimum appearance of tyranny in the eyes of all who had means of resistance. Somehow or other he must profiteer justly.'[126] It may be useful to note that French historians have appeared more troubled by this issue than English historians. The reason seems to be that fourteenth-century French kings, and the historians who have written about them, have had to deal with St Louis as the father figure in the history of French secular reform. Given the incidence of saintliness in the world and the probabilities of its recurrence in the Capetian or early Valois lines, most royal efforts after Louis IX could only appear to be backsliding into crass fiscality, particularly as hard-pressed governments struggled to carry out their policies in the troubled conditions of the fourteenth century. One

123 Lewis, *Later Medieval France*, 263.

124 McLane, 'The Royal Courts', ch. 3.

125 The easy blending of piety and profit is illustrated, for example, in the letters of the Luccese company of the Riccardi, whose agents operated in both France and England in this period; see Kaeuper, *Bankers to the Crown*, 227-8.

126 Smalley, 'Capetian France', 64.

127 Langlois, 'Doléances', 1.

of the arguments entered in support of Louis's canonization, after all, was his unusual love of justice as witnessed by the *enquêtes* he commissioned.[127] And even St Louis had held strongly that royal rights, too, must be defended in a just state.[128] The marvel is not the mixed motives of lesser mortals, but the unusual reform effort of Louis IX, motivated by an intense personal piety focused on the crusade.[129] Movements to canonize Robert Burnell or Walter Langton, Enguerran de Marigny, or Henri de Sully were not much in evidence.

Rather than thinking of two opposed conceptions emerging from radically different worlds of thought, we might consider reform to operate on a single scale shared by all concerned: kings and their subjects would locate somewhere on this continuum of desirability a reasonable degree of efficiency and some degree of profit for royal government (the degree being a matter of debate), the establishment of rules for the good conduct of royal officers (toward the king and all others), the detection and punishment of official misconduct, the granting, confirming, or regulating of administrative or jurisdictional rights on the basis of requests from particular individuals or communities. As J. C. Holt said of England at the time of the Great Charter, the king and his opponents were not so much fighting over opposing principles as clashing interpretations of shared principles.[130] The heritage of nineteenth-century constitutionalism (which sometimes still weighs heavily on our views) cannot mislead us into thinking that we can award credit to the good or true reform and condemn crass fiscality in easy confidence that our views reflect those of the fourteenth century.

Three particular examples, one from thirteenth-century England and two from fourteenth-century France, may be useful in illustrating the cross-currents of motivation at work in any measure of reform. Across the first half of the thirteenth century the office of the English sheriff was considerably changed in the name of reform. As D. C. Carpenter shows,[131] the changes reflect

[128] Brown, 'Corruption, Finance, and Reform', ch. 3, p. 16; cf. ch. 5, p. 1.

[129] This is the theme developed in Jordan, *Louis IX and the Challenge of the Crusade*, chs. 3, 6. See also the views of Jean Glénnison, 'Les Enquêtes administratives', 16-20.

[130] Holt, *Magna Carta*, 80-1, 90.

[131] The following discussion is based on Carpenter, 'The Decline of the Curial

crown efforts for fiscal reform in the interests of efficiency and profit, skilfully coupled with a concern for remedy of the grievances of county society against the local government headed by the sheriff. Two basic issues were at stake, shrieval personnel and shire revenues. At the opening of the thirteenth century sheriffs were only ceasing to be great *curiales* who served in effect as regional governors and military commanders; the profit expected of them by the crown may have been as much political and military as financial, since they were usually allowed to farm shire revenues (at considerable personal profit) and, as powerful men, were hard for the exchequer to control. The exchequer ideal was rather an agent of lower status who could be held accountable for shire revenues, even for the profits exceeding the old set figures of the shire farms, either by paying a fixed increment above the farm, or by a straightforward custodial accounting for all revenues received (in which case he would cease to be a farmer but would receive an allowance). Clearly this weighing of profits versus patronage would have to take into account the political stability of the realm as well as the current state of the king's coffers and the willingness of the community of the realm to co-operate with royal taxation. In 1232, after the fall of the last great justiciar, Hubert de Burgh, the regime of Peter des Roches and Peter des Rivaux presented itself as an agency of financial reform, but basically placed favoured men in the counties and on the issues of curial sheriffs and farmed revenues made little change. The watershed came four years later when a new regime, with William of Savoy, bishop-elect of Valence, as the king's chief adviser, implemented the plan long-favoured by the exchequer. Having no party in the country to reward with lucrative shrievalties, William of Savoy and his circle seem to have accepted the exchequer idea of appointing new men of lower social status in the counties. Nearly half the counties of England were given the new sheriffs between mid-April and the end of May 1236; moreover, all the new sheriffs were expected to account as custodians for every penny of revenue from their shire. 'At the same time', Carpenter notes, 'these changes were cleverly packaged and proclaimed as reforms to meet the

Sheriff'. Other useful sources include Morris, *The Medieval English Sheriff*; Powicke, *King Henry III and the Lord Edward*, ch. 3; Templeman, 'The Sheriffs of Warwickshire'.

aspirations and grievances of county society so that in several respects the measures of 1236 anticipated the reforms of local government in 1258.'[132] If Matthew Paris can be taken as a reflection of county society, the attempt succeeded; he praised the new sheriffs, noting that they were under oath not to take bribes, not to demand excessive entertainment; he predicted success for the reform. But the 1236 reforms by the crown did not merge simply with the 1258 reforms of the baronial opponents of the crown. In 1241 the exchequer, attempting to drive the tightest bargains it could with the sheriffs (at a time when Henry III was being denied tax grants), returned to a policy of farms and increments, now set so high that pressure on sheriffs was painfully intensified. The sheriffs, of course, passed on the burden to the residents of their counties in a way dramatically revealed by the complaints about corruption and oppression in local government so prominent in 1258-65. Several local inquests and the addition of a number of articles about sheriffs to the *capitula* of the general eyre were insufficient to correct perceived abuses. The reforming barons of 1258 thus reversed the course of the preceding seventeen years and returned to the policy of 1236-41: non-curial sheriffs, often local men appointed with a generous amount of exchequer influence, accounting for the profits of a county with an allowance provided for the sheriff.

If the royal reforms of 1236 were useful to the baronial reformers of 1258, these baronial efforts were likewise precedents for the inquests of 1274-5 which led to the great burst of legislative activity in the first half of the reign of Edward I; many of the articles of the so-called Hundred Inquests of 1274 and after can be matched article for article with those of the baronial eyre of 1259.[133] Similarly, the 1236 changes were important to continuing reform by reducing the curial sheriff to a status more closely approximating that of crown servant; the complaints against sheriffs and other local officials actively solicited by the crown as an important feature of the reform movement from the mid-thirteenth century can scarcely be imagined while the king's familiars and important political allies held office in the shires.

The interconnections between politics and reform, royal fiscality and local governmental oppression, central control of the

132 Carpenter, 'The Decline of the Curial Sheriff', 17.

133 Cam, *Studies in the Hundred Rolls*, 14.

king's own local officials, and attention to local grievances (all evident in the mid-thirteenth-century English reform of sheriffs) appear again in a French reform mission dispatched to Languedoc by Philip V in 1318-19. As Elizabeth Brown has shown in her detailed study of this mission,[134] behind the king's action lay concern over Languedocian support of the anticipated campaign in Flanders and the political and religious unrest feared as Pope John XXII reopened the case against Bernard Délicieux (with Philip V's support) as part of his attack on the spiritual Franciscans.[135] Philip considered the mission important enough to send Jean I, Count of Forez, and Raoul Rousselet, Bishop of Laon, as his commissioners with wide powers to advance the reform, peace, and welfare of his subjects. Yet, as Brown argues, the king's interests and especially his financial interests were primary, as appears from the prominent role played by the Chamber of Accounts in supervising the reform mission. Before travelling to Languedoc the count and bishop submitted a carefully prepared memorandum to the Chamber of Accounts seeking advice on important points; more than once in the course of their work decisions were supervised, approved, or overturned by Chamber officials, and the Chamber continued to sanction acts of the commissioners well after the conclusion of their mission.[136] Likewise, the reformers seem to have played a significant role, if sometimes at second hand, in the negotiations for a subsidy for the Flanders campaign. At first in collaboration with Henri de Sully (Philip's chief minister) and then acting on their own in his absence, they played a significant role as supervisors and directors of tax negotiations.[137] Financial motives are again evident in the money they collected for confirming existing local rights or for redressing legitimate grievances.[138] Complex negotiations over the royal salt staple of Carcassonne produced the most significant sum promised to the crown; whatever the difficulties raised by the specifics of the settlement, the crown could count on significant subsidies paid

[134] What follows is based on Brown, 'Corruption, Finance, and Reform', which she generously sent me in TS.

[135] Ibid., ch. 3, pp. 1-4.

[136] Ibid., chs. 2, pp. 9-17; 5, pp. 11, 12, 19; 6, p. 1; 8, p. 4.

[137] Ibid., ch. 4, pp. 14-15.

[138] Ibid., ch. 5, pp. 13, 26.

over three years.[139] In all, the Count of Forez and Bishop of Laon collected more than 200,000*l.t.* in cash or obligations for the crown during their two year tour.

On the other hand, many individuals and communities benefited from the visitation. Presumably there was considerable popular approval when three officials of the seneschals of Carcassonne, two judges and an acting treasurer, were tried and sentenced for their misdeeds. The same might be said when the reformers launched the trial of the consuls of one important town, charged with unusually serious offences (though the case was finished in Parlement) and were themselves judges in a second, similar case. The correctional record was somewhat tarnished, however, by the total disregard of the misdeeds of others and by the mercy of remission granted by the king or his reformers to some of those convicted.[140] Yet an ordinance promulgated by the reformers on the institution of guardianship in Toulouse was obviously valued (even beyond Toulouse) and was carefully registered in the statutes of the seneschal's court. General approval also seems likely for the supervision of such public works as improvements on one of the bridges in Narbonne and in the navigability of the river Aude. Certainly many subjects were eager to purchase privileges in the king's power to grant through the agency of his commissioners. Benefits continued even after the reformers had left. Within a year after the conclusion of the mission a proclamation, which seems to draw on their experience, mandated oaths to be sworn by all *baillis* and seneschals, rehearsing and strengthening the code of conduct prescribed by St Louis and Philip IV. More significant, Philip V ordered the wholesale removal of serjeants, the object of so much complaint, the selection of the minimal number suitable in each district, the choice of only the best men, and the provision of surety for loyal performance.[141]

A third example demonstrates the similarities between the motives, problems, and responses of a great French feudatory and those involved in crown attempts at reform. The 'affaire' of 1342 and the reform of 1343 in Burgundy resulted from the malversations of three members of the prominent Bourgeoise

[139] Ibid., chs. 6, p. 16; 8, p. 12.
[140] Ibid., chs. 7, *passim*; ch. 5, pp. 1-8; 8, pp. 13-14.
[141] Ibid., chs. 7, pp. 5-7, 21-5; 7, pp. 5-7.

family of Dijon, Jean, Jean le Petit, and Helié, all members of the entourage of Duke Eudes IV with special financial duties.[142] Although the initial charges brought against Jean Bourgeoise in October 1342 were the malicious devices of his Dijon enemies, the investigation ironically brought to light charges against all three members of the family, and especially Helié, which could be substantiated. The Duke's outrage, and something of his motivation, appeared in his claim that Helié had kept for himself at least 500,000*l.t.* of ducal revenue. As was often true in administrative reforms, a particular scandal created an opportunity, perhaps a need, for a general house-cleaning. Eudes IV named commissioners in September and invited his subjects to bring charges against Jean. Jean compromised with the duke in October, promising him 24,000*l.t.*, a sum which seems not to have seriously damaged the family fortune. But the general reform began after Helié's actions came to light; a new commission in 1343 opened the investigation to include charges against all ducal officers and all unpunished offences in the duchy. When the council of Dijon, more watchful of urban jurisdiction than anxious for ducal reform, complained against infringements of its rights and threatened an appeal to the king of France, the reform commission was more strictly limited for Dijon and a new commission was issued for the area of Franche-Comté and the Outre-Saone (beyond the reach of appeals to the Parlement of Paris). Surviving records from this reform commission in imperial territory show that *prévôtés* were a principal target and that 6,697 livres in fines were collected.[143]

At the conclusion of each of her surveys of English local administration, Helen Cam was drawn to a judgement made by a monastic chronicler on the great inquests of 1274-5, and by extension on the entire effort of reform under Edward I. The monk of Dunstaple noted that the king had sent his investigators everywhere to inquire into the conduct of sheriffs and other officers, 'but no good came of it (*sed nullum commodum inde*

142 The evidence is discussed (and some of it is printed) in Richard, 'L'Affaire des bourgeoise'.

143 'Dans le cas de la réformation de 1343', Richard notes, 'dont nous connaissons les origines, ce n'est sans doute pas le désir de faire rentre dans ses caisses le montant des "exploits" qui avait été le souci dominant d'Études IV. . . .'

venit)'. In 1921 she thought the evidence 'explained if not justified' this judgement; in 1930 she again quoted the Dunstaple analyst, but closed with praise for the ideals and real achievements of Edward I.[144] The sense of balance, of the difficulty of making so large a judgement is interesting in one whose admiration for William Stubbs included praise for 'the perfect hedger'.[145] Miss Cam has been by no means alone in her caution over the results of medieval reform. Not surprisingly, the debates over royal motives are reproduced in the assessments of the success or failure of governmental reform in this period.

Those who judge medieval rule by an ideal standard can only record their disappointment. Even if the historian can thrust aside modern notions, accept a seemingly high level of violence as a concomitant of medieval governance, accept a link between justice and profit, accept that local officers were royal agents rather than civil servants, still the ideal standard clearly proclaimed in the thirteenth and fourteenth centuries prevents too optimistic a reading of the outcome of reform. Both royal pronouncements in statutes, ordinances, mandates and writs, and royal actions such as soliciting plaints and trying offending officials, show the existence of high standards. A similarly impressive body of evidence produced largely by the itinerant commissioners shows that these standards were widely violated.

The punishment of erring officials snared in the investigators' net provides the clearest case in point.[146] A handful of truly heroic offenders suffered execution.[147] In moments of great stress significant numbers or even entire classes of officials might be replaced, as were most of the sheriffs of England in 1170, 1236, 1258, 1278, 1341.[148] Louis IX replaced many *baillis* after 1254. But though there were spectacular exceptions, most officials

[144] Cam, *Studies in the Hundred Rolls*, 192; ead., *The Hundred and the Hundred Rolls*, 240-7.

[145] Quot.: J. G. Edwards, *William Stubbs*, 7.

[146] See the comments of Strayer, *The Reign of Philip the Fair*, 402-4; Jordan, *Louis IX and the Challenge of the Crusade*, 57-8; Cam, *The Hundred and the Hundred Rolls*, 242; ead., *Studies in the Hundred Rolls*, 190-1.

[147] Strayer, *The Reign of Philip the Fair*, 403.

[148] Warren, *Henry II*, 287-91; Carpenter, 'The Decline of the Curial Sheriff'; Paris, *Chronica Majora*, iii. 412; Tout, *Chapters in the Administrative History of Medieval England*, iii. 9, 35, 122; Cam, *The Hundred and the Hundred Rolls*, 43-4, 64; *Annales Monastici*, iii. 279; Fryde, 'Edward III's Removal of his Ministers and Judges.'

could expect to hold their posts without serious worry; even if charges were brought against them they could usually make fine with the king, or if dismissed could expect later pardon, often with reinstatement or a new position. Demonstrated competence was a sufficient cloak to cover most misdeeds, especially if the injured party was not the crown and the injury was committed in an excess of zeal for the king's business. Guillaume de Mussy held several *bailliages* under Philip IV, made a large fine with the crown when charges of corruption were brought against him, became an *enquêteur*, and continued to act in the fashion he had punished in others.[149] Guichard de Marzi was sacked as seneschal of Toulouse and fined in 1301, but ended his career as a member of Parlement and as an *enquêteur*.[150] At the condemnation of Bernard Délicieux in 1319, alongside the reformers sat Aimeri du Cros (the seneschal of Toulouse whose misdeeds the reformers had chosen to disregard) Damas de Marzi (implicated in the charges brought against his brother, Guichard, but promoted to acting seneschal of Toulouse in 1316, and of Carcassonne in 1319) and Raimond Costa (sacked as chief judge of Carcassonne in 1303, absolved and made a royal judge in the *sénéchaussée* of Toulouse in 1309).[151] Many of the English judges charged in showy trials in 1289 and 1341 were simply fined; some of those dismissed were, sooner or later, reinstated.[152] Sheriffs accused and fined for a great variety of offences often appear in the records serving again as sheriffs, or as oyer and terminer justices, escheaters, and tax collectors.[153] Although the outcry against purveyance produced various statements of official resolve to treat those convicted of illegal purveyance as felons, even outlawed purveyors and local officers might be employed again in similar positions.[154] The more complete English evidence reveals an even more basic weakness in the prosecution of officials; as was true for the accused in any other category, the crown found it difficult to compel them even

149 Bautier, 'Guillaume de Mussy', 64-98.

150 Strayer, *The Reign of Philip the Fair*, 403.

151 Brown, 'Corruption, Finance, and Reform', ch. 7, p. 20.

152 Tout and Johnstone, *State Trials*, pp. xxxvi-xxxix; Fryde, 'Edward III's Removal of his Ministers and Judges', 156-8.

153 Jones, 'Keeping the Peace', 316; McLane, 'The Royal Courts', ch. 3.

154 Ibid. 184-6, citing *Articuli Super Cartas* (1300 cl. 2, Ordinances of 1311, cl. 10, and the statute of 1331, cl. 2).

to appear in court and answer charges.[155] If outlawry were pronounced against them it was in effect an admission that they were beyond reach; as we have seen, the outlawry was often disregarded by the crown itself when looking for men to fill administrative positions. The French may have more frequently dismissed officials and barred them from office in some particular district or through the realm;[156] French kings seem to have had a larger pool of potential officers and relied more heavily on paid service than the English kings, whose dependence on unpaid service of local gentlemen may have increased their reluctance to dismiss the erring. But even the French crown showed a general reluctance to sack guilty officials.[157] The royal attitude on both sides of the Channel was concisely summarized by Hilda Johnstone: 'why . . . break a tool which might still have its uses?'.[158]

Fines were the most common punishment in either country and added revenue to royal coffers even as they added lustre to the royal reform image. The crown interest was not simply financial, since kings sometimes required the guilty to make restitution to victims (perhaps several times the value of goods extorted) as well as to offer fines to offset their offence to the royal majesty. [159] A comprehensive study of fines in either country has yet to be written; such studies would allow a comparison of the pain inflicted on the guilty and the revenue secured by the crown. Lower level officials were more likely to feel the force of fines than their superiors,[160] but the relentless increase in the numbers of such officers in England and France suggests that many men were willing to take the jobs and act as required for success; the risks cannot have been perceived as daunting.

155 McLane, 'The Royal Courts', 179-83.

156 Scores of sentences against French royal officials of various ranks appear in the *Actes du Parlement de Paris*; many of these bar the offender from holding any public office (e.g., *Actes*, 2nd ser. 2, 3, 35) or from holding office in some particular locality (e.g., *Actes*, 2nd ser. 128, 2975) or from holding a particular office again (e.g., *Actes* 4221, *Actes*, 2nd ser. 3987, 4785).

157 Fiétier, 'Le Choix des baillis'.

158 Tout and Johnstone, *State Trials*, p. xxxvii.

159 Jordan, *Louis IX and the Challenge of the Crusade*, 57-8; Thomson, *A Lincolnshire Assize Roll*, pp. cxi ff; McLane (ed.), *The 1341 Royal Inquest*, introd.

160 As Jordan notes in *Louis IX and the Challenge of the Crusade*, 57-8.

That medieval governments did not meet their own ideal standards can hardly cause shock. The efforts of governments since then stand as an antidote against too selective a cynicism. But cynicism is an element best admitted into historical analysis in small doses. Medieval men tended to see the need for reform in terms of a corruption of personal morality and were reluctant to believe in the importance of institutional change. As modern analysts of their world, we run the danger of committing a double injustice. We tend to use a medieval sense of personal causality, blaming problems on royal greediness, and condemning royal policies based on mere fiscality. At the same time we use a thoroughly modern scale of efficiency for judging the small measure of success achieved by reform. It is more useful to recognize that both the institutions of governance and standards for the proper conduct of those who directed them were constantly changing as the medieval state emerged.

Considering the reform movement as an important feature of one phase of the history of the state obviates idealistic defence of stated medieval goals or shallow cynicism over the distance between these goals and reality. Kings vigorously pursued what may appear to us to be contradictory ends: they sought to rule justly, as God required of them, and to rule efficiently so as to maximize power and profits; they turned a blind eye to the methods of officials who could extract revenue from the countryside, but reacted with righteous indignation when their officials cheated the crown or caused dangerous countryside clamour in their search for funds or their exercise of jurisdiction. Subjects, with more logical consistency to their aims, demanded reform to match the sense of their place in the emerging state; they usually accepted the costs associated with such reforms, though (especially in France) with as much demonstrative complaint as possible. In England, where the king's jurisdiction was all-encompassing, subjects wanted redress against local officials, but not the eyre which exposed the faults of all to the king's profit.[161] But, by and large, the process went on relatively peacefully through one of the most significant eras of governmental expansion in early European history. Even if judged a failure by ideal standards, the effort for reform generally kept the strains within tolerable limits. Yet the process must not be viewed

161 See Jones's comments, 'Keeping the Peace', 319.

through a rosy haze; if there was an element of game in the entire process, the play was serious and it sometimes became violent. Reform meant compromise rather than contentment; popular protest could be bitter and serious by the fourteenth century.

2. THE EVIDENCE OF LITERATURE

The same period in which the medieval state developed in England and France saw the emergence of highly sophisticated vernacular literatures in each country—Anglo-Norman and then Middle English on one side of the Channel, Old French on the other. Moreover, at this period 'literature was, to a much greater degree than today, a collective phenomenon whose modes of creation and dissemination involved the community as a whole.'[162] We can expect this literature to reveal something about the range of opinion on the expanding sphere of royal government; the works created between the eleventh and fourteenth centuries were certainly not produced by writers, underwritten by patrons, and heard or read by audiences freed from the particularities of their age. Thus we might expect, on the one hand, that the increasing tendency of kings and their agents to demand obedience, submission to royal judgment, payment of taxes, might leave its imprint on at least some aspects of both French and English literature; on the other hand, given the differing timetable and natures of governmental growth in the two realms, we might also expect that any expression of critical opinion would take different form on either side of the Channel and would come at different times. Might not the earlier and more forceful consolidation of an English state result in an earlier and deeper royal imprint on literary works produced in England? In France might not the characteristic time-lag appear in literature relating to the state no less than in royal finance or law? By considering the image of the state in literary works produced in France and England in the late twelfth and early thirteenth

[162] Bloch, *Medieval French Literature and Law*, 1. W. T. H. Jackson suggests that the epic form (to be discussed below) appeared 'at times and in societies when the distinction between literature, history, philosophy, and didactic composition was blurred or nonexistent and that even when such distinctions were known, it was often only to a small literate elite not particularly concerned with the vernacular epic', *The Hero and the King*, 135-6.

centuries and again in the late thirteenth and fourteenth centuries we will in fact find two sets of striking and important contrasts.

Repeatedly in previous chapters claims have been advanced for the precociousness of the English state which much earlier than the state in France claimed a comprehensive jurisdiction and was served by effective local administrators. Not surprisingly, the English also early created and regularly added to a literature of government—administrative manuals, law books, and the like. The list would include Richard FitzNeal's *Dialogue of the Exchequer* (probably written in the 1170s), the *De Legibus et Consuetudinibus Regni Angliae*, attributed to Glanville (1189), the work of Bracton by the same title (mid-thirteenth century), the *Brevia Placitata*, *Casus Placitorum*, *Fleta*, and *Britton* (all in the later thirteenth century), and the fourteenth century *Novae Narrationes* and *Modus Tenendi Parliamentum*.[163] But if we take literature in its usual and more important meaning and if we think in terms of an imaginative literature which may be in some degree *about* the state, rather than this administrative and legal literature *of* the state, then France must be considered the leader. It seems at first glance paradoxical, but France much earlier produced what R. Howard Bloch has termed 'a first literature of protest'.[164]

Scholars studying the evolution of the *chanson de geste* across the twelfth and early thirteenth centuries have generally agreed that the changes in medieval epic form cannot be explained on the grounds of literary adaptation and amplification alone. 'There must have been', in the words of William C. Calin, 'some more profound, external, non-artistic motives. . . .'[165] A number of scholars find one of the major motivating themes of the genre in the search for the proper relationship between the crown and great feudal lords.[166] W. T. H. Jackson has even suggested that

[163] For comments on the precocious English development of literature about the art of governance, see Southern, *Medieval Humanism and Other Studies*, 174-9; Thompson, 'England and the Twelfth-century Renaissance', 11, 20-1.

[164] Bloch, *Medieval French Literature and Law*, 101.

[165] Calin, *The Old French Epic of Revolt*, 122-3. Jackson notes in general terms that 'Epics always have strong social overtones'; *The Hero and the King*, pref.

[166] In addition to the works of Calin and Bloch already cited, see Bezzola, *Les Origines*, 317-23; id., 'De Roland à Raoul de Cambrai', 195-213; id., 'A propos de la valeur littéraire', 183-95; Matarasso, *Recherches historiques et littéraires; Adler, Rückzug in epischer Parade*; Bender, *König und Vassal*. The

conflict between an established but ineffective king and a powerful and intruding hero stands at the centre of the epic in all ages. 'The pattern of the conflict between settled king and intruder-hero is thus essentially a study of transfer of power or, in other terms, of the problem of kingship.'[167] The flourishing of epic in the formative period of Capetian kingship thus occasions no surprise. The medieval epic was hardly a static form and its changes might reveal a literary parallel to the struggle between the historical forces of kingship and feudality as they co-operated and clashed in the changing political environment of Capetian France. This development of the chanson de geste need not be thought of as linear, moving from a relatively positive or at least benign view of kingship to one openly critical or even hostile. More than one type of epic poem may have been present from the start; *Gormond et Isembard* is older than *Roland*, yet it contains the theme of feudal revolt and passages of a realism easily thought to be a late development.[168] But the genre does seem to become increasingly concerned with relationships between the king and the great feudatories; the writers in the epic form do seem to be struggling with the range of issues posed in the minds of nobles by the power of the nascent French state and its jurisdiction. 'Arthurian kingship', as R. Howard Bloch has written, 'resembles the feudal monarchies of the late Carolingians and early Capetians as seen from the increasingly national perspective of a Philippe-Auguste or St Louis. From this point of view, the death of Arthur and the destruction of the Round Table along with its baronage of *bons seigneurs* look like the failure of feudal organization to deal with the problems of a new, more centrally-oriented era.'[169]

This concern with the growing power of kingship is especially apparent in the set of poems known variously as the cycle of the rebellious barons, the feudal cycle, or the cycle of Doon de Mayence, written in the late twelfth and thirteenth centuries.

views of these authors are discussed by Bloch, *Medieval French Literature and Law*, 100-2. Most recently, see Jackson, *The Hero and the King*, 15-16.

[167] Jackson, *The Hero and the King*, 15, 111. If epic form regularly addresses these issues, the historian's interest is drawn to the recurrent problem of kingship and acceptable order.

[168] Calin, *The Old French Epic of Revolt*, 124.

[169] Bloch, *Medieval French Literature and Law*, 4. Cf. ibid. 100 and Calin, *The Old French Epic of Revolt*, 113-15.

Two other traditional cycles in the three fold categorization of the Old French epic find their unity in their chief characters: the cycle of the king (including the *Chanson de Roland*) deals with the deeds of Charlemagne; the cycle of Garin de Monglane (including *Le Couronnment de Louis*, *Chanson d'Orange*) deals with the faithful vassal Guillaume d'Orange. But the unity of the feudal cycle stems not from an individual but a common subject matter. As William Calin writes of these epics and their patrons:

To the feudal barons the increase in royal power was a hated innovation and violation of long-standing rights, a gross misuse of authority placing all society in jeopardy. The theme of revolt was their only positive answer to a keenly-felt danger; it crystallized the general feeling of discontent which was taking hold of the feudal nobility. These social and economic conditions were not solely responsible, in some magical deterministic way, for the epic of revolt. But they did provide the *necessary* if not sufficient milieu in which such poetry could thrive.[170]

For present purposes two significant differences measure the thematic distance between such poems from this cycle of rebellious barons as *Raoul de Cambrai, La Chevalerie Ogier, Les Quatre Filz Aymon, Girart de Roussillon*, and an earlier and much better-known epic like the *Chanson de Roland*. In the first place, the heroic panorama of the united knights of Christendom in the tens of thousands battling paynim hordes numbering hundreds of thousands in *Roland* has given way in the feudal cycle to much more local struggles between particular noble families and the crown, or even between one family and another. Lords fight not to preserve Christianity and the order of the empire but to preserve their region or even their own lignages and fiefs.[171] *Raoul de Cambrai*, for example, portrays two feudal wars, several single combats, the razing of a nunnery, a judicial duel, and finally a reconciliation of aristocratic enemies who combine against the king and burn Paris.[172] But even more significant than this reduction in geopolitical scale is the changed view of royalty. Charlemagne in the *Chanson de Roland* is in one sense a figure almost above mundane limitations: he is the epitome

[170] Ibid. 9, 131. The quots. appears on the latter page.

[171] See the comments of Bezzola: 'A propos de la valeur littéraire', 184-6, 190: id., 'De Roland à Raoul de Cambrai', 198-213.

[172] Calin provides a convenient plot summary, see *The Old French Epic of Revolt*, 10.

of Christendom; archangels whisper advice and exortation in his ear while he strokes his 200-year-old beard; if not the very wrath of God, his anger is the closest approximation to it likely to be encountered on earth. But in another sense he is a remote figurehead, a leader of a warrior band writ large, a symbol of militant Christianity[173] and sweet France, rather than the head of an administration that could ever prove troublesome, demand taxes, interfere in seigneurial jurisdiction, or question the particulars of local inheritance. In the later feudal cycle, by contrast, the king is either weak and incompetent or forceful but tyrannical; again and again the king acts unjustly, failing to heed the established principles of feudal relationships.[174] The lords often see themselves as injured and oppressed fighters for right order in the world, especially if (as Calin and Bloch suggest) they felt squeezed between an innovating crown and the emerging force of the bourgeoisie.[175]

Yet there is enough variety and complexity in the epic of revolt to support conflicting scholarly interpretations.[176] Feudal resentment at the growing power of Capetian kingship from Louis VII to Louis IX seems to be a well-established theme. The poems are often placed in the archaic setting of the post-Carolingian era and may have drawn inspiration and incident from an age in which kingship was less threatening than it was under the later Capetians. The epics often read as if ninth-century legends were being rewritten in terms of twelfth-century problems; elements of collective fantasy or day-dreams about ineffectual kings are evident, drawing on memories of the chaotic First Feudal Age when the disappearance of effective kingship over most of France allowed each lord to hold what he could.[177] Jackson notes that

[173] Eric Auerbach notes that Charlemagne is 'almost . . . a Prince of God . . . the head of all Christendom and . . . the paragon of knightly perfection'; *Mimesis*, 101.

[174] Bezzola, 'A propos de la valeur littéraire', 188-9; id., 'De Roland à Raoul de Cambrai', 205; Calin, *The Old French Epic of Revolt*, *passim*; Bloch, *Medieval French Literature and Law*, 100-1; Jackson, *The Hero and the King*, 54-78.

[175] Bloch, *Medieval French Literature and Law*, 9-10; Calin, *The Old French Epic of Revolt*, 128 ff.

[176] See the sources cited in n. 166.

[177] On the mixture of myth and history see Frappier, 'Réflexions'. For general interpretive comments, see Bloch, *Medieval French Literature and Law*, 101; Calin, *The Old French Epic of Revolt*, 125-7; Jackson, *The Hero and the King*, 15-16, 69-72, 89, 118, 135-6.

the defence offered by Ganelon in the famous trial scene in the *Song of Roland* highlights the cherished right of noblemen to conduct private feuds, whatever the king's opinion. 'Medieval history is in many ways an account of the struggle of central authority to suppress private war', he suggests, 'and the *Chanson de Roland* undoubtedly had a message-for the nobles of the twelfth century . . .'[178] Many lords may have been willing to consider this message. Their feelings about private rights and the role of royal authority seem to have been mixed and involved strong conflicts; resentment against royal failure appears in some epics as well as the more expected anger at royal intrusion. Some scholars note that the rebellious barons usually lose in the end, and they contend that the poems show not a nostalgic longing for the good old days of near anarchy, decorated with misty memories of archaic Carolingian legend, but rather a keen frustration at a kingship lacking the power to maintain elementary order. In this view, the incapacity of kingship, not its interference, is at the root of the implied criticism; the reaction is directed not so much against monarchy as against anarchy. The French epics show clearly the fears Jackson finds central to epic form: 'At the center of the conflict is the fear which haunted all warrior societies, that of the chaos which would inevitably ensure if the ruler were to be too weak to carry out his office adequately or if an outsider were to take over who was determined to force alien ideas on their societies.'[179] Thus, this view assumes that the issue of some degree of public order, some adequate political control, provided a measure of common ground on which both king and feudal lords could meet.

The opinions of twelfth- and thirteenth-century French lords, expressed in epic literature, may have been sufficiently complex and sufficiently contradictory for all shades of scholarly interpretation to share some claim to truth. It would scarcely be surprising if French nobles harboured ambivalent feelings about a kingship which looked as if it might reverse the course it had followed for several centuries and become effective. Likewise the harsh, almost Hobbesian atmosphere of violence and vendetta which had run unchecked for several hundred years since the collapse of Carolingian authority might produce alongside the delight in knightly prowess so evident in the epic a certain war-weariness; if

[178] Ibid. 69. [179] Ibid. 15-16.

monarchy could guarantee a slight softening of this state of chaos and savagery, perhaps not every lord and vassal in France would consider it a personal affront.[180] In fact, the epics may tell us that like people in other ages, twelfth-century Frenchmen were guilty of holding contradictory political desires. As R. Howard Bloch writes:

> . . . the trouvères' difficulty was compounded by the fact that they and their public, without the slightest conscious recognition of ambiguity, desired both a strong and a weak king at the same time. Looking back on the late Carolingians and early Capetians, they wanted someone powerful enough to keep peace in the realm and lead triumphant military expeditions against the Saracens; reacting against the more powerful Capetians of their own time (and legends of Carolingian autocracy), they sought a distant ruler who would not interfere with their local prerogatives.[181]

Moreover, their concern for order may have finally submerged a large part of their fear about seigneurial autonomy. 'In reality', as R. Howard Bloch suggests, 'the paradox of the feudal epic implies the preeminence of neither monarchy nor aristocracy *per se*. It points, rather, to the more general failure of war, like the duel, to provide adequate responses to the problems of the post-feudal age.' Bloch argues that in the late epic the central issue 'is not who wins, but the price of victory'.[182]

In his illuminating study, *Medieval French Literature and Law*, Bloch, in fact, uses this insight more generally to elucidate the close relationship between the judicial transformation carried out under the aegis of the late Capetian monarchy—the attempt at suppression of private war and judicial duel and the substitution of procedure by inquest—and the literary transformation which produced 'the major "aristocratic" forms—epic, courtly novel,

[180] F. Carl Riedel comments on the conflict in men's attitudes between vengeance and sheer force on the one hand and organized justice on the other; this tension is frequently used by the writers of the thirteenth-century romances he studied in *Crime and Punishment in the Old French Romances*. See his comments, p. 98. See also Jackson, *The Hero and the King*, 15-16.

[181] Calin, *The Old French Epic of Revolt*, 139. Cf. pp. 130-1, where he suggests a modern parallel in the desire both for strong government and considerable individual liberty. Cf. Bezzola, *Les Origines*, 321-2.

[182] Bloch, *Medieval French Literature and Law*, 103. Cf. Calin, *The Old French Epic of Revolt*, 136 ff.

and lyric'.[183] If the epic reveals the inadequacy of unrestricted feudal warfare as tempered only slightly by its formalization and reduction in the judicial duel, courtly romance and lyric each respond to this dilemma in a manner which parallels, rather than merely reflects, the monarchical legal changes set in motion by St Louis.[184] The lyric, like the judicial inquest, involves a disputation as a socially acceptable verbal combat substituted for disruptive physical violence. The romance, like the judicial deposition, distils into a written record an account of violence which has taken place in the literary, symbolic forest or in the 'real' world beyond the civil space of peace represented by Arthurian court or Capetian court of law.

Though a bald summary risks distortion of a rich and complex argument, it at least suggests again the likelihood that basic social attitudes towards legitimate authority, violence and restraint stand behind the changes in each realm.

If major forms of French literature in the twelfth and thirteenth centuries so closely parallel the evolution of French kingship and its judicial structures, the absence of a simultaneous or even earlier development in England will seem all the more surprising. The epic in England cannot be compared to that in contemporary France, for no epics were written at the same period in Anglo-Norman, the language of most literature in England between the Conquest and the fourteenth-century triumph of Middle English as vernacular.[185] We have been taught to regard Medieval England (at least in most regards, and before the fourteenth century) as an intellectual colony of a powerful French civilization;[186] we know, moreover, that people living in England must have read French epics, as they sometimes state

183 Bloch, *Medieval French Literature and Law*, 10. Cf. Riedel, *Crime and Punishment in the Old French Romances*, *passim*.

184 Bloch insists (p. 12) that we understand 'the literary artifact as an organic part, and not just the reflection, of a broad social mutation'.

185 Legge, *Anglo-Norman Literature and its Background*, 3, finds 'no trace of an Anglo-Norman *chanson de geste*. . . . Cf. p. 5. Brian Merilees makes the same point in his art.: 'Anglo-Norman Literature'. I am indebted to Prof. Merilees for providing an advance copy of this art. Both Miss Legge and Prof. Merilees note that some literary works in Anglo-Norman have literary characteristics similar to the epic. But none shows the concern over kingship and feudal independence so important in the Old French epic.

186 Southern, *Medieval Humanism and Other Studies*, 140. Thompson challenges this view in 'England and the Twelfth-century Renaissance'.

explicitly.[187] That they copied French epics is evidenced by the 'Oxford Roland', the earliest surviving manuscript of the *Chanson de Roland*. But although they patronized a lively and even pioneering literature in Anglo-Norman,[188] and could draw on an insular epic tradition,[189] the lords and ladies of England apparently demanded no epics from poets in their own homeland. 'It is strange' writes M. Dominica Legge, 'that no *chanson de geste* seems to have been composed in England, although the genre was popular.' No epics were produced, in other words, by those who lived under the governance of 'the most highly developed secular administrative machine in Europe'.[190] This absence of any Anglicized epic is surely striking. Patrons and writers who utilized other French literary forms and patrons who readily borrowed and creatively adapted continental architectural forms showed virtually no interest in producing native epics (whether in Anglo-Norman or Middle English), even at a time when interest in the English past, English traditions, English saints, was becoming rather fashionable among the descendants of the transplanted Norman aristocracy.[191]

The obvious reason may in this case be the best. If the French *chanson de geste* was deeply rooted in the political soil of France, in the transition out of centuries of political and juridical

[187] See Chardry's 'Set Dormanx', 11. 50-61, and 'Josaphaz', 11. 2931-8, Koch (ed.), *Chardry's Josaphaz, Set Dormanz, und Petit Plet*. (Heilbronn, 1879). I owe these references to Prof. Merilees. R. W. Southern notes that the daughter of Henry II, who became the bride of the Emperor Henry the Lion in 1168, took with her a German tr. of the *Chanson de Roland* as a gift for her husband, *Medieval Humanism and Other Studies*, 139. Cf. the comment of Miss Legge, *Anglo-Norman Literature and its Background*, 7.

[188] The vitality of this literature is stressed ibid., and Merilees, 'Anglo-Norman Literature', 259-72.

[189] As Jessie Crossland comments, *The Old French Epic*, 230-1: 'In England one might . . . have expected a better fate, considering the close ties which existed between the two countries after the Norman Conquest. English poetry had, moreover, an epic tradition behind it which might have made it more ready to embrace its foreign relation. Unfortunately, however, there is a scarcity of English productions for a long period before and after the year 1100, just about the time when epic poetry was at its height in France.'

[190] Legge, 'The Rise and Fall of Anglo-Norman Literature', 4-5. The phrase describing the English government is borrowed from Southern, *Medieval Humanism and Other Studies*, 152.

[191] Ibid. 135-58: 'England's First Entry into Europe'; Legge, *Anglo-Norman Literature and its Background*, 28-36.

disintegration following the Carolingian collapse, and in centuries of virtually unrestricted private warfare, then it could scarcely be expected to take root and flower in the very different political soil of England. English lords would not have felt the deep need of their continental cousins to lament the waning of a golden age of feudal independence nor to worry over the attempts of monarchy to reduce the self-evident right of nobles to settle all disputes by warfare on any scale they could manage. To overstate the case only slightly, these conditions did not obtain in England which had, in effect, skipped the long period of disintegration experienced by ninth- and tenth-century France, and which had passed from a kingdom recognizable by Charlemagne to one harshly ordered by William the Conqueror.

In the twelfth century, once the troubles of Stephen's reign were surmounted, the lords of the Anglo-Norman realm were even able to view English kingship with pride, as the focal point of the powerful political society they shared. They seem vastly to have enjoyed Geoffrey of Monmouth's *History of the Kings of Britain*, built around a panegyric of King Arthur whose empire had bridged the Channel and the North Sea, whose power had even toppled a haughty emperor of Rome. Perhaps their French cousins beyond the Narrow Seas could match them in arrogant self-assurance, but the difference in the role assigned to kingship in the two visions of superiority is surely striking. The popularity of Geoffrey's book telling the glorious past of English kingship, culminating in the towering figure of Arthur, speaks to the long-established tradition of a royal role in England and a view of the governance of kings much less troubled by the polarities of *fainéantise* or tyranny which so exercised the French.

The absence of an 'English epic' and the evidence of a veritable celebration in literature of potent kingship need not be taken to mean that the politically powerful in the realm were thoroughly or continually pleased with the governance provided by the crown. Reading a few clauses of the Great Charter dispells any such illusion quickly. But the difference seems to be that the English lords and London bourgeoisie were engaged in the business of dealing with royal government as an accepted if somewhat troublesome given in their lives. In short, the English, as we have seen, were already engaged in the political give and take which might be characterized as a secular reform movement; it was an important process, but one unlikely to generate a heroic literature.[192] The French nobles were, by contrast, making the difficult adjustment to the very idea of royal government, with its mixed offerings of benefits and intrusions. After two centuries of further development and expansion, the king's government in England did in fact become a subject of a large and even a great literature of protest; but in the twelfth and early thirteenth centuries that time had not yet come. In the age of the epic, royal governance in England was simply not a topic for epic treatment; only over the next several generations—and especially after the great increase in the level of warfare—did the increasing burden of the king's government and the development of a more broadly based vernacular literature combine to produce a telling critique.

Our first comparison, then, shows a striking contrast between the image of the state and its actions found in the literature enjoyed on either side of the Channel in the twelfth and early thirteenth centuries. But the contrast takes on a very different character by the late thirteenth and fourteenth centuries. If in the twelfth century a French genre, the *chanson de geste*, demands our close attention, two centuries later we must concentrate on an English genre, what is commonly termed the literature of satire and complaint.[193] This English 'literature of protest' was coming for a long time; the first thin rivulets of what would become the broad fourteenth-century stream can, in fact, be detected as far back as the twelfth century. A developing money economy and an increasingly complex and legalistic cast to major institutions, especially those of the church, generated a remarkable body of Latin satire in all of western Europe.[194] But the relative power and sophistication of the royal government in England, comparable

[192] Geoffrey of Monmouth's story certainly has heroic overtones, but he wrote at the end of what R. W. Southern has suggested was the 'heroic age of government'. From the time of Henry II 'instinct cooled into calculation' and the problem of regulating the growing capacity of the English royal administration loomed larger in contemporary minds. See *Medieval Humanism and Other Studies*, 193-233.

[193] G. R. Owst used this designation with regard to preaching in the title to ch. 5 of his *Literature and Pulpit in Medieval England*.

[194] An informative treatment is given by John A. Yunck, *The Lineage of Lady Meed*. Lester K. Little studied the effect of the economic changes in perceptions of the most socially significant virtues and vices, drawing especially on the evidence of medieval art, in 'Pride Goes Before Avarice'. The systematic expression of the new economic ideas is discussed in John F. McGovern, 'The Rise of New Economic Attitudes'.

even to that of the much criticized Roman *curia*, early attracted a satirical attention unique to secular government. If John of Salisbury's *Policraticus* represents 'the revival of the satirical theme in secular clothing', it is also worth emphasizing that this work is especially a commentary on the English court,[195] however much John's later career is a model of twelfth-century internationalism. Walter Map's more caustic *De Nugis Curialium* is even more interesting for our theme. Map, who knew the government of Henry II at first hand as a clerk in the royal household and as an itinerant justice, shows a concern for the action of a working local administration long in place. His book opens with an elaborate comparison of the English court to Hell: 'I say not, however, that it is Hell (which doth not follow), but it is as nearly like it as a horse's shoe is like a mare's.' Yet this work is not simply anti-courtier satire; within the opening discussion, Map manages to denounce the local royal foresters as monsters who 'eat the flesh of men and drink their blood', and to characterize sheriffs, under-sheriffs, and beadles as night-birds who greedily feed on dead bodies, tear the fleece from lambs, but, swayed by bribes, leave the foxes unharmed.[196] Complaint about the action of the English state is already being added to the older tradition of criticism of the moral failings of courtiers as a particular class of powerful men.

By the late thirteenth and fourteenth centuries, such Latin complaints and satires were still being written,[197] but even more significant is the emergence of vernacular complaint, composed first in Anglo-Norman and soon in Middle English. These texts broadened and secularized the earlier satirical tradition; they were obviously intended to meet the taste of a wider audience than the Latin poems and they often fired their barbs at government agents and actions. Thus, although many of the works are 'heartbreakingly pedestrian',[198] some, 'generally the most dreary',[199] had

195 Yunck, *The Lineage of Lady Meed*, 14.

196 Thomas Wright edited the Latin text for the Camden Society, *Gualteri Mapes: De Nugis Curialium*. A tr. was made by Frederick Tupper and Marbury Bladen Ogle, *Master Walter Mape's Book*. The quot. is from p. 9. Comments on local officers appear on pp. 6-7.

197 See the 'Song of the Venality of the Judges', in Wright (ed.), *The Political Songs of England*, 224-31. Cf. Yunck, *The Lineage of Lady Meed*, 165.

198 The evaluation of Isabel S. T. Aspin, *Anglo-Norman Political Songs*, p. xiii.

199 The phrase of Rossell Hope Robbins, *Poems Dealing with Contemporary Conditions*, 1387.

extensive circulation and 'reflect the reactions of the ordinary man to the public events of the time'.[200] As Thomas Wright noted more than a century ago, when English vernacular satire begins, it concerns 'the whole English public'.[201] If the fourteenth century complaint literature is popular in language, it is likewise popular in increasingly taking as its level of social focus 'the official venality which impinges directly on the average man, the poor but loyal subject.'[202] Equally interesting is the tone of these poems, the depth of bitter feeling and moral outrage which is apparent and sometimes even eloquent, despite the clumsiness of word and phrase.[203] The king's government was not an abstraction to the writers who penned these poems nor to the audience which heard or read them.

The surviving corpus of critical writing points to the much larger body of complaint literature which must have circulated. Of course much of the political verse must always have been essentially oral and thus lost to the historian; but a large part even of the written criticism has likely disappeared, especially the most topical.[204] A number of surviving pieces 'present criticism which is general enough to refer to more than one historical occasion.'[205] Though such general applicability creates problems of dating for scholars, it also suggests that the continuing policies of the English government, rather than the foibles or excesses of particular rulers or favourites, are the object of the complaint.

The *Song of the Husbandman*, written in a southern dialect around 1300, illustrates two common themes of the genre—oppressive taxation and extortionate officials.

I heard men on the earth make much lamentation, how they are injured in their tillage; good years and corn are both gone, they keep here no saying and sing no song. 'Now we must work, there is no other custom, I can no longer live with my gleaning; yet there is a bitterer asking for the boon, for ever the fourth penny must go to the king.'

200 Aspin, *Anglo-Norman Political Songs*, p. xiii.

201 Wright is quot. by Owst, *Literature and Pulpit in Medieval England*, 215. Cf. Yunck, *The Lineage of Lady Meed*, 301-3, for comments on the popular level of criticism.

202 Ibid. 302.

203 Owst, *Literature and Pulpit in Medieval England*, 215-16; Yunck, *The Lineage of Lady Meed*, 5.

204 Wright (ed.), *The Political Songs of England*, p. x; Scattergood, *Politics and Poetry*, 13-35; Wilson, *The Lost Literature of Medieval England*, ch. 10.

205 Kendrick, 'Criticism of the Ruler', 432.

Thus we complain for the king and care full coldly, and think to recover and ever are downcast; he who hath any goods, expects not to keep them, but ever the dearest we lose at last. . . .

Thus will walketh in the land and law is destroyed . . .

Still there come beadles with very great boast, 'Prepare me silver for the green wax [*used in seals on exchequer summons*]. Thou are entered in my writing, that thou knowest well of.' More than ten times I paid my tax. Then must I have hens roasted, fair on the fish day lamprey and salmon; forth to the market gains not cost, though I sell my bill and borstax.

I must lay my pledge well if I will, or sell my corn while it is but green grass. Yet I shall be a foul churl though they have the whole, what I have saved all the year I must spend then. . . .

There the green wax grieveth us in our life, so that they hunt us as a hound doth the hare. . . .

To seek silver for the king I sold my seed, wherefore my land lies fallow and learneth to sleep. Since they fetched my fair cattle in my fold, when I think of my weal I very nearly weep; thus breed many bold beggars.[206]

206 Ich herde men upo mold make muche mon,
 Hou he beth i-tened of here tilyynge,
Gode zeres and corn bothe beth a-gon,
 Ne kepeth here no sawe ne no song syng.
'Now we mote worche, nis ther non other won,
 Mai ich no lengore lyve with my lesinge;
zet ther is a bitterore bid to the bon,
 For ever the furthe peni mot to the kynge.'

Thus we carpeth for the kyng, and carieth ful colde,
 And weneth for te kevere, and ever buth a-cast;
Whose hath eny god, hopeth he nout to holde,
 Bote ever the levest we leoseth a-last.

. . .

Thus wil walketh in londe, and lawe is for-lore,

. . .

Zet cometh budeles with ful muche bost,—
 'Greythe me selver to the grene wax:
Thou art writen y my writ that thou wel wost.'
 Mo then ten sithen told y my tax.
Thenne mot ych habbe hennen a-rost,
 Feyr on fyhshe day launprey ant lax;
Forth to the chepyn geyneth ne chost,
 Thah y sulle mi bil ant my borstax.

Ich mot legge my wed wel zef y wolle,
 Other sulle mi corn on gras that is grene.
Zet I shal be foul cherl, thah he han the fulle,

These criticisms are driven home time and again in the Anglo-Norman poem *Against the King's Taxes*, dated by Wright to *c.*1297 and by Isabel Aspin to 1337-40:

Now the fifteenth runs in England year after year, thus doing harm to all; by it those who were wont to sit upon the bench have come down in the world; and common folk must sell their cows, their utensils, and even clothing. It is ill-pleasing thus to pay the fifteenth to the uttermost farthing.

Still more hard on simple folk is the wool collection; commonly it makes them sell their possessions. It cannot be that such a measure, crushing the poor under a grievous load, is pleasing to God. The law that makes my wool the king's is no just law.

Since the king wants to take such a huge amount. he will be able to find enough among the rich. And indeed in my opinion, he would have done both more and better to have taken something from the mighty, and to have spared the lowly. He who takes money from the needy without good cause commits sin.[207]

That ich alle zer spare thenne y mot spenc.

. . .

Ther the grene wax us greveth under gore,
That me us honteth ase hound doth the hare.

. . .

To seche selver to the kyng y mi seed solde,
Forthi mi lond leye lith anti leorneth to slepe.
Seththe he mi feire feh fatte y my folde,
When y thenk o mi weole wel neh y wepe;
Thus bredeth monie beggares bolde,

Wright (ed.), *The Political Songs of England*, 149-53.

207 Ore court en Engletere de anno in annum
Le quinzyme dener, pur fere sic commune dampnum;
E fet avaler que soleyent sedere super scannum,
E vendre fet commune gent vaccas, vas et pannum.
Non placet ad summum quindenum sic dare nummum.

. . .

Unquore plus greve a simple gent collectio lanarum,
Que vendre fet communement divicias earum.
Ne puet estre que tiel consail constat Deo carum
Issi destrure le poverail pondus per amarum.
Non est lex sana quod regi sit mea lana.

. . .

Depus que le roy vodera tam multum cepisse,
Entre les riches si purra satis invenisse.
E plus a ce que m'est avys et melius fecisse
Des grantz partie aver pris et parvis pepercisse.
Qui capit argentum sine causa peccat egentum.

Several poems attest that the king's purveyors practised a form of oppression considered especially onerous. The late fourteenth-century Middle English *King Edward and the Shepherd* pictures a chance meeting between sovereign (who has gone hawking in disguise) and a shepherd in which the latter tells the king:

I am so robbed by the King that I must flee from my dwelling and therefore woe is me. I had cattle; now I have none; they take my beasts and slay them and pay only a stick from a tree [*i.e. a wooden tally*] . . . They took my hens and my geese and my sheep with all the fleece and led them away. They lay by my daughter all night.

The shepherd and his wife have been put out of their own house by purveyors and thrust rudely into the carthouse:

I have three fine chambers but may not stay in any of them while they are there. They drove me into my carthouse; they put my wife out the door.[208]

The complaints of the shepherd are amplified, with appropriate changes of tone and language, in the Latin *Speculum Regis* written about 1331.[209] The author is particularly outraged by

Aspin, *Anglo-Norman Political Songs*, 112.
See also Wright (ed.), *The Political Songs of England*, 182.

208 I am so pylled with the Kyng
That i most fle fro my wonyng
And therfore woo is me.
I had catell; now haue I non;
Thay take my bestis and don thaim slone
And payen but a stik of tre
. . .
Thei toke my hennes and my geese
And my schepe with all the fleese
And ladde them forthe away.
Be my doztur thei lay alnyzt.

I have fayre chamburs thre
But non of theim may be with me
While that thei be thore.
Into my carthaws thei me dryfe;
Out at the dur their put my wyfe.

Pr. French and Hale (eds.), *Middle English Metrical Romances*, ii. 951, 956.

209 Moisant (ed.), *De Speculo Regis Edwardi Tertii*. The quots. are drawn from Robinson, 'Royal Purveyance'. Cf. Tait, 'The Date and Authorship of the

the number of great horses kept by the king's household and fed on grain and hay while poor men starve; four or five of the poor could survive on the daily cost of half a bushel of grain for the horse and the penny wage for the groom who tends him. But the author is even more effective in picturing a hen taken for a pittance from a poor woman and cooked for the king's dinner. How can he eat while she goes hungry? How can he dress in cloth of gold while she goes in rags? How can he feed a crowd of soldiers and followers while her children cry for bread? What finally produces the greatest show of outrage is the spectacle of the very poor, in a panic at the purveyor's approach, desperately consuming all of their provisions, willing to gorge as much as possible even of their store against starvation, before the purveyors take even that. The author pours out a 'cascade of lamentations' ending:

> Oh Fear! Oh Scandal to you, O King, and to the whole English people, that such things can happen at your coming! Fie! Fie! Alas! Alas! That such things are permitted to be done.

The *Song of the Times of Edward II* written in Middle English around 1308, also rails against the oppressors of the poor, but illustrates another common theme as well, the wrongs and extortions practised in the king's courts. Only if Holy Church and the king's law exert their might will covetousness and injustice be banished from the land. The author especially blames the light horsemen or hobblers ('hoblurs')[210] so important in the army of the time for robbing the husbandman of the tillage of the soil; they ought to be denied burial in sacred ground and their bodies thrown out like dogs. Higher officials get no higher marks:

> Those king's ministers are corrupted; they who should take heed for right and law to amend all the land take bribes from thieves. If the man who acts lawfully is brought to death and his property taken away, they take no account of his death, but have a share of the prey. If they have the silver and the bribe and the property received, they take no heed of felony; every trespass is allowed to pass.[211]

"Speculum Regis Edwardi" '; Boyle, 'The *Oculus Sacerdotis*'; id., 'William of Pagula'.

[210] See the discussion of A. E. Prince, *The English Government at Work*, i. 338-40, and the sources cited there.

[211] Thos Kingis ministris beth i-schend
To rizt and law that ssold tak hede,

To illustrate his point the author introduces a traditional animal fable. The lion, 'king of all beeste', summoned Ass, Wolf, and Fox to answer charges. Though guilty, the Wolf and Fox gave presents to the Lion and secured their pardon; but the simple Ass, completely innocent, trusted the Lion's royal justice and was condemned.

A Song on the Venality of the Judges, written in Latin at about the same time opens with the mocking lines 'Blessed are they who hunger and thirst, and do justice, and hate and avoid the wickedness of injustice; whom neither abundance of gold nor the jewels of the rich draw from their inflexibility, or from the cry of the poor. . . .' The personnel and agents of the court are scrutinized group by group. The clerks 'are like people half-famished, gaping for gifts'. Of the sheriffs he asks 'who can relate with sufficient fulness how hard they are to the poor'.[212]

A much more specific treatment of the charge of royal misuse of legal machinery appeared in the wake of Edward I's famous trailbaston commissions of 1305. An Anglo-Norman 'rhyme . . . made in the wood . . . and thrown on the highway that people

And al the lond for t'amend
  Of thos thevis hi taketh mede.
Be the lafful man to deth i-brozt,
  And his catel awei y-nom;
Of his deth ne tellith hi nozt.
  Bot of har prei hi hab som
Hab hi the silver, and the mede,
  And the catel under-fo,
Of feloni hi ne taketh hede,
  Al thilk trespas is a-go.

Wright (ed.), *The Political Songs of England*, 224-30

212 Beati qui esuriunt
Et sitiunt, et faciunt
  justitiam,
Et odiunt et fugiunt
  injuriae nequitiam;
Quos nec auri copia
Nec divitum encennia
  trahunt a rigore,
  nec pauperum clamore;

Wright (ed.), *The Political Songs of England*, 224-30.

should find it' curses those who established judicial inquests so comprehensive in their competence, so harsh in judgment, so readily corrupted.

> Sir, if I want to punish my boy with a cuff or two, to correct him, he will take out a plaint against me and have me attached, and made to pay a big ransom before I get out of prison.
>
> They take forty shillings for my ransom, and the sheriff comes for his reward for not putting me into a deep dungeon. Now judge, sirs, is this right? . . .
>
> But the ill-favoured people on whom may God never have pity, out of their deceitful mouths they have indicted me for wicked thefts and other misdeeds, so that I do not dare to be received by my friends. . . .
>
> Formerly I knew little that was worth while, now I am less wise; this is what the bad laws do to me by so great abuse, that I dare not come into peace among my kinsfolk. The rich are put to ransom, the poor dwindle away.[213]

By the late fourteenth century these telling complaints have even moved beyond the level of doggerel and broadside to become a prominent theme in literature of great mastery and beauty. Janet Coleman argues that the literary greats writing at the end of the century, Chaucer, Gower, and Langland, had inherited from

[213] Sire, si je voderoi mon garsoun chastier
De une buffe ou de deus, pur ly amender,
Sur moi betera bille, e me frad atachier,
E avant qe isse de prisone raunsoun grant doner.

Quaraunte souz pernent pur ma raunsoun,
E le viscounte vint a son guerdoun,
Qu'il ne me mette en parfounde prisoun.
Ore agardez seigneurs, est ce resoun?

. . .

Mes le male deseynes, dount Dieu n'eit ja pieté,
Parmi lur fauce bouches me ount enditee
De male robberies e autre mavestee,
Que je n'os entre mes amis estre receptee.

. . .

Avant savoy poy de bien, ore su je meins sage;
Ce me fount les male leis par mout grant outrage,
Qe n'os a la pes venyr entre mon lignage.
Les riches sunt a raunsoun, povres a escolage.

Isabel S. T. Aspin, *Anglo-Norman Political Songs*, 67-78.

the humble and usually anonymous authors of earlier complaint literature a keen sense of satire, 'a scornful comparison of what *is* the case with what ought to be.' She proposed, in fact, that 'relatively few works were meant merely to entertain but were intended rather to instruct, exhort and, ultimately, to inspire readers to criticize and eventually to reform social practice, by which was meant the behaviour of church officials and the politically and economically powerful.' Although the French literary tradition may have been important in forming the art of Chaucer and Gower, 'it is their topical political and social commentary—what strikes us as their very English view of their fictional society—that rests more on the sixty-odd-year complaint verse tradition created out of the English experience, of war and its consequences on home policy.'[214]

The power and presence of the king's government and the hopes and fears focused on it are especially evident in the Lady Meed episode which fills three passus of Langland's *Piers Plowman* (II, III, IV).[215] When Theology interrupts the marriage of Fraud to Lady Meed (who is the daughter of Falsehood and represents the morally ambiguous quality of reward or fee), the case is— significantly—taken before the royal court at Westminster. As the procession sets off, we are treated to an unforgettable spectacle of the great lady herself mounted on a Sheriff, newly shod, while Fraud rides a gently-trotting Juryman. Warned of the king's intent to arrest them, most of her party flee and Meed alone is brought to the royal court. There she quickly provides gifts to win the favour of the lawyers and clerks and for a time is able to withstand the attacks of Conscience and Reason. In a test case which arises, Peace brings a petition (a 'bille') against Wrong, clearly a royal purveyor, whose sins in this fictional petition are only amplifications of the charges encountered in many an historical petition against purveyors. In the king's name Wrong has violently seized poultry and livestock without payment, broken down barn doors, and carried off corn, paying only a wooden tally. The additional charges provided by Langland are sexual: Peace says the purveyor has run off with his wife and

214 Coleman, *Medieval Readers and Writers*, 16, 93, 126, 134-5.

215 A new edition of the B-Text has been provided by A. V. C. Schmidt, *The Vision of Piers Plowman*. Yunck, *The Lineage of Lady Meed*, 5 ff, 288 ff, gives a useful discussion.

raped his daughters. Lady Meed offers to make all right with a gift of pure gold to Peace, and winks knowingly at the lawyers. But the court decides against her, and against Wrong; Conscience tells the king that he must rule with the support of the common folk; and the king proclaims that he will henceforth rule with Reason at his side. The fate of Lady Meed (and her die-hard supporters, a juror, an ecclesiastical summoner, and a sheriff's clerk) is left uncertain.

Langland's vivid portrayal of the struggle against venality and injustice, and of the central role of the crown, takes on even deeper meaning when his work is set in the context of popular preaching. G. R. Owst has convincingly argued that in *Piers Plowman* Langland, among much else, sums up a fourteenth-century pulpit tradition.[216] In England, even more than in contemporary France, corrupt royal courts and grasping officials seem to have furnished material for many a sermon.[217] Even if their *exempla* were repetitive and uninspired, they show an awareness of the force of the royal administration and the royal courts and a critical attitude towards their many failings.

Though they are not part of the frankly didactic literature of satire and complaint, other fourteenth-century vernacular poems can add to the evidence in the texts which make up this genre. Most prominent are the outlaw ballads, with emphasis especially on the Robin Hood tales. The *Geste of Robyn Hode* may have been written as early as the 1330s and it was certainly already popular in the second half of the fourteenth century.[218] The meaning of the Robin Hood tales for social history has sparked lively debate,[219] but for present purposes the important fact is the focus on the local royal administration; the *Geste* is in fact a running commentary on the corrupt power of the sheriff in local

[216] Owst, *Literature and Pulpit in Medieval England*, 216 ff, 223-4.

[217] Compare the comments of Owst, ibid. ch. 5: 'The Preaching of Satire and Complaint', with Lecoy de la Marche, *La Chaire francaise au moyen âge*, pt. III: 'La Société d'après les sermons'. Cf. Yunck, *The Lineage of Lady Meed*, 253.

[218] Maddicott, 'The Birth and Setting of the Ballads of Robin Hood'.

[219] See Keen, *The Outlaws of Medieval Legend* and the following *Past and Present* arts.: Hilton, 'The Origins of Robin Hood'; Holt, 'The Origins and Audience of the Ballads of Robin Hood'; Keen, 'Robin Hood—Peasant or Gentleman?'; Aston, 'Robin Hood'. The most recent contributions are: Dobson and Taylor, *Rhymes of Robyn Hood*; Maddicott, 'The Birth and Setting of the Ballads of Robin Hood'; Holt, *Robin Hood*.

society, and it provides a visit by a corrupt chief justice from Westminster as well. In this sense John Maddicott suggests that the *Geste* can be read 'as another work from the same diffuse genre' as the *Song Against the King's Taxes* or the *Song of the Husbandman*. Though 'more popular, less learned and less mannered in tone than these other pieces', it shared with them 'the same antipathy toward the agents of royal government and the same sympathy with its victims'.[220]

Though it has been less often studied, the same point can be made regarding the mid-fourteenth-century *Tale of Gamelyn*.[221] The hero, whose estate has been kept from him by an evil brother (who becomes sheriff) is forced into outlawry, and only obtains justice by overawing the corrupted court. He hangs the procured judge and the bribed jury, supplying the place of the former himself, the latter by his followers. No doubt the tale was meant to amuse and entertain an audience (admittedly with a very dark variety of humour), but perhaps we can hear in the lines of the poem echoes of the 'fierce, mocking laughter, that bursts out suddenly without warning here and there, filled often with the spirit of mad exasperation and a reckless despair' which Owst detected in the literature of satire and complaint.[222] If not a part of this *genre*, the tales of Robin Hood and Gamelyn are close adjuncts, testifying like these other texts to the force of the king's government in the countryside and the likelihood that it could be both venal and oppressive.

It is a commonplace of scholarship on the outlaw tales that the authors and audience assume a beneficent king; only let him see the wrongs committed and justice will be done—or more frequently, the justice already done by an outlaw hero will receive royal recognition and approval. If we bear in mind this tendency to idealize and exonerate the monarch and if we remember as well the glowing portrayal of Arthur presented by Geoffrey of Monmouth in the twelfth century, we can only find fascinating ambiguities in the late fourteenth century telling of the Arthurian story known as the *Alliterative Morte Arthure*.[223] What

[220] Maddicott, 'The Birth and Setting of the Ballads of Robin Hood', 298-9.

[221] Skeat (ed.), *The Tale of Gamelyn*. A text with useful commentary is also provided in Sands, *Middle English Verse Romances*. Cf. Kaeuper, 'An Historian's Reading of *The Tale of Gamelyn*'.

[222] Owst, *Literature and Pulpit in Medieval England*, 216.

[223] Brock (ed.), *Alliterative Morte Arthure*.

heightens interest is the debated identification of the mythical Arthur of the poem with the historical King Edward III. Though too close an identification may be unwise,[224] Larry Benson has suggested that 'Arthur is too clearly a fourteenth-century king to fit into the fictional past of romance or the heroic past of epic. . . .'[225] The poem gives a graphic account of Arthur's wars of continental conquest. Before the great combat with the Roman emperor Lucius (who is playing the tyrant with Arthur's French subjects), the English king vanquishes a local tyrant, the giant of *Mont St Michel*, in single combat. A prophetic dream had already informed Arthur that this brute 'tourmentez thy pople'. But once Arthur has defeated Lucius, the fourteenth-century author departs from his twelfth-century source and adds an Arthurian conquest of Lorraine, Lombardy, and Tuscany. As this campaign progresses the ambiguity in the portrayal of Arthur deepens; the poet now states that it is Arthur who 'turmentez the pople', using the very terms which earlier had described the tyranny of the giant and the emperor.[226] Arthur, however, moves from triumph to triumph until, offered the imperial crown, he exults in the idea of world conquest: 'We salle be ouerlynge of alle that one the erthe lengex' (3211). But not long after this moment of exultation he learns of the treachery of Mordred in England. Arthur must return to the island for the last battles and the collapse of his kingship, based on the support and fellowship of his knights of the Round Table.

On all questions of literary form and intent (the poem as epic, as romance, as tragedy), we must leave the lists to the literary contenders, as was likewise prudent with literary issues involved in the French epics considered earlier. But the historian seeking evidence on attitudes toward the action of the state can only be fascinated by the parallel between scholarly debate over the view of kingship and war in the French epics and debate over the same topics in the *Alliterative Morte Arthure*. In both cases there is enough ambiguity in the texts to generate differing opinions on essential questions of meaning. But the striking fact is that much

[224] For the strongest argument linking Arthur and Edward and interpreting the conquests as unjust see Matthews, *The Tragedy of Arthur*. For a qualifying view see Keiser, 'Edward III and the *Alliterative Morte Arthure*'.

[225] Benson, 'The *Alliterative Morte Arthure* and Medieval Tragedy'.

[226] Lumiansky, 'The *Alliterative Morte Arthure*'.

of the ambiguity concerns the same issues. In both the French works and the later English poem there is an obvious concern about the role of kingship and, in a more hesitant and tentative way, the role of war.[227]

Of course Edward III was a popular warrior king (at least through most of his long reign); criticism of the French war was anemic so long as the English expectation of victory flourished. Such criticism as was voiced seldom extended to war in principle. Medieval pacifism was exceedingly rare and was often associated with heresy.[228] But some scholars sense in the *Alliterative Morte Arthure* (as they did in the epics) tremors of uncertainty about the enterprise of war. We cannot calibrate a moral Richter scale to measure these faint tremblings; not all would agree that they exist, at least during the reign of Edward III. But it would not be surprising to find that some of the uneasiness associated with monarchy and war in twelfth- and early thirteenth-century France would trouble some observers in England by the late fourteenth century; and it is instructive to note that the warfare in the twelfth-century French case is largely private war, while in the fourteenth-century English case it is the king's war of continental conquest.

227 This broad subject is the theme of a series of studies by German scholars; see Göller (ed.), *The Alliterative Morte Arthure*. In varying degrees the contributors to this volume read the poem as an anti-war tract. Göller states that it destroys 'commonplaces of chivalry and knightly warfare through inversion, irony and black humour' and that the author was 'simultaneously a patriot and an opponent of war—at times holding positions that would nowadays be called pacifist' (pp. 16-17). Jena Ritzke-Rutherford writes that the author 'has constructed a war poem with an anti-war bias. . . .' (p. 95). In addition to the vol. ed. by Göller and the sources cited in the previous two notes, see the comment of John Gardner that the early battle scenes 'set up the favorable view of war *which the poem is to reverse* . . .' (my italics), *The Alliterative 'Morte Arthure'*, 250. He also notes (pp. 249-50) the emphasis on destruction of convents, hospitals, churches, and homes in the siege of Metz (11. 3034-41). Some debate has turned on the justness of Arthur's late continental campaigns. John Finlayson argued that initially just wars became wars of oppression; see his edn., *Morte Arthure*, 81. George Keiser countered with the point that the entire series of campaigns was accepted by Arthur's court; 'The Theme of Justice'. There is a danger of too narrowly construing the issue. Perhaps the poet was aware that even wars begun with 'consent' led to excesses.

228 Barnie, *War in Medieval English Society*, chs. 2, 5. Cf. Haines, 'Attitudes and Impediments to Pacifism in Medieval Europe'; Coleman, *Medieval Readers and Writers*, 65-6, 71-9, 84-92, 95-113.

Moreover, evidence uncovered by Juliet Vale allows us to posit the existence of more or less open debate about the war even amidst the trumpet calls and tournaments of the warrior king's court. The alliterative poem *Wynnere and Wastoure*[229] takes the form of a debate between two 'armies' before a king who is obviously Edward III. One group, the army of Waster, is representative of the military classes; Waster charges that his opponents are miserly and avaricious. In turn, Winner, representing merchants, friars, and lawyers, claims that in their pride the military classes waste what he has gained through diligent labour. The debate pictured by the poem, with each group standing uniformed beneath its respective banners before the king, may have actually transpired as part of the court games, the Christmas *ludi*, in 1352.[230] Vale suggests that the *ludi* show the close connections between some of the alliterative poets and the court, and thinks that they show as well the possibility of 'a taste for the topical and satirical' in the court circle. In the case of *Wynnere and Wastoure* and whatever elaborate court game it may reflect, the king's judgment on the two positions is equivocal; he recognizes a need for both points of view. As Vale notes

> It would be naive to imagine that Edward identified himself so completely with warfaring interests that he was unaware of, and unresponsive to, other points of view within the kingdom. Indeed, one would expect him to be particularly aware of the mercantile and clerical viewpoints; finance had after all been a particular factor in earlier campaigns and the issue which had precipitated the domestic crisis of 1340, while clerics were to be found in administrative circles close to the king.[231]

Most of the criticism of war was directed at its misconduct and high cost, not against war in the abstract. Yet in some minds within court circles could more general and even more principled doubts have been gnawing as early as 1352? Certainly by the reign of Richard II significant anti-war sentiment is clearly

229 Gallancz (ed.), *Wynnere and Wastoure*.

230 Vale, *Edward III and Chivalry*. Another example of this connection of *ludi*, politics, and poets may appear in Chaucer's *Legend of Good Women*, in which he insists he is not of the 'leaf' nor the 'flower'. Barnie suggests a link with 'an apparently innocent court game which may, nevertheless have had political overtones'; *War in Medieval English Society*, 131 and n. 51.

231 Vale, *Edward III and Chivalry*, 73-5.

documented. John Barnie asserts that 'by 1380 there is not a single moralist or chronicler who wholeheartedly supports the war.' Wyclif, Gower, and (with more circumspection) Chaucer show in their writings the effects of 'two generations of war between Christian kings . . .'.[232] As Janet Coleman points out, a similar voice is heard in such poems as *Mede and Muche Thank*. Indeed, she argues, all of the complaint literature, moving away from the romance convention of glorifying war, shows an acute awareness of the horrors and destruction inseparably linked with war.[233] Thus, the evidence of literature dovetails with other indications that many in England associated war with oppressive financial burdens and with exacerbated problems of internal justice and order; it also suggests that a few thinkers had yet more basic objections.

The tales, poems, and sermons heard by fourteenth-century Englishmen, then, are invaluable historical evidence. Scholars have long recognized that this body of literature reveals a new concern for 'the woes of a voiceless multitude of common men and women suffering from daily wrongs and injustice of all kinds.'[234] They have less often pointed to the omnipresence of the early English state in this literature. It has been argued that the 'commercial revolution of the High Middle Ages', the economic renewal operative across the eleventh, twelfth, and thirteenth centuries,[235] stands behind the general flowering of the Western satirical tradition; these changes created a new economic order in which most men were 'caught between the . . . terrifying marriage to Lady Poverty and the morally repulsive marriage to Lady Meed.'[236] It can likewise be argued that the massive increase in the capacity of the king's government in England in the same period created a particular form of satire and complaint directed against royal taxation, the injustices of royal courts, and the oppression of royal officials, and provided as well an eager

232 Barnie, *War in Medieval English Society*, 129-31; Coleman, *Medieval Readers and Writers*, 96-8. I am grateful to Dr Coleman for providing me with a TS copy of her book.

233 Ibid. 97.

234 Owst, *Literature and Pulpit in Medieval England*, 215.

235 See the comments and citations provided by Lester Little in 'Pride Goes Before Avarice', 27 ff.

236 Yunck, *The Lineage of Lady Meed*, 160.

audience for the outlaw ballads. The force of the king's government acting in daily life and at the level of county society, in other words, provided the subject matter and the impetus for a literary genre. We ignore the particular world in which these English writers and preachers lived if we imagine them simply issuing the timeless strictures of moralists upon a world forever going wrong.

If this link between government power and literary forms is true for England, the virtual absence of this type of literature in fourteenth-century France is significant. Writers in France of course contributed to the general revival of satire evident from the eleventh and twelfth century. Writing first in Latin and later in the vernacular they pilloried the traditional targets—the pope and his *curia*, bishops, the lesser clergy, and in time judges and lawyers—often for the traditional sin of venality.[237] But if satire in both England and France shares the same point of origin and initial direction, the course of satire in the two countries soon diverges. By the mid-thirteenth century, Rutebeuf's *Lections d'Ypocrisi et d'Umilitei* might show the essentials of the Meed episode in *Piers Plowman*, but significantly the court is here the papal rather than the royal *curia*. Lawyers merit very little attention from Rutebeuf, only a short passage in another of his works.[238] If the lawyers and judges are increasingly objects of satire in the generations which follow, they are, unlike their English counterparts, not exclusively agents of a system of royal justice with claims to nearly all secular jurisdiction above the level of petty seigneurial courts. Across the thirteenth and fourteenth centuries, criticism is directed against rulers, but it seems to consist mainly of *ad hominem* attacks on particular faults of kings and courtiers rather than protests against the sheer weight of the emerging royal apparatus of government. Rutebeuf's hostility to St Louis, for example, seems grounded in his intense dislike of the friars so favoured by the king. A century later the criticisms Eustache Deschamps brings against Charles VI are of the same type: the young king listens to the wrong group of counsellors, favouring a new group of advisers over older and wiser men (to whom Deschamps was himself linked) who had

237 Ibid., ch. 5.
238 Ibid. 197 ff.

served Charles V.[239] Such ruler criticism is historically significant, but in a fashion far different from that of the poems written in England during the same time to protest against the weight of royal taxation, the corruption and oppression of royal officials, the venality and injustice of all-pervasive royal courts.[240]

The officials and institutions of the Capetian state seem likewise to have been handled with relative gentleness, or rather with benign neglect, by the French pulpit. It is true that tradition held that Philip Augustus had nearly been damned, that only by the dramatic intervention of St Denis and other saints could his soul be snatched away from the devil's clutches. But in the popular mind might not the dramatic rescue have been as impressive as the king's peril? And by the late thirteenth century the image of kingship was unambiguous; St Louis was established in an honoured place in the prayers ending homilies. Even more important, since English kings themselves must have been subject to direct pulpit criticism only in times of great political crisis, is the relative absence of complaint specifically directed against the officers of the French royal administration the *baillis*, *prévôts*, *serjeants*. The injustices and oppressions of all possessors of power were denounced in sweeping and non-specific terms. In fact, the king was more likely to appear as an agency of justice, punishing errant lords, than as the source of exactions and injustices.[241]

Possible exceptions to this general contrast in the thirteenth and fourteenth centuries appear at just those times when the French crown was actively extending its capacities (as in the judicial measures of St Louis) or when the cumulative weight of royal wartime expectations produced an outburst of resentment and reaction (as in the leagues which formed at the end of the reign of Philip the Fair). Two poems, for example, reflect the trial of Enguerran de Couci in 1258, which became a test case of the royal jurisdiction claimed by Louis IX and of his preference for inquest over trial by battle. One of these poems, the anonymous

239 Kendrick, 'Criticism of the Ruler', chs. 3, 4; Arié Sarper, *Rutebeuf, poète satirique*, *passim*, and esp. ch. 3.

240 Pauline Smith notes (*The Anti-courtier Trend*, 38-40) that late Medieval invective against court life and courtiers often makes no attempt to link particular instances of corruption in court circles with the general plight of the country as a whole.

241 See above, n. 216.

Gent de France complains that the king is forcing trial by inquest on nobles who, as truly free men (*Francs*) have the freedom to settle their disputes by the traditional means of force (*voie de fait*); under misguided clerical direction, Louis IX is actually imposing on the nobles a slavery contrary to God's will. This criticism stands very much in the tradition of some poems in the cycle of the rebellious barons; in fact, *Gent de France* was probably written for the lords, or the sons of lords, who had joined the rebellions early in Louis's reign and who in 1258 backed Enguerran de Couci in the *cause célèbre*.[242]

Two sets of poems from roughly 1310-18 are more significant for our comparison with English literary protests because they seem intended for a broader audience. In the troubled reigns of the sons of Philip the Fair, Geffroi de Paris, 'the earliest Parisian journalist',[243] wrote at least eight historical poems, six in the vernacular, as well as two in Latin. He was a cleric and was probably of middling social rank, a status he praises more than once in his poems.[244] He opens one of his longest and most interesting works, *Les avisemens pour le Roy Loys*,[245] with references to the current topical, moralizing poems or *dits* (presumably now lost) which had been written ostensibly for the king's instruction. Though they seem to have taken a critical line, he professes to be tolerant:

> People should not contradict in their entirety
> 'Dits' wherein there is something to criticize;
> Rather should the good be taken therefrom
> And, what will cause reproof
> Gently should be put in truth
> And corrected in charity
>
> (11. 7-12)

[242] See the discussion by Kendrick, 'Criticism of the Ruler', 241-6; she prints the text of the poem (pp. 304-8). Cf. Faral, 'Le Procés d'Enguerran IV de Couci'.

[243] 'Geffoi de Paris est, en réalité, le premier en date des nouvellistes parisiens, experts à resumer les faits du jour en petits vers prosaiques, mais coulants, vifs et malicieux, non sans charme.' This evaluation of Petit de Julleville is quot. by Walter H. Storer and Charles A. Rochedieu, *Six Historical Poems of Geffroi de Paris*, p. vii.

[244] Ibid. 50.

[245] Pr. ibid. 1-41, with tr.

After all, he says, the authors have had three sensible aims: that the king 'pay well / In order to have his people satisfied'; that he 'reign sincerely / And without extortion'; and that he 'live generously' (11. 25-35). Geffroi would add only the scriptural admonition drawn from the story of Solomon, that wisdom is most to be desired as the true link between all other desirable royal virtues (11. 41-50). To Geffroi, as the following 1,300 lines in his poem amply demonstrate, wisdom means especially to honour and consult clerics above all others. It is not the presumption involved in criticizing royalty that bothers him, but the anti-clerical tone of the *dits*. Yet he recognizes that some wicked clerics at court have themselves given bad advice and that:

> Ever since such people were anchored
> At court and not set adrift
> There has been only war and conflict.
> Each one has taken his shovelful,
> So, the people are stripped,
> And in the realm wars born.
> (11. 594-9)

Thus, he counsels Louis X:

> King, think how thou wilt have
> To bring to an end the wars of thy father.
> See to it that thy people are no longer pay for
> The things of evil counsel
> Whereof everyone speaks upon his threshold;
> Whence France has many a vexation.
> (11. 873-8)

In so doing he hopes that Louis will observe measure in all things, to a greater degree than did his father. In another poem, Philip V is given the same advice.[246] Ever a traditionalist,[247] he urged both Louis X and Philip V to 'live of their own' without imposing needless financial burdens on subjects.[248] In *Un Songe*[249] he suggests that Philip the Fair, a great hunter, had

[246] 'Du Roy Philippe qui ores régne', 11. 81-5; ibid. 55. The entire poem runs pp. 53-7.

[247] Charles-Victor Langlois considered him a man of the age of Louis IX writing later, *Histoire littéraire de la France*, xxxv, 335-6.

[248] Storer and Rochedieu, *Six Historical Poems of Geffroi de Paris*: 'Les Avisemens', 11. 606-8; 'Du Roy Phelippe', 11. 81-6; Cf. the comments on v.

caught Jews, Templars, and Christians. But the financial yield of the hunt was largely lost to the king through corruption and 'he had the least of it' (1. 205):

> Of one hundred sous he had only one penny,
> For at the game he was last.
>
> (11. 207-8)

And the result of the financial exactions and official venality was the appearance of the leagues in 1314:

> That game was like that for a long time,
> For that reason, began the quarrel
> Of the allies, just as one knows.
>
> (11. 209-11)

But Geffroi was at heart a royalist. In both French and Latin poems on the leagues of 1314, he denounced the allies in bitter terms. His position is clearly stated in 'Des Allies':[250]

> Their predecessors put their thinking
> Entirely on the advancement
> Of our sacred crown;
> And they are for destruction;
> There is here evil engendering;
> Bad fruit and evil brood.
>
> (11. 55-60)
>
> For the king had not denied justice.
> Do they not have the right to come and go
> . . .
> Both to the King and to the Parlement?
> And one will hear them kindly,
> And without doing excess
> One will listen to their claim.
>
> (11. 101-5)

Other writers were not so generous in their estimates of those in power. Enguerran de Marigny, the chief minister of Philip IV at the end of the reign, seems a lightning-rod hit time and again by poetic bolts. Often his personal qualities, his pride (which led him to place several portraits of himself in prominent locations in

83-8 of 'De Alliatis', 59-60.

[249] Pr. ibid. 61-71, with tr.

[250] Pr. ibid. 73-80 with tr. A part of the Latin poem 'De Alliatis' is pr. pp. 58-60.

the royal palace),[251] his greed, his driving ambition which led to his swift rise to power, sparked the lightning flashes of satire. But something of a response to larger policy also is present in the attacks; on him fell much abuse for royal taxation and the seemingly endless struggle for Flanders. The anonymous clerk who wrote the last branch of the Reynard the Fox stories during Marginy's lifetime has harsh things to say of him, and Jean Favier has convincingly argued that contemporaries identified Marigny not only with Reynard and the quality of 'renardie', but as well with that other great symbol of venality, Fauvel the horse. Although both the fox and horse symbols antedate Marigny, the reddish colour of his hair made natural the link between the greedy politician and the red fox or especially the roan horse.[252] The concluding portion of the *Roman de Fauvel* was, in fact, written by Gervais de Bus, Marigny's chaplain.[253] To this day we testify to the set of qualities associated with the royal minister when we describe venal, flattering behaviour as 'currying favour' (an English corruption of 'currying Fauvel').[254]

Undoubtedly a more thorough search of French literature than is possible here would produce further examples of what might be broadly classified as criticism of the emerging French state. Eustache Deschamps, for example, could be critical of excessive taxation late in the fourteenth century, or perhaps more accurately, critical of the waste of tax revenues by an ill-advised king.[255] But it seems unlikely that such further examples will overturn the contrast between the occasional, relatively mild, and often narrowly *ad hominem* French complaint in the fourteenth century and the entire *corpus* of English complaint (including the outlaw ballads), so strikingly different in its volume, its frequent bitterness, and the apparent scope of its audience. The contrast

[251] Favier, 'Les Portraits d'Enguerran de Marigny'.

[252] Smith, (*Anti-Courtier Trend*, 49) seems almost to have predicted some such conclusion: 'Some of these attacks, it is true, concentrate on shortcomings which would be thought typical of courtiers of any epoch . . . but in the *Roman de Fauvel, Renart le Contrefait* and some of the *ballads* of Deschamps we are left with the impression that such portraits are more specific, drawn by an observer on the spot and not simply by a moralist generalizing on the profession.'

[253] Favier, *Un Conseiller de Philippe le Bel*, 67, 191-9. Cf. id., *Philippe le Bel*, 132-3.

[254] Ruth Mohl, *The Three Estates*, 52.

[255] Kendrick, 'Criticism of the Ruler', ch. 4.

between the response to the state in two literatures points clearly to the greater impact of the English king's government as it touched more people in more aspects of their lives than was yet true in France.

3. THE EVIDENCE OF POPULAR REVOLT

The direct and forceful evidence of popular risings might seem a welcome relief after the obscurities encountered in extracting the political content from difficult poems written in two countries and several languages. In fact, analysis of the Jacquerie of 1358 and the English rising of 1381 and any attempt to compare them may take us into even more hazardous territory than the realms of literature. If there is no dearth of scholarship on the English rising, there is also no lack of controversy. 'The great revolt', R. B. Dobson wrote in 1970, 'has hitherto defeated the attempts of historians who have tried to solve all its problems, proving too mysterious in its motivation and too complex in its ramifications for entirely satisfactory analysis.'[256] The absence of a great, synthetic modern work on the English rising is perhaps not surprising, especially in view of the tendency to make the rising a lodestone to guide us to interpretations of agrarian society across many centuries of medieval English history. For the French rising the problem is almost the reverse: the classic work on the Jacquerie was written in 1859, with a second edition in 1894;[257] though subsequent discussion of the events of 1358 is not lacking, it is much less full than discussion of the events of 1381, and it has tended to appear in broad, comparative discussions of late medieval unrest,[258] or in regional studies with necessarily comprehensive agendas.[259] Attempts to compare the two great fourteenth-century risings have been limited to a few sentences in general works.

[256] Dobson, *The Peasants' Revolt of 1381*, 10.

[257] Luce, *Histoire de la Jacquerie*.

[258] Mollat and Wolff, *Ongles bleus* and the English tr., Lytton-Sells, *The Popular Revolutions of the Late Middle Ages*. The English edn. omits the valuable bibliog. in the original. See also Fourquin, *Les Soulèvements populaires au moyen âge*.

[259] Fourquin, *Les Campagnes de la région parisienne*. A brief summary is provided in Cazelles, 'La Jacquerie', *The English Rising of 1381*.

A detailed comparison is thus conspicuously absent from historical scholarship on fourteenth-century France and England. Fortunately, our present concern requires nothing so vast and can be relatively limited. We need only ask what the risings can tell us about widespread perceptions of government and criticisms of governance in the two realms. An emphasis on the political dimensions of the revolts seems hardly out of place. Historical scholarship, especially in the English case, has been tilting in this direction for some time.[260] In his survey of the economic and social history of medieval England, M. M. Postan has concluded that it is 'very difficult to find a direct economic cause behind the rising'; he thinks that the economic historian 'can therefore do little more than warn other historians against too naïve or too economic a sociology of rebellion . . .'.[261] More recently, C. C. Dyer has declared that the 'frustration of historians who despair of finding a social explanation of the rising is understandable, as causes suggested in the past have been shown to be inadequate.'[262] Lords apparently did not increase their demands for labour services late in the fourteenth century; feudal society cannot be thought (in some simplistic way) to have been dissolving as a money economy advanced; peasants and wage-earners improved their conditions in the period after the plague. The question thus becomes whether landlords frustrated the rising expectations of villagers by actions constituting a 'seigneurial reaction'.

The present discussion makes no effort to deal with the vast and disputed issues of the sociology of rebellion; but it proceeds on the assumption that close attention to the political dimension of the two risings is not naïve, and that a cross-Channel comparison of rebellion may reveal differences in attitudes towards the crown and governmental policies in England and France. As George Holmes has concisely suggested, with the events of both 1358 and 1381 in mind, 'the combination of political weakness and social conflict was essential.'[263] What

[260] Dobson, *The Peasants' Revolt of 1381*, 20, 51. R. H. Hilton disapprovingly notes the same trend in *Bond Men Made Free*, ch. 5, and a comment on p. 220.

[261] *The Medieval Economy and Society*, 154.

[262] Dyer, 'The Social and Economic Background to the Rural Revolt of 1381', 1.

[263] Holmes, *Europe: Hierarchy and Revolt*, 127.

were the causes, the nature, and the consequences of this political weakness in England and France?

The highly-developed royal capacity for warfare seems likely to be an important key. From one point of view the great fourteenth-century revolts in England and France may be interpreted as risings against the war, as results not of some abstract distaste for fighting, but of utter exasperation with the consequences of the current war felt by those who had to pay in one way or another. Of course, warfare on the fourteenth-century scale produced strains along dangerous faultlines long in existence. But if we recognize the importance of long-range tensions in social relationships, of continued lordly oppression of villagers whose aspirations may have been rising in the changed circumstances after the mortality inflicted by the Plague,[264] we ought also to take account of the widespread effects produced by the demands of governments vigorously at war from the closing decades of the thirteenth century.[265]

Throughout the fourteenth century in France 'peasant disorder was endemic wherever there was military disorder.'[266] In the case of England, with its better documentation, we know that throughout the century, and especially in periods of heavy taxation, there was gnawing fear of a rising. The Ordinances of 1311 state the fear openly, both in a preamble and in a clause on the royal right of prise.[267] Though the capricious rule of Edward II is the major concern of the ordinances, the fear of a rising is obviously an outgrowth of the war taxation and purveyance begun late in the reign of Edward I. Early in Edward III's reign the author of the *Speculum Regis* warned the king that if they had a leader the people would rise up against royal exactions.[268] Several chroniclers and the author of the *Song Against the King's Taxes* likewise thought a rebellion was possible in the wake of the purveyance and taxation which accompanied the campaigns

[264] Hilton, *The Decline of Serfdom in Medieval England*; id., *Bond Men Made Free*, chs. 5-10; Dyer, 'The Social and Economic Background', 21.

[265] For specific comments in this vein, see Keen, *England in the Later Middle Ages*, 259; Dobson, *The Peasants' Revolt of 1381*, 20-1 (and his interesting comments on fifteenth-century rebellions, pp. 336-7); Dyer, 'The Social and Economic Background', 21. The effects of war are discussed in ch. 1, above.

[266] Lewis, *Later Medieval France*, 286.

[267] *Statutes of the Realm*, i. 157.

[268] Moisant (ed.), *De Speculo Regis Edwardi Tertii*, 96.

which have traditionally been considered the opening of the Hundred Years War. What might have happened if a dynamic leader had emerged, or perhaps even more important, if the English crown had not made important concessions (abandoning large-scale purveyance, reducing the burden of the tax of the 'ninth' in 1340, ordering broad commissions of inquiry into governmental abuses in 1340-1)?[269] The spectre of a rising was again in men's minds in the years before their fears became fact, and again these were years of excessively heavy war taxation. A commons petition in the 1377 parliament stressed the need 'to avoid a danger of the sort that recently occurred in the realm of France because of a similar rebellion and confederation of villeins against their lords.'[270] John Wyclif was writing of the possibility of a rising early in 1381; he recognized the strains of heavy taxation (which he blamed on the stinginess of the possessionate clergy).[271]

The strains and disillusionment caused by war may have accumulated and made their weight felt only slowly among the privileged ranks of society.[272] But for England, as we have noted, the fear of a general rising against war taxation and purveyance supporting the early campaigns of the Hundred Years War (and indeed the similar fears associated with the warfare of the last years of Edward I) suggest a different interpretation in so far as the great bulk of the population is concerned. For France at only a slightly later date there is the evidence of a governmental crisis building up by 1347 followed by the Parisian rising and the Jacquerie a decade later. The French crises both in 1347 and 1356-8 followed shocking battlefield defeats, at Crécy in 1346 and at Poitiers in 1356, and involved charges of inefficiency and corruption voiced in meetings of the Estates; both produced demands for a purge of royal financial officers and for war taxation

[269] Maddicott, 'The English Peasantry and the Demands of the Crown', 23-4, 64-6; Fryde, 'The English Parliament and the Peasants' Revolt of 1381', 83-4.

[270] *Rotuli Parliamentorum*, iii. 21-2, quot.: Dobson, *The Peasants' Revolt of 1381*, 77. What apparently stood behind this petition was the 'great rumour' of 1377, a movement for peasant freedom affecting at least forty villages in Wiltshire, Hampshire, and Surrey. See Faith, 'The "Great Rumour" of 1377'.

[271] Wilks, 'Reformatio Regni', 125. As Wilks points out, he expected a revolt to draw upon discontents other than those that motivated the rebels.

[272] Barnie, *War in Medieval English Society*.

controlled by *élus* (responsible to the Estates) rather than by members of the regular domainal administration.[273]

Thus, the strains of financing major warfare had appeared in both countries within a decade of the opening campaigns; in England fears of 'peasant' revolt troubled the sleep of authorities and forced a range of concessions, while recriminations over the conduct and financing of the war generated the 'constitutional' crisis of 1341. Six years later the French were embroiled in a broadly similar governmental crisis with war finance at the centre.

Can it then be accidental that the major risings come at the moment when grinding war taxation coincided with disastrous, humiliating defeat in France, or with a sense of utter exhaustion and frustration in England? Frenchmen could somehow swallow the bitter pill of defeat of Crécy. The chronicler Jean de Venette, who seems often to reflect common opinion, could attribute the defeat to accidents of nature and the general untrustworthiness of foreigners: a sudden rain had wet the cords of the crossbows of the hired Genoese archers, who were after all only foreigners of low degree.[274] Moreover, if the defeat had brought increased difficulties for the French monarchy, it had not created an utterly disastrous situation. The English took and garrisoned Calais, but their main force went home and the war went on.[275] Ten years later, after the defeat at Poitiers, the prospects quickly appeared quite different: the king was a captive; his son was faced with newly assertive claims of the Estates he felt compelled to summon and especially with their most active element, the Parisian bourgoisie led by the provost of the merchants, Étienne Marcel; the ambitions of the dauphin's brother-in-law, Charles of Navarre, threatened an anti-Valois alliance and civil war.[276] Worst of all, the countryside of much of northern France was beginning to suffer the scourge of lawless bands of men-at-arms operating under one banner or another, or under no banner at all.

[273] Henneman, *Royal Taxation in Fourteenth-century France* (1976), ch. 1, *passim*; Perroy, *The Hundred Years War*, 126-35; Cazelles, *La Société politique et la crise de la royauté*, 151-261; id., 'Le Parti navarrais'.

[274] *The Chronicle of Jean de Venette*, 43-4, 176-7.

[275] Perroy, *The Hundred Years War*, 125-6.

[276] Henneman, *Royal Taxation in Fourteenth-century France* (1976), ch. 1, esp., pp. 20-1.

One such brigand captain, reflecting on his activities in a speech attributed to him by Froissart, thought that all things considered he had a good life: 'Par ma foi, ceste vie estoit bonne et belle.'[277] His victims, who took a different view, were chiefly commoners. Though the bands might come to an understanding with local nobles, who sometimes joined in the brigandage, they appeared to be veritable devils to the men of the local villages and to the merchants who travelled through them. The nobles who had failed conspicuously on the field of Poitiers were thus likewise failures in the most elementary defence of their own tenants.[278] If traditional medieval social theory had any meaning, it required alongside the labour of one estate and the prayers of another, the vigorous defence of all by the nobility. Jean de Venette suggests the current climate of opinion by retelling the fable of the dog who befriended the wolf and joined him in devouring the sheep he was set to guard. Jean says the story was commonly told and 'seemed to have come true'.[279] A similar point of view appears in the *Complainte sur la bataille de Poitiers*.[280] The attitudes behind such literary complaints must occasionally have produced actual physical assaults on nobles. By chance we know of an incident in which Jean, sire de la Ferté-Fresnel et de Gracé, was assaulted by his tenants when he returned from captivity to collect his ransom. How many more such incidents Délachenal wondered, are simply lost to us?[281] Jean de Venette offers no excuse for the nobles after Poitiers. Many nobles are pusillanimous sluggards, given over to ostentatious and obscene costume, who spend war taxes on gambling and frivolous occupations such as tennis:

From that time on all went ill with the kingdom, and the state was undone. Thieves and robbers rose up everywhere in the land. The nobles despised and hated all others and took no thought for the mutual usefulness and profit of lord and men. They subjected and despoiled the peasants and the men of the villages. In no wise did they defend their country from its enemies. Rather did they trample it underfoot, robbing and pillaging the peasants' goods.[282]

277 Quot. Luce, *Histoire de la Jacquerie*, 17-18.

278 Fourquin, *Les Soulèvements populaires au moyen âge*, 176-7.

279 *The Chronicle of Jean de Venette*, 113.

280 Lewis, *Later Medieval France*, 48-9.

281 Délachanel, *Histoire de Charles V*, i. 396-97.

282 *The Chronicle of Jean de Venette*, 66. He returned repeatedly to criticisms of nobles in writing of the events of the following years. See pp. 67, 78,

Though the documentation is not as full for France as for England, it is likely that in the spring of 1358 some peasants in the Paris region found themselves expected to pay not only taxation for what seemed a war rapidly being lost, but also ransoms for captured lords who were losing that war, protection money to ward off deprivations of English, Navarrese or even royal soldiery, and (if they were buying off non-royal brigands) fines to the crown for dealing with the enemy; at the same time their lords seem to have increased their demands and the hated right of prise was being activated to place strategic fortresses in the region on a suitable war footing.[283] The Jacquerie broke out in Champagne, Picardy, and Beauvaisis in late May with a ferocity that was more surprising to contemporaries than to modern historians. As the nineteenth-century historian of the rising, Siméon Luce, suggests,[284] the Jacquerie of the peasants and the counter-jacquerie of the nobles who suppressed the rising, had been preceeded by the Jacquerie of the brigands. Perhaps historians should avoid a terminological surfeit of Jacqueries, but the point of three connected waves of violence related to the warfare between England and France is useful. The heavy demands of the war, the failures and consequences of the war, set this cycle of reciprocal violence in motion.

For the English rising, the importance of the poll tax of 1380 has been a commonplace of analysis. But this tax has not always been viewed in the full context of the conduct and financing of the war. As Edmund Fryde has demonstrated,[285] though Englishmen paid no direct royal taxes between 1359 and 1371, in the decade between 1371 and the revolt no fewer than eight separate parliamentary grants assessed a total of £382,000 on the lay population, with somewhat more than half this sum falling in the

94-5, 97, 102, 105, 111, 123-4.

283 Délachanel, *Histoire de Charles V*, 401; Luce, *Histoire de la Jacquerie*, 9-43. Raymond Cazelles argues that a number of fortresses were provisioned by the regent and his allies among the nobles in their effort to blockade the commerce of Paris via the Seine, Marne, and Yvonne; *Société politique, noblesse et couronne*, 318, 329-330; 'La Jacquerie: Fûtelle un mouvement paysan?', 663-4.

284 Luce, *Histoire de la Jacquerie*, 9 ff.

285 The following discussion is based on Fryde's introd. to Oman, *The Great Revolt of 1381*, 2nd edn., and Fryde, 'The English Parliament and the Peasants' Revolt of 1381'.

five years preceding the rising.[286] Parliament not only imposed heavy taxation, it experimented with the forms in an effort to find enough money to fuel the voracious machinery of war. Such experimentation was necessary because the tax system developed in the thirteenth and early fourteenth centuries, based on tenths and fifteenths of movable wealth, was unpopular, subject to abuses, and out of touch with the economic and demographic realities of post-plague England. Instead of reassessing the regional sums fixed since 1334, parliament experimented with a series of taxes on people rather than on property; after the parish tax of 1371, which proved lucrative but cumbersome and complex, parliament turned to three poll taxes in 1377, 1379, and 1380. Following the unusually heavy tax of two tenths and two fifteenths in 1378, parliament provided some relief by the carefully graduated poll tax of 1379, 'probably the most equitable tax of the fourteenth century.' Since it was unfortunately also one of the less productive taxes, another tenth and fifteenth in 1380 was levied and was quickly followed by the infamous poll tax of 1380, assessed at a rate three times that of the first such tax in 1377, and expected to raise 100,000*m*. from the laity. In justifying the heavy tax, the lord chancellor spoke openly in parliament of only one major military expedition, that of the earl of Buckingham in Brittany; the need to reinforce the same army was stressed by the speaker for the Commons, who may have feared the government would divert the money for an expedition to Portugal in support of the ambitions of John of Gaunt. Any such fears erred only in that John of Gaunt may have coveted the money for two expeditions, an invasion of Castile from Gascony as well as the expedition to Portugal. Buckingham's army, Gaunt's ambitions, and the continuing need to guard the Channel and the Scottish border thus underlay the government's sense of urgency, though only the first need in this list was publicly acknowledged. 'John of Gaunt's Spanish plans, which the government was concealing from parliament', as Fryde suggests, 'appear to have played a

[286] In his discussion of the problems standing behind the Good Parliament of 1376, George Holmes suggests that the heavy papal taxes imposed on the clergy by Gregory XI may be linked with a sudden expansion in the use of the hitherto rare writ *de excommunicato capiendo* which ordered the arrest by royal officers of those who persistently resisted clerical coercion backed by excommunication; *The Good Parliament*, 17. This suggests that clerics must have experienced troubles in collecting from their tenants.

considerable part in causing the Great Revolt in 1381.'[287] The failure of Buckingham's expedition was certainly known by the time the revolt erupted, and it may have been known with particular force in Essex, one centre of revolt, where Buckingham owned extensive estates; if misuse of tax funds to further Gaunt's schemes was also known, as seems possible, another reason for the widespread and well-nurtured hatred of Gaunt in 1381 becomes apparent.[288] As Edmund Fryde points out, the massive tax evasion in 1381 (in effect a 'disappearance' of one-third of those taxed in 1377) amounted to a first act of rebellion, a serious though a passive step.[289] Even a summary account of royal taxation in 1371-81 thus helps to explain the urgency with which the government reacted to the widespread evasion and underassessment which threatened to reduce the expected yield of the poll tax, and to explain why the reassessment and the hated special commissioners were ordered. We can better appreciate how the rising of 1381 can be interpreted as the 'outcome of a war which seemed incapable of a successful ending and where each successive effort produced only new failures or disasters.'[290]

Whereas in France the war-related issues standing behind the rising seem to have been defence first and taxation second, in England the order should be reversed; but the issue of actual defence cannot be ignored. England was largely spared a war fought on her own soil, but the contrast with France may not be as complete as might appear at first glance.

One reason is the regularity with which the French carried the war to English shores.[291] The sea-borne threat was apparent as early as 1338, when a French fleet sacked Southampton; but the real danger came later. In the great raid of 1360 the French sacked Winchelsea and spread fear and destruction into the

[287] Fryde, 'The English Parliament and the Peasants' Revolt of 1381', 81. See also his introd., Oman, *The Great Revolt of 1381*, 13-14.

[288] Gaunt would have been hated even if the expedition had been successful, but in fact it degenerated into mere plunder, Fryde, 'The English Parliament and the Peasants' Revolt of 1381', 85; Russell, *The English Intervention*, 306-43.

[289] Fryde, *The Great Revolt of 1381*, 11.

[290] Id., introd., Oman, *The Great Revolt of 1381*, p. xxvii. In a similar vein see Keen, *England in the Late Middle Ages*, 259, 272; McKisack, *The Fourteenth Century*, 422-3; Dobson, *The Peasants' Revolt of 1381*, 20-1.

[291] The following discussion is based on Searle and Burghart, 'The Defense of England and the Peasants' Revolt'.

surrounding countryside. Once Charles V secured an alliance with Castile in 1372, the swift and deadly Castilian galleys began to appear as an added and yet more feared menace off the south coast of England. In 1377 they burned Rye, Folkestone, and Hastings on the southern coast and Yarmouth, Newport, and Newton on the Isle of Wight. Though Winchelsea was defended against this force, it too was sacked three years later. Eleanor Searle and Robert Burghart have argued that such major raids (and the continual, if less officially noticed and documented, piracy and minor raiding) had a dramatic effect on the climate of opinion and a drastic effect on the economy of south-eastern England. The ports and native shipping declined; the population tended to move away from dangerous coastal areas; the cultivation of lands exposed to raids declined, lowering the agricultural production in the area.

Such broad issues take on the specificity of personalities when we consider the reactions of men in the south-east to three major lords with lands in the region. In addition to hating him as director of a royal administration gone wrong, the villagers of the region could hone their hatred of John of Gaunt by repeating stories that he had left Pevensey castle without a garrison, despite the appeals of local men, during the great Franco-Castilian raid of 1377; he could, the stories reported him saying, rebuild what the French destroyed. A chronicler likewise reports that the Earl of Arundel, though he was jointly with the Abbot of Battle arrayer for Sussex, fled during the raids, leaving Lewes castle undefended. Again, a local appeal for aid had been rejected; he had refused to help unless the town agreed to pay costs for 400 lances. Gaunt's property was, of course, a chief target in 1381; his great palace of the Savoy was utterly demolished. In the continuing discontent after the rebellion, an armed crowd smashed its way into Lewes castle through gates, doors, and windows, refreshed itself with ten casks of wine, threw down the earl of Arundel's buildings, and burned his rolls, rentals, and other muniments.[292] How different was the popular reaction to Abbot Hamo de Offyngton of Battle who, as already noted, was arrayer of Sussex with Arundel. More than once he led the local defence forces against French raiders,

[292] Evidence from a commission of oyer and terminer of 20 Feb. 1383, *CPR 1381-1385* 259, cited Searle and Burghart, 'The Defense of England and the Peasants' Revolt', 366.

showing courage and even personal bravery. During the Great Revolt, although he was head of a wealthy house with extensive lands, Abbot Hamo went without fear for a holiday to one of his manors; he even soon entertained the new archbishop of Canterbury at Battle for a hunting vacation.[293] The English rebels could certainly be discriminating and at least along the southern coast they noted carefully who had done his duty against the French raids.

But in England as in France the official enemy was not the only source of danger and devastation feared by villagers. Medieval armies on either side of the Channel were more easily collected than they were fed, paid, and disciplined. English troops from an inland county collected for coastal defence or waiting for long weeks to embark for France from some port, poorly paid and fed, if paid and fed at all, showed a discouraging tendency to pillage the surrounding countryside. According to a complaint from the commons of Hampshire, the expedition of John Neville, Lord of Raby, created so much havoc before setting off for Brittany in 1372 that local people had to arm themselves.[294] Petitions in parliament in 1379-80 charged that houses in coastal counties had been robbed and even destroyed by the troops of soldiers 'venantz et passantz . . . et par lour long demoer';[295] but even as early as the inquests regarding the tax of the ninth in 1340, there were complaints that guardians of the coast, 'sailors and others', stole lambs and ewes and caused great destruction and expense to local people; much land lay uncultivated the inquest jurors said, for fear of 'foreigners and sailors'.[296] Governing 'a realm that was not yet a community', the English crown 'had developed a machinery for control and total mobilization before it or its people had developed a sense of the realm as a single people.'[297] The local county feeling which became so apparent in 1381[298] had long been evident in the willingness of village conscripts to take

293 Ibid. 381-3, 386, 387, and n. 85. Searle, *Lordship and Community*, 346-7.

294 Holmes, *Good Parliament*, 130.

295 *Rotuli Parliamentorum*, iii. 80, quot.: Searle and Burghart, 'The Defense of England and the Peasants' Revolt', 385.

296 *Inquisitiones Nonarum*, 125-6, 354-5, quot.: Searle and Burghart, 'The Defense of England and the Peasants' Revolt', 369.

297 Ibid.

298 McKisack, *The Fourteenth Century*, 420-1.

what they wanted or needed by force in the 'foreign' counties to which they might be sent as defenders or through which they passed on their way to some campaign in Scotland or France.

It is difficult to assess the exact toll of wartime devastation in England as a causal factor in the Great Rising. To some extent, the men of south-eastern England, as the Frenchmen who became Jacques, were exploited by a state war mechanism which was nevertheless unable to defend them. Yet wartime exploitation coupled with a failure of protection cannot be read as a major factor in the formula of revolt. The geographical area of the 1381 rising did not coincide with the area affected by war: there were no risings in the war-torn border country in the north; there were hardly any French raids on the coasts of Essex or East Anglia, where the rising was prominent; the raids may have troubled Kent, a centre of rebellion, less than Hampshire and Sussex, which were relatively quiescent in 1381.[299] Moreover, the rebels' grievances presented in London did not include complaints about defence. Yet we cannot assume that the effects of the raids and the English counter-measures were limited to a radius of a few miles from the coastal ports. The effects on shipping, merchants, cultivation, and grain prices, even population patterns, the attempts to muster defence forces, the costs of paying troops and building or improving defences could well have affected all of south-east England. The villages involved in the initial act of rebellion in 1381 included villagers who were angry not only about war taxation but also about the government's impressment of fishermen and boatmen for service in the navy.[300] The sack of Winchelsea may not have occupied major space in the thoughts of men in Northumberland; but the impact of war on the southern coast may well have added its force to the shock waves which passed through villages on both sides of the Thames in 1381.

Thus, war taxation and to a much lesser extent actual wartime devastation help to explain the Great Rising in England. Taking into account the different weights attributable to these two consequences of war policy in England and in France (and even in different regions of England which revolted), it is possible to assert that 'as much as the Jacquerie rebellion of 1358 in France,

299 Hilton, *Bond Men Made Free*, 158.
300 Fryde, *The Great Revolt of 1381*, 5.

though less obviously, the Peasants' Revolt was the fruit of the Hundred Years' War.'[301] In both countries the war effort generated, or at least revealed, the political weaknesses which fused with long-standing social tensions to produce violent reactions.

Public debate over war policies may likewise have acted as a positive catalyst for rebellion. Rebels in both countries seem to have been influenced by the open and stringent questioning of the government by those in higher social ranks; in each case, revolt followed a period of debate and criticism over the conduct of the war in important assemblies. English discontent flared in the parliament of 1371 and five years later the Good Parliament 'popularized for the first time the idea that the war was being lost and that the country was wretchedly misgoverned through corruption and even treason in high places.' These charges would be made in much more extreme form and with more serious consequences by the rebels of 1381; Richard Lyons, impeached in the parliament of 1376, would be murdered in the rising of 1381; John of Gaunt, the *bête noire* of the Good Parliament, would stand at the head of the rebels' list of 'traitors' in the Great Revolt.[302] In France, pungent criticism of the management of the realm and the prosecution of the war in the crisis of 1346 became virtual civil war, as we have seen, in the crisis of 1358. The voices of criticism and the atmosphere of confusion can only have intensified as the nobles separated themselves from the Estates meeting in Paris and as the dauphin and Charles of Navarre competed for support.[303] These criticisms in each country seem to have diffused easily into the countryside around the capitals; a higher degree of receptivity near London and Paris might be expected in any case; these regions probably possessed a more lively political consciousness than more distant areas. But historians have not always pointed to the obvious fact that both revolts originated and were concentrated in the areas close to the capitals.[304]

[301] Searle and Burghart, 'The Defense of England and the Peasants' Revolt', 316.

[302] Fryde, introd., Oman, *The Great Revolt*, p. xxvii. Cf. Dobson, *The Peasants' Revolt of 1381*, 84.

[303] Cazelles, *La Société politique et la crise de la royauté*, 253-61, 427-36; Henneman, *Royal Taxation in Fourteenth-century France* (1975), ch. 1.

[304] Fourquin comments on this situation, *Les Soulèvements populaires au*

The role of government war policy appears in an even less obvious way in both revolts. The exigencies of war led to specific royal policies which may, unwittingly, have helped to produce at the village level the mentality and the rudimentary degree of organization necessary for revolt. In the great crises after Poitiers the French crown several times authorized peasants to take up arms against the brigands who so troubled their lives. In the ordinance of 3 March 1357 peasants were told that they could use force and that they could bring together the men of the neighbourhood: 'que chacun puisse résister de fait à leurs forces par toutes voyes et manières que ils pourront mieulx, appeller ad ce les gens des villes voisines par son de cloche ou autrement si comme bon leur semblera.'[305] Such forces might well act with feelings of full legitimacy against lordly brigands as against English or Navarrese troops. Just such a clash was the spark igniting one of the opening fires of the Jacquerie; slightly later a clash was only narrowly averted between the seigneur de St-Pizer et de Vignory (who was ruthlessly suppressing rebels) and the troops raised in the *bailliages* of Chaumont and Vitry as a defence force against maurading Germans and Lorrainers.[306] In England the crown efforts early in the war to raise troops for French campaigns and to defend the coasts produced 'generations of men and boys of a customarily exploited class . . . trained in arms and hardened in bivouacking and in real combat.' Though reliance on troops conscripted in the localities for French service may have declined after the statute of 1352 and as indentured retinues became more prominent in the campaigns, the needs of coastal defense became even more pressing.[307]

Yet stressing the important common link between war and rebellion tends to obscure differences between the risings in England and France which are critically important in understanding the reaction to crown policy at the local level, differences which in fact are important in understanding the different character

moyen âge, 178. Cf. the general observations of Hilton, *Bond Men Made Free*, 160, and the comment of Dobson, *The Peasants' Revolt of 1381*, 18.

305 Quot. Flammermont, 'La Jacquerie en Beauvaisis', 128-9. Cf. *Ordonnances*, iii. 133-4, 139; Luce, *Histoire de la Jacquerie*, 161-3.

306 Ibid. 90; Flammermont, 'La Jacquerie en Beauvaisis', 130.

307 Searle and Burghart, 'The Defense of England and the Peasants' Revolt', 366.

of the two governments. The risings themselves show strikingly differing characteristics.[308] Jacquerie has, in fact, become in historical writing almost a generic term, signifying a brutal, seemingly irrational peasant rising, an almost blind striking out to destroy all those perceived as oppressors. An examination of the incidents of the early summer of 1358 reveals the origin of such a concept. In the concise words of the chronicler Jean le Bel, 'ces gens assemblez sans chief ardoient et roboient tout et murdrissoient gentilz hommes et nobles femmes, et leur enfans, et violoient dames et puchielles sans misericorde quelconques'.[309] The lurid stories told by Froissart and other chroniclers seem to be no exaggeration; the letters of pardon later issued by the French crown and the well-known letter of Étienne Marcel to the Flemish towns in July 1358 confirm the impression that this may have been the most bloody rising of the fourteenth century.[310] Lords and even their wives and children were killed if caught, their houses were pillaged and burned. Once they recovered from the shock and organized themselves, the nobles of the region, especially under the leadership of Charles of Navarre, exacted their own revenge which was ruthless and largely independent of any formal legal process.[311] The rising of the Jacques lasted only two weeks; the noble reaction went on for years.[312]

While the English rising two decades later involved violence, some ugly scenes, and much destruction of property, it was never a Jacquerie. Had the rebels caught him they would surely have

[308] Fryde, introd., Oman, *The Great Revolt*, p. xxx. Cf. ibid. 40-1; Fryde, *The Great Revolt of 1381*, 30.

[309] *Chronique de Jean le Bel*, ii. 257.

[310] This is the evaluation of Holmes, *Europe: Hierarchy and Revolt*, 128. For discussions of the Jacques' excesses and lordly vengeance see the following medieval historians: Birdsall and Newhall (ed.), *The Chronicle of Jean de Venette*, 76-9; Viard and Déprez (eds.), *Chronique de Jean le Bel*, 256-60; Luce (ed.), *Chronique des quatre premiers valois (1327-1393)*, 71-6; *Œuvres de Froissart*, i, ch. 80. For comments by modern historians, see Luce, *Histoire de la Jacquerie*, 24 f., 31-43, 62, 116-19, 166-9 and his 'Pièces justicatives', *passim*; Flammermont, 'La Jacquerie en Beauvaisis', 133-4, 139-43; Fourquin, *Les Soulèvements populaires au moyen âge*, 179-80 and *Les Campagnes de la région parisienne*, 232-40; Cazelles, *Société politique, noblesse et couronne*, 322, 330.

[311] In addition to the sources in the previous n., see Fryde's evaluation in his introd., Oman, *The Great Revolt*, p. xxx.

[312] Cazelles, *Société politique, noblesse et couronne*, 330.

murdered John of Gaunt; they did kill the treasurer and chancellor and some local officials. But there was no movement against the entire class of landlords and no mention of assaults and murder committed against women and children. The relatively few landlords killed in England seem to have been hated for their role in local government more than their propertied status.[313] Likewise, when the tide of fury ebbed and the repression of the rebels began, it seems much more restrained than in France and in most cases it very quickly took the form of recognized legal procedures.[314] An English rebel properly hanged by a justice holding a commission of oyer and terminer might have considered academic the difference between his execution and the death of a French rebel beneath a noble's sword swung in hot and extra-legal wrath. But the differences between the two cases are significant to the historian as, in general, the differing qualities of the two risings are revealing.

In the first place each revolt shows its own distinct interaction between social and political problems. In France the defeat and capture of John II at Poitiers created the tangled political web which in 1358 stretched across three major points of power and influence: the dauphin and his allies; Charles of Navarre and his allies; the bourgeoisie of Paris, led by Étienne Marcel, allied with the ruling élites of a number of cities in the region between the Seine and the Marne (Meaux, Senlis, Montdidier, Amiens). Raymond Cazelles has argued with force that the crisis of war revealed and intensified a basic social division between nobles and non-nobles that greatly complicated the three-cornered contest for political power.[315] Rural and urban non-nobles were moving closer together as towns rather than castles became the centres of security in the countryside so necessary in an era of invasion and the breakdown of order. The non-nobles viewed castles not as

[313] Most landowners in Kent, for example, simply had to pay blackmail and take an oath to King Richard and the Commons. See Oman, *The Great Revolt*, 41; Fryde, *The Great Revolt of 1381*, 30; Dyer, 'The Social and Economic Background', 5-6.

[314] Fryde, introd. Oman, *The Great Revolt*, pp. xxx, 40-1, 45, 82, 86-9, 152-3; Reville, *Le Soulèvement*, 159 and the many documents he prints in the appends. to this book; Dobson, *The Peasants' Revolt of 1381*, 16, 262, 303-4.

[315] Cazelles, *Société politique, noblesse et couronne*, 318, 332. His discussion draws upon the more detailed analysis he provides in 'La Jacquerie: Fût-elle un mouvement paysan?' John Henneman kindly provided a copy of this article.

havens of security but as nest of oppressors. Country folk hated the nobles who had failed to defend the region, and whose financial demands now mounted to cover costs of provisioning castles and often the payment of ransoms. Townsmen in the region, especially the Parisians, reached for a generous measure of control over the royal administration nominally headed by the dauphin who (at their insistence) assumed the title of regent. The Parisians had shown their power and audacity by murdering the noble marshals of Champagne and Normandy in the dauphin's presence. They seem to have worked initially through the Estates meeting in Paris without nobles in attendance, and they continued to co-operate with the representatives of the other towns after the Estates rose. Cazelles sees this informal but effective coalition of townsmen in the Paris basin as the critical organizing force responsible for the success of the Jacquerie in dismantling so many castles throughout the region in a period of only two weeks. To the rage of the Jacques the various *échevinages* brought a directing hand and additional force. The bourgeois interest is clear: the castles destroyed were those blocking the crucial riverine trade of these cities. The regent and his allies were using strategic castles to snip these arteries one by one, correctly seeing this policy as the means of bringing the towns to terms. The explosion of the Jacques altered matters dramatically. 'L'exaspération du plat pays a été utilisée, exploitée par la bourgeoisie de quelques villes, sous la direction des autorités parisiennes, contre une noblesse qui se refuse à collaborer avec elle. . . .'[316] The union of rural and urban forces was limited to this objective; most towns would not harbour the Jacques within their walls before or after co-operating with them on expeditions to smash local castles, but the smouldering ruins of castles in a wide territory around Paris (roughly from Amiens to Orléans on a north/south axis, and from Rouen to Laon east to west), clearly marked its temporary success. The Anglo-French war was a catalyst for a social war, but the non-noble alliance was only briefly effective and the traditional military force of the nobility soon made its weight felt with terrible effect.

England was scarcely a peaceful Arcadia in which all social tensions were resolved in communal accord. Yet class differences

[316] Cazelles, *Société politique, noblesse et couronne*, 330-1.

and class privileges do seem less marked in England than in France. The English nobility by and large lacked the quality of caste which so marked the French nobility and set it apart as a target of non-noble wrath as matters went from bad to worse in the realm of France. In fact, despite the obvious differences in wealth and importance among Englishmen, English society showed a series of gradations merging one into another, an unbroken spectrum rather than a ladder of clearly stratified social ranks. 'The privileges of the English gentry were tacit ones based on power and wealth without the sanction of legally defined status.'[317] Even the fifteenth-century English peers had no formal fiscal privileges and, in contrast to France, England knew no restrictions on alienations of fiefs to commoners. In corresponding political terms, England had earlier and more completely than France produced a political community, much more easily achieved, of course, in a kingdom the size of a single French province. Major issues of land tenure, felony, and trespass were settled in a single set of judicial agencies, the royal courts, in accordance with a single code of law, the Common Law of the realm of England. Even resistance to the royal administration had acquired communal form, as the movement for Magna Carta revealed as early as 1215.[318]

This difference in political form seems especially important—as important as social differences to which it was related—in understanding the particular character of each of the revolts. For in each case the target of the rebels' fury indicates what force in the hierarchy of control they considered responsible for their misery, where, in other words, in their view lay the power that had gone wrong.

The contrast could scarcely be more clear. The Jacques butchered noble families and pillaged noble houses, showing with brutal clarity where they placed blame. Those under the leadership of Guillaume Cale first moved away from Paris, and thus away from the dauphin. Cale may have wanted to move his force

[317] Introd. McFarlane, *The Nobility of Later Medieval England*, p. xxv.

[318] For a general comment see Keen, *The Pelican History of Medieval Europe*, 192-206. Cazelles discusses the French nobility and its increasingly caste quality in *Société politique, noblesse et couronne* (pp. 60-84). For a contrast between the English and French nobilities see James Campbell's introd., McFarlane, *The Nobility of Later Medieval England*, pp. xxii-xxv, and McFarlane's discussions, *passim*.

toward Paris just before his defeat at Mello, but he was unable to convince the rebels of this course of action; they preferred to fight the noble army led by Charles the Bad then and there.[319] Thus, the French rebels totally ignored the agency of the royal government and never approached the capital. The French monarchy was, of course, in one of its worst crises, with John II a captive and a civil war gathering force. But it is none the less suggestive that the rebels (although they respected the king, carried banners with fleurs-de-lis, and shouted the royal battle cry, 'Mountjoy!')[320] approached neither the dauphin nor even his rival for the throne, Charles of Navarre, and made no appeal for relief to the crown. The Jacques were manipulated and joined by townsmen when the issue was destroying troublesome local fortresses, but they made no permanent alliance with the townsmen with whom they shared a common enemy; they could never effect more than a tentative alliance with the Parisians, never marched on Paris to try to influence the shifting balance of forces in the capital. Though the Parisian rising and the struggle between the dauphin and Charles of Navarre are part of the same crisis as the Jacquerie, the peasant rising seems in most respects curiously separate, only a part of the political crisis in that it greatly heightened tensions, gave leaders in Paris and the other towns a very temporary ally for destroying troublesome fortifications in the Paris region, and gave Charles the Bad a chance to achieve a rather cheap victory on the field of Mello. Marcel's brief link with the Jacques, John Henneman suggests, was not of decisive importance: 'It is merely calling attention to the obvious to point out that Marcel, the supporter of the peasants, and Charles of Navarre, their destroyer, very quickly resumed their alliance.' The French crown likewise refused to take the Parisian involvement with the Jacques seriously; the letters of pardon granted later in the summer excluded those who had tried to make Charles the Bad king of France and those who had impeded the ransom of King John, but made no mention of encouraging or supporting the Jacquerie.[321]

[319] *Chronique des quatre premiers valois*, 73-4; Flammermont, 'La Jacquerie en Beauvaisis', 140.

[320] Luce, *Histoire de la Jacquerie*, 78. Cf. Mollat and Wolff, *The Popular Revolutions of the Late Middle Ages*, 125-6.

[321] Henneman, *Royal Taxation in Fourteenth-century France* (1975), 77-81; the quot. is taken from p. 77.

The political dimensions of the Great Revolt in England loom very large by contrast. Though the scattered risings in regions at some distance from London concentrated on local issues, the two major bodies of rebels in the south-east very quickly organized themselves to march on London. Here they found enough support to enter the city and presented demands for the execution of 'traitors' and for a conference at which they could voice their grievances to the boy king Richard II. However we interpret the demands made at Mile End on 14 June and the even more controversial demands in the famous interview at Smithfield on 15 June,[322] for present purposes what is important is the rebels' focus on the crown and its agents from the beginning, their assumption that the essential task was to turn the direction being taken by the government (at least by a purge of leadership below the level of the king himself), and to use the authority of the crown as a seal of approval on any changes to be made in the conditions of their lives. Intense frustration with the royal government and a long-nurtured belief in the essential role of the royal government were opposite sides of the same coin in England.

If the risings, then, reflect in part the weakness of the king's government in England and France, these weaknesses were not identical. The French political problem was a fairly straightforward incapacity caused by or at least revealed by the war, which produced a complex political crisis and which helped generate the Jacquerie. Since Crécy, as John Henneman writes, 'Frenchmen no longer feared the tyranny of a strong and ruthless government, but rather the incompetence of a weak one.' The great reform ordinance of 1357 illustrates the level of concern; the legislation set salaries for officials, ordered them to be at work by sunrise, prescribed that no work was to be done by unqualified subordinates or deputies, and ordered officials to deal with matters in the order of urgency.[323]

322 The problem is whether to interpret the radical demands at Smithfield as representative of the views of most rebels or as a deliberately provocative programme devised by Wat Tyler in the hopes of maintaining his initiative and control. See Hilton, *Bond Men Made Free*, ch. 9; Wilkinson, 'The Peasants' Revolt of 1381'; Faith, 'The "Great Rumour" of 1377'; Prescott, 'London in the Peasants' Revolt'.

323 Henneman, *Royal Taxation in Fourteenth-century France* (1975), 45.

The English political problem was not incapacity but rather the overreaching we have noted more than once; as Maurice Keen suggests, the rising was at least in this political dimension 'a remarkable demonstration of the way in which distrust of all concerned in government and administration had percolated right down to the grass roots social level.'[324] Of course, the intense hatred and suspicion of John of Gaunt was a great catalyst, helping to link the discontents of countrymen with those of a great many Londoners. But as Bertie Wilkinson argued, 'A common hatred of John of Gaunt was only the spear point of a more general hatred against the government as a whole based on wider discontents . . .'.[325]

Heavy war taxation (often for dubious ends and with disappointing results) and the failure to defend the southern coast do not exhaust the list of causes for this grass roots political alienation. Another likely cause is the gap between ambitious claims to provide decent administration, good justice, and some measure of internal order on the one hand, and, the actual conduct of officials, the workings of courts, and the worrisome state of the public peace on the other. As Edmund Fryde has pointed out, the chancellor, Michael de la Pole, in a speech at the opening of parliament in 1383 and a similar speech by the speaker of the Commons in the parliament of 1382 ascribed the origins of the revolt to hostility against local officials which then mounted the rungs of the ladder of state to become an attack on its great officers:

These two well-informed men were prepared, in a moment of truth, to recognize that misgovernment by royal agents and the prevailing judicial abuses had reached alarming proportions. Manifestations of hatred towards the royal judges, the justices of the peace and, in general, towards all lawyers were a universal feature of the risings. . . . Clearly to understand the causes of the revolts we must learn much more about the malfunctioning of local government and justice in medieval England.[326]

324 Keen, *England in the Later Middle Ages*, 272.

325 Wilkinson, 'The Peasants' Revolt of 1381', 31 and 29-32 generally.

326 Fryde, introd. Oman, *The Great Revolt*, pp. xxviii-xxix, and ibid. 46, 58. Oman points out that the rebels at Canterbury acted against Sudbury as chancellor, not as archbishop; they sacked his palace, not the monastic buildings; ibid. 39. Cf. Dobson, *The Peasants' Revolt of 1381*, 23.

Criticism of royal justices, in the opinion of John Maddicott, had developed into outright and widespread antagonism by the 1370s; the conduct of the justices, and especially their link to the magnates who so regularly disturbed order, then became a major political issue for the great mass of people below the level of the judges and magnates themselves. If the Great Rising was provoked by wartime taxation, it also made special targets of lawyers, justices, and jurors. 'Both the words of rebels and their actions make it plain that what they wanted was a society free from corrupt justice, in which the poor and uninfluential could obtain their rights, and that they saw the removal of lawyers and justices as a necessary preliminary to the achievement of this Utopia.'[327] Maddicott rejects as unconvincing both the 'millenarian' and 'manorial' explanations of this hostility to the entire apparatus of the law:

> The central issue, the common denominator uniting all the rebels, was surely an intense dislike of corruption in the courts, a corruption which was as prevalent in the provincial sessions of the justices of the peace, assize and gaol delivery as in the central courts of King's Bench, Common Bench, Exchequer and Chancery, or in the private courts of lords. The concurrent attacks on false jurors, which were extremely common throughout the area affected by the rising, are more easily explicable in similar terms, as a part of a general resentment against the corrupt administration of the law, than as an attempt to pursue the millenium or throw off the burden of lordship.[328]

The rebels, according to the chronicler Walsingham, 'declared that the land could not be fully free until the lawyers had been killed.'[329] They attacked the Temple in London with double fury for it was both the symbolic headquarters of the lawyers of the realm and the symbolic base of the treasurer, Hales.[330] Perhaps a very long ancestry stands behind the well-known Shakespearian line given to a follower of Jack Cade, Dick the butcher of Ashford, in *Henry VI*, 'The first thing we do, let's kill all the lawyers.'[331]

[327] 'Law and Lordship', 47, 59-71; the quot. is from p. 61.

[328] Ibid. 63.

[329] Dobson, *The Peasants' Revolt of 1381*, 133. Maddicott cites other chronicles to the same effect, 'Law and Lordship', 62.

[330] Oman, *The Great Revolt*, 58. He cites a contemporary description of the flight of the lawyers: 'it was marvelous to see how even the most aged and infirm of them scrambled off, with the agility of rats or evil spirits'.

[331] *King Henry VI*, III. ii.

This may not sound very much like a reform programme, even if G. K. Chesterton described the vendetta against lawyers as 'a comprehensible and (relatively) even commendable course.'[332] Yet medieval men more often sought redress by replacing personnel than by altering major institutions; and often their ideas of the appropriate methods were none too gentle. In the *Tale of Gamelyn*, the solution to local corruption of justice is for a local hero to hang all the offenders on his own authority: the corrupt justice from Westminster, the corrupt sheriff, the corrupt jurors.[333]

For contemporaries the relationship between rebellion and the problems of justice, administration, and order was painfully clear. The poem *What Profits a Kingdom* contained in the Digby 102 collection of occasional complaint verse from *c.*1400, for example, notes the public ramifications of private illegality; misuse of the developed legal system may provoke rebellion. The poem suggests that righteous action by men in power is the only guarantee of peaceful order, the only cure for the legitimate grievances which inspired the rising of 1381. The poem *Love God and Drede* in this same collection contains the following admonitory line: 'And lawe be kept, no folk wyl ryse. . . .'[334] The matter was raised repeatedly in the parliaments following the rising. Petitions urged measures for an end to the retaining of justices by great lords, for more equitable justice and more equitable taxation; the Commons warned that if remedy were not found for excessive taxation and corrupted justice a new rising could be expected. In this sense, Maddicott argues, the effects of the Great Revolt (which may have been negligible as far as the fortunes of the governed are concerned) may have been quite powerful in shaping the political attitudes of the governors by fuelling the sense of a need for reform of a government which was widely considered corrupt and inefficient.[335] Thus, the revolt,

[332] Quot.: Prescott, 'London in the Peasants' Revolt, 133.

[333] Kaeuper, 'An Historian's Reading of *The Tale of Gamelyn*', 51-62.

[334] Quot.: Coleman, *Medieval Readers and Writers*, 100. The same sentiment, stated in almost the same words, appears in *What Profits a Kingdom:* 'And lawe be kept, folk nyl not ryse. / That kingdom shal have reste an pes.' (Ibid. 104.)

[335] Maddicott, 'Law and Lordship', 64 ff. See also the comments of Keen, *England in the Later Middle Ages*, 272, and Dobson, *The Peasants' Revolt of 1381*, 125.

like the popular literature of protest which was written both long before and long after it, gives evidence that the consequences of the over-extension and failures of the English government were keenly felt by a very large body of Englishmen.

Perhaps ordinary Englishmen were all the more likely to feel the political malaise because of the way in which political and social grievances were mutually reinforcing. In many ways the power of the English state fused these two categories which historians often strive to separate. Contemporary literature provides an illustration; many complaint poems blend themes modern scholars want to analyse separately as political, social, or religious.[336] The former two categories easily dissolve into one and even the latter is sometimes a common part of an undifferentiated disillusionment with those in authority. Likewise, the rebels of 1381 acted on the basis of the same generalized discontent with authorities below the level of the king himself. In view of their actions C. C. Dyer suspects that 'the rebels recognized the close connection between lordship and government, so that "political" and "social" grievances were linked in their minds.' They thus 'saw their enemies as part of a single system of corrupt authority.'[337] All those with hands on the reins of power were liable to vitriolic criticism poured out by authors who thought their world was going swiftly to hell, and many in positions of power witnessed the wrath of rebels as they attacked local exemplars of misgovernment or burned hated manorial records. In the eyes of subjects the crown was responsible not only for such explosive 'political' problems as the burden of taxation, but also for the equally explosive 'social' problems of regulating the supply and compensation of labourers. Historians have long noted this connection between the justices of labourers and the revolt. Significantly, the fury of revolt seems to have been most intense in the area for which we have evidence of the greatest efforts to enforce the labour laws. Though the crown resisted demands for desperate measures to ensure a labour supply at acceptable cost to landowners, the existing labour laws were retained and the existing records suggest an increasing number of labour cases in the decade before the revolt. When the rising

336 This theme is developed in Coleman, *Medieval Readers and Writers*, 60-2.

337 Dyer, 'The Social and Economic Background', 28.

came, the justices of the peace, who had intermittently enforced the labour legislation, were special targets; moreover, the rebels destroyed large numbers of the rolls recording enforcement of the hated laws.[338]

To a significant degree, then, the functioning of the precocious English government was itself the focus of the 1381 revolt; though the rebels accepted the framework of kingship (and may not have shared *en masse* the millenarian, egalitarian, or apocalyptic dreams of John Ball or Wat Tyler),[339] they seem deeply to have resented the obvious malfunctioning of the king's government, the painful gap between the ideal it professed and the actuality of its practice, not as some abstraction of political philosophy, but as a powerful force working in their daily lives.

In a curious fashion, however, this profound resentment may have helped to temper the revolt in England and to give it, at least in comparison with the Jacquerie, the relatively restrained characteristic so often noted. For the English rebels had a political outlet and could imagine a programme of action. Those in the south-east, at least, could march on London, confront the boy king, remove the traitors, secure the needed charters. Indeed, the absence of this outlet may have been one cause for the greater violence and incoherence of some of the English risings at a distance from London, such as that in western Norfolk characterized by André Reville as 'un immense et presque fantastique pillage'.[340] Such a focus or outlet did not exist in France in any comparable fashion, for crown claims and popular expectations of royal control were much slighter than in England. Thus the only outlet for the rage of the Jacques was an explosion of pillage, arson, and savage killing. Likewise, the presence or absence of such an outlet may have affected the denouements of revolt on either side of the Channel in 1358 and 1381. Many English rebels seem to have gone home after the march on London, the spectacular executions of 'traitors' on Tower Hill,

[338] Plucknett, introd., Putnam, *Proceedings*, p. xciii; Hilton, 'Peasant Movements in England Before 1381', 135; Putnam, *Enforcement*, 93-4; Fryde, introd., Oman, *The Great Revolt*, xviii-xix, xxxi-xxxiii.

[339] See the opinions of Maddicott, 'Law and Lordship', 63, and of Wilkinson, 'The Peasants' Revolt of 1381', 27, casting doubt on the likelihood that most rebels expected the millenium. Hilton argues against such doubts, *Bond Men Made Free*, 221-30.

[340] Reville, *Le Soulèvement*, 78. Cf. Oman, *The Great Revolt*, 99, 112-13.

and the royal concessions committed to parchment and wax after the Mile End meeting. Even the force still present at Smithfield was rendered harmless with surprising ease. But in the Jacquerie any vision of the final outcome of revolt must have been as obscure to the rebels as it has always seemed tragically inevitable to historians.

4. PUBLIC OPINION AND ROYAL ACTION

The movements for governmental reform, the literature of protest, and the great risings in England and France provide valuable evidence of popular dissatisfactions felt with varying degrees of intensity across a spectrum of social levels and regional differences. Trying to form general conclusions from this evidence involves all of the hazards and problems mentioned at the outset; but at least an approach to two basic questions should be possible: for both England and France we obviously want to consider who was objecting, by listening to literature of complaint and satire, by patronizing these works, by writing them, or (at a different level) by joining in a band of rebels. Likewise, we want to consider what crown policies or conditions linked to governmental actions were the object of widespread criticism. That these questions are obvious does not enable confident answers. That they can be notionally separated does not mean the questions do not overlap in analysis.

Lords, gentlemen, and leading townsmen tended to express similar discontents in regular meetings of the English parliament or in the more periodic meetings of French Estates. The wisdom of a war policy *per se* was not at issue, but rather its cost, and the proper expenditure and supervision of the war chests collected. Though the emphasis and expectations varied, both English and French assemblies also wanted less corrupt administrations, along with whatever law and order measures the crown could encourage. Though they could always be troublesome to the crown, as the English parliament proved to be regarding war finance from the very beginning of the Hundred Years War,[341] and could prove in times of crisis to be quite prickly, as in the

[341] Fryde, 'Parliament and the French War'.

English crises of 1341 or 1376,[342] or the French crises of 1347, 1356-8,[343] the members of these assemblies accepted the broad, existing framework of monarchical government in England and in France and showed no thought to remodel it. They basically wanted to make government more efficient and less corrupt, to make it live more closely in consonance with the guidelines of its own pronouncements and with common expectations. Their attitude toward the state and state officials had much in common with the outlook of ecclesiastical reformers toward the institutional church and churchmen in more than one age. But were these attitudes and criticisms regarding royal governance shared at social levels below that of the members who attended parliaments and Estates?

The social range of the literature of satire and complaint in fourteenth-century England is hardly self-evident. In the most recent treatment of the topic, Janet Coleman suggests that 'The literature of complaint does not . . . appear to be a literature of the "peasantry" at all, even when it deals with the poor ploughman.' She locates this literature rather in the ranks of 'urban merchants and guild members ranging from the rich to the relatively poor, country gentry ranging from those bearing arms to lesser squires and humble free tenant farmers.' A combination of increasing literacy and increasing government service produced in this 'middle class' a heightened sensitivity to complaint and criticism which took the royal government as its focus; the pressure to produce such works owes much to their experience and to their views.[344]

Yet even if we locate the great bulk of the literature of protest in the rather privileged and prosperous middling strata of society there are still a few windows through the wall which separates us from the views of the great mass of people below that social level. As Coleman notes, 'there is also a small but trenchant corpus of poetry written by lesser lights expressing a particular grievance against the practices of . . . a rising gentry and bourgeoisie, reminding the nouveaux riches of their origins amongst the poor . . .'.[345]

342 McKisack, *The Fourteenth Century*, 152-82, 384-97; Holmes, *The Good Parliament*.

343 Cazelles, *Société politique, noblesse et couronne*, 253-61; Henneman, *Royal Taxation in Fourteenth-century France* (1975), ch. 1.

344 Coleman, *Medieval Readers and Writers*, 64.

345 Ibid. 61.

Equally interesting is the corpus of outlaw tales and ballads, not always considered when the literature of complaint and satire is discussed; stories of Robin Hood and Gamelyn reflected broad views about legitimate authority and law in society, even while spinning a good yarn.[346] The numbers of people familiar with ballads of Robin Hood must have been vast, if the fourteenth-century moral strictures of Langland and the twentieth-century scholarly conclusions of R. B. Dobson and J. Taylor are accepted.[347] Most Englishmen, it would seem, enjoyed stories which implied that at least much of local order and authority was upside down and needed righting by outlaw heroes.

Something of the world of thought of the most ordinary Englishman can also be recovered in the style and content of the preaching which the Church thought effective in instructing them.[348] This preaching must have reached as truly popular an audience as can be imagined for fourteenth-century England. Though the sermons featured moralistic criticism which pointed out the failures of each social rank, the uncompromising scriptural passages and the powerful *exempla* of the preachers could furnish ample material for radical preachers like John Ball; and they likewise provide links with the 'dark sayings' embodied in the obscure vernacular letters which circulated at the time of the rising and in the text of *Piers Plowman* itself. As Dobson suggests, 'the correspondence reveals two essential characteristics of the author and his audience—a strong sense of personal identification with the ideal of a social brotherhood, and a deeply personal devotion to the most simple and literal truths of the Christian religion.'[349]

We would do well to take careful note of the blending of this powerfully simple Christian idealism into complaint with clear political and social thrust. However valiantly we may work at separating the poems into distinct political or social or religious categories, the types seem to have merged in the consciousness of writers who felt a powerful disenchantment with *all* the authorities who gave shape to contemporary life, whether manorial, ecclesiastical, or royal. The complaint conveys a brooding sense of

346 See above, ch. 4, pt. 2

347 Dobson and Taylor, *Rhymes of Robin Hood*.

348 Owst, *Literature and Pulpit in Medieval England*.

349 Dobson, *The Peasants' Revolt of 1381*, 380.

malaise, the conviction that those in charge (whatever their wands of office) were failing badly. The Czechoslovakian historian Frantisek Graus, writing of the Hussite revolt in particular, has suggested that the essence of a social crisis is a widespread perception that essential values and symbols are menaced. 'What is really important', he insists, 'is that *the people of those times* held those values to be vital and nevertheless menaced.' Though historians can identify various factors contributing to a crisis, 'for those who must live through it, there is the overall feeling that *everything* is in decline, and hence an effort must be made to restore the *whole*.'[350]

Perhaps the widespread feelings of unease in fourteenth-century England did not reach the depths Graus suggests for Bohemia in the century following; but something of the same phenomenon seems to be present. Justice undoubtedly ranked among the potent values of fourteenth-century society and the forceful satire and complaint against misuse or denial of justice show a sense of menace to a valued symbol. The crown role in providing justice formed no small piece in the pattern of discontent. Were the royal courts an acceptable agency for transforming violence into litigation? Should peaceful courtroom process replace the strongly felt right to violent self-help? Even the formally proclaimed standards of royal governance might be found wanting if measured against the idealistic standards derived from religious conviction: the actual practices of royal government missed by a country mile. The prevalence and the biting tone of so much fourteenth-century English satire, so often directed against corrupted justice and administration, suggest that many Englishmen felt the dilemma keenly.

When in each country discontent was spectacularly transformed into rebellion, what social levels and what mass of the populace were involved? Most historians now agree that the risings cannot be characterized simply as 'peasant revolts', but then confess that the exact composition of rebel forces remains elusive.[351] On both sides of the Channel some townsmen joined, as did some bailiffs and members of the gentry in England, some *prévôts* and

[350] Graus, 'The Crisis of the Middle Ages', 81-2.

[351] Ibid. 13; Hilton, *Bond Men Made Free*, ch. 7; Luce, *Histoire de la Jacquerie*, 63-4; Mollat and Wolff, *The Popular Revolutions of the Late Middle Ages*, 125. Cf. Prescott, 'London in the Peasants' Revolt'.

serjeants and even some lesser nobles in France. 'The most striking common characteristic of our sample of rebels [in four south-eastern counties of England], C. C. Dyer observes, 'is their prominent role in the government of their manor, village, or hundred, either at the time of the revolt or within a few years of 1381.' Thus he concisely suggests that 'leadership in the revolt was exercised by the village elite.'[352] Representatives of the lesser clergy were relatively prominent in both revolts and artisans and petty merchants may have been more prominent than agricultural workers *per se*.[353] Indeed, we cannot think of the English and French peasantry itself as a homogenous mass; even to separate this group simply into villeins and wealthier kulaks may be too crude.[354] Questions of composition may well turn on questions of definition. In France the Parisian rising shook the realm at the same time as the Jacquerie, and was surely related to some of the same problems, yet it basically ran a separate course. Although the Parisian rebels were not part of the Jacquerie, their rising is highly important to any assessment of widespread dissatisfaction. Londoners in some numbers supported the mass of English rebels who marched on the city and opened the city gates to them; yet R. H. Hilton prefers to think of the countrymen as the rebels and the Londoners as 'allies'; this distinction takes on importance if one is trying to discover what common aims the rebels held.[355]

Even if we could establish with confidence what social ranks were represented in the risings, there would remain the question of what part of the population in any or all of these ranks actually rebelled. Guy Fourquin notes that the Jacques numbered thousands if not tens of thousands; but he suggests that in a densely populated region of France this can only mean that most villagers did not revolt.[356] Our sense of numbers for the various areas of English revolt is certainly no more precise. Moreover, in both England and France the rebels' recruitment through compulsion

[352] Dyer, 'The Social and Economic Background', 8.

[353] For the Jacquerie this issue is carefully analysed by Raymond Cazelles, 'La Jacquerie: Fût-elle un mouvement paysan?'.

[354] Fourquin, *Les Soulèvements populaires au moyen âge*, 184.

[355] Hilton, *Bond Men Made Free*, ch. 8; Wilkinson, 'The Peasants' Revolt of 1381', 31-2. Cf. Prescott, 'London and the Peasants' Revolt'.

[356] Fourquin, *Les Soulèvements populaires au moyen âge*, 184.

complicates any attempt to determine what the numbers and social ranks mean for an analysis of anti-government sentiment. Letters of pardon granted to men of any status found among French or English rebels regularly record the claim that they were coerced; in some cases it may well have been true.[357] Force may also have recruited humbler rebels. According to several chroniclers, after he had gained the upper hand at the end of the Smithfield meeting, Richard II refused to allow any slaughter of the cowed rebels, asserting that many had come unwillingly, out of fear.[358] Richard's perception was translated into law: a statute allowed acquittal if four men swore the defendant had been compelled to join the rebellion.[359] Threats of reprisals—often the burning of the reluctant rebel's house, or of entire unco-operative villages—appear frequently in French sources.[360]

The evidence we have considered is characterized by gaps and problems of interpretation. Yet it allows us to see basic similarities and contrasts between criticism of crown action voiced in England and France. We may have underestimated the importance of popular opinion about government as it was shaped by crown action in an era of extensive warfare. In his study of French political society under John the Good and Charles V, Raymond Cazelles turns repeatedly to public opinion which he considers 'without doubt the most important element for understanding these reigns.'[361] Though it is a difficult element to capture, public opinion was evidently recognized as a factor of great importance by those who ruled or those who would rule; their estimation of its role appears in every placard nailed to a church door, in every sermon preached with a political message, in the paintings displayed as propaganda in the royal palace, in the ferocious executions of those holding traitorous views. Writing of England in the same era, John Maddicott has stressed the 'new awareness of the need to direct and control the attitudes of the localities.'[362] The fourteenth-century English government

[357] See for example Dobson, *The Peasants' Revolt of 1381*, 262.

[358] Walsingham and the Continuator of the 'Eulogium Historiarum' both give the king's opinion, ibid. 180, 208.

[359] Prescott, 'London in the Peasants' Revolt', 127, citing 6 Ric. II Stat 2 caps, 4-5 and examples of procedure under this statute in KB 27/487 m. 41d.; CP 40/495 m. 340.

[360] Luce, *Histoire de la Jacquerie*, 84-5, 1379.

[361] Cazelles, *Société politique, noblesse et couronne*, 3-4.

[362] Maddicott, 'The County Community', 35.

attempted to steer opinion by a stream of directives, information, and legislation sent from Westminster and insisted that sheriffs inform Chancery of the dates and places at which the material was proclaimed; the king and his advisers wanted to reach local audiences not only in the various county courts, but also in some 200 county towns across England. Maddicott suggests that local men, even those of no great social standing, were very well-informed about crown action and the means of seeking redress for grievances, and that beside them we should picture the professional lawyer who 'made his own contribution to the legal and political self-consciousness of the shires.' Thus 'the novelty in the fourteenth century lay . . . in the intensity of the government's efforts to influence opinion and in the activity in public affairs of a well-attended country court.'[363]

Yet if public opinion was increasingly important and vocal in both England and France and if the governments of both realms were aware of the need to shape opinion through a judicious mixture of propaganda and reform, the outcome nevertheless was different on either side of the Channel. The earlier and more forceful character of governmental reform in England, the existence of an English literature of protest and the divergent character of the revolts in the two countries show how profound the differences were. In England an earlier start to the process of state-building and the higher level of crown activity over centuries seem to have produced a more political society or rather a political society with royal governance more firmly at its centre. As we have seen, the objections of Englishmen, whether expressed in writing or in action, seem to cover the whole range of ambitious royal activity and to involve more people in more of the ranks of society in a direct way. If ancient social tensions were important in both countries, if the more recent strains of war led to charges of waste and corruption among the possessors of political and economic power, the social diffusion and the comprehensive quality of the criticism in England stands apart.

In France the first stirrings of effective governmental power in the twelfth century had sent shock waves of mixed hope and fear through the traditionally independent feudal lords and had helped to generate a literature which took up these very themes. By the

[363] Maddicott, 'The County Community', 38, 43.

fourteenth century the crises brought on largely by war showed that these issues connected with royal power could be a matter of periodic concern to an even wider body of Frenchmen, now including the townsmen and especially the politically sophisticated Parisians. The absence of a literature of protest similar to that in fourteenth-century England suggests, however, that the pressure of royal demands in France had not yet forced the crown into the forefront of men's vision, as had evidently occurred in England. The diffusion of political sensibility linked to the crown seems to have become more faint with each lower social stratum. The demands of the French crown, even in wartime, were still so regularly diffused to the great mass of villagers through the nobility that such political consciousness at this local level, across the vastness of France, seems to have been quite weak.

This situation in the second and third quarters of the fourteenth century could, however, produce surprisingly different results by the fifteenth century. The great fourteenth-century crises of both monarchies were closely linked with the war. But English discontent was focused on a monarchy which was clearly failing either to win the war it had launched or to carry out with real success its ambitiously claimed internal functions with regard to law and justice. By contrast, the French monarchy could simultaneously appear in the guise of victim and claim with some credibility to be the only hope for unity and victory. From the early fourteenth century it was acquiring administrative and judicial capacity and had even won loyalty occasionally expressed with some intensity of feeling.[364] Royal striving had not so outstripped royal achievement in France as to bring disillusionment which could cripple a major role for the crown in the recovery of the fifteenth century. Several historians have noted the paradox of early English royal capacity and her later limited form of government in comparison with early French royal weakness and her later absolutism.[365] The history of royal jurisdiction and of efforts to secure public order amply reinforces that paradox. The kings of France at the end of the Middle Ages

364 Strayer, 'Defense of the Realm'; id., 'France'.

365 The paradox in overall governmental development seems to have been noted first by J. R. Strayer in Strayer and Taylor, *Studies in Early French Taxation*, 94. J. P. Dawson suggested the point in a legal vein in *A History of Lay Judges*, 48. Recently Peter Lewis stated the paradox in terms similar to Strayer's in 'La Formation des états nationaux', 36.

were able to build on a theory of legal centralization which was just barely put into practice before the Hundred Years War but which was readily revived in the recovery of French unity based on monarchy which followed the war. The late medieval kings of England had, in a sense, to pay the price for the precocious legal development achieved by their twelfth- and thirteenth-century predecessors. Lordly appropriation of a large part of the royal jurisdiction, expanded beyond the capacity of the tiny corps of professionals, was well underway in England as the Hundred Years War began; this tendency was scarcely reversed in the last medieval century, nor for a long time thereafter. In the twelfth century Philip II looked enviously at the royal power and governmental machinery possessed by Henry II; he longed to govern in the English manner. After the fourteenth-century crises, however, the phenomenon of Jeanne d'Arc is much less surprising in a French than an English setting, and movement toward a limited monarchy was much more explicable in England. By the seventeenth century the shift was complete: Charles I would long to govern in the French mode.

5

Conclusion

By the thirteenth century the Western state was launched on its remarkable course as the agency defining and practising legitimate violence while working to suppress the illicit violence of private persons at every social rank within its boundaries. Across the previous several centuries the state had begun to establish this position as arbiter of questions of war, justice, and public order in European society; in the kingdoms of England and France it was acquiring something of its basic administrative structure and some of its most basic powers. Royal governments increasingly made good their claims to superior jurisdiction and provided courts of law which attracted an increasing volume of litigation. They augmented their revenues dramatically and (with different degrees of success) launched experiments in direct taxation. Combining feudal obligations with yet older notions of service and with the enabling medium of cash, they increased their military capacities significantly. Within the bounds of their respective realms they claimed a special responsibility (sometimes working indirectly) for the regulation of the violence of their subjects, noble and non-noble alike. Although Englishmen and Frenchmen kept their eyes on the kings' agents and their hands on their purses, they basically supported the massive growth of royal power which was such a feature of the twelfth and thirteenth centuries. The support of a large percentage of the growing number of those people whose opinions counted was, in fact, a necessary condition for this movement towards state power. The cry for reform, it is true, came from subjects interested in lowering costs and raising standards of administrative practice as often as from crown agents interested in efficiency; the exchange of views could, moreover, be hot-tempered and might bring parties in armour on to the field; but the role of the state as a major arbiter of disputes, an enactor and enforcer of laws, a leader in war, a dispenser of patronage—along with the rather generous range of powers which such roles required—was not in question by the late thirteenth century on either side of the Channel.

Yet within this broad framework of the growth of state powers, we must take into account the critically important differences in England and France. As we have seen repeatedly, the development of the state did not proceed at an equal pace on either side of the Channel. The existence of significant royal power and its sporadic growth were much more in evidence in England. By the twelfth century the heirs of Alfred the Great, Anglo-Saxon, Norman, and Angevin alike, worked within and built upon a powerful tradition of effective kingship; the Carolingian and early Capetian heirs of Charlemagne, by contrast, had to rebuild slowly and painstakingly, beginning with a very limited functional and geographical scope. Time and again the French monarchy appears to be behind the English monarchy in developing some characteristic aspect of state authority; as a rough rule of thumb we can consider it generally a century later. A system of public taxation reaches back to the eleventh-century geld in Anglo-Saxon England; the characteristic high medieval English form of percentage taxes on personal property appeared in the first half of the thirteenth century; in France the crown had to abandon the experiments of the late thirteenth century and could initiate public taxation only in the fourteenth century. After the middle of the twelfth century when the French crown sent out its first *baillis* in imitation of the English itinerant justices of Henry I and Henry II, it found that the more pressing need was for administrators with responsibility for local districts similar to the sheriffs in place in the shires of England since the tenth and eleventh centuries; the *baillis* had to be given territories and the role of itinerant commissioners went to the *enquêteurs* only in the mid-thirteenth century. In England the first major, widespread reaction to the dangers of governmental power came in the famous movement of 1215; the comparable French movement (though it took a provincial rather than a national character) came in 1314-15. Though the use of informal plaints or *querelae* appeared in both countries in the second half of the thirteenth century, it represented (in Alan Harding's phrase) a second stage of growth for English royal jurisdiction, in effect a first stage for French royal jurisdiction.[1] Even though we

[1] Harding, 'Plaints and Bills in the History of English Law, 65.

could find instances of chronologically parallel developments in the elaboration of the apparatus of the state, the important fact remains that much earlier and much more fully than in France the king's government in England acquired some degree of control over its subjects' lives, litigation, and purses. The precocious English government touched the lives of a wider range of people, affecting their lives more immediately and directly than was true of the French king in his realm. The English crown was thus a more major factor in English society than the French crown could be across the expanse of France. We can even detect something of a 'tight little island' feeling as early as the twelfth century, at least as far as governance is concerned. England was, as Maitland reminds us, 'a much governed land'.[2]

By the fourteenth century the growth of state power on both sides of the Channel and in particular the precocious capacity of the English state were factors of the greatest importance. Especially from the 1290s, the emphasis of the two most important among the emerging European states turned to war. Of course, war was an old companion of the state, an important part of its very *raison d'être*. But the warfare conducted by the kingdoms of England and France from the 1290s brought significantly new effects in its wake; these effects would appear both in the late medieval state and, more broadly, in late medieval society.

The very momentum of state development and the increased emphasis on warfare altered the state and the political society which sustained it. The late medieval state would not play the innovative role in society that had so characterized its actions across the High Middle Ages. Stated baldly, by the end of the thirteenth century the royal governments of England and France could not carry out all of their ambitious programmes nor reach the high goals they had so often proclaimed at the same time as they waged warfare on the scale they so wanted. The failure of royal administration was especially apparent in the related areas of justice and public order. Heavy involvement in war seems to have brought shifts in the centre of gravity of royal administrations, with the voices of those men devoted to war becoming predominant. As Raymond Cazelles suggests, 'La guerre . . . est la revanche des hommes de force physique, d'audace, voire de brutalité et de ruse, sur les hommes de droit,

[2] Maitland, *History of English Law*, i. 688.

de conseil, de procédure qui ont fourni une part important du personnel administratif de la royauté.'[3] Historians in medieval England might think of competing impulses within the men who governed rather than distinct, competing groups of 'hawks' and 'doves'. Yet in both kingdoms many non-military activities took distinctly second place to the voracious demands of war: the satisfactory resolution of disputes through courts of law with some claim to fairness, the definitions of illicit violence and some measure of control over its ravages (especially as practised by the privileged), the watchful reform of the oppressions and malfeasance so common among royal agents (particularly when they were hard pressed by the crown for funds to fill war chests). The kings of England and France had been known both for their innovative justice and their vigorous warfare across the twelfth and thirteenth centuries; in the fourteenth century their image as dispenser of justice by and large yielded to that of warrior. Given the finite amount of time, administrative talent, and treasure at the command of a fourteenth century administration, strained and over-extended even by its peacetime commitments, the enterprise of almost continuous warfare on a major scale could only reduce the attention to non-military concerns. Much of the formerly creative work of the state was thus reduced or badly mismanaged.

Both England and France show the change in the work of the state but it took different forms and produced significantly different results in the two realms. The French crown had developed its capacities in the area of justice and order less swiftly and less completely than the English crown. Nevertheless, from the efforts of Louis IX in the mid-thirteenth century to the more ambitious programme of Philip IV and his sons reaching into the first several decades of the fourteenth century, kings of France viewed with evident seriousness their responsibilities as agents of peace and order. The issue, of course, was royal power and prerogative as well as kingly responsibility: jurisdiction was both the symbol and the means of sovereignty. In fact, under Philip IV or Philip V the action of the French crown more closely than at any other time paralleled the sweeping efforts of royal administration in England. The subsoil of theory on which royal peace measures rested was basically similar in either realm: the king took on final

3 Cazelles, *Société politique, noblesse et couronne*, 14.

responsibility for the peace of the realm; his government provided courts and procedures either to act directly, as in England, or on appeal from lower jurisdictions, as in France. To the older category of felonies royal courts in both realms added the important new judicial action of trespass (including complaints against royal officials) brought by means of informal *querelae*. The social ranks which royal justice could reach were expanding significantly. Of course, kings in both countries used the stick as well as the carrot. Those who broke the king's peace might feel royal wrath, whether they had acted 'with force and arms and against the king's peace' (as in England) or 'with an open display of prohibited arms' (as in France). Though royal administration was a less intrusive force in daily life and concerns in France than in England, the activism of the late Capetians appeared excessive to the influential subjects who made their views quite clear in the movement of the leagues of 1314–15.

But this degree of similarity in the theory informing royal action in peace and justice was not matched by a similarity of kingly clout; within the relatively restricted space of his realm the English king exercised a much more direct and comprehensive jurisdiction than was within the capability of the French king across the vaster expanse of his realm. Moreover, the ambitious effort so apparent under Philip IV and Philip V diminished markedly in the reign of Charles IV and then was largely submerged by the tide of war which swept over France from the 1330s. By the early fourteenth century, then, the French administration, actively expanding the role of royal government in society and actively pursuing expensive war (persistent in Flanders, periodic in Aquitaine), made demands on its subjects which in their view outweighed the benefits it conferred. A few decades later the beginning of persistent English invasions blurred the distinction between the question of public order and the basic matter of public safety across wide stretches of the realm. For generations the judicial initiatives which St Louis had announced and which his grandson and great grandson tried to effect had to be put aside. Their Valois successors, insecurely seated on the throne and occupied above all with the recurrent threat of the English and their allies, could not carry the effort forward.

In England greater royal power magnified the problem and made it less straightforward. Close royal involvement in justice and public order first ironically complicated the state of public order and then slackened markedly in the period of extensive warfare culminating in the great war in France. Given its earlier development and the more powerful and pervasive role it had established in English society, more was expected of the king's government in England; in the area of justice, broadly defined, the crown had achieved much and claimed even more. The problem was that the gap between what was claimed and what could be achieved widened, or at least came to be more widely perceived. As the general eyre, the great workhorse of twelfth- and thirteenth-century royal justice, staggered and collapsed under the heavy load imposed on it by the crown and by an increasing number of litigants, royal experiments with *ad hoc* commissions of local men as replacements for the eyre produced mixed results. The problems arising from commissions of oyer and terminer give the clearest insights into the difficulties of a medieval government which had expanded its jurisdictional claims beyond its administrative capacities. Since the expansion of royal justice could not be managed by a parallel expansion of the small corps of professional justices on which the English had so long relied, the crown followed its administrative reflex and turned to local men, first as occasional justices and then increasingly as justices of the peace. Unfortunately, this localization of a good deal of judicial authority was no boon to public order, for men busily engaged in the struggle for local power quickly found the royal wand of office a convenient weapon to use on their opponents. An expanding judicial system, reaching down through the social strata and touching more peoples' lives operated with decreasing control from the centre. The prime attention of the crown was focused instead on the demands of war from the late years of Edward I. By the time of Edward III the direction of the English state was yet more closely set on war. To keep the ship of state on this course much of its former cargo had to be jettisoned. Across the entire fourteenth century, and with increasing volume by its end, voices of protest were raised against the miscarriage of royal justice and the strains of the war with France (by mid-century no longer masked by showy victories). English writers at various social levels created a literature of protest and directed a stream of vitriolic complaint at the gap between crown claims and demands and crown achievements. Complaint was transformed into action in 1381; war taxation ignited the Great Rising and the rebels took local officials and especially agents of local justice as their favourite targets. The central place of the crown in the aspirations and bitter disappointments of fourteenth-century Englishmen is clear. In Langland's *Piers Plowman* those concerned with the proposed marriage of Wrong to Lady Meed, who represents roughly the power of money, set off (Meed and her allies grotesquely mounted on sheriffs, jurymen, and the like, easily controlled by the silver bridles in their mouths) to ride to Westminster where they will present their problem before the king. The rebels of 1381 took the same route. Reliance on royal power and bitter resentment over its failures were opposite sides of the same coin in fourteenth-century England.

The contrast between English and French claims and capacities in justice and public order, as the royal administrations simultaneously advanced the business of war, had an important bearing on the constitutional histories of the two countries. Any mention of constitutionalism may raise fears about the introduction of Ideal Forms, political teleology, or notions of inherent national characteristics, all the legacy of nineteenth-century views. Yet questions of war, justice, and public order stand at the heart of what we might without apology call constitutional history, if we mean simply our analysis of the continuous consideration (sometimes conducted on the battlefield) of the respective rights and duties of kings and various social ranks of subjects operating within a broadly accepted but far from static framework of the state and law. This process came to a critical phase in the fourteenth century. No doubt the difficult setting of economic decline and demographic catastrophe was important, but the setting was common to both sides of the Channel and during this time of severe testing the political courses of England and France diverged more than ever before. To many modern historians and even to contemporary observers of these states, such as the English Chief Justice Sir John Fortescue (1385–1479?), the 'constitutionalism' of England contrasts sharply with the 'absolutism of France. If these terms have troubling connotations, we can still speak of the English concern to limit and control the action of the crown and the French tendency to exalt the monarchy and to emphasize its necessary role from the later Middle Ages.

Our evidence suggests that the constitutionalism evident in later medieval England, far from being the result of elusive traits of national character or of some yet more doubtful unfolding of providential will, represents the understandable reaction of English political society to a combination of royal over-extension and the high costs of war. In the eyes of most Englishmen whose views carried weight, royal government, if carefully watched, manipulated to the best of one's ability and now and again sharply rebuked, was worth the cost, as the history of parliament and the volume of litigation in royal law courts amply demonstrate. But enthusiasm for continued expansion of royal capacity cooled considerably as an over-extended crown failed to meet widespread expectations for public order and justice at the same time that it was failing to achieve a speedy conquest of France. In 1215, with a generous measure of control in their hands, the barons and the London bourgeoisie had demanded more, not less, crown action, even as they regulated it in particular ways. Such a confident endorsement of the central and growing role of the crown in English society could scarcely be imagined two hundred years later. The curious domestic result of English governmental precocity was a clear and widespread sense of the problems and liabilities which could accompany the growth of governmental power, especially when the machinery of state was geared for war.

In France the political problems came less from the over-reaching of royal activism than from uncertainties over the Valois succession to the throne and the significant political divisions existing within a large kingdom. If the enemy were to be expelled and an acceptable measure of order restored, the monarchy had to be strong. Thus, in French political consciousness 'the very misfortunes of France reinforced the image of the king as saviour of France.'[4] Nothing guaranteed the integrity of the territory of France as it had existed under the Capetian and early Valois kings, but the notion of a French realm had achieved some reality by the late thirteenth century and the king of France was the logical focus for a great many hopes. In contrast to the situation in England, French memories of royal oppressiveness or over-extension were too dim and too few to trouble the identity of king and realm at the close of the Hundred Years War.

4 Lewis, *Later Medieval France*, 80.

The emphasis on war and the tension between the goals of the state in peace and war affected society at large no less than they altered the focus and shaped the character of the state itself in England and France. The social effects of fourteenth-century war were particularly related to matters of scale and timing. By the late thirteenth century the considerable powers of the developed medieval state produced a capacity for war not duplicated since the height of the Roman Empire. The kings of England and France filled war-chests from the wealth of their prosperous realms (and kings of England even anticipated the income by means of elaborate credit mechanisms); they raised large armies with combinations of paid and volunteer troops and kept them in the field longer than their ancestors had dreamed possible. Large numbers of men were thus doing the traditional work of the medieval soldier over extended periods of time: looting and burning, bringing about 'the destruction of the means by which life is maintained.'[5] The expanded and extended scale of such military activities takes on all the more importance when viewed in the context of social and economic changes in north-western Europe. The thirteenth century had brought a rare respite of widespread peace to this region, at least as far as major campaigning is concerned.[6] Certainly both in England and across wide stretches of France generations grew up without witnessing warfare on a scale beyond local feuding. Of course, the entire period of the High Middle Ages had scarcely been free of the troubles of war; the late twelfth-century struggles of the kings of England and France, in fact, appear as scaled-down anticipations of their grander fourteenth-century efforts. Yet, as such generalizations go, the High Middle Ages was the time of flourishing of the medieval economy; the costs of raising troops and of paying for what they destroyed rested on an economy that most economic historians take to have been healthy. By contrast, the expanded scale of warfare in the fourteenth century operated within an economy that stood at considerably less than its peak; the destructive and disruptive effects of war between the great realms added its effects

[5] Hewitt, *Organization of War*, 93.

[6] The English campaigns in Wales in the last quarter of the thirteenth century are something of an exception to this generalization. But they might well be considered as the first signals of the more expanded warfare to come in the fourteenth century.

to economic depression and demographic crises (overpopulation and then the Plague).

In fact, it seems likely that nearly continuous, destructive, and highly costly warfare helped to create the late medieval depression. The attention which has been given to the profits and losses of individual war captains and the attempt to draw up a balance sheet for England may have diverted attention from this broader economic consequence of war. Though France obviously suffered more heavily and directly than England, the destructive and disruptive effects of war seem to have had a seriously negative impact on the economy of north-western Europe as a whole. In any long-range view such an effect looms larger than supposed changes in the quantity of bullion on one side of the Channel or the other, and even somewhat lessens the contrast usually drawn between ravaged France and England safe 'against . . . the hand of war'. In terms of the economy, the Anglo-French warfare produced no winner, but only a widespread zone within which losses were immediately experienced to a greater or lesser extent and eventually were felt by all.

The causation was, of course, complex. Given the vast social and economic transformations at work in north-western Europe in the fourteenth century we must be wary of the danger M. M. Postan pointed out of attributing to the war what would be attributed to the hundred years.[7] Historians possess no magnet to separate the metal from the non-metal. But surely the war and its social and economic setting were so fused that separation is, in fact, impossible. The task is not thus to find 'political' as opposed to economic forces, or to evaluate the weightiness of each with some spurious precision, but rather to see how these forces worked together to effect the transformation of European history brought about in the fourteenth century. If, as seems likely, war helped to usher in economic decline (even if it did not of itself cause it); if it helped to slow the growth of the medieval state and to alter its focus, then it must be considered among the major forces at work in late medieval Europe. The very human factor of war must be added to a list of such impersonal factors as the Black Death and demographic change, secular economic, or climactic changes.

[7] Postan, 'The Costs of the Hundred Years' War', 53.

Evaluating the effects of the great Anglo-French war on the economic life of north-western Europe is difficult, but it is harder still to reach an exact sense of how the kaleidoscopic changes in governmental activity in law and war affected the daily lives of people at various times and at various social levels. Did lords, gentlemen, townspeople and rural folk sleep more soundly in one decade or another because the action of the crown shielded them from fear of violence and injustice? Or did the king's wars and the heavy and heavy-handed demands of war finance actually multiply their fears for their bodies and goods? The modern historian, even when backed by the modern computer, can only realize how slim is the hope of answering such questions in a convincing manner; the evidence is too patchy, too intractable.

Yet we can observe lines of development which seem significant. Violence among the great mass of unprivileged men and women occupied much governmental attention, especially in England where the king's courts had direct jurisdiction over most categories of serious crime. But the proud violence of the social ranks who professed the code of chivalry may well have troubled the peace even more; this chivalric violence, however, long resisted the label of crime and the governmental repression that could accompany it. Thus, perhaps the most important factor for the public peace of each realm was not the prosecution of the crimes committed by people in the broad lower social strata but rather the attempt by the crown to reduce the violence practised by habit and by right among the privileged. This effort, which reached maximum force in the late thirteenth and early fourteenth centuries, was a new factor in the formula of public order. Stern royal justices hanging thieves in England may have been no more or less effective in securing public order than proud French possessors of their own gallows. But both the English and French crown did make a difference whenever they dampened the enthusiasm of lords and gentlemen who so often reached for their swords to settle quarrels in their own way. Royal success was not overwhelming: lawsuits at best accompanied rather than replaced violent self-help by the privileged across our period; yet even this transitional phase between an earlier era largely characterized by violent self-help and a subsequent era largely characterized by feuding sublimated into courtroom confrontations is worthy of notice. The effort was an important start to a characteristic feature of the Western state, its claim to a monopoly of licit violence. Of course, the great eagerness of the state to put this monopoly into action also led to the Anglo-French war which ground on across the later Middle Ages, changing so much in state and society.

In fact, the relationship between kingship and chivalry best reveals the complex and even contradictory impulses at work in the creation of medieval states. The knightly ethos, however much it civilized behaviour in certain categories of life, glorified direct and violent responses to any challenge to honour; it likewise reinforced in lords and gentlemen the knightly sense of legitimate possession of rights to dispense justice on their own, to act as the policemen of Christian society as the founding myth of chivalry (created with memories of an age of generally weak or absent kingship) pictured knights. Complexities were multiplied by royal acceptance and even enthusiastic royal participation in the chivalric life, which were much more pronounced in the late thirteenth and fourteenth centuries than in the preceding age. If knights celebrated their defence of honour through violence, and remembered their origins as kinglets, kings loved to be knights and depended on the knighthood of their realms for the warfare so close to their hearts. Yet their sense of mastery and every trace of Christian teaching on kingship lodged in their minds compelled kings to think about the public peace and to try to achieve some control over the open violence of the privileged ranks of warriors. In both England and France royal efforts along these lines reached a peak in the last decades of the thirteenth century and the early decades of the fourteenth century, but fell off decidedly with the exigencies of continuous Anglo-French war.

The medieval state and the code of chivalry were inextricably intertwined with questions of violence and order, of justice and war. Analysis of these major issues in fourteenth-century society does not yield a story of villains, nor any temptation to Dantean judgements; in fact, the story is rich in paradox and it is more than a little sad.

Bibliography

Actes du Parlement de Paris, 1st ser., 1254-1328, ed. E. Boutaric, 2 vols. (Paris, 1863-7) 2nd ser., 1328-1350, i (1328-1342) ed. Henri Furgeot (Paris, 1920; repr. Neudeln, Liechtenstein, 1977).

Adler, A., *Rückzug in epischer Parade* (Frankfurt, 1963).

D'Alauzier, L., 'Les Viguiers de Figeac du début du XIVe siècle au milieu du XVIe siéle', *Comité des travaux historiques et scientifiques, bulletin philologique et scientifique* (1963), 457-64.

Alexander, N., 'The Raid on Beaume's Manor, Shinfield, Berks, Good Friday 1347', *Berkshire Archaeological Journal*, 35 (1935), 144-53.

Allmand, C. T., 'The War and the Non-combatant', *The Hundred Years War*, ed. K. Fowler (London, 1971).

—— (ed.), *Society at War: The Experience of England and France During the Hundred Years War* (New York, 1973).

Altschul, M., *A Baronial Family in Medieval England: The Clares, 1217-1314* (Baltimore, 1965).

Artonne, A., *Le Mouvement de 1314 et les chartes provinciales de 1315* (Paris, 1912).

Aspin, I. S. T., *Anglo-Norman Political Songs* (Oxford, 1953).

Aston, T. H., 'Robin Hood', *Past and Present*, 20 (1961), 7-9.

L'Atlas des châteaux forts en France, ed. C.-L. Salch, J. Burnouf, and J.-F. Fino (Strasbourg, 1977).

L'Atlas des villes et villages fortifiés en France (moyen age), ed. J. Burnouf and P. Dollinger (Strasbourg, 1978).

Aubert, F., *Le Parlement de Paris de Philippe le Bel à Charles VII (1314-1422), son organisation* (Paris, 1886).

Auerbach, E. *Mimesis: The Representation of Reality in Western Literature*, tr. W. R. Trask (Princeton, 1953).

Autrand, F., and P. Contamine, 'La France et l'Angleterre: histoire politique et institutionelle, onzième-quinzième siècles', *Revue historique*, 531 (1979), 117-68.

Bailey, V., 'Crime, Criminal Justice, and Authority in England', *Bulletin of the Society for the Study of Labour History*, 40 (1980), 36-46.

Baker, R. L., 'The English Customs Service, 1307-1343', *Transactions of the American Philosophical Society*, NS, 51 (1961).

Barber, R., *The Knight and Chivalry* (London, 1974).

Barnie, J., *War in Medieval English Society: Social Values in the Hundred Years War, 1337-1399* (Ithaca, 1974).

Barrow, G. W. S., *Robert Bruce and the Community of the Realm of Scotland* (Berkeley, 1965).

Baudot, M., 'L'Éviction de Normandie des Evreux-Navarre', *Actes du colloque international de Cocheral; les cahiers vernonnais*, 4 (1964), 141-8.

Bautier, R.-H., 'Guillaume de Mussy: bailli, enquêteur royal, pannetier de France sous Philippe le Bel', *Bibliothèque de l'école des chartes*, 105 (1944), 64-98.

—— 'Recherches sur les routes de l'Europe médiévale', i, 'De Paris et des foires de Champagne à la Méditeranée par le Massif Central', *Comité des travaux historiques et scientifiques, bulletin philologique et historique* (1960), 99-143; ii, 'Le Grand axe routier est-ouest du Midi de la France d'Avignon à Toulouse', ibid. (1961), 277-308.

—— 'Recherches sur la chancellerie royale au temps de Philippe VI', *Bibliothèque de l'école des chartes*, 122 (1964), 89-176; 123 (1965), 313-459.

Beardwood, A., *Records of the Trial of Walter Langton, 1307-1312*, (Royal Historical Society, Camden Fourth Series, 6 (London, 1969).

—— 'The Trial of Walter Langton, Bishop of Litchfield, 1307-1312', *Transactions of the American Philosophical Society*, NS, 54 (1969).

Beaumanoir, P. de, *Coutumes de Beauvaisis*, ed. A. Salmon (Paris, 1899-1900).

Bellamy, J. G., 'The Coterel Gang: An Anatomy of a Band of Fourteenth-century Criminals', *English Historical Review*, 79 (1964), 698-717.

—— *The Law of Treason in England in the Later Middle Ages* (Cambridge, 1970).

—— *Crime and Public Order in England in the Later Middle Ages* (London, 1973).

Bender, K.-H., *König und Vassal: Untersuchungen zur Chanson de geste des XII Jahrhunderts* (Heidelberg, 1967).

Benson, L. D., 'The Alliterative *Morte Arthure* and Medieval Tragedy', *Tennessee Studies in Literature*, 11 (1966), 75-87.

Berben, H., 'Une Guerre économique au moyen âge: l'embargo sur l'exportation des laines anglaises (1270-1274)', *Études d'histoire dédiées à la mémoire d'Henri Pirenne* (Brussels, 1937).

Berman, H. J., *Law and Revolution: The Formation of the Western Legal Tradition* (Cambridge, Mass., 1983).

Beugnot, A. (ed.), *Les Olim ou registres des arrêts rendus par la cour du roi, sous les règnes de Saint Louis, de Philippe le Hardi, de Philippe le Bel, de Louis le Hutin et de Philippe le Long, publiés par le comte Beugnot*, 3 vols. in 4 pts. (Paris, 1839-48).

Bezzola, R., *Les Origines et la formation de la littérature courtoise en ocident*, 2 vols. (Paris, 1944).
—— 'De Roland à Raoul de Cambrai', *Mélanges Hoepffner* (Paris, 1949).
—— 'Á propos de la valeur littéraire des chansons féodales', *La Technique littéraire des chansons de geste* (Paris, 1959).
Billacois, F., 'Pour une enquête sur la criminalité dans la France d'ancien régime', *Annales*, 22 (1967), 340-9.
Birdsall, J. (tr.) and R. A. Newhall (ed.), *The Chronicle of Jean de Venette* (New York, 1953).
Bisson, T. N., *Assemblies and Representation in Languedoc in the Thirteenth Century* (Princeton, 1964).
Blaauw, W. H., *The Barons' War* (London, 1871).
Bloch, M., *Feudal Society*, tr. L. A. Manyon, 2 vols. (Chicago, 1961).
Bloch, R. H., *Medieval French Literature and Law* (Berkeley, 1977).
Bois, G., *Crise du féodalisme* (Paris, 1976).
—— 'Noblesse et crise des revenus seigneuriaux en France aux XIVe et XVe siècles: essai d'interprétation', *La Noblesse au moyen âge*, ed. P. Contamine (Paris, 1976).
Bongert, Y., *Recherches sur les cours laïques du Xe au XIIIe siècle* (Paris, 1949).
Bonnaud-Delamare, R., 'La Paix en Flandre pendant la première croisade', *Revue du Nord*, 39 (1957), 147-52.
—— 'Les Institutions de la paix en Aquitaine au XIe siècle', *Recueils de la société Jean Bodin*, 14 (1961), 415-87.
Borst, A., 'Knighthood in the High Middle Ages: Ideal and Reality', *Lordship and Community in Medieval Europe*, ed. F. L. Cheyette (New York, 1968), 180-91.
Bouguet, M., *et al.* (eds.), *Recueil des historiens des Gaules et de la France*, 24 vols. (Paris, 1738-1904).
Boussard, J., 'Les Mercenaires au XIIe siècle: Henri II Plantagenet et les origines de l'armée de métier', *Bulletin de l'école des chartes*, 106 (1945-6), 189-224.
—— *Le Gouvernement d'Henri II Plantagenet* (Paris, 1956).
—— 'Services féodaux, milices et mercenaires dans les armées, en France, aux Xe et XIe siècles', *Ordinamenti militari in Occidente nell'Alto Medioevo, settimane di studio del centro Italiano di studi sull'Alto Medioeveo*, 15 (Spoleto, 1968), 131-68.
Boutaric, E., *La France sous Philippe le Bel* (Paris, 1861).
Boutruche, R., La Crise d'une société; seigneurs et paysans du Bordelais pendant la guerre de cent ans (Paris, 1947).
—— 'La Dévastation des campagnes pendant la guerre de cent ans et la reconstruction agricole de la France', *Études historiques*, Publications de la faculté des lettres de l'université de Strasbourg, (Paris, 1947).

Bowsky, W. M., *A Medieval Italian Commune: Siena Under the Nine, 1287-1355* (Berkeley, 1981).
Boyle, L. E., 'The *Oculus Sacerdotis*, and some other Works of William of Pagula', *Transactions of the Royal Historical Society* 5th ser., 5 (1955), 81-110.
—— 'William of Pagula and the *Speculum Regis Edwardi III*', *Medieval Studies*, 32 (1970), 329-36.
Brandt, W., *The Shape of Medieval History* (New Haven, 1966).
Bridbury, A. R., *Historians and the Open Society* (London, 1972).
—— 'The Black Death', *Economic History Review*, 2nd ser., 26 (1973), 577-92.
—— 'The Hundred Years War: Costs and Profits', *Trade, Government, and Economy in Pre-industrial England*, ed. D. C. Coleman, and A. H. John (London, 1976).
—— 'Before the Black Death', *Economic History Review* 2nd ser., 30 (1977), 393-410.
Brock, E. (ed.), Alliterative Morte Arthure (1871; repr. London, 1961).
Brooks, N., 'The Development of Military Obligations in Eighth- and Ninth-century England', *England Before the Conquest, Studies in Primary Sources Presented to Dorothy Whitelock*, ed. P. Clemoes, and K. Hughes (Cambridge, 1971), 69-84.
Broome, D. M., 'The Ransom of John II, King of France, 1360-1370', *Camden Miscellany*, 3rd ser., 14 (1926).
Brown, E. A. R., 'Assemblies of French Towns in 1316: Some New Texts', *Speculum*, 46 (1971), 282-301.
—— 'Subsidy and Reform in 1321: The Accounts of Najac and the Policies of Philip V', *Traditio*, 27 (1971), 399-431.
—— '*Cessante Causa* and the Taxes of the Last Capetians: The Political Applications of a Philosophical Maxim', *Studia Gratiana*, 15 (1972), 565-87.
—— 'Customary Aids and Royal Fiscal Policy under Philip VI of Valois', *Traditio*, 30 (1974), 191-258.
—— 'Royal Salvation and Needs of State in Late Capetian France', *Order and Innovation in the Middle Ages*, ed. W. C. Jordan, B. McNab, and T. Ruiz (Princeton, 1976), 365-79.
—— The Tyranny of a Construct: Feudalism and Historians of Medieval Europe', *American Historical Review*, 79 (1979), 1063-88.
—— 'Corruption, Finance, and Reform', unpub. TS.
Brown, P., 'Society and the Supernatural', *Daedulus*, 104 (1975), 133-51.
Brown, R. A., *English Castles* (London, 1962).
Calendar of the Close Rolls, HMSO (1892-1954).
Calendar of the Fine Rolls, HMSO (1911-1913).
Calendar of the Patent Rolls, HMSO (1901-1909).

Calendar of Various Chancery Rolls (Supplementary Close Rolls, Welsh Rolls, Scutage Rolls), 1277-1326 (London, 1912).

Calin, W. C., *The Old French Epic of Revolt* (Paris, 1962).

Cam, H., *Studies in the Hundred Rolls: Some Aspects of Thirteenth-century Administration* (Oxford, 1921).

—— 'The General Eyres of 1329-1330', *English Historical Review*, 39 (1924), 241-52.

—— *The Hundred and the Hundred Rolls* (London, 1963).

Campbell, J., 'England, Scotland, and the Hundred Years War in the Fourteenth Century', *Europe in the Later Middle Ages*, ed. J. R. Hale *et al.* (London, 1965).

—— 'Observations on English Government from the Tenth to the Twelfth Century', *Transactions of the Royal Historical Society*, 5th ser., 25 (1975), 39-54.

—— (ed.), *The Anglo Saxons* (Ithaca, 1982).

Capua, J. V., 'The Early History of Martial Law in England from the Fourteenth Century to the Petition of Right', *Cambridge Law Journal*, 36 (1977), 152-73.

Carbasse, J.-M., 'Le Duel judiciare dans les costumes méridionales, *Annales du Midi*, 87 (1975).

Carolus-Barré, L., 'Benoit XII et la mission charitable de Bertrand Carit dans les pays dévastés du nord de la France, Cambrésis, Vermandois, Thiérache, 1340', *Mélanges d'archéologie et d'histoire* (1950), 165-232.

—— 'L'Organisation de la jurisdiction gracieuse à Paris, dans le dernier tiers du XIIIe siècle: l'officialité et le châtelet', *Moyen âge*, 69 (1963), 417-35.

—— 'La Grand ordonnance de réformation de 1254', *Académie des inscriptions et belles-lettres, comptes rendus* (1973), 181-6.

—— 'La Grand ordonnance de 1254 sur la réforme de l'administration et la police du royaume', *Septième centenaire de la mort de Saint Louis* (Paris, 1976).

Carpenter, D. A., 'The Decline of the Curial Sheriff in England, 1194-1258', *English Historical Review*, 91 (1976), 1-32.

Carreau, M.-E., 'Les Commissaires royaux aux amortissements et aux nouveaux acquêts sous les capétiens, 1275-1328', *École des chartes, positions des thèses* (1953), 19-22.

Carus-Wilson, E. M. and O. Coleman, *England's Export Trade 1275-1547* (Oxford, 1963).

Castelnau, J., *Étienne Marcel: une révolutionnaire au XIVe siècle* (Paris, 1973).

Cazelles, R., *La Société politique et la crise de la royauté sous Philippe de Valois* (Paris, 1958).

—— 'Le Parti navarrais jusqu'à la mort d'Étienne Marcel', *Bulletin philologique et historique* (1960), 839-69.

Cazelles, R., 'Quelques réflexions à propos des mutations de la monnaie royale française', 1295-1360', *Moyen âge*, 72 (1966), 83-105, 251-78.

—— 'La Réglementation royale de la guerre privée de Saint Louis à Charles V et la précarité des ordonnances', *Revue historique de droit française*, 4th ser., 38 (1960), 530-48.

—— 'Les Mouvements révolutionnaires du milieu du XIVᵉ siècle et le cycle de l'action politique', *Revue historique*, 228 (1962), 279-312.

—— 'Une exigence de l'opinion depuis Saint Louis: la réformation du royaume', *Société de l'histoire de France, bulletin* (1962-3), 91-9.

—— 'Un problème d'évolution et d'intégration: les grands officiers de la couronne de France dans l'administration nouvelle au moyen âge', *Fondazione Italiana per la storia administrativa, Annali* (1964), 183-9.

—— 'La Peste de 1348-1349 en Langue d'oïl: épidémie prolétarienne et enfantine', *Comité des travaux historiques et scientifiques, bulletin philologique et scientifique* (1965), 293-305.

—— 'Jean II le Bon: quel homme? quel roi?', *Revue historique*, 251 (1974), 5-26.

—— 'La Stabilisation de la monnaie par la création du franc (décembre 1360)—blocage d'une société', *Traditio*, 32 (1976), 293-311.

—— 'La Jacquerie: Fût-elle un mouvement paysan?', *Académie des inscriptions et belles-lettres, comptes rendus* (Paris, 1979), 654-66.

—— 'La Jacquerie', *The English Rising of 1381*, Past and Present Conference (1981).

—— *Société politique, noblesse et couronne sous Jean le Bon et Charles V* (Geneva and Paris, 1982).

Chaplais, P., 'Un message de Jean de Fiennes à Edouard II et le projet de démembrement du royaume de France (janvier 1317)', *Revue du Nord*, 43 (1961), 145-8.

—— 'La Souveraineté du roi de France et le pouvoir législatif en Guyenne au début du XIVᵉ siècle', *Moyen âge*, 69 (1963), 449-69.

Chenu, M.-D., *Nature, Man, and Society in the Twelfth Century* Chicago, 1968).

Cheyette, F., 'Suum cuique tribuere', *French Historical Studies*, 6 (1967), 287-99.

Chotzen, T. M., 'Welsh History in the Continuation of the "Spiegel Historiael" by Lodewijk Van Velthem', *Bulletin of the Board of Celtic Studies*, 7 (1933), 42-54.

The Chronicle of Jean de Venette, tr. J. Birdsall and ed. R. A. Newhall (New York, 1953).

Chronicon Galfridi le Baker, ed. E. M. Thompson (Oxford, 1889).

Chronique de Jean le Bel, ed. J. Viard and E. Déprez, 2 vols. (Paris, 1905).

Chronique des quatre premiers valois (1327-1393) ed. S. Luce (Paris, 1867; rep. New York, 1965).

Cipolla, C. M., 'Economic Depression of the Renaissance?', *Economic History Review*, 2nd ser., 16 (1963-4), 519-24.
—— (ed.), *The Fontana Economic History of Europe: The Middle Ages* (London, 1972).
Clanchy, M. T., 'Law, Government, and Society in Medieval England', *History*, NS, 59 (1974), 73-8.
Clark, G., *War and Society in the 17th Century* (Cambridge, 1958).
Cohen, E., 'Patterns of Crime in Fourteenth-century Paris', *French Historical Studies*, 11 (1980), 307-27.
Coleman, J., *Medieval Readers and Writers, 1350-1400* (New York, 1981).
Colvin, H. M. (gen. ed.), *The History of the King's Works*, i-ii, *The Middle Ages*, ed. R. Allen Brown, H. M. Colvin, and A. J. Taylor (London, 1963).
Constant, M., 'La Justice dans une châtellenie savoyarde au moyen âge: Allinges-Thonon', *Revue historique de droit français*, 4th ser., 50 (1972), 374-97.
Contamine, P., 'Batailles, bannières, compagnies: aspects de l'organisation militaire française pendant la première partie de la guerre de cent ans', *Actes du colloque international de Cocherel, les cahiers vernonnais*, 4 (1964), 19-32.
—— *Guerre, état, et société* (Paris, 1972).
—— La Guerre de cent ans en France: une approche économique', *Bulletin of the Institute of Historical Research*, 47 (1974), 125-49.
—— (ed.), *La Noblesse au moyen âge, XIe-XVe siècles: essais à la mémoire de Robert Boutruche* (Paris, 1976).
—— 'De la puissance aux privilèges: doléances de la noblesse française envers la monarchie aux XIVe et XVe siècles', in: *La Noblesse au moyen âge*, ed. P. Contamine (Paris, 1976), 237-50.
—— 'Consommation et demande militaire en France et Angleterre, XIIIe-XVe siècles', *Instituto internazionale di storia economica F. Datini: atti della sesta settimana di Studio (27 Aprile-3 Maggio, 1974)* (1978).
—— La Guerre au moyen âge (Paris, 1980).
Coss, R. R. 'Sir Geoffrey de Langley and the Crisis of the Knightly Class in Thirteenth-century England', *Past and Present*, 68 (1975).
Coulson, C. H., 'Seignorial Fortresses in France in Relation to Public Policy: c.864 to c.1483', Ph.D. thesis (London, 1972).
—— 'Rendability and Castellation in Medieval France', *Château gaillard*, 6 (1973), 59-67.
Coupland, G. W., 'Crime and Punishment in Paris: September 6, 1389 to May 18, 1392', *Medieval and Middle Eastern Studies in Honor of Aziz S. Atiya*, ed. S. A. Hanna (Leiden, 1974), 64-85.
Cowdrey, H. E. J., 'The Peace and the Truce of God in the Eleventh Century', *Past and Present*, 46 (1970), 42-67.

Crook, D., 'The Later Eyres', *English Historical Review*, 283 (1982), 241-68.

Crossland, J., *The Old French Epic* (Oxford, 1951).

Cutler, S. H., *The Law of Treason and Treason Trials in Later Medieval France* (Cambridge, 1981).

Cuttino, G. P., 'Medieval Parliament Reinterpreted', *Speculum*, 41 (1966), 681-7.

Davies, J. C., *The Baronial Opposition to Edward II* (Cambridge, 1918).

Davies, R. G., and J. H. Denton (eds.), *The English Parliament in the Middle Ages* (Philadelphia, 1981).

Davies, R. R., 'The Survival of the Bloodfeud in Medieval Wales', *History*, 54 (1969), 338-57.

—— 'Kings, Lords, and Liberties in the March of Wales, 1066-1272', *Transactions of the Royal Historical Society*, 5th ser., 29 (1979), 41-61.

Davis, R. H. C., *King Stephen* (Berkeley), 1967).

Dawson, J. P., *A History of Lay Judges* (Cambridge, Mass., 1960).

Déclareuil, J., *Histoire générale du droit français des origines à 1789* (Paris, 1925).

Délachanel, R., *Histoire de Charles V (1338-1358)*, 3 vols. (Paris, 1909-16).

Delatouche, R., 'La Crise du XIVe siècle en Europe occidentale', *Les Études sociales*, NS, 42-3 (1959), 1-55.

Denholm-Young, N., 'Feudal Society in the Thirteenth Century: The Knights', *History*, 29 (1944), 107-19.

—— 'The Tournament in the Thirteenth Century', *Studies in Medieval History Presented to Frederick Maurice Powicke*, ed. R. W. Hunt, W. H. Pantin, and R. W. Southern (Oxford, 1948).

—— *The Country Gentry in the Fourteenth Century, with Special Reference to the Heraldic Rolls of Arms* (Oxford, 1969).

Denifle, H., *La Désolation des églises, monastères, et hôpitaux en France pendant la guerre de cent ans*, 2 vols. (Paris, 1897, 1899).

Deprez, E., *Les Préliminaires de la guerre de cent ans: la papauté, la France, et l'Angleterre (1328-1342)* (Paris, 1902; repr. Geneva, 1975).

—— 'La double trahison de Godefroi de Harcourt (1346-1347)', *Revue historique*, 99 (1908), 32-4.

Dobson, R. B., *The Peasants' Revolt of 1381* (London, 1970).

Dobson, R. B., and J. Taylor, 'The Medieval Origins of the Robin Hood Legend: A Reassessment', *Journal of Northern History*, 7 (1972), 1-30.

—— *Rhymes of Robyn Hood: An Introduction to the English Outlaw* (London, 1976).

Dossat, Y., 'Un viguier de Toulouse au début de XIVe siècle: Philippe de Fontanes (1303-1310), *Comité des travaux historiques et scientifiques, bulletin philologique et scientifique 1971* (1978), 627-43.

Douglas, D. C., *William the Conqueror* (London, 1964).

Dubois, P., *Les Asseurements au* XIIIe *siècle dans nos villes du Nord* (Paris, 1900).

DuBoulay, F. R. H., 'Law Enforcement in Medieval Germany', *History*, 63 (1978), 345-55.

Duby, G., 'Les Laics et la Paix de Dieu', *I laici nella 'Societas Christiana' dei secoli* XIe *e* XIIe *: Atti della terza settimana internationale de studi della Mendola* (Milan, 1966), 548-81.

—— 'Medieval Agriculture, 900-1500', in: *The Fontana Economic History of Europe: The Middle Ages*, ed. C. M. Cipolla (London, 1972).

—— 'Guerre et société dans l'Europe féodale: la guerre et l'argent', *Concetto storia, miti, e immagini del Medio Evo, atti del XIV corso internazionale d'alta cultura*, ed. V. Brance (Florence, 1973).

—— 'The Evolution of Judicial Institutions: Burgundy in the Tenth and Eleventh Centuries', *The Chivalrous Society*, tr. C. Postan (Berkeley, 1977), 15-58.

—— 'Laity and the Peace of God', tr. C. Postan, *The Chivalrous Society* (Berkeley, 1977), 123-33.

—— 'Les Origines de la chevalerie', *Ordinamenti militari in Occidente nell'Alto Medioevo*, ii (Spoleto, 1968); tr. C. Postan, 'The Origins of Knighthood', *The Chivalrous Society* (Berkeley, 1977), 158-70.

Du Cange, C. D., *Glossarium ad scriptores mediae et infirmae latinitatis*, ed. G. A. L. Henschel, vol. x (Paris, 1887).

Ducoudray, G., *Les Origines du Parlement de Paris et la justice aux* XIIIe *et* XIVe *siècles* (Paris, 1902).

Dufayard, C., 'La Réaction féodale sous les fils de Philippe le Bel', *Revue historique*, 54 (1894), 241-72; 55 (1895), 241-90.

Dupont-Ferrier, G., 'Le Rôle des commissaires royaux dans le gouvernement de la France spécialement du XIVe and XVe siècle', *Mélanges Paul Fournier* (Paris 1929), 1-13.

Dyer, C. C., 'The Social and Economic Background to the Rural Revolt of 1381', *The English Rising of 1381*, Past and Present Conference, London, (1981).

Edwards, J. G., '*Confirmatio Cartarum* and Baronial Grievances in 1297', *English Historical Review*, 58 (1943), 147-69, 273-300.

—— 'Edward I's Castle-building in Wales', *Proceedings of the British Academy*, 32 (1946), 17-81.

—— *William Stubbs*, Historical Association (1952).

—— 'The Normans and the Welsh March', *Proceedings of the British Academy*, 42 (1956), 155-77.

—— *Historians and the Medieval English Parliament* (Glasgow, 1960).

Ehrlich, L., *Proceedings Against the Crown (1216-1377)* (Oxford, 1921).

Faith, R. J., 'The "Great Rumour" of 1377 and Peasant Ideology', *The English Rising of 1381*, Past and Present Conference (1981).
Faral, E., 'Robert le Coq et les États-Généraux d'octobre 1356', *Revue historique de droit français et étranger*, 23 (1945), 171-214.
—— 'Le Procès d'Enguerran IV de Couci', *Revue historique de droit français et étranger*, 26 (1948), 213-58.
Favier, J., 'Enguerran de Marigny et la Flandre', *Revue du Nord*, 39 (1957), 5-20.
—— *Un conseiller de Philippe le Bel: Enguerran de Marigny* (Paris, 1963).
—— 'Les Portraits d'Enguerran de Marigny', *Annales de Normandie*, 15 (1965), 517-24.
—— Les Légistes et le gouvernement de Philippe le Bel', *Journal des savants* (1969), 92-108.
—— 'Les Finances de Saint Louis', *Septième centenaire de la mort de Saint Louis* (Paris, 1976).
—— *Philippe le Bel* (Paris, 1978).
Favreau, R., 'Comptes de la sénéchausée de Saintonge (1360-1362)', *Bibliothèque de l'école des chartes*, 117 (1959), 73-88.
Fawtier, R., 'Parlement d'Angleterre et États-Généraux de France au moyen âge', *Académie des inscriptions et belles-lettres, Paris, comptes rendus* (1953), 275-84.
—— 'Comment le roi de France, au début du XIVe siècle, pouvait-il se réprésenter son royaume?', *Mélanges offerts à Paul E. Martin, Société d'histoire et d'archéologie de Genève*, 40 (1961), 65-77.
—— *The Capetian Kings of France*, tr. L. Butler and R. J. Adam (London, 1962).
—— and F. Lot, *Le Premier Budget de la monarchie française* (Paris, 1932).
—— and —— *Histoire des institutions françaises au moyen âge*, 3 vols. (Paris, 1958-62).
Fedou, R., *Les Hommes de loi lyonnais à la fin du moyen âge* (Paris, 1964).
—— 'Les sergents à Lyon aux XIVe et XVe siècles: une institution—un type social', *Comité des travaux historiques et scientifiques, bulletin philologique et historique* (1964), 283-92.
—— *L'État au moyen âge* (Paris, 1971).
Fesler, J. W., 'French Field Administration: The Beginnings', *Comparative Studies in Society and History*, 5 (1962-3), 76-111.
Fietier, R., 'Le Choix des baillis et sénéchaux aux XIIIe et XIVe siècles (1250-1350)', *Société pour l'histoire du droit et des institutions des anciens bourguignons, comtois, et romands, mémoires*, 29 (1968-9), 255-74.

Finlayson, J., *Morte Arthure* (Evanston, Illi., 1967).

Flammermont, J., 'La Jacquerie en Beauvaisis', *Revue historique*, 9 (1879), 123-43.

Fliche, A., *La Réforme grégorienne* (Paris, 1946).

Fontaine, F. de, 'Revue des recueils périodiques', *Revue des questions historiques*, 42 (1887).

Fortescue, J., *The Governance of England*, ed. C. Plummer (Oxford, 1926).

Foss, E., *The Judges of England*, 9 vols. (London, 1848-64).

Fossier, R., *Histoire sociale de l'occident médieval* (Paris, 1970).

—— 'Fortunes et infortunes paysannes au Cambrésis à la fin du XIIIe siècle', *Économies et sociétés au moyen âge, mélanges offerts à Edouard Perroy* (Paris, 1973).

Fournial, É., 'Enquêteurs, réformateurs, et visiteurs généraux dans le comté de Dorez au XIVe siècle', *Bulletin de la Diana*, 36 (1959), 22-35.

—— 'L'Indexation des créances et des rentes au XIVe siècle (Forez, Lyonnais, et Dauphine)', *Moyen âge*, 69 (1963), 583-96.

Fournier, G., *Le Château dans la France médiévale* (Paris, 1978).

Fourquin, G., *Les Campagnes de la région parisienne à la fin du moyen âge du milieu de XIIIe siècle au début du XVI siècle* (Paris, 1964).

—— *Les Soulèvements populaires au moyen âge* (Paris, 1972).

Fowler, G. H. (ed.), *Quarto Memoirs of the Bedfordshire Historical Record Society*, iii, *Rolls from the Office of the Sheriff of Bedfordshire and Buckinghamshire, 1322-1334* (1929).

Fowler, K., 'Les Finances et la discipline dans les armées anglaises en France au XIVe siècle', *Cahiers vernonnais*, 4 (1965), 55-84.

—— (ed.), *The Hundred Years War* (London, 1972).

Frappier, J., 'Réflexions sur les rapports des chansons de geste et de l'histoire', *Zeitschrift für Romanische Philologie*, 73 (1957), 1-19.

French, W. H., and C. B. Hale (eds.), *Middle English Metrical Romances*, 2 vols. (New York, 1964).

Fryde, E. B. (ed.), *Book of Prests of the King's Wardrobe for 1294-5, presented to John Goronwy Edwards* (Oxford, 1962).

—— 'Materials for the Study of Edward III's Credit Operations, 1327-1348', *Bulletin of the Institute of Historical Research*, 22 (1949), 105-38; 23 (1950), 1-30.

—— 'Loans to the English Crown, 1328-1331', *English Historical Review*, 70 (1955), 198-211.

—— 'Edward III's Wool Monopoly of 1336: A Fourteenth-century Royal Trading Venture', *History*, NS, 37 (1957), 8-24.

—— 'The English Farmers of the Customs, 1343-1351', *Transactions of the Royal Historical Society*, 5th ser., 9 (1959), 1-17.

Fryde, E. B. (ed.), 'The Last Trials of Sir William de la Pole', *Economic History Review*, 2nd ser., 15 (1962-3), 17-30.
—— *The Wool Accounts of William de la Pole*, Borthwick Institute of Historical Research, St Anthony's Hall Publications, No. 25 (York, 1964).
—— 'Financial Resources of Edward I in the Netherlands, 1294-1298: Main Problems and Some Comparisons with Edward III in 1337-1340', *Revue belge de philologie et d'histoire*, 40 (1962), 1168-87; 45 (1967), 1142-216.
—— 'The English Parliament and the Peasants' Revolt of 1381', *Liber Memorialis George De Lagarde* (Louvain, 1968).
—— 'Parliament and the French War', in: *Historical Studies of the English Parliament*, ed. E. B. Fryde and E. Miller, 2 vols. (Cambridge, 1970), i. 247-63.
—— 'Financial Policies of the Royal Governments and Popular Resistance to Them in France and England c.1270-c.1420', *Revue belge de philologie et d'histoire*, 57 (1979), 824-60.
—— *The Great Revolt of 1381*, Historical Association (London, 1981).
—— and M. M. Fryde, 'Public Credit, with Special Reference to North-western Europe', *Cambridge Economic History of Europe*, III, ed. M. M. Postan, E. E. Rich, and E. Miller (Cambridge, 1963), 430-553.
—— and E. Miller, *Historical Studies of the English Parliament* 2 vols. (Cambridge, 1970).
Fryde, N. 'Edward III's Removal of his Ministers and Judges, 1340-1341', *Bulletin of the Institute of Historical Research*, 48 (1975), 149-61.
—— 'Antonio Pessagno of Genoa, King's Merchant of Edward II of England', *Studia in memoria di Federigo Melis*, ii (Naples, 1978), 159-78.
—— *The Tyranny and Fall of Edward II, 1321-1326* (Cambridge, 1979).
Funck-Brentano, F., 'Document pour servir à l'histoire des relations de la France avec l'Angleterre et l'Allemagne sous le règne de Philippe de Bel', *Revue historique*, 39 (1888), 5-40, 238-53.
Galbert of Bruges, *The Murder of Charles the Good*, tr. and ed. J. B. Ross (New York, 1967).
Galbraith, V. H., 'Good Kings and Bad Kings in Medieval English History', *History*, 30 (1945), 119-32.
Gallancz, I. (ed.), *Wynnere and Wastoure* (Oxford, 1921; repr. Cambridge, 1974).
Gardelles, J., *Les Châteaux du moyen âge dans la France du sud-ouest: la Gascogne anglaise de 1216 à 1327* (Geneva, 1972).
Gardner, J. (ed.), *The Alliterative 'Morte Arthure'*, (Carbondale, Ill., 1971).

Gaudemet, J., Le rôle de la papauté dans le règlement des conflits entre états aux XIIIe et XIVe siècles', *Recueils société Jean Bodin*, 15 (1961), 79-106.

Genicot, L., 'Crisis: From the Middle Ages to Modern Times', *Cambridge Economic History of Europe*, ed. M. M. Postan, 2nd edn. (Cambridge, 1966), i. 660-741.

Geremek, B., 'La Lutte contre le vagabondage à Paris', *Ricerche storiche ed economiche in memoria di Corrado Barbagallo*, 3 vols. (Naples, 1970), ii. 213-36.

—— *Les Marginaux parisiens aux XIVe et XVe siècles*, tr. D. Beuvois (Paris, 1976).

Gillingham, J., 'Richard I and the Science of War in the Middle Ages', *War and Government in the Middle Ages*, ed. J. Gillingham and J. C. Holt (Cambridge, 1984).

Giraldus Cambrensis Opera, ed. J. S. Brewer, 8 vols. (London, 1861-91).

Given, J. B., *Society and Homicide in Thirteenth-century England* (Stanford, 1977).

Glasson, E., *Histoire du droit et des institutions politiques, civiles, et judiciaires de l'Angleterre comparés au droit et aux institutions de la France depuis leur origine jusqu'à nos jours*, 6 vols. (Paris, 1882).

Glénisson, J., 'Les Enquêteurs-réformateurs de 1270 à 1328', *École des chartes, positions des thèses* (1946), 81-8.

—— 'Les Enquêtes administratives en Europe occidentale aux XIIIe et XIVe siècles', *Beihefte der Francia*, 9 (1950).

Gollancz, M. (ed.), *Rolls of Northamptonshire Sessions of the Peace: Roll of the Supervisors, 1314-1316, Roll of the Keepers of the Peace, 1320*, Northamptonshire Record Society, (1940).

Göller, K.-H. (ed.), *The Alliterative Morte Arthure: A Reassessment of the Poem* (Bury St Edmunds, 1981).

Goodman, A., *A History of England from Edward II to James I* (London, 1977).

Grabois, A., 'Le Privilège de croisade et la régence de Suger', *Revue historique du droit français et étranger*, 62 (1964), 458-64.

—— 'De la trêve de Dieu à la paix du roi: étude sur les transformations du mouvement de la paix au XIIe siècle', *Mélanges offert à René Crozet*, ed., P. Gallais and Y. J. Riou, 2 vols. (Poitiers, 1966).

Gras, N. S. B., *The Early English Customs System* (Cambridge, Mass., 1918).

Graus, F., 'The Crisis of the Middle Ages and the Hussites', tr. J. Heaney, in: *The Reformation in Medieval Perspective*, ed. S. E. Ozment (Chicago, 1971).

Green, J. A., 'The Last Century of Danegeld', *English Historical Review*, 96 (1981), 241-58.

Griffiths, Q., 'Les Origines et la carrière de Pierre de Fontaines, jurisconsulte de Saint Louis (une reconsideration avec documents inédits)', *Revue historique de droit français*, 4th ser., 48 (1970), 544-67.

Guenée, 'La géographie administrative de la France à la fin du moyen âge: élections et bailliages', *moyen âge*, 67 (1961), 293-323.

—— *Tribunaux et gens de justice dans le bailliage de Senlis à la fin du moyen âge (vers 1380 vers 1550)* (Paris, 1963).

—— 'État et nation en France au moyen âge', *Revue historique* 237 (1967), 17-30.

—— 'L'Histoire de l'état en France à la fin du moyen âge vue par les historiens français depuis cent ans', *Revue historique*, 237 (1967), 331-60.

—— *L'Occident aux XIVe et XVe siècles: les états* (Paris, 1971).

—— 'Y'-a-t-il un état des XIVe et XVe siècles?' *Annales*, 26 (1971), 399-406.

Gurr, T. R., 'Historical Trends in Violent Crime: A Critical Review of the Evidence', *Crime and Justice: An Annual Review of Research*, 3 (1961), 295-353.

Haines, K., 'Attitudes and Impediments to Pacifism in Medieval Europe', *Journal of Medieval History*, 7 (1981), 369-89.

Hallam, E., *Capetian France, 987-1326* (London, 1980).

Hallem, H. E., 'The Postan Thesis', *Historical Studies*, 15 (1972), 203-22.

Hanawalt, B. A., 'Economic Influences on the Pattern of Crime in England, 1300-1348', *American Journal of Legal History*, 18 (1974), 281-97.

—— 'The Peasant Family and Crime in Fourteenth-century England', *Journal of British Studies*, 13 (1974), 1-18.

—— 'Fur-collar Crime: The Pattern of Crime Among the Fourteenth-century English Nobility', *Journal of Social History*, 8 (1975), 1-17.

—— 'Violent Death in Fourteenth- and Early Fifteenth-century England', *Comparative Studies in Society and History*, 18 (1976), 297-320.

—— 'Community Conflict and Social Control: Crime and Justice in the Ramsey Abbey Villages', *Medieval Studies*, 39 (1977), 402-23.

—— *Crime and Conflict in English Communities, 1300-1343* (Cambridge, Mass., 1979).

Hanning, R. W., 'The Social Significance of Twelfth-century Chivalric Romance', *Mediaevalia et Humanistica*, 3 (1972), 3-29.

Harding, A., 'The Origins and Early History of the Keeper of the Peace', *Transactions of the Royal Historical Society*, 5th ser., 10 (1960), 85-109.

—— *The Law Courts of Medieval England* (London, 1973).

—— *A Social History of English Law* (Gloucester, Mass., 1973).

—— 'Plaints and Bills in the History of English Law Mainly in the Period 1250-1350', *Legal History Studies 1972*, ed. D. Jenkins (Cardiff, 1975), 65-87.

—— 'Early Trailbaston Proceedings from the Lincoln Roll of 1305', *Medieval Legal Records edited in Memory of C. A. F. Meekings*, ed. R. F. Hunnisett and J. B. Post (London, 1978), 144-68.

Harriss, G. L., 'Parliamentary Taxation and the Origins of Appropriation of Supply in England, 1207-1340', *Recueils de la Société Jean Bodin*, 24 (1966), 165-79.

—— *King, Parliament, and Public Finance in Medieval England to 1369* (Oxford, 1975).

—— 'War and the Emergence of the English Parliament, 1297-1360', *Journal of Medieval History*, 2 (1976), 35-56.

—— 'The Formation of Parliament, 1272-1377', *The English Parliament in the Middle Ages*, ed. R. G. Davies and J. H. Denton (Philadelphia, 1981), 29-61.

Harvey, P. D. A., 'The English Inflation of 1180-1220', *Past and Present*, 61 (1973), 3-31.

Haskins, C. H., *The Renaissance of the Twelfth Century* (Cambridge, Mass., 1927).

Haskins, G. L., 'Three Early Petitions of the Commonalty, *Speculum*, 12 (1937), 314-18.

—— 'Executive Justice and the Rule of Law: Some Reflections on Thirteenth-century England', *Speculum*, 30 (1955), 529-38.

Hebert, M., 'Guerre, finances, et administration: les états de Provence de novembre 1359', *moyen âge*, 83 (1977), 103-30.

Heers, J., 'Difficultés économiques et troubles sociaux en France et en Angleterre pendant la guerre de cent ans: le problème des origines', *Actes du colloque international de Cocheral, les cahiers vernonnais*, 4 (1964), 47-53.

Henneman, J. B., 'Financing the Hundred Years War: Royal Taxation in France in 1340', *Speculum*, 42 (1967), 275-98.

—— 'Enquêteurs-réformateurs and Fiscal Officers in Fourteenth-century France', *Traditio*, 24 (1968), 309-49.

—— 'Taxation of Italians by the French Crown (1311-1363)', *Medieval Studies*, 31 (1969), 15-43.

—— *Royal Taxation in Fourteenth-century France: The Development of War Financing, 1322-1356* (Princeton, 1971).

—— 'The French Ransom Aids and Two Legal Traditions', *Studia Gratiana*, 15 (1972), 615-29.

—— *Royal Taxation in Fourteenth-century France: The Captivity and Ransom of John II, 1356-1370* (Philadelphia, 1976).

—— 'The Military Class and the French Monarchy in the Late Middle Ages', *American Historical Review*, 83 (1978), 946-65.

—— 'Nobility, Privilege, and Fiscal Politics in Late Medieval France', *French Historical Studies*, 13 (1983), 1-17.

Hewitt, H. J., *The Black Prince's Expedition of 1355-1357* (Manchester, 1958).

Hewitt, H. J., *The Organisation of War Under Edward III* (Manchester, 1966).
Hibbert, A. B., 'The Economic Policies of Towns', *The Cambridge Economic History of Europe*, iii, ed. M. M. Postan, E. E. Rich, and E. Miller (Cambridge, 1963), 198-229.
Hilton, R. H., 'Peasant Movements in England before 1381', *Economic History Review*, 2nd ser., 2 (1949), 117-36.
—— 'The Origins of Robin Hood', *Past and Present*, 14 (1958), 30-43.
—— 'Freedom and Villeinage in England', *Past and Present*, 31 (1965), 3-19.
—— *A Medieval Society: The West Midlands at the End of the Thirteenth Century* (London, 1967).
—— *The Decline of Serfdom in Medieval England* (London, 1969).
—— *Bond Men Made Free: Medieval Peasant Movements and the English Rising of 1381* (London, 1973).
—— and J. Le Goff, 'Féodalité et seigneurie', in: *De Guillaume le Conquérant au Marché Commun*, ed. F. Bedarida, F. Couzet, and D. Johnson (Paris, 1979), 41-68.
Histoire littéraire de la France; ouvrage commencé par des religieux benedictins de la congrégation de Saint Maur, et continué par les membres de l'institut (académie des inscriptions et belles-lettres), 40 vols. (1865-).
Hoffman, H., *Gottesfriede und Truga Dei* (Stuttgart, 1964).
Holdsworth, C. J., 'Ideas and Reality: Some Attempts to Control and Defuse War in the Twelfth Century', *Studies in Church History*, 70 (1983), 59-78.
Hollister, C. W., *Anglo-Saxon Military Institutions on the Eve of the Norman Conquest* (Oxford, 1962).
—— *The Military Organization of Norman England* (Oxford, 1965).
—— 'Military Obligation in Late Saxon and Norman England', *Ordinamenti Militari in Occidente nell'Alto Medioevo*, 15 (Spoleto, 1968).
—— and J. W. Baldwin, 'The Rise of Administrative Kingship: Henry I and Philip Augustus', *American Historical Review*, 83 (1978), 867-905.
Holmes, G., *Europe: Hierarchy and Revolt, 1320-1450* (London, 1975).
—— *The Good Parliament* (Oxford, 1975).
Holt, J. C., 'The Origins and Audience of the Ballads of Robin Hood', *Past and Present*, 18 (1960), 89-110.
—— *Magna Carta* (Cambridge, 1965).
—— 'The Prehistory of Parliament', *The English Parliament in the Middle Ages*, ed. R. G. Davies and J. H. Denton (Philadelphia, 1981), 1-29.
—— *Robin Hood* (London, 1982).
Housley, N., *The Italian Crusades* (Oxford, 1982).

Hubrecht, G., 'La Juste Guerre dans la doctrine chrétienne, des origines au milieu du XVIe siècle', *Recueils de la société Jean Bodin*, 15 (1962), 107-23.

Hughes, D., *A Study of Social and Constitutional Tendencies in the Early Years of Edward III* (London, 1915).

Huizinga, J., *The Waning of the Middle Ages* (New York, 1954).

—— 'The Political and Military Significance of Chivalric Ideas in the Late Middle Ages', *Men and Ideas* (Cleveland, 1959), 196-206.

Hurnard, N. D., *The King's Pardon for Homicide Before AD 1307* (Oxford, 1969).

Hyams, P. R., 'Trial by Ordeal: The Key to Proof in the Early Common Law', *On the Laws and Customs of England: Essays in Honor of Samuel E. Thorne*, ed. M. S. Arnold, T. A. Green, *et al.* (Oxford, 1979), 90-126.

Jackson, W. T. H., *The Hero and the King* (New York, 1982).

Jolliffe, J. E. A., *Angevin Kingship*, 2nd edn. (London, 1963).

Jones, M., *Ducal Brittany, 1364-1399* (Oxford, 1970).

Jones, T., *Chaucer's Knight* (London, 1980).

Jones, W. R., '*Rex et ministri*: English Local Government and the Crisis of 1341', *Journal of British Studies*, 13 (1973), 1-20.

—— 'Keeping the Peace: English Society, Local Government, and the Commissions of 1341-1344', *American Journal of Legal History*, 18 (1974), 307-20.

Jordan, W. C., *Louis IX and the Challenge of the Crusade* (Princeton, 1979).

Kaeuper, R. W., *Bankers to the Crown: The Riccardi of Lucca and Edward I* (Princeton, 1973).

—— 'The Frescobaldi of Florence and the English Crown', *Studies in Medieval and Renaissance History*, 10 (1973), 41-97.

—— 'The Role of Italian Financiers in the Edwardian Conquest of Wales', *Welsh History Review*, 6 (1973), 387-403.

—— 'Royal Finance and the Crisis of 1297', *Order and Innovation in the Middle Ages: Essays in Honor of Joseph R. Strayer*, ed. W. C. Jordan, B. McNab, and T. Ruiz (Princeton, 1976), 103-10, 450-2.

—— 'Law and Order in Fourteenth-century England: The Evidence of Special Commissions of Oyer and Terminer', *Speculum*, 54 (1979), 734-84.

—— 'An Historian's Reading of *The Tale of Gamelyn*', *Medium Aevum*, 52 (1983), 51-62.

Kantorowicz, E. H., *The King's Two Bodies: A Study in Medieval Political Theology* (Princeton, 1957).

—— 'Kingship under the Impact of Scientific Jurisprudence', *Twelfth-century Europe and the Foundations of Modern Society*, ed. G. Post, M. Claggett, and R. Reynolds (Madison, Wis., 1961), 89-111.

Keen, M. H., *The Outlaws of Medieval Legend* (London, 1961).
—— 'Robin Hood—Peasant or Gentleman?' *Past and Present*, 19 (1961), 7-15.
—— *The Laws of War in the Late Middle Ages* (London, 1965).
—— 'The Political Thought of the Fourteenth-century Civilians', *Trends in Medieval Political Thought*, ed. B. Smalley (Oxford, 1965), 105-26.
—— *The Pelican History of Medieval Europe* (Harmondsworth, 1969).
—— 'Chivalry, Nobility, and the Man-at-Arms', *War, Literature, and Politics in the Late Middle Ages*, ed. C. T. Allmand (Liverpool, 1976).
—— *England in the Later Middle Ages* (London, 1977).
—— 'Huizinga, Kilgour, and the Decline of Chivalry', *Medievalia et Humanistica*, NS, 8 (1977), 1-20.
—— *Chivalry* (New Haven, 1984).
Keeney, B. C., 'Military Service and the Development of Nationalism in England, 1272-1327', *Speculum*, 22 (1947), 534-49.
Keiser, G. R., 'Edward III and the Alliterative *Morte Arthure*', *Speculum*, 48 (1973), 37-51.
—— 'The Theme of Justice in the Alliterative *Morte Arthure*', *Annuale Medievale*, 16 (1975), 94-109.
Kendrick, L. 'Criticism of the Ruler, 1100-1400, in Provençal, Old French, and Middle English Verse', Ph.D. thesis (Columbia University, New York, 1978).
Kershaw, I., 'The Great Famine and Agrarian Crisis in England, 1315-1322', *Past and Present*, 59 (1973), 3-50.
Kirwin, H. W., 'James J. Walsh—Medical Historian and Pathfinder', *Catholic Historical Review*, 45 (1959-60), 409-35.
Koch, J. (ed.), *Chardry's Josaphaz, Set Dormanz, und Petit Plet* Heilbronn, 1879).
Ladner, G., *The Idea of Reform: Its Impact on Christian Thought and Action in the Age of the Fathers* (Cambridge, Mass., 1959).
Lane, F.C., 'The Economic Consequences of Organized Violence', *Journal of Economic History*, 18 (1958), 401-17.
Langlois, C.-V., *Le Règne de Philippe III le Hardi* (Paris, 1887).
—— 'Project for Taxation Presented to Edward I', *English Historical Review*, 4 (1889), 517-21.
—— *Saint Louis—Philippe le Bel: les derniers Capétiens directs (1226-1328)*: vol. iii of E. Lavisse (ed.), *Histoire de France depuis les origines jusqu'à la révolution* (Paris, 1901).
—— 'Doléances recueilles par les enquêteurs de Saint Louis et des derniers Capétiens directs', *Revue historique*, 92 (1906), 1-41.
—— 'Les Doléances des communautés du Toulousain contre Pierre de Latilli et Raoul de Breuilli (1297-1298)', *Revue historique*, 95 (1907), 23-53.

Langlois, M., and Y. Lanhers, *Confessions et jugements de criminels au Parlement de Paris (1319-1350)* (Paris, 1971).
Langmuir, G. I., 'Community and Legal Change in Capetian France', *French Historical Studies*, 7 (1970), 275-86.
Lanhers, Y., 'Crimes et criminels au XIVe siècle', *Revue historique*, 240 (1968), 325-38.
Lartigaut, J., 'Témoignages sur la dépopulation du Quercy au XIVe siècle', *Annales du Midi*, NS 84 (1972), 5-15.
Latham, R. E., and C. A. F. Meekings, 'The Veredictum of Chippenham Hundred, 1281', *Collectanea: Wiltshire Archaeological and Natural History Society*, 12 (1956), 50-128.
Lauriere, E.-J. de, *et al.* (eds.), *Ordonnances des roys de France de la troisième race: recueillies par ordre chronologique*, 22 vols. (Paris, 1723-1849).
Leclercq, J., 'Un sermon prononcé pendant la guerre de Flandre', *Revue du moyen âge latin*, 1 (1945), 165-72.
Lecoy de la Marche, A., *La Chaire française au moyen âge* (Paris, 1886).
Legge, M. D., *Anglo-Norman Literature and its Background* (Oxford, 1963).
—— 'The Rise and Fall of Anglo-Norman Literature,' *Mossaic*, 8 (1975), 1-6.
Le Goff, J., 'Le temps du travail dans la "crise" du XIVe siècle: du temps mediéval au temps moderne', *Moyen âge*, 69 (1963), 597-613.
Leguai, A., *De la seigneurie à l'état: le Bourbonnais pendant la guerre de cent ans* (Moulins, 1969).
—— *La Guerre de cent ans* (Paris, 1974).
—— 'Les troubles urbains dans le Nord de la France à la fin du XIIIe au début du XIVe siècle', *Revue d'histoire économique et sociale*, 54 (1976), 281-303.
Lehugeur, P., *Histoire de Philippe le Long, roi de France (1316-1322)*, 2 vols. (Paris, 1897-1931; repr. Geneva, 1975).
Le Patourel, J., 'L'Occupation anglaise de Calais au XIVe siècle', *Revue du Nord*, 33 (1951), 228-41.
—— 'The King and the Princes in Fourteenth-century France', *Europe in the later Middle Ages*, ed. J. R. Hale *et al.* (London, 1965), 155-83.
Lettenhove, Kervyn de (ed.), *OEuvres de Froissart*, 25 vols. in 26 pts. Brussels, 1867-77).
Lewis, N. B., 'The Organization of Indentured Retinues in Fourteenth-century England', *Transactions of the Royal Historical Society*, 5th ser., 27 (1945), 29-39.
Lewis, P. S., 'The Failure of the French Medieval Estates', *Past and Present*, 23 (1962), 3-17.
—— *Later Medieval France: The Polity* (New York, 1968).
—— (ed.), *The Recovery of France in the Fifteenth Century* (New York, 1971).

Lewis, P. S., 'La Formation des états nationaux', *De Guillaume le Conquérant au Marché Commun*, ed. F. Bedarida, F. Couzet, and D. Johnson (Paris, 1979).
Little, L. K., 'Pride Goes Before Avarice: Social Change and the Vices in Latin Christendom', *American Historical Review*, 76 (1971), 16-49.
Lloyd, T. H., *The Movement of Wool Prices in Medieval England* (Cambridge, 1973).
—— *The English Wool Trade in the Middle Ages* (New York, 1977).
—— 'Overseas Trade and the English Money Supply in the Fourteenth Century', *Edwardian Monetary Affairs (1279-1344)*, ed. N. J. Mayhew, British Archaeological Reports, 36 (1977).
Loomis, R. S., 'Edward I, Arthurian Enthusiast', *Speculum*, 28 (1953), 114-127.
Lopez, R. S., and H. A. Miskimin, 'The Economic Depression of the Renaissance', *Economic History Review*, 2nd ser., 14 (1962), 408-26, 525-9.
Lorcin, M.-T., 'Les Paysans et la justice dans la région lyonnaise aux XIVe et XVe siècles', *Moyen âge*, 74 (1968), 269-300.
Lot, H., 'Des frais de justice au XIVe siècle', *Bibliothèque de l'école des chartes*, 33 (1872), 217-53, 558-94; 34 (1873), 204-32.
Luard, H. R. (ed.), Matthew Paris, *Chronica Majora*, Rolls Series, 7 vols. (1872-83).
Lucas, H. S., *The Low Countries and the Hundred Year Wars, 1326-1347* (Ann Arbor, 1929).
—— 'The Great European Famine of 1315, 1316, and 1317', *Speculum*, 5 (1930), 343-77.
Luce, S., *Histoire de la Jacquerie*, 2nd edn. (Paris, 1894; repr. Geneva, 1978).
Luchaire, A., *Louis VI le Gros, annales de sa vie et de son règne* (Paris, 1890).
—— *Manuel des institutions françaises* (Paris, 1892).
Lumiansky, R. M., 'The Alliterative *Morte Arthure*, the Concept of Medieval Tragedy, and the Cardinal Virtue, Fortitude', *Medieval and Renaissance Studies*, 3 (1968), 95-118.
Lydon, J. F., 'The Bruce Invasion of Ireland', *Irish Conference of Historians: Historical Studies*, 4 (1964), 111-25.
Maddicott, J. R., *Thomas of Lancaster, 1307-1322* (Oxford, 1972).
—— 'The English Peasantry and the Demands of the Crown, 1294-1341', *Past and Present Supplement*, i (1975).
—— The Birth and Setting of the Ballads of Robin Hood', *English Historical Review*, 93 (1978), 276-99.
—— 'The County Community and the Making of Public Opinion in Fourteenth-century England', *Transactions of the Royal Historical Society*, 5th ser., 28 (1978), 27-43.

—— 'Law and Lordship: Royal Justices as Retainers in Thirteenth- and Fourteenth-century England', *Past and Present Supplement*, 4 (1978).
—— 'Parliament and the Constituencies', *The English Parliament in the Middle Ages*, ed. R. G. Davies and J. H. Denton (Philadelphia, 1981), 61-88.
Maillard, F., 'Mouvements administratifs des baillis et des sénéchaux sous Philippe le Bel', *Comité des travaux historiques et scientifiques, bulletin philologique et scientifique 1960* (1959), 407-30.
Maitland, F. W., *The Constitutional History of England*, ed. H. A. L. Fisher (Cambridge, 1908).
—— *Doomsday Book and Beyond* (New York, 1966).
—— and F. Pollock, *The History of English Law Before the Time of Edward I*, 2nd edn., reissued with introd. by S. F. C. Milsom, 2 vols. (Cambridge, 1968).
Mansi, G. D. (ed.), *Sacrorum conciliorum*, 53 vols. in 60 pts. (Paris, 1901-27).
Master Walter Mape's Book, 'De Nugus Curialium (Courtiers' Trifles), tr. F. Tupper and M. B. Ogle (New York, 1924).
Matarasso, P., *Recherches historiques et littéraires sur 'Raoul de Cambrai'* (Paris, 1962).
Mate, M., Monetary Policies in England 1272-1307', *British Numismatic Journal*, 41 (1972), 34-79.
—— 'The Indebtedness of Canterbury Cathedral Priory 1215-1295', *Economic History Review*, 26 (1973), 183-97.
—— 'High Prices in Early Fourteenth-century England: Causes and Consequences', *Economic History Review*, 2nd ser., 28 (1975), 1-16.
Matthews, W., *The Tragedy of Arthur* (Berkeley, 1960).
Mayhew, N. J., 'Numismatic Evidence and Falling Prices in the Fourteenth Century', *Economic History Review*, 27 (1974), 1-15.
—— 'Crockards and Pollards; Imitation and the Problem of Fineness in a Silver Coinage', *Edwardian Monetary Affairs (1277-1344)*, British Archaeological Reports, 36 (1977).
McFarlane, K. B., 'England and the Hundred Years War', *Past and Present*, 22 (1962), 3-18.
—— 'Had Edward I a "Policy" towards the Earls?' *History*, 50 (1965), 145-59.
—— *The Nobility of Later Medieval England* (Oxford, 1973).
McGovern, J. F., 'The Rise of New Economic Attitudes—Economic Humanism, Economic Nationalism—During the Later Middle Ages and the Renaissance, AD 1200-1550', *Traditio*, 26 (1970), 217-53.
McHardy, A. K., 'The English Clergy and the Hundred Years War', *Studies in Church History*, 20 (1983), 171-8.
McKisack, M., *The Fourteenth Century* (Oxford, 1959).

McKisack, M., 'Edward III and the Historians', *History*, NS 45 (1960), 1-15.
McLane, B. W., 'The Royal Courts and the Problem of Disorder in Lincolnshire, Ph.D. thesis (University of Rochester, New York, 1979).
—— 'A Case Study of Violence and Litigation in Early Fourteenth-century England: The Feuds of Robert Godsfield of Sutton-le-March', *Nottingham Medieval Studies*, 28 (1984), 22-44.
—— 'Changes in the Court of King's Bench: The Preliminary View from Lincolnshire', *England in the Fourteenth Century: The Proceedings of the 1985 Harlaxton Symposium*, ed. M. Ormrod (Woodbridge, Suffolk, 1986), 152-60.
—— (ed.), *The 1341 Royal Inquest in Lincolnshire*, Lincoln Record Society, 78 (forthcoming).
Merilees, B., 'Anglo-Norman Literature', *Dictionary of the Middle Ages*, i. ed. J. R. Strayer (New York, 1982), 259-72.
Mezieres, P. de, *Letter to King Richard II: A Plea Made in 1395 for Peace between England and France*, tr. G. W. Coopland (Liverpool, 1975).
Michel, R., 'L'Administration royale dans la sénéchaussée de Beaucaire au Temps de Saint Louis', *Mémoires et documents publiés par la société de l'école des chartes*, 9 (Paris, 1910).
Miller, E., 'The State and Landed Interests in Thirteenth-century England and France', *Transactions of the Royal Historical Society* 5th ser., 2 (1952), 109-29.
—— 'The Economic Policies of Governments', *Cambridge Economic History of Europe*, III, ed. M. M. Postan, E. E. Rich, and E. Miller (Cambridge, 1963), 281-430.
—— 'The English Economy in the Thirteenth Century: Implications of Recent Research', *Past and Present*, 28 (1967), 21-40.
—— 'War, Taxation, and the English Economy in the Late Thirteenth and Early Fourteenth Centuries', *War and Economic Development: Essays in Honour of David Jaslin*, ed. J. M. Winter (Cambridge, 1975).
—— and J. Thatcher, *Medieval England—Rural Society and Economic Change, 1086-1348* (London, 1978).
Miskimin, H. A., *Money, Prices, and Foreign Exchange in Fourteenth-century France* (New Haven, 1963).
Mitchell, S. K., *Taxation in Medieval England* (New Haven, 1951).
Mohl, R., *The Three Estates in Medieval and Renaissance Literature* (New York, 1933).
Moisant, J. (ed.), *De Speculo Regis Edwardi Tertii* (Paris, 1891).
Mollat, M., and P. Wolff, *Ongles bleus, Jacques et Ciompi* (Paris, 1970), tr. A. L. Lytton-Sells, *The Popular Revolutions of the Late Middle Ages* (London, 1973).

Morris, C., "Equestris Ordo": Chivalry as a Vocation in the Twelfth Century', *Studies in Church History*, 15 (1978), 87-98.
Morris, J. E., *The Welsh Wars of Edward I* (Oxford, 1901).
Morris, W. A., *The Medieval English Sheriff* (Manchester, 1927).
Mortet, C., 'Le Livre des constitutions démenées le chastelet de Paris', *Mémoires de la société de l'histoire de Paris et de l'Île de France*, 10 (1863).
Munro, J. H. 'Bullionism and the Bill of Exchange in England', *The Dawn of Modern Banking* (New Haven, 1979).
Nelson, J. L., 'The Church's Military Service in the Ninth Century: A Contemporary Comparative View?', *Studies in Church History*, 20 (1983), 15-30.
Nicholas, D. M. 'Town and Countryside: Social and Economic Tensions in Fourteenth-century Flanders', *Comparative Studies in Society and History*, 10 (1967-8), 458-85.
—— 'Crime and Punishment in Fourteenth-century Ghent', *Revue belge de philologie et d'histoire*, 48 (1970), 289-334, 1141-76.
Nichols, F. M., 'Original Documents Illustrative of the Administration of the Criminal Law in the Time of Edward I, with Observations', *Archaeologia*, 40 (1866), 89-105.
Nicholson, R., *Edward III and the Scots* (Oxford, 1965).
North, D. C., and R. P. Thomas, 'An Economic Theory of the Growth of the Western World', *Economic History Review*, 2nd ser., 23 (1970), 1-17.
—— and ——, *The Rise of the Western World: A New Economic History* (Cambridge, 1973).
Les Olim ou registres des arrêts rendus par la cour du roi, sous les règnes de Saint Louis, de Philippe le Hardi, de Philippe le Bel, de Louis le Hutin et de Philippe le Long, publiés par le comte Beugnot, 3 vols. in 4 pts. (Paris, 1839-48).
Olivier-Martin, F., *Histoire du droit français des origines à la révolution* (Montchrestien, 1948).
Oman, C., *The Great Revolt of 1381*, 1st edn. (1906), 2nd edn., with introd. by E. B. Fryde (Oxford, 1969).
Ordonnances des roys de France de la troisième race: recueillies par ordre chronologique, ed. E.-J. de Lauriere *et al.*, 22 vols. (Paris, 1723-1849).
Owst, G. R., *Literature and Pulpit in Medieval England* (Cambridge, 1933).
Painter, S., *William Marshal: Knight-errant, Baron, and Regent of England* (Baltimore, 1933).
—— *French Chivalry* (Ithaca, 1969).
Palmer, J. J. N., 'The Parliament of 1385 and the Constitutional Crisis of 1386', *Speculum* 46 (1971), 477-90.
Pegues, F. J., *The Lawyers of the Last Capetians* (Princeton, 1962).

Pena, N. de, 'Vassaux gascons au service du roi d'Angleterre dans la première moitié du XIVe siècle: fidelité ou esprit de profit?', *Annales du Midi*, NS, 88 (1976), 5-21.

Perrot, E., *Les Cas royaux* (Paris, 1910).

Perroy, E., 'La Fiscalité en Beaujolais aux XIVe et XVe siècles', *Moyen âge*, 38 (1928), 5-68.

—— 'L'Administration de Calais en 1371-1372', *Revue du Nord*, 33 (1951), 218-77.

—— 'Social Mobility Among the French Noblesse in the Later Middle Ages', *Past and Present*, 21 (1962), 25-36.

—— *The Hundred Years War* (New York, 1965).

—— 'Carolingian Administration', *Early Medieval Society*, ed. S. Thrupp (New York, 1967), 129-46.

Petit-Dutaillis, C., 'Querimoniae Normanorum', *Essays in Medieval History presented to T. F. Tout*, ed. A. G. Little and F. M. Powicke (Manchester, 1925), 99-118.

Pistrono, S. P., 'Flanders and the Hundred Years War: The Quest for the Trêve Marchande', *Bulletin of the Institute of Historical Research*, 59 (1976), 185-97.

Pitt-Rivers, J., 'Honour and Social Status', in: *Honour and Shame: The Values of Mediterranean Society*, ed. J. Peristiany (London, 1965).

Plucknett, T. F. T., *The Legislation of Edward I* (Oxford, 1949).

Poole, A. L., *From Domesday Book to Magna Carta* (Oxford, 1951).

Porteau-Bitker, A., 'L'Emprisonnement dans le droit laïque du moyen âge', *Revue historique de droit français*, 4th ser., 46 (1968), 211-45, 388-428.

Post, G., 'Law and Politics in the Middle Ages: The Medieval State as a Work of Art', *Perspectives in Medieval History*, ed. K. F. Drew (Chicago, 1963), 59-76.

—— *Studies in Medieval Legal Thought* (Princeton, 1964).

Post, J. B., 'The Peace Commissions of 1382', *English Historical Review*, 91 (1976), 98-101.

Postan, M. M., 'Some Social Consequences of the Hundred Years War', *Economic History Review* 12 (1942), 1-12.

—— 'The Costs of the Hundred Years War', *Past and Present* 27 (1964), 34-53.

—— *The Medieval Economy and Society: An Economic History of Britain, 1100-1500* (Berkeley, 1972).

Pounds, N. J. G., 'Overpopulation in France and the Low Countries in the Later Middle Ages', *Journal of Social History* 3 (1970), 225-47.

Powell, E., 'Arbitration and the Law in England in the Later Middle Ages', *Transactions of the Royal Historical Society*, 5th ser., 33 (1983), 49-69.

Power, E., *The Wool Trade in English Medieval History* (Oxford, 1941).

Powicke, F. M., *The Loss of Normandy*, 2nd edn. (Manchester, 1961).
—— 'Reflections on the Medieval State', *Transactions of the Royal Historical Society*, 4th ser., 19 (1936), 1-8.
—— *King Henry III and the Lord Edward*, 2 vols. (Oxford, 1947).
—— 'King Edward I in Fact and Fiction', *Fritz Saxl, 1890-1948, A Volume of Memorial Essays from his Friends in England*, ed. D. J. Gordon (London, 1957).
—— *The Thirteenth Century* (Oxford, 1962).
Powicke, M., *Military Obligation in Medieval England* (Oxford, 1962).
Prescott, A., 'London in the Peasants' Revolt: A Portrait Gallery', *London Journal*, 7 (1981), 125-43.
Prestwich, J. O., 'War and Finance in the Anglo-Norman State', *Transactions of the Royal Historical Society*, 5th ser., 4 (1954), 19-43.
—— 'The Military Household of the Norman Kings', *English Historical Review*, 96 (1981), 1-35.
Prestwich, M., 'Edward I's Monetary Policies and their Consequences', *Economic History Review*, 2nd ser., 22 (1969), 406-16.
—— *War, Politics, and Finance* (Totowa, NJ, 1972).
—— 'Exchequer and Wardrobe in the Later Years of Edward I', *Bulletin of the Institute of Historical Research*, 46 (1973), 1-9.
—— 'Italian Merchants in Late Thirteenth- and Early Fourteenth-century England', The Dawn of Modern Banking (New Haven, 1979), 77-104.
—— (ed.), *Documents Illustrating the Crisis of 1297-1298 in England* (London, 1980).
—— *The Three Edwards: War and the State in England, 1272-1377* (London, 1980).
—— 'English Armies in the Hundred Years War: A Scheme in 1341', *Bulletin of the Institute of Historical Research*, 133 (1983), 102-13.
Prestwich, M. C., 'Currency and the Economy of Early Fourteenth-century England', *Edwardian Monetary Affairs (1279-1344)*, ed. N. J. Mayhew, British Archaeological Reports, 36 (1977).
Proctor, E. S., *The Judicial Use of the Pesquisa in Leon and Castile*, EHR Supplement no. 2 (London, 1966).
Putnam, B. H., *Enforcement of the Statute of Labourers, 1349-1359* (New York, 1908).
—— 'The Transformation of the Keepers of the Peace into the Justices of the Peace, 1327-1380', *Transactions of the Royal Historical Society*, 4th ser., 12 (1929), 19-48.
—— *Proceedings Before the Justices of the Peace in the Fourteenth and Fifteenth Centuries, Edward III to Richard III* (London, 1935).
—— 'The Keepers and Justices of the Peace', in: *English Government at Work, 1327-1336*, vol. iii, ed. J. F. Willard, W. A. Morris, and W. H. Dunham, jun., (Cambridge, Mass., 1950).

Ramsay, J. H., *A History of the Revenues of the Kings of England* (Oxford, 1925).

Reedy, jun., W. T., 'The Origins of the General Eyre in the Reign of Henry I', *Speculum*, 41, 688-724.

Registre criminel du Châtelet de Paris du 6 septembre 1389 au mai 1392, ed. M. Duplès-Agier, 2 vols. (Paris, 1941).

Renouard, Y., *Les Relations des papes d'Avignon et les compagnies commerciales et bancaires de 1316 à 1378* (Paris, 1941).

—— 'L'Ordre de la jarretière et l'ordre de l'étoile: étude sur la genèse des ordres laïcs de chevalerie et sur le développement progressif de leur caractère national', *Moyen âge*, 54-5 (1948-9), 281-300.

—— '1212-1216, comment les traits durables de l'Europe occidentale moderne se sont définis au début du XIIIe siècle', *Annales de l'université de Paris* (1952), 5-21.

Reville, A., *Le Soulèvement des travailleurs d'Angleterre en 1381* (Paris, 1898).

Rey, M., *Le Domaine du roi et des finances extraordinaires sous Charles VI, 1388-1413* (Paris, 1965).

Richard, J., 'Le Droit de guerre du noble comtois', *Mémoires, société pour l'histoire du droit et des institutions des anciens pays bourguignons, comtois et romands*, 12 (1948-9), 107-15.

—— 'L'Affaire des bourgeois et la réformation de 1343 en Burgogne', *Annales de Bourgogne*, 27 (1955), 7-32.

Richardson, H. G., and G. O. Sayles, *Select Cases of Procedure Without Writ Under Henry III*, Selden Society, 60 (1941).

Riedel, F. C., *Crime and Punishment in the Old French Romances* (New York, 1939).

Robbins, R. H., *Historical Poems of the XIVth and XVth Centuries* (New York, 1959).

—— *Poems Dealing with Contemporary Conditions*, A Manual of the Writings in Middle English, 1050-1500, ed. A. E. Hartung (New Haven, 1975).

Robinson, C., 'Royal Purveyance in Fourteenth-century England in the Light of Simon Islip's *Speculum Regis*', *Annual Report of the American Historical Association for 1910* (Washington, 1912), 91-9.

Roover, R. de, 'Le marché monétaire au moyen âge et au début des temps modernes', *Revue historique*, 244 (1970), 5-40.

Rosenthal, J. T., 'Feuds and Private Peace-making: A Fifteenth-century Example', *Medieval Studies*, 14 (1970), 84-90.

Rothwell, H., 'The Confirmation of the Charters, 1297', *English Historical Review*, 60 (1945), 16-35, 177-91, 300-15.

—— 'Edward I and the Struggle for the Charters, 1297-1305', *Studies in Medieval History presented to F. M. Powicke*, ed. R. W. Hunt, W. H. Pantin, and R. W. *Southern*, (Oxford, 1948), 319-32.

Rotuli Parliamentorum, ed. J. Strachey *et al.*, 6 vols. (London, 1767).
Russell, E., 'The Societies of the Bardi and Peruzzi and their Dealings with Edward III, 1327-1345', *Finance and Trade Under Edward III*, ed. G. Unwin (Manchester, 1918).
Russell, F. H., *The Just War in the Middle Ages* (Cambridge, 1975).
Russell, J. C., 'Recent Advances in Medieval Demography', Speculum, 40 (1965), 84-101.
—— 'Effects of Pestilence and Plague, 1315-1385', *Comparative Studies in Society and History*, 8 (1965-6), 464-73.
—— The Pre-plague Population of England', *Journal of British Studies*, 5 (1966), 1-21.
Russell, P. E., *The English Intervention in Spain and Portugal in the Time of Edward III and Richard II* (Oxford, 1955).
Rymer, T., *Foedera, Conventiones, Litterae*, ed. A. Clarke and F. Holbrooke, vols. i-ii (London, 1859).
Sands, D. B., *Middle English Verse Romances* (New York, 1966).
Sarper, A., *Rutebeuf, poète satirique* (Paris, 1969).
Sayles, G. O., *Select Cases in the Court of King's Bench Under Edward III*, x, Selden Society, 58 (1939).
—— *Select Cases in the Court of King's Bench Under Edward II*, iv, Selden Society, 74 (1955).
—— *The Medieval Foundations of England* (New York, 1961).
—— *The King's Parliament of England* (New York 1974).
Scammel, J. 'Robert I and the North of England', *English Historical Review*, 73 (1958), 385-403.
—— 'The Rural Chapter in England from the Eleventh to the Fourteenth Century', *English Historical Review*, 86 (1971), 1-21.
Scattergood, V. J., *Politics and Poetry in the Fifteenth Century* (London, 1971).
Schmidt, A. V. C. (ed.), *William Langland: The Vision of Piers Plowman* (London, 1978).
Searle, E., *Lordship and Community: Battle Abbey and its Banlieu, 1066-1538* (Toronto, 1974).
—— and R. Burghart, 'The Defense of England and the Peasants' Revolt', *Viator*, 3 (1972), 365-88.
Shennan, J. H., *The Parlement of Paris* (Ithaca, 1968).
Sherborne, J. W., 'Indentured Retinues and English Expeditions to France, 1369-1380', *English Historical Review*, 79 (1964), 718-46.
—— 'The Cost of English Warfare with France in the Later Fourteenth Century', *Bulletin of the Institute of Historical Research*, 50 (1977), 135-50.
Sivwery, G., 'Les Orientations actuelles de l'histoire économique du moyen âge dans l'Europe du nord-ouest', *Revue du Nord*, 55 (1973), 207-18.

Skeat, W. W. (ed.), *The Tale of Gamelyn* (Oxford, 1884).
Small, C. M., 'Appeals from the Duchy of Burgundy to the Parlement of Paris in the Early Fourteenth Century', *Medieval Studies*, 39 (1977), 350-68.
Smalley, B., 'Capetian France', *France: Government and Society, a Historical Survey*, ed. J. M. Wallace-Hadrill and J. Manners (London, 1957).
—— 'Church and State, 1300-1377: Theory and Fact', *Europe in the Later Middle Ages*, ed. J. R. Hale et al. (London, 1965).
Smith, P., *The Anti-courtier Trend in Sixteenth-century French Literature* (Geneva, 1966).
Southern, R. W., *Medieval Humanism and Other Studies* (New York, 1970).
Spiegel, G. M., 'The Cult of Saint Denis and Capetian Kingship', *Journal of Medieval History*, 1 (1975), 43-69.
Spufford, P., 'Assemblies of Estates, Taxation, and Control of Coinage in Medieval Europe', *Twelfth International Congress of Historical Sciences* (Vienna, 1966), 113-30.
Statutes of the Realm, Record Commission (London, 1810-28).
Stenton, D. M., *English Justice Between the Norman Conquest and the Great Charter* (Philadelphia, 1964).
Stephenson, C., and F. G. Marcham, *Sources of English Constitutional History* (New York, 1937).
Stone, L., 'Interpersonal Violence in English Society, 1300-1980', *Past and Present*, 101 (1983), 22-33.
Stones, E. L. G., 'Sir Geoffrey le Scrope (c.1285-1340)', Ph.D. thesis (Glasgow, 1950).
—— 'The Folvilles of Ashby-Folville, Leicestershire, and their Associates in Crime, 1326-1347', *Transactions of the Royal Historical Society*, 5th ser., 7 (1957), 117-36.
Storer, W. H., and C. A. Rochdieu (eds.), *Six Historical Poems of Geffroi de Paris, Written 1314-1318* (Chapel Hill, 1950).
Strayer, J. R., *The Administration of Normandy under St Louis* (Cambridge, Mass., 1932).
—— 'The Laicization of French and English Society in the Thirteenth Century', *Speculum*, 15 (1940), 76-86; repr. in: *Medieval Statecraft and the Perspectives of History: Essays by Joseph R. Strayer*, ed. J. F. Benton and T. N. Bisson (Princeton, 1971), 251-65.
—— 'Defense of the Realm and Royal Power in France', *Studi in onore di Gino Luzzato*, i (Milan, 1949), 289-96; repr. in: *Medieval Statecraft*, 291-9.
—— 'Economic Conditions in the County of Beaumont-le-Roger, 1261-1313', *Speculum*, 26 (1951), 277-87; repr. in: *Medieval Statecraft*, 13-27.

—— 'The Crusade Against Aragon', *Speculum*, 28 (1953), 102-13; repr. in: *Medieval Statecraft*, 107-22.

—— 'The Historian's Concept of Public Opinion', *Common Frontiers of the Social Sciences*, ed. M. Komarovsky (Glencoe, Ill., 1957).

—— 'The Promise of the Fourteenth Century', *Proceedings of the American Philosophical Society*, 105 (1961), 609-11; repr. in: *Medieval Statecraft*, 315-20.

—— 'Viscounts and Viguiers under Philip the Fair', *Speculum*, 38 (1963), 242-55; repr. in *Medieval Statecraft*, 213-31.

—— 'Pierre de Chalon and the Origins of the French Customs Service', *Festschrift Percy Ernst Schramm*, i (Wiesbaden, 1964), 334-9; repr. in: *Medieval Statecraft*, 232-8.

—— 'France: The Holy Land, the Chosen People, and the Most Christian King', *Action and Conviction in Early Modern Europe: Essays in Memory of E. H. Harbison*, ed. T. K. Rabb and J. Seigel (Princeton, 1969), 3-19; repr. in: *Medieval Statecraft*, 300-14.

—— 'Italian Bankers and Philip the Fair', *Economy, Society, and Government in Medieval Italy: Essays in Memory of Robert L. Reynolds*, ed. D. Herlihy, R. S. Lopez, and V. Slessarev (Kent, Ohio, 1969), 113-21; repr. in: *Medieval Statecraft*, 239-47.

—— 'Philip the Fair—A Constitutional King', *American Historical Review*, 62 (1969), 18-32; repr. in: *Medieval Statecraft*, 195-212.

—— *Les Gens de justice du Languedoc sous Philippe le Bel* (Toulouse, 1970).

—— *On the Medieval Origins of the Modern State*, (Princeton, 1970).

—— 'The Fourth and the Fourteenth Centuries', *American Historical Review*, 77 (1972), 1-14.

—— 'Economic Conditions in Upper Normandy at the End of the Reign of Philip the Fair', *Économies et sociétés au moyen âge: mélanges offerts à Edouard Perroy* (Paris, 1973), 283-95.

—— 'La Conscience du roi: les enquêtes de 1258-1262 dans la sénéchaussée de Carcassonne-Béziers', *Société d'histoire du droit et des institutions des anciens pays de droit écrit, recueil de mémoires et travaux*, 9 (1974).

—— 'The Costs and Profits of War', *The Medieval City*, ed. H. A. Miskimin, D. Herlihy, A. L. Udovitch (New Haven, 1977), 269-91.

—— *The Reign of Philip the Fair* (Princeton, 1980).

—— and C. H. Taylor, *Studies in Early French Taxation* (Cambridge, Mass., 1939).

—— and W. A. Morris (eds.) *The English Government at Work*, vol. ii, *Fiscal Administration* (Cambridge, Mass., 1947).

Sutherland, D. W., *The Assize of Novel Disseisin* (Oxford, 1973).

Strubbe, E. I., 'La Paix de Dieu dans le nord de la France', *Recueils de la société Jean Bodin*, 14 (1962), 489-501.

Stubbs, W., *The Constitutional History of England*, 3 vols. (Oxford, 1875).
—— (ed.), *Select Charters and other Illustrations of English Constitutional History from the Earliest Times to the Reign of Edward the First*, 9th edn., rev. H. W. L. Davis (Oxford, 1962).
Tait, J., 'The Date and Authority of the "Speculum Regis Edwardi"', *English Historical Review*, 16 (1901), 110-15.
Taylor, C. H., 'The Assembly of 1312 at Lyons-Vienne', *Études d'histoire dédiées à la mémoire d'Henri Pirenne* (Brussels, 1937).
—— 'French Assemblies and Subsidy in 1321', *Speculum*, 43 (1968), 217-44.
Tellenbach, G., *Church, State, and Christian Society at the Time of the Investiture Conflict* (Oxford, 1940).
Templeman, G., 'The Sheriffs of Warwickshire in the Thirteenth Century', *Dugdale Society Occasional Papers*, 7 (1948), 3-50.
—— 'Edward I and the Historians', *Cambridge Historical Journal*, 10 (1950), 16-35.
Thompson, E. M. (ed.), *Chronicon Galfridi le Baker* (Oxford, 1889).
Thompson, R. M., 'England and the Twelfth-century Renaissance', *Past and Present*, 101 (1983), 3-21.
Thomson, W. S., *A Lincolnshire Assize Roll for 1298*, Lincoln Record Society, 36 (1944).
Tierney, B., 'Medieval Canon Law and Western Constitutionalism', *Catholic Historical Review*, 52 (1966), 1-17.
Timbal, P.-C., *La Guerre de cent ans vue à travers les registres du parlement (1337-1369)* (Paris, 1961).
Tout, T. F., *Chapters in the Administrative History of Medieval England*, 6 vols. (Manchester, 1936).
—— *The Place of the Reign of Edward II in English History*, 2nd edn. (Manchester, 1936).
—— and H. Johnstone, *State Trials in the Reign of Edward the First, 1289-1293*, Camden Society, 3 ser., 9 (1906).
Trabut-Cussac, J.-P., 'Le Financement de la croisade anglaise de 1270', *Bulletin de l'école des chartes*, 119 (1961), 113-40.
Tupper, F., and Marbury Bladen Ogle, *Master Walter Mape's Book, 'De Nugis Curialium (Courtiers' Trifles)* (New York, 1924).
Vale, J., *Edward III and Chivalry: Chivalric Society and its Context, 1270-1350* (Woodbridge, Suffolk, 1982).
Vale, M., *War and Chivalry* (Norwich, 1981).
Van Caenegem, R. C., 'La Paix publique dans les îles britanniques du XIe au XVIIIe siècle', *Recueils de la société Jean Bodin*, 15 (1962), 5-25.
—— 'L'Histoire du droit et la chronologie: réflections sur la formation du "Common Law" et de la procédure romano-canonique', *Études*

d'histoire du droit canonique dédiées à Gabriel le Bras (Paris, 1965).
—— *The Birth of the English Common Law* (Cambridge, 1973).
—— 'Public Prosecution of Crime in Twelfth-century England', *Church and Government in the Middle Ages: Essays Presented to C. R. Cheney* (Cambridge, 1976), ed. C. N. L. Brooke *et al.*
Van Werveke, H., 'La Famine de l'an 1316 en Flandre et dans les régions voisines', *Revue du Nord*, 41 (1959), 5-14.
Verbruggen, J. F., *The Art of Warfare in Western Europe During the Middle Ages from the Eighth Century to 1340*, tr. S. Willard and S. C. M. Southern (Oxford, 1977).
Vercauteren, F., 'La Princesse captive: note sur les négociations entre le pape Jean XXII et le comte Guillaume Ier de Hainaut en 1322-1323', *Moyen âge*, 83 (1977), 80-101.
Vermeesch, A., *Essai sur les origines et la signification de la commune dans le nord de la France (XIe et XIIe siècles)* (Paris, 1966).
Wagner, A. R., 'The Swan Badge and the Swan Knight', *Archaeologia*, 97 (1959), 127-38.
Wallace-Hadrill, J. M., 'The Bloodfeud of the Franks', *The Long-haired Kings and Other Studies in Frankish History* (London, 1967), 121-47.
—— 'War and Peace in the Early Middle Ages', *Early Medieval History* (New York, 1975), 19-38.
Warren, W. L., *Henry II* (Berkeley, 1973).
Watts, D. G., 'A Model for the Early Fourteenth Century', *Economic History Review*, 2nd ser., 20 (1967), 543-7.
Waugh, S. L., 'The Profits of Violence: The Minor Gentry in the Rebellion of 1321-1322 in Gloucestershire and Herefordshire', *Speculum*, 52 (1977), 843-69.
White, A. B., *Self-government at the King's Command* (Minneapolis, 1933).
Wilkinson, B., 'The Peasants' Revolt of 1381', *Speculum*, 15 (1940), 12-35.
Wilks, M., '*Reformatio Regni*: Wyclif and Hus as Leaders of Religious Protest Movements', *Studies in Church History*, 9 (1972), 109-30.
Willard, J. F., 'The Scotch Raids and the Fourteenth-century Taxation of Northern England', *University of Colorado Studies*, 5 (1906-8), 237-42.
—— *Parliamentary Taxes on Personal Property, 1290-1334: A Study of Mediaeval English Financial Administration* (Cambridge, Mass., 1934).
Wilson, R. M., *The Lost Literature of Medieval England* (London, 1952).
Winter, J. M. (ed.), *War and Economic Development* (Cambridge, 1975).
Wolff, P., *Commerces et marchands de Toulouse (vers 1350-vers 1450)* (Paris, 1954).

Wolff, P., 'Pouvoir et investissements urbains en Europe occidentale et centrale du treizième au dix-septième siècle', *Revue historique*, 258 (1977), 277-311.

Wood, C. T., The French Apanages and the Capetian Monarchy, 1224-1328 (Cambridge, Mass., 1966).

—— 'The Mise of Amiens and Saint-Louis' Theory of Kingship', *French Historical Studies*, 6 (1969), 300-10.

—— 'Personality, Politics, and Constitutional Progress: The Lessons of Edward II', *Studia Gratiana*, 15 (1972), 519-36.

—— 'The Deposition of Edward V', *Traditio*, 31 (1975), 247-86.

—— 'The English Crisis of 1297 in the Light of French Experience', *Journal of British Studies*, 18 (1979), 1-13.

Wormald, J., 'Bloodfeud, Kindred, and Government in Early Modern Scotland', *Past and Present*, 87 (1980), 54-97.

Wright, T. (ed.), *The Political Songs of England*, Camden Society (London, 1839).

—— (ed.), *Gualteri Mapes: De Nugis Curialium* (London, 1850).

Wrottesley, G., *Extracts from the Plea Rolls of the Reign of Edward II, AD 1307-AD 1327*, William Salt Archaeological Society, 10 (1889).

Young, C. R., *Hubert Walter, Lord of Canterbury and Lord of England* (Durham, NC, 1968).

—— *The Royal Forests of Medieval England* (Philadelphia, 1979).

Yunck, J. A., *The Lineage of Lady Meed: The Development of Medieval Venality Satire* (Notre Dame, Ind., 1963).

Yver, J., 'Contribution à l'étude du développement de la compétence ducale en Normandie', *Bulletin de la société des antiquaires de Normandie*, 57 (1963-4), 139-83.

—— Le Développement du pouvoir ducal en Normandie de l'avènement de Guillaume le Conquérant à la mort d'Henri I, 1035-1135', *Convegno Internazionale di studi ruggeriani. Atti* (1955), 183-204.

Zagorin, P., *The Court and the Country* (New York, 1970).

Index

Printed in the United States
1292400001B/8

9 780198 228738